Imperium Christus

Imperium Christus

…the Big Picture of the Looming Clash Between the Emerging World System and the Coming Empire of Christ

OBINNA C.D. ANEJIONU

RESOURCE *Publications* • Eugene, Oregon

IMPERIUM CHRISTUS
The Big Picture of the Looming Clash Between the Emerging World System and the Coming Empire of Christ

Copyright © 2025 Obinna C. D. Anejionu. All rights reserved. Except for brief quotations in critical publications or reviews, no part of this book may be reproduced in any manner without prior written permission from the publisher. Write: Permissions, Wipf and Stock Publishers, 199 W. 8th Ave., Suite 3, Eugene, OR 97401.

Resource Publications
An Imprint of Wipf and Stock Publishers
199 W. 8th Ave., Suite 3
Eugene, OR 97401

www.wipfandstock.com

PAPERBACK ISBN: 979-8-3852-4887-2
HARDCOVER ISBN: 979-8-3852-4888-9
EBOOK ISBN: 979-8-3852-4889-6

To my late dad Chief S.N Anejionu (Ohamadike I)

Table of Contents

Acknowledgement xiii
Preface xv
Concealed Truth 1
    1.1 The Revelation of Concealed Truth 1
        1.1.2 Concealed Truth in Extrabiblical Texts 8
    1.2 In the Beginning–Creation of Heavens and Earth 12
    1.3 The Heavens: The Cosmic Realms and Hosts of Heaven 16
        1.3.1 Celestial Beings: Thrones, Dominion, Powers, Principalities, and Angels 18
        1.3.2 The "gods" 20
        1.3.3 The Divine Assembly–God's Heavenly Council 25
The World that Was 29
    2.1 Who were the Original Occupants of the Earth? 29
        2.1.1 Atlantis–one of the lost pre-adamic civilizations 35
        2.1.2 What About Dinosaurs? 38
    2.2 Satan's Coup D'état: The Rebellion of Satan and his angels 39
    2.3 The Cataclysmic War that Destroyed the Earth 41
    2.4 Expulsion from Heaven 43
Cosmic Interregnum and Recreation 45
    3.1 The Interregnum 45
    3.2. Let there be Light! 45
    3.3. Recreation of the Earth 46
    3.4. Restoration of Vegetation 48
    3.5. Lights in the Firmament 48
    3.6. Restoration of Marine life, Birds and Terrestrial Animals 49
    3.7. The Creation of Humans (Male and Female) 50
    3.8. The Wheat and Tares (Darnel)–Corruption of Humans 51

TABLE OF CONTENTS

The Adamic Era 54
- 4.1 The Man of Dust: The Creation of Adam 54
- 4.2 Eden–The Garden of God 61
- 4.3 Creation of Eve 63
- 4.4 The Fall - Corruption of Adamic DNA 64
- 4.5 Mandate to the children of men over the Earth 71

Disruption of God's Plan for Man 73
- 5.1 Satan's usurping of Adam's Authority over Earth 73
- 5.2 The seed of Satan 76
- 5.3 Cain's Civilization 80
- 5.4 The Rebellion of Men against God 82
- 5.5 The Rebellion of the Watchers: The brazen incursion of the Sons of God into the Earth 83
- 5.6 Consequences of the Fall of the Watchers 88
- 5.7 The Noah's Flood–The Great Reset 92

The New beginning 94
- 6.1 The World after the Flood 94
- 6.2 Spiritual interference and idolatry 96
- 6.3 Postdiluvian Giants 99
- 6.4 The Ancient Orders of Seth and Cain 111
- 6.5 The Rise of Evil after the Flood 112
- 6.6 Nimrod–Antichrist foreshadow 115
- 6.7 Tower of Babel 128
  - 6.7.1 Tower of Babel and the CERN Connection 130
  - 6.7.2 Nimrod and Ancient One World Government 135

Reordering of the World–Emergence of a New World Order 140
- 7.1 The Division of the Earth among the Sons of God 140
- 7.2 Rebellion of the Sons of God 146
- 7.3 The Fallen Ones and the renegade gods 149
- 7.4 The Supremacy of God 153
- 7.5 The Inheritance and Nation of God 157

Establishment of the Nation of God 160
- 8.1 The Patriarch: The Missing Early Life of Abram 160
- 8.2 Abram's Evangelism in Shinar and Encounter with Nimrod 166
- 8.3 The Custodians of God's Truth 168
- 8.4 God's Covenant with Abraham 169

8.5 Israel's Rescue from Egypt 171
8.6 The Battle of the Bloodlines 173
8.7 Genocidal War against the Post-Diluvian Giants 177

The World under Dark Forces 185
9.1 The World under the Captivity of Satan 185
9.2 The Structure of Satan's Government over the World 188
9.2.1 Principalities and their Modus Operandi 189
9.2.2 Demons and Modus Operandi 193
9.2.3 Mind Control 194
9.2.4 Dislodging Principalities and Demons - Christ's Encounter with Territorial Spirits 196
9.3 Ancient Egypt: The Epitome of the World Under Satanic Influence 199

The First Coming of Christ–Redemption of Man from Darkness 202
10.1 Cosmic Legalism 202
10.2 Man Ought to Redeem Himself 207
10.3 Intrigues Surrounding the First Coming of Christ 209
10.4 The Authority of Christ 213
10.5 The Gospel 218
10.6 The Kingdom of God 221
10.7 The Mystery of the Cross 223
10.7.1 Descent into Underworld 226
10.8 Resurrection of Christ 231
10.8.1 Presentation of the blood at the Heavenly Altar 232
10.9 Salvation: The Rectification Process 233
10.9.1 The Mystery of Salvation 240

The Way–Becoming a Follower of Christ 244
11.1 Law and Grace Conundrum 244
11.2 Faith vs Works: The James vs Paul Viewpoints 256
11.3 Walking the Righteous Path 266
11.3.1 The Narrow Path 275
11.3.2 Receiving the Holy spirit 277
11.3.3 Mercy of God 281
11.3.4 Grace at work 283
11.3.5 The Dynamics of Navigating the Narrow Path 290
11.4 Becoming a follower of Christ 291

TABLE OF CONTENTS

  11.4.1 The Repentance Process 292
    11.4.1.1 The trigger point 292
    11.4.1.2 The long wait 294
    11.4.1.3 Continual renewal of the mind 295
  11.4.2 Baptism and Being Born Again–The Rewiring of Man's DNA 296
  11.4.3 Bearing of Good Fruit 300
  11.4.4 Be Discerning 304
  11.4.5 Unequal Yoking 305
    11.4.6 The Great Commission 306
 11.5 Confrontational Gospel 308

New World Order: The Foundations of the Last Empire of Satan 310
 12.1 The Recreation of the Atlantean Civilization 311
 12.2 The Beast System–The Final Empire of Satan 316
 12.3 Satan's Master Plan to recapture the World 320
 12.3.1 The Emergence of the Antichrist and Establishment of the Beast System 325
  12.3.2 The False Prophet–The Beast System Executor 330
  12.3.3 The Great Tribulation–The Violent Takeover of the World and Establishment of the rule of Satan 332
  12.3.4 The Mark of the Beast: Satan Gene Top-up Super Max 342
  12.3.5 Satan's war on human DNA 346
  12.3.6 Deception to draw out the righteous 347
 12.4 The Resurgence of the worship of renegade gods 348
 12.5 Transhumanism to Posthumanism: Satan's False 'Evolution' Promise to Humans 351

The Second Coming of Christ 358
 13.1 Why is Christ coming back to Earth? 358
 13.2 Reclaiming the Nations 358
 13.3 Delivering the Earth to God 359
 13.4 Enforcement of God's Judgement on Earth 360
 13.5 The End Times–A Selection Period 361
 13.6 The Great Tribulation–A test of loyalty, refinement and inoculation process 364
  13.6.1 The Two Parallel Worlds of the Great Tribulation 367

13.7 The Slow Demise of the Beast System 371

13.8 The Fall of Babylon the Great 379

13.9 The Day of the Lord - The Battle of Armageddon and the Defeat of the Beast System 384

13.10 Takeover of the Kingdom of the World 392

13.11 Sanitisation of the Heavens 393

The Empire of Christ 395

14.1 The Empire of Christ–The Millennial Reign of Christ 395

14.2 The World After the Defeat of the Antichrist 400

14.3 Rationale for the Empire of Christ 403

14.4 The Gathering of the Elect (Second Exodus) 406

14.4.1 End-time Gathering versus 1948 Reconstitution of the State of Israel 413

14.4.2 Regrouping of the Nations 416

14.4.3 Are the Elects the 144000 people? 420

14.5 The Great Banquet: The Marriage Supper of the Lamb 421

14.5.1 End time Lessons from the Parable of the Ten Virgins 425

14.6 The First Resurrection and the Transformation of Humans 426

14.7 *Filii Dei* (Sons of God)–The Ultimate Prize for Humans 429

14.7.1 Priest from Every Nation 439

14.8 The Earth and not Heaven is the Final Residence of Humans 440

14.9 The Parallel Worlds During the Millennial Reign 447

14.10 Regimen Christus–The Government of Christ 448

14.11 Overthrowing of the Adversaries of God 451

14.12 Jerusalem the Capital of the Empire (World Capital) 453

14.13 The Final Battle–Gog and Magog Battle II 455

14.14 The Second Resurrection 457

14.15 The Final Judgement 458

14.16 Restoration of God's Kingdom 462

References 467

Acknowledgement

I WISH TO EXTEND my special thanks to my wife for her immense support and encouragement, as well as in reviewing this book alongside Sir Percy L. Ahiarammunnah. They proffered good suggestions that shaped the direction and contents of this book. I would also like to acknowledge my children for their understanding, especially during those times when daddy did not have enough time to play with them while writing this book.

Preface

⁹ The Lord will be king over the whole earth. On that day there will be one Lord, and his name the only name. (Zechariah 14:9 NIV).

ACROSS HUMAN HISTORY, THERE has been a quest for global dominance. This has resulted in conflicts that have caused the rise and fall of empires across generations. The *Imperium Christus* examines the underlying dynamics of these conflicts and presents the idea that this quest is not limited to humans but originates from invisible cosmic forces pulling the strings from behind the scenes. At the root of this conflict is the contest for the control of man and the earth. The Bible is replete with stories of the conflict between forces of good and evil – transcending the physical and spiritual realms. The culmination of this conflict between the opposing cosmic forces is the establishment the Empire of Christ, an empire-like system of governance that will have absolute control over every part of the earth.

The *Imperium Christus* tells the fascinating story about this emerging empire of Christ and the events that will lead to its materialization on earth. The book explores the various events that will orchestrate the return of Christ and his entourage of angelic army, leading to the establishment of the Empire of Christ. This empire will rule the entire world for a thousand years and would be a precursor to the full establishment of the Kingdom of God on earth.

In the contemporary world where democracy has pushed the monarchical system of governance into oblivion, the idea that the near future holds the prospects of a return to the imperial system, where the entire world will be governed by one king, seems absurd and radical. However, this is an underlying theme that is running through various passages in the Bible. The entire gospel of Jesus Christ pivots around this theme.

PREFACE

Regardless of its importance, this concept is generally glossed over and many hardly focus on the physicalization of the Kingdom of God.

The *Imperium Christus* highlights the kingdom-oriented aspects of the gospel of Christ by exploring this central theme in detail. It re-analyses the concept from a contemporary viewpoint and unpacks the dynamics of its materialization, while exploring its links to eschatological events and the ultimate destiny of humans. The ideas explored in this book deviate from the usual spiritual connotations of the Kingdom of God and tackles this from the perspective that the kingdom will physically be established on the earth and function almost like other previous worldly empires. The book forays into various core concepts and events in many ancient sacred texts and how they all tie up to the quest for global dominance.

The book presents an intriguing angle on the underlying cosmological dimensions and connections between the events and how they will orchestrate the establishment of the Empire of Christ. It reveals core hidden messages that underlies the entire essence of the humanity and its destiny, and what makes the earth so important that it draws the attention of powerful cosmic forces. In unravelling these mysteries, this book explores the connection between many core concepts presented in sacred texts including: the creation of the heavens and earth, the Gap Theory, Satan's coup d'état, the cosmic realms and hosts of Heaven (Thrones, Principalities, Dominion and Powers), God's Heavenly Council, recreation of the earth, the creation of humans, creation of Adam and Eve, the fall of Adam and Eve, Satan's usurpation of Adam's authority, the rebellion of the Watchers, the Nephilim and Demons, the Great Flood, the New Beginning, the Tower of Babel, the division of the earth among the Sons of God, the rebellion of the sons of God, the judgement of the gods, the rectification process, the second coming of Christ, law and grace, the return of the Nephilim, the Beast System, the Great Tribulation, transhumanism, the Final Battle, the sons of God, emergence of the Millennial Reign of Christ, the restoration of the Kingdom of God and other topics considered by many to be controversial.

This book is a journey of discovery into the hidden truth of God. It is intended to take the reader through a journey from the beginning of creations to the contemporary times, in an attempt to trace the origin of the strife between God and Satan, the connection between Satan and earth, and why the control of the earth is of such great importance to the cosmic beings. It tells a compelling tale of the grand plan of God to

PREFACE

establish a global empire under the authority of God. It connects several dots littered across the Bible to present a tale of humanity from the creation to the end of the present world as we know it.

Welcome aboard as we dig into these salient mysteries and hidden truths in the Bible in this exciting journey.

CAVEAT

This book was written not for average followers of Christ, but for those followers of Christ who have gained greater depth with the Holy Bible and realised that there are more to most of events presented in the Bible:

> [25] Now there are also many other things that Jesus did. Were every one of them to be written, I suppose that the world itself could not contain the books that would be written (John 21:25 ESV).

I strongly encourage any Christian who wants to read this book to first familiarise themselves with the core tenets of the Holy Bible.

This book is also targeting non-followers of Christ who have outrightly rejected the Bible, because of what they perceived to be outlandish stories, apparent contradictions, missing information, inaccurate historic accounts, and illogical conclusions and beliefs. For genuine seekers in this category, they must have also come to the realization that there is more to life than science and history can explain. Hence, it is only for those who are genuinely searching for the truth and back stories that fills the missing links in the Holy Bible.

The conclusions arrived at in this book are purely based on my interpretation of various sacred texts, as the spirit led. Readers are encouraged to re-examine the texts and arrive at their own conclusions.

CHAPTER 1

Concealed Truth

1.1 THE REVELATION OF CONCEALED TRUTH

For several reasons, many truths about our world, the Kingdom of God, and its operations are concealed from both humans and celestial beings. Paul alluded to this, when he opined that wisdom behind the coming of Christ and his grace to the Gentiles were concealed from the people and celestial beings:

> [9] and to make plain to everyone the administration of this mystery, which for ages past was kept hidden in God, who created all things. [10] His intent was that now, through the church, the manifold wisdom of God should be made known to the rulers and authorities in the heavenly realms, [11] according to his eternal purpose that he accomplished in Christ Jesus our Lord. (Ephesians 3: 9–11 NIV).

The truths are tightly controlled, and in most cases, wrapped in parables and prophetic riddles, that only a few can crack. Not everyone is entitled to have this truth:

> [10] And he said, *Unto you it is given to know the mysteries of the kingdom of God*: but to others in parables; that seeing they might not see, and hearing they might not understand. (Luke 8:10 KJV).

This is a deliberate act, and God reveals these truths to only those He wants to, and at a time He deems appropriate. Oftentimes, these mysteries are revealed to the humble and genuine seekers of truth:

> ²⁵ At that time Jesus answered and said, I thank thee, O Father, Lord of heaven and earth, because thou hast hid these things from the wise and prudent and *hast revealed them unto babes*. (Mathew 11:25 KJV).

There are various reasons for this strategy. Some of the truths are concealed such that only genuine and diligent seekers will find them. Others, because they are strategically important to the plans of God, cannot be allowed to fall into wrong hands or the enemies of God.

The mysteries of God and the operations of his Kingdom are not meant to be revealed to everyone or casual seekers. God expects diligent and wise seekers to find these hidden gems; he had deliberately concealed:

> It is the glory of God to conceal things, but the glory of kings is to search things out. (Proverbs 25:2 ESV).

Others are concealed to protect critical plans of God, by not allowing them to be unduly revealed:

> Truly, you are a God who hides himself, O God of Israel, the Savior. (Isaiah 45:15 ESV).

Such truths are only revealed at the appropriate time. This is particularly pertinent to plans of God concerning the end times. A key one being the uncertainty surrounding the day of the Lord, which is still shrouded in secrecy:

> ³⁶ But of that day and hour knoweth no man, no, not the angels of heaven, but my Father only. (Mathew 24:36 AKJV).

Daniel was also instructed to conceal some of the revelations he got about the end times:

> ⁴ But you, Daniel, shut up the words and seal the book, until the time of the end. Many shall run to and fro, and knowledge shall increase." (Daniel 12:4 ESV)

A careful observation of eschatological prophesies from the Old Testament to the New Testament, will reveal that God was progressively revealing the secrets about this period. Christ's take on this provided more insight into the end time than the prophets of old who prophesied about them. The revelation given to John expounds the information provided by Christ in the gospels about this period.

This concealment of the mysteries of God is essentially because the plans of God are very critical to his goal. Satan and his angels are keen to know about these plans so they can undermine it. Hence, these secrets are only to be revealed on a need-to-know basis. Even when revealed, the plans of God are often hidden or shrouded in parables, riddles and mysteries, so that the enemies of God will not get hold of them and twist/use them to their advantage:

> "To you it has been given to know the secrets of the kingdom of God, but for others they are in parables, so that 'seeing they may not see, and hearing they may not understand.' (Luke 8:10 ESV).

To grasp the full import of this, it must be understood that Satan and his cohorts are at war with God. Hence, they are out to undermine God's plans for his creations. As a result, the Bible, which contains critical information about God's plan for humanity and the earth is enmeshed in various mysteries. This is most evident in prophecies and parables. Christ essentially taught in parables, to prevent the undue revelation of the core purpose of his mission. While ramping up his messages to his disciples as his death was fast approaching, the disciples found it difficult to understand the messages Jesus Christ was reeling out, especially those concerning his crucifixion and resurrection. The clarity of these only came after the fact–the death and resurrection of Jesus Christ. This was the tactics used by God to completely fool Satan and his agents, such that God used them to accomplish the core purpose of Christ's mission in His first coming. Paul alluded to this, when he opined that:

> [8] None of the rulers of this age understood this, for if they had, they would not have crucified the Lord of glory.

The downside of the concealment of these truths, is that many followers of Christ wallow in ignorance and are deprived of grasping the mysteries and plans of God for them:

> [6] My people are destroyed for lack of knowledge; because you have rejected knowledge, I reject you from being a priest to me. (Hosea 4:6 ESV).

This high level of ignorance has led many believers into the hands of deceitful individuals claiming to represent Christ and have superior knowledge of the deep things of God, while leading many away from the truth:

> "For my people are foolish; they know me not; they are stupid children; they have no understanding. (Jeremiah 4:22)

This ignorance is also permeated by many Christian preachers and Biblical scholars who deliberately or inadvertently avoid some of the hard facts in the Bible, as some of these facts are perceived as inconvenient to their preconceived notions and doctrines or what they believe to be true or representative of God's opinion. Hence, they gloss over these truths in the Bible and only present what they are comfortable to teach their followers, which often are merely scratching the surface. However, ignorance of the mysteries of God is dangerous, as it could lead to destruction. The contents of the Holy Bible are meant to guide humans in their earthly sojourn, while maintaining a healthy relationship with God. To avoid being destroyed, there is an expectation that humans should endeavor to discover the truths of God. Hence, there is need for all to diligently search out the truths behind many mysteries of God contained in many sacred texts. This is especially important at this critical moment when the earth is dangerously spiralling out of control, with increasing deception and influence of dark forces, taking hold on the world.

One of the highlights of the gospel is the promise of the establishment of the Kingdom of God. This is the pinnacle of the gospel.

However, there are so many questions surrounding it, such as, is the Kingdom of God a spiritual or physical construct? Why does God have to establish a kingdom on earth? Does it mean the world has not been under God's kingdom. If it is not, under whose authority has it been? What is the composition of this kingdom and how would it come about? How will this kingdom operate?

Hence, it is imperative to understand the mysteries surrounding this concept. This is the focus of this book. However, unravelling these and their full import requires a diligent search and the help of the Holy Spirit, hinging on the promise of God that these mysteries will be revealed towards the end:

> [4] But thou, O Daniel, shut up the words, and seal the book, even to the time of the end: many shall run to and fro, and *knowledge shall be increased*. (Daniel 12:4).

To unravel these secrets, one must start from the sacred books in the Holy Bible. However, biblical texts are wrapped in symbology, parables, allegories, riddles, and mysteries that increases the complexity. Hence, biblical understanding has become problematic to many. The interpretation of biblical passages is so complex that often people arrive at different interpretations even for the simplest passages.

Bible interpretation is an arduous task due to several reasons. Firstly, the Bible we have today has gone through series of translations, making it almost impossible for an average reader to fully grasps the original context and contents. Hence, some of the meanings have been lost in translations. Secondly, no single book contains all the information. The Bible is like a puzzle with bits and pieces of the information littered across many books. Hence, requires putting them together to fully grasp the message. Thirdly, many ancient sacred books that contain some key information and missing links often encountered in the canonised books, have been lost or excluded from the canonised Bible. Even though the process of compilation, canonisation and standardisation of the Bible was a monumental and arduous task, with certain parameters deployed to select which books should be included,[1] this process may not have been without flaws. Thirdly, there are also indications that deliberate attempts were made in the past by individuals/organisations to hide or obscure much information in biblical texts that would have enlightened people. For instance, the name God (YHWH/YaHuWah) present in the original texts is hidden in most translations of the Bible and substituted with LORD. There have been few other substitutions and transliteration of the original texts in the Bible. A classic case of transliteration is that of Christ. The original name of Christ YHW'shua/Yahushua/Yehōšua was transliterated to the Greek word "Iesous". This was subsequently transliterated as Iesus in the Vulgate (Latin translation of the Bible). Further down the line, Iesus made its way in the English translation of the 1611 King James Version (KJV). It should be noted that the letter "I" was originally pronounced as "Y" so even though the spellings were different, the pronunciation of Iesous (Yesous) and Iesus (Yesus) sounded almost alike in both Greek and Latin. The letter "J" came into the picture through the Germans who pronounce J as Y (e.g. Ja for Ya/yes)[2]. This resulted in the final form (Jesus) that has been popularised in subsequent Bible versions.

1. O'Neal, "When Was the", 1; Reyna, "How Was The", 1

2. the consonant form of J was not known in the 14th century, therefore, both J and I used the Y sound, as in the word "yes"; The Christian Realist, "How did we get", 1

Another popular transliteration is that of Lucifer, which was used to substitute the original text (hê-lêl ben-šā-ḥar) in the Vulgate[3]. The translators of King James Bible carried this forward till date. Hence, the interpretation and analyses of biblical contents based on contemporary translations has remained problematic, with no guarantee for 100% accuracy. This further obfuscate the understanding.

Despite the inherent complexities, God also deliberately hides certain critical information so as not to reveal his hands untimely. Daniel was told not to reveal every information he was given until a certain time. John was also told not to write down certain information he heard regarding the end times:

> [4] And when the seven thunders spoke, I was about to write; but I heard a voice from heaven say, "Seal up what the seven thunders have said and do not write it down." (Revelation 10: 4 NIV).

In addition, there are several books that were referenced in the Bible that have essentially been lost (with no surviving records of them). For instance, the Book of the Wars of the Lord was referenced in Numbers 21:14. The Chronicles of the Kings of Israel and Chronicles of the Kings of Judah, which contain stories about events during the reigns of kings Jeroboam of Israel and Rehoboam of Judah respectively, were cited severally in the Book of Kings (1 Kings 14:19, 29). Likewise, several others that have been lost such as the Book of the Covenant, the Manner of the Kingdom (Book of Statutes), the Chronicles of King David, the Book of Samuel the Seer, the Book of the Acts of Solomon and so on. A complete list of the lost books can be found in a document provided by the Christian Resource Center (2024).[4]

Furthermore, many books in the Bible are very concise. Some of them tell stories that span generations that it becomes impossible to write everything down. Even John hinted at this regarding the gospels:

> And there are also many other things which Jesus did, the which, if they should be written every one, I suppose that even the world itself could not contain the books that should be written. Amen. (John 21:25 KJV).

Genesis might be the most concise book in the Bible, as the author needed to cover a lot of topics concerning the origin of man with stories

---

3. Biblical Hermeneutics, "Is Lucifer", 1; Christian Pure, "Lucifer in Latin", 1
4. Christian Resource Centre, "The Lost Books", 1

spanning several generations from the beginning to Abraham. The first few chapters of the Genesis are arguably the most concise as they told stories that span long periods of time. Hence, one should not expect the book to contain all the details.

At times it seems that some details were purposefully left out, hence, increasing the obfuscation. For instance, in Genesis 4, a surprising statement was added under Cain's genealogy, where Lamech was confessing to have committed murder. It seems like a statement that was dropped in there out of nowhere as the previous verses were tracing the genealogy of Cain and out of nowhere, the reader was being told that Lamech killed a man:

> [21] And his brother's name was Jubal: he was the father of all such as handle the harp and organ.
> [22] And Zillah, she also bare Tubal Cain, an instructor of every artificer in brass and iron: and the sister of Tubal Cain was Naamah.
> [23] And Lamech said unto his wives, Adah and Zillah, Hear my voice; ye wives of Lamech, hearken unto my speech: for I have slain a man to my wounding, and a young man to my hurt.
> [24] If Cain shall be avenged sevenfold, truly Lamech seventy and sevenfold. (Genesis 4: 21 - 24 KJV).

So, who was the man that Lamech killed? And why did Lamech commit such an egregious act? The answer to this was not provided in Genesis. Fortunately, there are other books that dwelt a little bit more on certain aspects of the stories in the Bible in greater detail. Some details about this event concerning Lamech were provided in other extrabiblical books such as the Writings of Abraham (Chapter 12) and Book of Jasher (Chapter 2:10–37). Hence, to unpack the mysteries in the books in the Bible, one must consider other sacred texts that complement the stories in the book. However, these books are usually not readily available or acceptable to many followers of Christ, as they were excluded from the canonised Bible. But believers have been charged to assiduously study to unravel the mysteries of God and our world:

> [15] Study to shew thyself approved unto God, a workman that needeth not to be ashamed, rightly dividing the word of truth. (2 Timothy 2:15 KJV)

Hence, in this book, in addition to passages in biblical texts, insights were also drawn from certain extrabiblical texts that were considered to illuminate the passages in the Bible.

1.1.2 Concealed Truth in Extrabiblical Texts

There are several justifications for extracting information from extrabiblical sources. Firstly, many of them provide contextual information that can be used to understand the events in the Bible even more. They serve as gap fillers, especially for the concise passages in the Bible, by providing the backdrop to some of the events narrated in the Bible. Certain details were left out in the books that made it to the Bible. Hence, to have a full picture of the events, there is a necessity to fill the gaps, with details extracted from other valid sources.

Secondly, some books in the Bible extracted information from some extrabiblical texts, hence, setting the precedence for this. For instance, Jude quoted directly from the Book of Enoch, which is among the collections from the Dead Sea Scrolls, and was not included in the canonised Bible. In the Epistle of Jude, the writer who identified himself as *Jude, the servant of Jesus Christ, and brother of James (Jude 1:1 KJV)*, while cautioning followers of Christ not to take the grace of God for granted, revealed several mysteries most of which came directly from the revelations contained in the Book of Enoch. Firstly, Jude hinted about the punishment of the fallen Watchers who abandoned their core responsibilities to descend to earth to fornicate with earthly women:

> [6] And the angels which kept not their first estate, but left their own habitation, he hath reserved in everlasting chains under darkness unto the judgment of the great day. (Jude 1:6 KJV).

The fall of the Watchers as will be discussed in detail in this book, is the central theme of the Book of Enoch.

Secondly, to confirm that he was quoting from the Book of Enoch, Jude cited Enoch in verse 14:

> [14] And Enoch also, the seventh from Adam, prophesied of these, saying, Behold, the Lord cometh with ten thousands of his saints,
> [15] To execute judgment upon all, and to convince all that are ungodly among them of all their ungodly deeds which they

have ungodly committed, and of all their hard speeches which ungodly sinners have spoken against him. (Jude 1:14-15 KJV).

There is no dispute whatsoever that the above quote from Jude came directly from Chapter 1 of the Book of Enoch:

> And behold! He cometh with ten thousands of [His] holy ones
> To execute judgement upon all,
> And to destroy [all] the ungodly:
> And to convict all flesh
> Of all the works [of their ungodliness] which they have ungodly committed,
> And of all the hard things which ungodly sinners [have spoken] against Him. (Book of Enoch 1:9).

What this clearly say is that Jude read the Book of Enoch! But there is no Book of Enoch in the Holy Bible. It must be considered that at that time, there was no Holy Bible as we have it today. Rather the various books that are contained in the Holy Bible were individual books/scrolls that people read. However, when the Church decided to put some of the books into a compilation, not all the books were adopted. Thus, if a book did not make it into the compilation known today as the Bible, it does not nullify its scriptural significance or authenticity. The apostles who followed Jesus read from some of these books that are contemporarily termed apocryphal or extrabiblical texts, to gain insight into the mysteries of the Kingdom of God. So, why would present day followers of Christ preclude themselves from reading these books? It appears that Jude did not only read the Book of Enoch, but also other books that did not make it into the Holy Bible. In verse 9, Jude made a reference about Archangel Michael and the devil contending for the body of Moses:

> [9] Yet Michael the archangel, when contending with the devil he disputed about the body of Moses, durst not bring against him a railing accusation, but said, The Lord rebuke thee. (Jude 1:9 KJV).

This story is not contained in any other book in the Bible. So where did Jude learn this from? Origen of Alexandria[5] suggested in *Chapter 2 of Book III of the De principiis*[6] that the backstory of this quote from Jude

---

5. An early Christian scholar, ascetic, and theologian. Origen | Early Christian Theologian & Scholar | Britannica

6. Origen at Alexandria. De Principiis (Book III). CHURCH FATHERS: De Principiis, Book III (Origen) (newadvent.org)

came from the Assumption of Moses also known as the Ascension of Moses or Jewish Testament of Moses:

> We have now to notice, agreeably to the statements of Scripture, how the opposing powers, or the devil himself, contends with the human race, inciting and instigating men to sin. And in the first place, in the book of Genesis, the serpent is described as having seduced Eve; regarding whom, in the work entitled *The Ascension of Moses (a little treatise, of which the Apostle Jude makes mention in his Epistle), the archangel Michael, when disputing with the devil regarding the body of Moses,* says that the serpent, being inspired by the devil, was the cause of Adam and Eve›s transgression. (De Principiis (Book III) Chapter 2:1)

Footnote *d* of Jude 1 (NIV) also suggested that this quote came from Jewish Testament of Moses: *Jude 1:9 Jude is alluding to the Jewish Testament of Moses (approximately the first century a.d.).*

Likewise, Paul mentioned Jannes and Jambres in his second letter to Timothy:

> [8] Just as Jannes and Jambres opposed Moses, so also these teachers oppose the truth. They are men of depraved minds, who, as far as the faith is concerned, are rejected. (2 Timothy 3:8 NIV)

To an average Bible reader these men and their names would seem strange, as those names were not mentioned in any other book in the Bible. Even though these seem to be a mystery, the event that Paul mentioned where these men opposed Moses is contained in the Bible. These men are the court magicians of Egypt that Pharaoh arrayed against Moses when he was demanding the exodus of Israelites from Egypt (Exodus 7:22, full story in Exodus Chapter 7 to Chapter 9). So where did Paul learn the names of these individuals from? Again, the answer lies in the so-called apocryphal books. Chapter 79 of the Book of Jasher narrated the same story contained in Exodus 7 to Exodus 9 about the encounter between Moses, Aaron, the Pharoah and the magicians with certain extra details that were left out in the Exodus. A snippet of this passage mentioned Jannes and Jambres:

> [25] And Pharaoh said to Moses, What do you require? and they answered him, saying, The Lord God of the Hebrews has sent us to thee, to say, Send forth my people that they may serve me.

> ²⁶ And when Pharaoh heard their words he was greatly terrified before them, and he said to them, Go today and come back to me tomorrow, and they did according to the word of the king.
> ²⁷ And when they had gone Pharaoh sent for Balaam the magician and to Jannes and Jambres his sons, and to all the magicians and conjurors and counsellors which belonged to the king, and they all came and sat before the king. (Book of Jasher 79: 25–27).

One can see from the above that even though the gist of the story in Exodus and the Book of Jasher were essentially the same, many details were added to the story, which provided a broader context to the story. Hence, if God has made effort to reveal some of the mysteries, why would man stop himself from searching out these? For instance, Enoch introduced his Book by saying that the mystery he has been shown pertains to a coming generation that will live through the time of Tribulation:

> The words of the blessing of Enoch, wherewith he blessed the elect [and] righteous, who will be living in the day of tribulation, when all the wicked [and godless] are to be removed. 2. And he took up his parable and said—Enoch a righteous man, whose eyes were opened by God, saw the vision of the Holy One in the heavens, [which] the angels showed me, and from them I heard everything, and from them I understood as I saw, but not for this generation, but for a remote one which is for to come. (Book of Enoch 1: 1–2).

Why would such generation refuse to dig through these mysteries freshly baked from heaven for them?

Therefore, the underlying impetus for this work is that there are many truths about God and his kingdom that are carefully hidden in various ancient books. Unfortunately, many of these books were not canonised and hence not readily available to many. However, this should not pose a hindrance to searching out the truths that enlighten the purpose of man. Thus, to grasp the import of the physicalization of the Kingdom of God on the earth, one must scour through some of these books that provide a broader perspective to the topic.

No doubt there might be some so-called extrabiblical text whose authenticity may be considered doubtful. Hence, it is recommended that any extrabiblical book should be read with utmost caution. As always, the books in the Bible should be used to calibrate and validate information contained in the other books. Any information that deviates from the core tenets of the gospel should be disregarded, because the gospel and truth of God doesn't change, but remains the same.

1.2 IN THE BEGINNING–CREATION OF HEAVENS AND EARTH

To fully grasp the genesis of the contest for earth between God and Satan and the coming empire of Christ, it is important to go back in history, to the beginning–the creation of earth:

> In the beginning, God created the heavens and the earth. (Genesis 1:1 ESV)

This verse clearly sets out who owns these objects, which makeup the universe. The heavens and the earth belong to God (God is their rightful owner), because he created them. This fact will become relevant in trying to understand the strife between God and Satan.

Here, one could also ask in the beginning of what? This beginning supposedly is not just pointing to the beginning of planet earth, but the beginning of all that God created–entire universe (*heavens and the earth*). It should be assumed that at this point (primordial era) nothing else really exists, other than God. So, the universe was more like a vacuum (an empty place). This must be the point God started to create the basic elements (air, fire, earth, and water) from which other elements/materials used in the creation of the heavens and earth were formed. After this, God created the heavens and the earth.

Despite the fact that details about this creation were not extensively proffered in *Genesis 1:1*, this is a complete creation, accomplished in the first epoch. Isaiah hinted that this was made perfect by God, who did not create it empty:

> For thus says the Lord, who created the heavens (he is God!),
> who formed the earth and made it
> (he established it; he did not create it empty, he formed it to be inhabited!)–(Isaiah 45:18 ESV).

This was also hinted in 2 Esdras:

> [38] I said, "O Lord, you spoke at the beginning of creation and said on the first day, 'Let heaven and earth be made,' and your word accomplished the work. (2 Esdras 6:38 New Revised Standard Version Updated Edition).

If God did not create the heavens and earth empty, it means both had some inhabitants. With regards, to the inhabitants of the earth, recall at this point (Genesis1:1) humans have not yet been created. This calls for the question of who were the inhabitants of the earth then, when it was first created alongside the heavens? This question is discussed further in Section 1.3.1.

The time it took for the creation of the heavens and the earth to be completed are not apparent from the Bible. However, it could have taken seconds, hours, days, hundreds, thousands, millions, or billions of years for the creations to be accomplished. The length of day as we know it today (24 hours) based on the apparent rotation of the earth around the sun cannot be the same day being referred to in Genesis 1, because the creation of the sun has not yet happened at this time. Hence, a day in Genesis is more like an epoch (stage or phase). Thus, Day 1 could be read as Epoch 1 or Stage 1. Recall that:

> [8]with the Lord one day is as a thousand years, and a thousand years as one day. (2 Peter 3:8).

Another important thing to note here is that the age of the earth is somewhat close to that of the heavens, because God created the heavens and the earth. Hence, the earth was a key agenda of God's plans and not an addendum. That said, it must be made clear that the creation of the heavens precedes that of the earth. This is made evident in Genesis 1:1 sequence, as well as in the following passage from 2 Peter:

> [5] But they deliberately forget that long ago by God's word the heavens came into being and the earth was formed out of water and by water. (2 Peter 3:5).

After this point the earth became void and without form:

> [2] And the earth was without form, and void; and darkness was upon the face of the deep. And the Spirit of God moved upon the face of the waters. (Genesis 1:2 KJV).

Genesis 1:2 presents a complexity that rattles many. What made the earth that has been completely created to become void and formless? From this verse it could be seen that some of these basic elements were already in place. The earth is already there–although void and formless. There was already water, the deep, and darkness. Something happened to render it formless. The rebellion of Satan which was hinted at in the

Bible, without elaboration happened within this period (between *Genesis 1:1 and Genesis 1:2)*. It is the opinion of this book that the war between the angels of God and angels of Satan was what led to the destruction of this earth and parts of the heavens.

Unfortunately, this aspect of creation history was glossed over (except for snippets and hints dropped here and there in few books of the Bible). Jeremiah saw a vision when the earth was without form and void. The exact same words used in Genesis 1:2:

> I looked on the earth, and behold, it was without form and void;
> and to the heavens, and they had no light.
> [24] I looked on the mountains, and behold, they were quaking,
> and all the hills moved to and fro.
> [25] I looked, and behold, there was no man,
> and all the birds of the air had fled.
> [26] I looked, and behold, the fruitful land was a desert,
> and all its cities were laid in ruins
> before the Lord, before his fierce anger. (Jeremiah 4:23-26).

The mere fact that the earth was mentioned in these texts, and its condition was being described (*The earth was without form and void*), confirms that this was at a time the earth has been created (already in existence). To buttress this post-creation destruction of the earth, the verse hinted on the destruction of the cities (all its cities were laid in ruins-Jeremiah 4:26). This indicates that the cities were already in place before they were ruined by the fierce anger of God. This is to clear up any notion that this verse was referring to the pre-creation period when the earth has not been created. The verse from (Jeremiah 4:23-26), clearly shows that the earth was in existence but was destroyed by God who was angry at it. Certainly, Jeremiah was not referring to the earth he lived on (the present earth). Since the creation of Adam, there has not been a record of the earth becoming formless and void, and without humans. This is also not a reference to the future condition of the earth, because even in the last days, not every person in the world would be killed. Hence, the future earth will not be void of people. So which earth did Jeremiah looked on in that vision, and saw it without form and void? Recall, in this vision there were mountains on that earth, which were "quaking", and hills that were moving "to and fro", and cities that have been laid in ruins. Hence, this is not a reference to a period when the earth has not yet been created. This is an earth that used to bubble with live (man, animals–birds, and vegetation–fruitful–Jeremiah 4:25-26) and properties (cities–Jeremiah

4:26) and was brought to ruin by a cataclysmic event, rendering it void and formless. This must be an earth like the one we have today, thus, making Jeremiah to recognise it as the earth. Jeremiah was taken back in time to see this period when the earth that was perfectly created was made void and formless, so as to understand the impact of the wrath of God when it blazes, as a lesson for the Jews he was prophesying to, at this time.

One may be drawn to think that Genesis 1:2 was an explanation of the state of things before the heavens and earth were created. More like the writer looping back after stating that in the beginning God created heavens and earth. However, considering that every verse in the bible was carefully written, it would have been easier for the writer to have started with: Gen 1:2, and then Gen1:1. Thus, if this was the case, the bible should have been written in the following form:

> [1] In the beginning, the earth was without form and void, and darkness was over the face of the deep. And the Spirit of God was hovering over the face of the waters. (Genesis 1:2)
>
> [2] God created the heavens and the earth. (Genesis 1:1 ESV).

Despite how ridiculous the above re-arrangement of the few verses of Genesis is, this is how many have interpreted the creation story presented in the Genesis. The Bible was concisely and carefully written such that even a subdivision of a verse could have tremendous meaning that spans thousands of years. For instance, when Jesus was handed over the scroll of the prophet Isaiah (Luke 4:18-19), he read only a portion of the prophecy that pertained to his first coming and left out the part that pertained to his second coming. Even though the last sentence was just a fraction of the second verse of Isaiah 61, he did not bother to read the rest of the verse:

> [1]The Spirit of the Lord God is upon me,
>   because the Lord has anointed me
> to bring good news to the poor;
>   he has sent me to bind up the brokenhearted,
> to proclaim liberty to the captives,
>   and the opening of the prison to those who are bound;
> [2] to proclaim the year of the Lord's favor,(Isaiah 61:1-2).

Hence, there seems to be a gap between Genesis1:1 and Genesis 1:2 that was not accounted for in the Bible. This theory regarding the apparent gap or disjoint in the history of the earth is commonly referred to as the Gap theory[7]. Although it is a controversial topic among Biblical scholars, and many followers of Christ are ignorant of it, several facts point that the event that resulted in the destruction of the earth, was the rebellion of Satan and the resultant war in heaven, which led to the expulsion of Satan and his angels from the First Heaven, where God's angels mainly reside. The roots of the strife between God and Satan emanated from this period. Prior to this time, there are indications that there were beings on the heaven and the earth, who were not like present day humans:

> What has been is what will be,
>   and what has been done is what will be done,
>   and there is nothing new under the sun. (Ecclesiastes 1:9 ESV).

The above passage is a very profound statement, that might also be pointing to the fact that the earth has been in existence longer than many think, and there have been many generations that have inhabited the earth. This means that a lot were happening on the earth long before the present humans came into existence. As would be seen later, these beings have some connection with Satan. Hence, when the angelic war happened that earth has to be destroyed. For that earth to have been destroyed shows that it was somehow linked, or important to Satan. In conventional warfare only objects that are considered strategically or tactically important are normally targeted either for takeover or destruction.

1.3 THE HEAVENS: THE COSMIC REALMS AND HOSTS OF HEAVEN

In addition to the creation of the earth, God also created billions of galaxies with billions of stars and planets that are many light years away from the earth, as well the invisible nonphysical realms:

> [9] who made the Bear and Orion,
>   the Pleiades and the chambers of the south;
> [10] who does great things beyond searching out,
>   and marvelous things beyond number. (Job 9: 9–10 ESV).

---

7. DivineNarratives Team, "The Gap Theory", 1; Fairchild, Mary. "Exploring Gap", 1

These are the heavens referred to in Genesis 1:1 that God created before the earth. The psalmist dropped a hint about these, where he listed some of the beings and entities that occupy this space:

> ² Praise ye him, all his angels: praise ye him, all his hosts.
> ³ Praise ye him, sun and moon: praise him, all ye stars of light.
> ⁴ Praise him, ye heavens of heavens, and ye waters that be above the heavens.
> ⁵ Let them praise the name of the Lord: for he commanded, and they were created. (Psalm 148: 2–5 KJV).

In religious circles the invisible realms and dimensions are referred to as the spiritual realms. The equivalent of this in astronomy and quantum physics is classified into the dark matter and dark energy. The 'dark' portraying their immaterial nature and invisibility (their presence can only be discerned from sensing their influence (gravitational attraction) rather than their luminosity). As a matter of fact, the universe is composed mainly of these invisible realms (dark matter makes up 30.1% of the matter-energy composition of the universe and dark energy–69.4%), than of the physical realm–0.5%.[8] These invisible aspects of the universe are the cosmic realms where celestial beings reside:

> 18 While we look not at the things which are seen, but at the things which are not seen: for the things which are seen are temporal; but the things which are not seen are eternal. (2 Corinthians 4:18 KJV).

One can merely guess what is out there. In this realm the hosts of heaven, comprising of beings of multifaceted nature and classes and their domain or phase of influence, exercise the authority given to them by God. Few of the hosts of heaven have been revealed to humanity, many have not yet been revealed. In this realm, there exist various levels and dimensions. Some spaces are pre-dominated by beings that are loyal to God's authority, and other realms predominated by those beings that at one point or the other rebelled against the authority of God and are mostly loyal to Satan or have forged some form of alliance with Satan to undermine the authority of God and his son. Hence, the constant strife in the heavens between the cosmic forces of good and evil, which eventually spills over to the earth. There are indications that about one-third of the heavenly hosts rebelled alongside Satan, when they plotted

---

8. Riess, "Dark matter," 1

to overthrow God. There was also the case of the Watchers who fell after the rebellion of Satan. They have also become the adversaries of God and may have partnered with Satan in his plot to undermine God. In addition to these two angelic camps opposed to God, another group that may have joined the camp of the adversaries of God, are the sons of God, who were judged in Psalm 82. These last sets were given charge of the nations after the flood, but they went beyond their remit. These are discussed in detail further down the line in this book (Section 7.2). What has been outlined here is not an exhaustive list of all the adversaries of God, these are only the ones that could be gleaned from the Bible, there may be others who have rebelled or disobeyed God at one time or the other that were not made known to man.

The heavenly realm is broadly classified into two: the Third Heaven, where the throne of God is and the good beings reside; and the Second Heaven, where the fallen ones mainly occupy. Under this categorisation, the earth is usually considered the First Heaven. Even though, the good cosmic beings reside in the Third Heaven, they occasionally come into the Second Heaven and First Heaven where they encounter the fallen ones and humans respectively. The invisible realm is tightly woven with the physical realm and there is consistent interplay between these two. The stories in the Bible are a constant reminder of the interplay between the cosmic and the physical realms. The encounter between Gabriel and the prince of Persia is an example of such encounters (Daniel 10:13–21). Gabriel also interacted with Mary at the Annunciation of the coming of Christ. A being from a higher heaven has default access to lower realms, whereas one from a lower realm will require extra permission to access. Isaiah, John, and Paul, were granted access to these realms in visions, likewise other holy mean such as Enoch.

1.3.1 Celestial Beings: Thrones, Dominion, Powers, Principalities, and Angels

The celestial beings are the beings God created to reside in the celestial realms. These beings are created to serve God by carrying out various functions for the actualization of God's plans across the universe. There are indications that these beings are of different nature and classes. In the Bible, some of these were introduced through their interactions with humans. In the epistle of Paul to the Colossians, he mentioned some of these beings, while introducing Christ as the first creature of God:

> [15] Who is the image of the invisible God, the firstborn of every creature:
> [16] For by him were all things created, that are in heaven, and that are in earth, visible and invisible, whether they be thrones, or dominions, or principalities, or powers: all things were created by him, and for him:
> [17] And he is before all things, and by him all things consist. (Colossians 1: 15–17 KJV).

Also, in Ephesians, Paul identified various levels of cosmic authorities:

> [12] For we wrestle not against flesh and blood, but against principalities, against powers, against the rulers of the darkness of this world, against spiritual wickedness in high places. (Ephesians 6:12 KJV).

Generally, 9 choirs of angels are recognised, largely based on Thomas Aquinas's *Summa Theologica*, where he classified and described the roles of the angelic classes[9]. Prominent ones include the angels (mal'ākh) who tend to appear like humans, archangels who are chief angels, often referred to as princes with territorial powers (principalities e.g. Michael), the seraphim, and the cherubim, who have very frightening nature and demeanour. These last two sets are found around the throne of God and perform protective functions (guard the throne of God). Others that are commonly recognised by humans include the Thrones, Dominions, Powers, Authorities, the Watchers, and rulers. Obliviously, this is not an exhaustive list as the chances of the existence of other classes are great. These beings are relevant to humans as even though they do not reside here, they influence the happenings on the earth. Hence, Paul's caution about them (Ephesians 6:12).

These beings tend to have permanent areas of residence designated to them in the cosmic realms. In the vision recorded in Chapter 7 of the Ascension of Isaiah, he was shown eight realms outside of the earth. The first realm identified as the firmament, had a close resemblance to the earth and the beings there were the fallen ones loyal to Satan. There, Isaiah saw continuous war and strife:

---

9. Catholic Adventurer, "The Choirs of Angels", 1; Catholic Online, "The Nine Choirs, 1"

> 9. And we ascended to the firmament, I and he, and there I saw Sammael and his hosts, and there was great fighting therein and the angels of Satan were envying one another.
>
> 10. And as above so on the earth also; for the likeness of that which is in the firmament is here on the earth (Ascension of Isaiah 7: 9–10).

This realm is generally referred to as the Second Heaven (astral plane), using the three-tier heavenly structure. Beyond this realm, are 7 realms (which the passage associated with heavens), where the holy ones of God reside. Each of these realms (except the sixth heaven) had a Throne in charge of the realm, to whom the praises go to. A careful read of the passage suggest that the thrones are rulers of the realms, who in turn are subject to God, and channel the praises from their respective realms to God:

> 16. And I asked the angel who conducted me, and I said unto him: "To whom is this praise sent?"
>
> 17. And he said unto me: "(it is sent) to the praise of (Him who sitteth in) the seventh heaven: to Him who rests in the holy world, and to His Beloved, whence I have been sent to thee. [Thither is it sent.]" (Ascension of Isaiah 7: 16–17).

The Thrones are a class of celestial beings that oversee different realms or aspects of the cosmos. They are kings in their respect and normally have thrones and crowns that matches their status. The twenty-four elders with golden crowns and sitting on thrones usually found around the throne of God, when important divine businesses are being convened, bowing and worshipping him are mostly likely Thrones:

> [10] The four and twenty elders fall down before him that sat on the throne, and worship him that liveth for ever and ever, and cast their crowns before the throne, saying,
>
> [11] Thou art worthy, O Lord, to receive glory and honour and power: for thou hast created all things, and for thy pleasure they are and were created. (Revelation 4: 10–11 KJV).

1.3.2 The "gods"

The Bible is replete with references to gods. These are usually ascribed to beings that pretend to have great authorities and powers equal to God's, and hence, demand worship and loyalty from humans.

There is a consistent narrative about the contention between these gods and God, running across the Bible. So, this begets the question, are there other gods? If there are, how does that fit into the monotheist narrative? What are the origins of these gods? Are they of equal power and status or is there a special one among them with greater power and status? These are some of the questions this section attempts to answer.

Throughout the Holy Bible there are references to God, as *God of gods* (El Elyon), the *Most-High God, Lord of lords, King of kings*. The adjectives used to qualify God is usually comparative. All these appellations and titles point towards the fact that there are entities in the celestial realm identified as gods that are subject to God. For example, the title "Most-High God" suggests there are other gods, but this one is the highest. Similarly, El Elyon (God of gods) suggests the same thing, likewise the "Only True God", which suggest others are inferior. Even God addressed some of the entities, who he identified as sons of the Most-High, as gods (Psalm 82:6). Jesus Christ later affirmed this (*John 10:34-38*):

> [34] Jesus answered them, "Is it not written in your Law, 'I said, you are gods'? [35] If he called them gods to whom the word of God came—and Scripture cannot be broken— [36] do you say of him whom the Father consecrated and sent into the world, 'You are blaspheming,' because I said, 'I am the Son of God'?

All these point to the fact that there is a category of supernatural entities that have attained the godlike status. But this is not to say that they can be compared to God, who created them:

> [11] "Who is like you, O Lord, among the gods?
> Who is like you, majestic in holiness,
> awesome in glorious deeds, doing wonders? (Exodus 15: 11 ESV).

It was God's prerogative to elevate these sons of God to this level/rank. Just the same way he elevated Jesus above every rule, authority, power, and dominion in heaven after his resurrection:

> [19] and what is the immeasurable greatness of his power toward us who believe, according to the working of his great might [20] that he worked in Christ when he raised him from the dead and seated him at his right hand in the heavenly places, [21] far above all rule and authority and power and dominion, and above every name that is named, not only in this age but

also in the one to come. ²² And he put all things under his feet (Ephesians 1: 19–22).

However, despite all these glaring facts, many Christians are in denial of this truth. Many tend to contend the idea of the existence of other gods. They resent the idea of other gods and usually present certain passages in the Bible where the gods are described as inanimate objects (idols) that cannot do anything; to back up their doctrinal positions. 1 Corinthians 8:4 is a go to verse:

> ⁴ Therefore, as to the eating of food offered to idols, we know that "an idol has no real existence," and that "there is no God but one." (1 Corinthians 8:4 ESV).

However, they ignore the rest of the passage where Paul acknowledged the *so-called gods in heaven or on earth*:

> ⁵ For although there may be so-called gods in heaven or on earth—as indeed there are many "gods" and many "lords"— ⁶ yet for us there is one God, the Father, from whom are all things and for whom we exist, and one Lord, Jesus Christ, through whom are all things and through whom we exist. (1 Corinthians 8:5–6 ESV).

Again, another verse presented is Moses declaration that there is no one else besides God, while addressing Israelites:

> ³⁵ Unto thee it was shewed, that thou mightest know that the Lord he is God; there is none else beside him. (Deuteronomy 4:35 KJV).

However, looking at the context of this, Moses was telling the Israelites who had witnessed what God did to the worshipers of Baal Peor, that God has demonstrated that none of the gods can withstand his powers:

> ³ Your eyes have seen what the Lord did because of Baalpeor: for all the men that followed Baalpeor, the Lord thy God hath destroyed them from among you.
> ⁴ But ye that did cleave unto the Lord your God are alive every one of you this day. (Deuteronomy 4:3–4 KJV).

The mere fact that the first and second commandments was aimed at dissuading Israelites from worshipping these gods, suggests that there are powerful entities behind these idols that could challenge the authority of God. Otherwise, why would God be so much concerned with people going after inanimate objects that are nothing?

Although many followers of Christ and scholars think that the Bible suggests that idols are nothing–just inanimate objects, what it is rather being communicated by the writers is that those lesser deities cannot be compared to the Most-High God–they pale in significance before God Almighty. Hence, those passages are grammatical expressions used in comparability rather than denials of these entities. Hence, even though some passages contain phrases such as "idols are nothing, who can neither see nor hear." (Isaiah 44:9, 1 Corinthians 8:4), the writers were not trying to deny the existence of the entities behind the idols but rather using such expression to demonstrate clearly that these are incomparable to God, to the extent that they are worth nothing if you place them side-by-side with God. The writers were essentially saying that those gods inhabiting those idols are nothing compared to God. For instance, a passage in Psalm 97, that portrays these idols as nothing, went ahead to compel them to worship God:

> All worshipers of images are put to shame,
>   who make their boast in worthless idols;
>   worship him, all you gods! (Psalm 97:7 ESV).

Hence, if these were truly nothing or inanimate objects why would the psalmist urge the gods to worship God, as in the case above? The psalm, which was declaring that God is reigning over all, further noted in the following verse that God is exalted far above all gods.

> For you, O Lord, are Most-High over all the earth;
>   you are exalted far above all gods. (Psalm 97:9 ESV).

Hence, these verses, which appear to suggest there are no other gods are merely establishing the supremacy of God over these other entities and not denying their existence (see Section 7.4). Moses referred to these entities inhabiting the idols as demons and gods:

> [16] They stirred him to jealousy with strange gods;
>   with abominations they provoked him to anger.
> [17] They sacrificed to demons that were no gods,
>   to gods they had never known,
> to new gods that had come recently,
>   whom your fathers had never dreaded.
> [18] You were unmindful of the Rock that bore you,
>   and you forgot the God who gave you birth.
> (Deuteronomy 32:17 ESV).

Paul in 1 Corinthians 10, also confirmed that behind these idols are demons:

> [19] What do I imply then? That food offered to idols is anything, or that an idol is anything? [20] No, I imply that what pagans sacrifice they offer to demons and not to God. I do not want you to be participants with demons. [21] You cannot drink the cup of the Lord and the cup of demons. You cannot partake of the table of the Lord and the table of demons. [22] Shall we provoke the Lord to jealousy? Are we stronger than he? (1 Corinthians 10: 19–22 ESV).

One thing that is clear is that the mere fact the Israelites struggled to stay away from these gods, shows that they had powerful seductive influences that kept entrapping them. Obviously, there were some forms of benefits their worshippers were receiving from them, such as solving some problems for them or some other things that were physically manifested among the people, for them to have continued to be relevant or attractive to the society. Even evil spirits can bestow some gifts to their worshippers to keep them loyal. This is not farfetched, because God gave certain powers to these beings, which they can deploy to mesmerise humans. During the temptation of Jesus Christ, Satan offered him the kingdoms of this world if he bowed to him. Satan could not have offered Jesus what he does not have. In the same vein, these gods, supposedly were offering the people certain benefits, to lure them to worship them.

Having established the existence of these entities, referred to as gods, the next line of questioning is to probe who these gods are and where they came from. The origins of these gods are not clearcut, because there are so many things that have not been revealed to humans. One thing we know about them from Biblical passages is that they were created by God, since he called them sons of the Most-High (Psalm 82:6). What is usually not clear is whether they attained the rank of being called gods by God, or they were made so from the beginning by God. It is common knowledge that there are different hierarchies of supernatural beings. Paul suggested the following strata of heavenly authorities: rule, authority, power, and dominion. These may be various hierarchies of celestial beings or positions of authorities that can be granted to the sons of God. We also know about the angels, archangels, cherubim, seraphim, ophanims, etc. It is my supposition that the gods emanated from some of the hierarchies or classes of celestial beings, because at some point in their lifetime, they enjoyed the favor of God. When they fell out with

God, they became adversaries. One of the ways they contend with God is to demand worship from humans, who God created, to divert their attention away from their creator. They are determined to undermine God by sharing his glory among men.

1.3.3 The Divine Assembly–God's Heavenly Council

The concept of Divine Assembly or Divine Council is the idea that there is a consultative forum in God's royal heavenly court made up of selected members of the sons of God, who regularly sit to deliberate on various issues pertaining to God's creation. God presides over this council, where the celestial beings participate in making critical decisions with God and execute these decisions. Some of these decisions pertain to how the earth (as revealed in the Bible) is governed, and by extension, to other parts of the universe[10]. The specific composition of this council is not certain, but there are various references in the Bible of this council meeting to decide on different matters. The clearest reference to how this council functions was documented in Psalm 82:

> 82 God has taken his place in the divine council;
> in the midst of the gods he holds judgment: (Psalm 82: 1 ESV).

There is really no dispute as to what is going on in the passage. There is a divine council, and God has a presiding role in that council made up of other celestial beings. There was another snapshot of the divine council meeting that Micaiah was given a scoop of. In this instance, the council was deliberating on what could be done to King Ahab. In this meeting, God allowed the sons of God to present different ideas regarding how best to *treat the Ahab's malady,* by enticing him to go to a battle that would lead to his demise:

> [19] ... I saw the Lord sitting on his throne with all the multitudes of heaven standing around him on his right and on his left. [20] And the Lord said, 'Who will entice Ahab into attacking Ramoth Gilead and going to his death there?'
> "One suggested this, and another that. [21] Finally, a spirit came forward, stood before the Lord and said, 'I will entice him.'
> [22] "'By what means?' the Lord asked.

---

10. Heiser, *The Unseen Realm*, 23–43; Heiser, "Divine Council", 1; Minton, "What is the Divine Council", 1

"'I will go out and be a deceiving spirit in the mouths of all his prophets,' he said.

"'You will succeed in enticing him,' said the LORD. 'Go and do it.'

(1 Kings 22: 19–22 NIV).

This passage reveals a lot on how the council functions. God raises the topic for discussion; he then allows members of this assembly to proffer their opinions. After sampling the opinions, he decides on which opinion should be taken forward. A key question that jumps out here is the identity of the deceiving spirit and why God chose his suggestion. The deceptive spirit in this council might even be Satan. The good guys were providing solutions that were not perfect, but the deceptive spirit came up with a plot that fits his résumé. This suggestion that the deceptive spirit might be Satan, may be shocking to many, but it must be recalled that in Job, Satan appeared in such assembly of the sons of God:

> [6] Now there was a day when the sons of God came to present themselves before the Lord, and Satan came also among them. (Job 1: 6 KJV).

Satan's impetus to appear before this assembly might be linked to the fact that at that time, he might be usurping Adam's authority to represent the earth in the council. Adam, being a son of God, would have probably been at such assembly, had he not fallen, and handed over his mandate to Satan. It is, however, unlikely that Satan still has access to the divine assembly after the death and resurrection of Christ, having reclaimed the mandate of Adam from Satan.

Daniel was also given a vision of this council:

> "I watched till thrones were put in place,
> And the Ancient of Days was seated;
> His garment was white as snow,
> And the hair of His head was like pure wool.
> His throne was a fiery flame,
> Its wheels a burning fire;
> [10] A fiery stream issued
> And came forth from before Him.
> A thousand thousands ministered to Him;
> Ten thousand times ten thousand stood before Him.
> The court was seated,
> And the books were opened. (Daniel 7:9–7:10 NKJV).

In this vision, there was a mention of thrones being setup, which suggests that the occupants of these thrones are regarded as kings in this respect. Thrones are usually reserved for kings or those in positions of power. This begs the question of who those thrones were setup for? However, there was a differentiation of the throne of God, which was "fiery flame", from the other thrones that were setup. This points to some form of hierarchical structure in this council. Hence, from this vision, we can start stratifying this divine assembly comprising of God (who presides over this assembly), some beings at a high level of authority who sit on thrones, myriads of beings ministering to God, and possibly another myriads of beings observing the proceedings of the court. These thrones in the divine council were also sighted by John in the vision of the court of God, where end time proceedings were being deliberated:

> ² Immediately I was in the Spirit; and behold, a throne set in heaven, and One sat on the throne. ³ And He who sat there was like a jasper and a sardius stone in appearance; and there was a rainbow around the throne, in appearance like an emerald. ⁴ Around the throne were twenty-four thrones, and on the thrones I saw twenty-four elders sitting, clothed in white robes; and they had crowns of gold on their heads. ⁵ And from the throne proceeded lightnings, thunderings, and voices. (Revelation 4:2–5 NKJV).

Here John identified the number of thrones that were set up before the throne of God. The beings seated on the 24 thrones; he identified as elders. Although, mostly misunderstood, the use of the world elders tends to suggest the rank of these beings in the divine council. Many Christians view these 24 elders as the patriarchs or some saints who are given such position before God. But this is not so, considering the foregoing. These are rather special class or rank of celestial beings that have risen to a high position of authority that is equivalent to kingship. These might be rulers of different planets or other aspects/dimensions or realms of the universe. To confirm they have kingly authority, these 24 elders had crowns on their heads. However, they are still subject to God. They bow before God to demonstrate their status and loyalty to God:

> the twenty-four elders fall down before Him who sits on the throne and worship Him who lives forever and ever, and cast their crowns before the throne. (Revelation 4:10 NKJV).

The idea of the existence of other kings in the cosmic realm is not absurd considering that God is referred to as the King of kings and God of gods. These appellations are not figurative. Hence, there must be other kings and gods that are subjects to God.

The existence of the divine council is simply God's prerogative, and he can do with or without it. There is a clear hierarchy (levels of authorities) in heaven, as the council is more or less a council of unequal, as opposed to polytheistic view of council of equals. The position of Christ in this assembly is usually not apparent, however, these can be gleaned from the celestial hierarchy as mentioned in many biblical passages, which suggest that God precedes everything, then followed by Christ, and other creatures:

> [22] Who is gone into heaven and is on the right hand of God; angels and authorities and powers being made subject unto him. (1 Peter 3:22 KJV).

This hierarchy was also reiterated in Ephesians:

> [20] Which he wrought in Christ, when he raised him from the dead, and set him at his own right hand in the heavenly places,
> [21] Far above all principality, and power, and might, and dominion, and every name that is named, not only in this world, but also in that which is to come:
> [22] And hath put all things under his feet, and gave him to be the head over all things to the church (Ephesians 1: 20–22 KJV).

A comprehensive discussion on the divine council was presented by Heiser.[11]

---

11. Heiser, "Divine Council", 1; Heiser, *The Unseen Realm*, 23–43.

CHAPTER 2

The World that Was

2.1 WHO WERE THE ORIGINAL OCCUPANTS OF THE EARTH?

There is a lingering question on the age of the earth and whether Adam and Eve were the first beings that walked on the planet. A casual interpretation of biblical account would place the age of the earth to roughly six thousand years, matching the time of the creation of Adam and Eve. However, various evidence found through archaeological discoveries, geology, and radiocarbon dating tend to suggest that the earth has been around for much longer than six thousand years.[1] Some estimates place the age of the earth to be around four and half billion years. It must be caveated that radiocarbon dating is not perfect. However, the wide gap between six thousand and four and half billion years that has been estimated by science is worth a second look. Fossil records points to the existence of various species of humanoids, some of which have lived on this planet longer than six thousand years such as the Denisovan, Neanderthals–Homo Neanderthalensis[2]. Neanderthals are believed in the scientific circle to be extinct species of ancient predecessors of modern humans (Homo Sapiens) who walked the earth between four hundred thousand and forty thousand years ago[3]. There have been discoveries

---

1. Hendricks, "Geological time", 1; National Geographic Society, "How Did Scientists", 1; Blakemore, "How archaeologists, 1"

2. Cooke, "What's the difference", 1; Croft, "Denisovan vs Neanderthal", 1; Stringer, "Are Neanderthals", 1

3. Blakemore, "What were Neanderthals", 1

of many ancient cities pre-dating the time of Adam found buried deep under the oceans, such as the Dwarka in India[4], and the Yonaguni Monument in Japan[5], estimated to have been in existence about nine thousand and ten thousand years respectively.

There are key questions that pop out regarding the age of the earth. Could this seemingly divergent views between the biblical account and scientific evidence about the age of the earth be reconciled, based on breadcrumbs littered in the Bible? Were biblical writers given the full creation story or were some portions considered not particularly relevant at the time the books were written, left out? Or perhaps, the Bible has been misread for a long time that certain details were skipped. If the earth is far older than six thousand years, were there no beings occupying it? If other beings occupied the earth before six thousand years ago, that means that Adam and Eve were not the first beings to have lived on earth. However, if Adam and Eve were the first beings or occupiers of the earth, were they the beings that occupied the planet after its creation?

These have been the questions that have nagged biblical scholars and historians. Many want to solve the enigma that surrounds the identity and nature of the original inhabitants of the earth. This quest to uncover the original occupants of the earth has persisted for generations and the jury is still out. This chapter examines the world that existed on earth immediately after its creation, to uncover what it was like and the beings that occupied it. The term 'beings' is used here to suggest that the entities being considered may not necessarily be humans, but some form of humanoid entities with intelligence.

One of the indicators of a pre-homo sapiens world is the age of the earth. Based on biblical account, it has only been about six thousand years since the creation of Adam. However, considering that the earth was created in the beginning (soon after the heavens were created), it does not add up that it has only been six thousand years from the beginning of creation.

There are pointers in the Bible that suggest that soon after the creation of the earth, it was filled with some beings, who occupied it. This earth was bubbling with lives and properties (cities) before it was destroyed as can be gleaned from (Jeremiah 4:25–26).

---

4. Archaeology World, "India", 1; BBC, "Dwarka", 1
5. BBC, "Japan's mysterious", 1

Another indication is the mandate God gave the male and female after their creation to replenish the earth:

> ²⁸ And God blessed them, and God said unto them, Be fruitful, and multiply, and replenish the earth, and subdue it: and have dominion over the fish of the sea, and over the fowl of the air, and over every living thing that moveth upon the earth. (Genesis 1:28 KJV).

This suggests that there was something on the earth before, which needed to be replenished and subdued. To buttress this point, God gave Noah and his sons the same mandate, after the cataclysm of the flood:

> And God blessed Noah and his sons, and said unto them, Be fruitful, and multiply, and replenish the earth.
> ² And the fear of you and the dread of you shall be upon every beast of the earth, and upon every fowl of the air, upon all that moveth upon the earth, and upon all the fishes of the sea; into your hand are they delivered. (Genesis 9:1-2 KJV).

For the case of Noah, we know exactly what was to be replenished and what was to be subdued, but in the case of the first man and woman, the Bible did not say, and one can only rely on conjectures and snippets dropped here and there in biblical texts.

There is also a pointer to this pre-human world by Solomon in Ecclesiastes, where the writer was pointing to an age before us that has been forgotten:

> What has been is what will be, and what has been done is what will be done, and there is nothing new under the sun. ¹⁰ Is there a thing of which it is said,
> "See, this is new"?
> It has been already
>   in the ages before us.
> ¹¹ There is no remembrance of former things,
>   nor will there be any remembrance of later things yet to be among those who come after. (Ecclesiastes 1:9-11 ESV).

A curious mind would wonder what age that was before Solomon's generation that there is no remembrance of? This cannot be the age that commenced with Adam, because key events of this age were documented in sacred texts. Hence, Solomon must be referencing another age in time past, that has been forgotten.

Looping back to Genesis 1:1, it is clear that there was no human (as we know humans to be now) immediately after the heavens and earth were created. Man only came into the scene in day 6. However, Isaiah 45:18 indicates that God did not create the earth empty, but to be inhabited. Therefore, he must have created some form of beings to occupy the freshly created earth. Who were these beings? The answer to this could be gleaned from Job when God was interrogating Job:

> [4] Where wast thou when I laid the foundations of the earth? declare, if thou hast understanding.
> [5] Who hath laid the measures thereof, if thou knowest? or who hath stretched the line upon it?
> [6] Whereupon are the foundations thereof fastened? or who laid the corner stone thereof;
> [7] *When the morning stars sang together, and all the sons of God shouted for joy?* (Job 38:4–7).

First, for God to have posed this question to Job, it clearly implies that there was no man when the earth was created. Even though, the question was posed to Job, it is clear from the passage that God was generalising humanity with Job. The passage indicates that the sons of God were already present and watching as the foundations of the earth were being laid. Here we see that the morning stars sang, and all the sons of God shouted together. But why did the morning stars sing together when the foundations of earth were laid. Why were they singled out among the sons of God to be mentioned in this passage, in connection with the creation of the earth? Was there a special affinity to the earth as it was being formed? Perhaps, the sons of God were just onlookers or also helping God (stretching the measuring lines across the earth) as he laid the foundations. This might also be a clue to suggest that these were the first inheritors of the new creation of God, hence their happiness and joy which made them to sing, while the rest of the sons of God were equally joyful.

Secondly, the fact that the sons of God were present when the foundations of the earth were laid, demonstrates their existence long before the creation of the earth. Thus, one can infer that after the heavens were created, angelic beings were created to fill it (hence, confirming that it was not created empty). Subsequently, God started the creation of the earth, and these beings were joyous at the prospects of a new abode. Furthermore, the writer of Hebrews opined that God created man a little lower than angels:

> ⁷ You made them a little lower than the angels;
> you crowned them with glory and honor (Hebrews 2: 7 NIV).

This implies that angels (or the celestial beings being refereed here) have already been created before man. You cannot create something lower than another thing that has not existed. If it was the other way round, the passage ought to have read, you created the angels higher than man.

From the foregoing, it may seem that the freshly created earth was initially inhabited/controlled by these angelic beings, referred to as the *morning stars*, because in the passage they were distinguished from the rest of the sons of God for emphasis. One can hypothesise that Adam and Eve were not the first set of beings to have walked this earth, but rather the first of their kind to have lived and walked on this planet (this angle is explored further in Chapter 3).

So, who are the morning stars? A search through the scriptures shows some passages where morning stars were mentioned. In Revelation, Jesus Christ referred to himself as the bright morning star:

> ¹⁶ "I, Jesus, have sent my angel to testify to you about these things for the churches. I am the root and the descendant of David, the bright morning star." (Revelation 22:16 ESV).

Satan was also referred to as morning star in some Bible translation (NIV, WEB, CEB etc):

> ¹² How you have fallen from heaven,
> morning star, son of the dawn!
> You have been cast down to the earth,
> you who once laid low the nations! (Isaiah 14:12 NIV).

Although, other translations such as the ESV translates the key word Hê-lêl, which is the name of the entity the passage was referring to, as Day Star, or Lucifer (KJV).

> ¹² "How you are fallen from heaven,
> O Day Star [hê-lêl] son of Dawn [ben-šā-ḥar!]
> How you are cut down to the ground,
> you who laid the nations low! (Isaiah 14:12 ESV).

> ¹² How art thou fallen from heaven, O Lucifer, son of the morning! how art thou cut down to the ground, which didst weaken the nations! (Isaiah 14:12 KJV).

Despite the ambiguity in the meaning of 'morning star', the term seems to be referring to a certain group of celestial beings. There are pointers in the Bible that tend to suggest that Satan had a form of responsibility given to him by God over the earth, which he has refused to relinquish.

In Isaiah 14, the entity that the prophesy was referring to, had some form of control over the earth (he shook the earth and made the kingdoms to tremble). He essentially subdued the earth. This same entity was aspiring to ascend to the heavens to set his throne above the stars of God. This is a suggestion that the entity's throne was not in heaven but in a lower realm, most likely on earth where he held sway, and his plan was to raise this throne to the heavens where he can tower above other stars:

> [13] You said in your heart,
> "I will ascend to the heavens;
> I will raise my throne
> above the stars of God;
> I will sit enthroned on the mount of assembly,
> on the utmost heights of Mount Zaphon.
> [14] I will ascend above the tops of the clouds;
> I will make myself like the Most-High."
> [15] But you are brought down to the realm of the dead,
> to the depths of the pit.
>
> [16] Those who see you stare at you,
> they ponder your fate:
> "Is this the man who shook the earth
> and made kingdoms tremble,
> [17] the man who made the world a wilderness,
> who overthrew its cities
> and would not let his captives go home?" (Isaiah 14:12 NIV).

Furthermore, when the sons of God gathered to present themselves to God (probably to render account of what they have been up to), Satan also came. To acknowledge his presence, God asked him where he had come from, and the first thing he blurted out was that he was patrolling the earth:

> [7] The Lord said to Satan, "From where have you come?" Satan answered the Lord and said, "From going to and fro on the earth, and from walking up and down on it." (Job 1:7 ESV).

This seems to suggest that Satan had some links or responsibility to the earth, and possibly other parts of the universe. God wouldn't have asked him the question, if he only oversees the earth. Patrolling the earth may have been one of the assignments God gave him before the rebellion and he still held onto that, after usurping Adam's mandate. This is clear from how God responded. He did not reproach Satan on why he was patrolling the earth, which indicates that somewhat Satan was acting within his remit. If he was overreaching or contravening the command of God by patrolling the earth, God would have rebuked and explicitly told him he was out of line, and possibly mete out an appropriate punishment to him, as he did to the angels who left their first estate as noted in Jude 1:6.

Based on the foregoing, one can safely assume that Satan was put in charge of the earth and by extension the beings who initially occupied it. Hence, even after he lost it after the rebellion, he found a way to take it back from Adam. My supposition is that this world that was thriving on earth after its creation, is linked to several lost civilizations such as Lemuria (Mu)[6] and the Atlantean civilization (which may have spanned hundreds of thousands or millions of years). This world developed to a very advanced level and slowly became proud of their achievements to the extent that their angelic leader, Satan (O Day Star, son of Dawn) began to aspire to be like God. This aspiration led to the rebellion and the subsequent angelic war in heaven, when Satan was stripped of his authority and position. The impact of this war was catastrophic, resulting in the demise of this pre-human world, with its inhabitants forced into the deep.

2.1.1 Atlantis–one of the lost pre-adamic civilizations

At the fringes of mythology, where it meshes with history lies the story of Atlantis, an ancient civilization that once existed on earth. Although, largely dismissed, the existence of Atlantis and perhaps other ancient cities and kingdoms is an idea that is worth entertaining in the view of the possibility of a pre-adamic world. Although, currently classed as a myth or fable, the central story is that Atlantis was a civilization that was destroyed and submerged underwater, because they became proud and greedy[7]. It is generally believed that it once lied somewhere within the

---

6. DeLong William. "The Lost Continent of Lemuria", 1; Grey, "What Is the Lost", 1
7. Harvey, "The true story of Atlantis", 1

Atlantic Ocean. Alongside Atlantis is another mythical ancient civilization, the Lemurian civilization, that is believed to lie below the Pacific Ocean.

According to the legends, the Atlantean civilization was characterised by advanced technology, great wealth (the land was rich in various kinds of precious minerals and natural resources). Plato narrated the story of the cataclysmic destruction of Atlantis, in two of his dialogues (Timaeus and Critias). He claimed the knowledge of Atlantis had been passed down by poets, priests, and other ancient sources (most likely from Solon[8]; student of Pythagoras; and initiates of ancient Egyptian secret brotherhood guarding hidden wisdom). According to Plato, the founders of Atlantis were hybrids (half god and half human). Plato estimated that the Atlantean civilization existed about nine thousand years prior to his time (before 350 BC when Plato wrote the story). This timing places the Atlantean civilization to an era that was prior Adam. Hence, the obfuscation of its existence. This aligns with the hypothesis in the previous section, which hinted that long before humans were created, Satan and other angelic beings inhabited the earth.

The Bible has references to cities and people who were submerged because they disobeyed God. A key one can be found in Ezekiel 26, where God was warning the inhabitants of Tyre, and points to a world of old, that was destroyed when waters from the deep covered those cities as reference:

> [19] "For thus says the Lord God: When I make you a city laid waste, like the cities that are not inhabited, when I bring up the deep over you, and the great waters cover you, [20] then I will make you go down with those who go down to the pit, to the people of old, and I will make you to dwell in the world below, among ruins from of old, with those who go down to the pit, so that you will not be inhabited; but I will set beauty in the land of the living. [21] I will bring you to a dreadful end, and you shall be no more. Though you be sought for, you will never be found again, declares the Lord God." (Ezekiel 26:19–21 ESV).

In this passage God raised various salient points, which the current generation casually dismiss. The key fact here is that there are people of old, who dwell in a world that has been submerged by water. Unlike the

---

8. Solon, Athenian statesman, law maker and poet most likely got the from his travels to Egypt where he might have interacted with members of Egyptian mystical society, who were custodians of ancient knowledge.

people who died in Noah's flood, the people whose cities were ruined and submerged in this passage somehow managed to stay alive. Somehow, they manage to survive the cataclysm, which points to the fact that they may have acquired some form of immortality or were created to be immortal. Perhaps they are part of the angelic beings, that were corrupted by Satan.

Going by several biblical passages, it is hard for one not to conclude that there are beings inhabiting the underbellies of the earth. Paul while commenting on the high authority of Christ, also alluded that there are beings under the earth:

> [10] so that at the name of Jesus
> every knee should bend
> *of those in heaven and on earth and under the earth* (Philippians 2: 10 NCB).

In Exodus, reference was also made to beings under the earth, that humans could worship. The mere fact that humans could worship these beings suggests that beings being referred here are not just mere animals inhabiting these regions:

> [4] "You shall not make for yourself an image in the form of anything in heaven above or on the *earth beneath* or in the waters below. [5] You shall not bow down to them or worship them; for I, the Lord your God, am a jealous God, punishing the children for the sin of the parents to the third and fourth generation of those who hate me, (Exodus 20: 4–5 KJV).

According to legends, the Atlantean civilization was built to an enviable state with the help of aliens (extraterrestrial beings) and they eventually became proud and bellicose. This seems to tally with the pride of Satan that led to his downfall. Satan was so proud to the extent that he became too ambitious and aspired to be like God. He wanted to ascend and place his throne, which was on earth in heaven. This aspiration led to the war in heaven as Satan had to be cut down to size, and the civilization he built destroyed:

> [12] "How you are fallen from heaven,
> O Day Star, son of Dawn!
> How you are cut down to the ground,
>   you who laid the nations low!
> (Isaiah 14:12 ESV)

The beings that were living in this civilization were submerged into the oceans alongside their cities. The earth became utterly destroyed (without form and void–Genesis 1:2), as a result of this war:

> ² The earth was without form and void, and darkness was over the face of the deep. And the Spirit of God was hovering over the face of the waters. (Genesis 1:2).

2.1.2 What About Dinosaurs?

Archaeological findings have revealed that there was a point in time that certain gigantic animals such as various species of dinosaurs lived on this earth. Based on the dating of the various dinosaurs' fossils, the era of dinosaurs apparently spans beyond the six thousand years adamic era. Hence, they must have existed on this planet prior the time of Adam. The description of Behemoth in Job 40, suggests that it may be a class of dinosaur, that pre-dated humans:

> ¹⁵ "Behold, Behemoth,
>   which I made as I made you;
>   he eats grass like an ox.
> ¹⁶ Behold, his strength in his loins,
>   and his power in the muscles of his belly.
> ¹⁷ He makes his tail stiff like a cedar;
>   the sinews of his thighs are knit together.
> ¹⁸ His bones are tubes of bronze,
>   his limbs like bars of iron.
> ¹⁹ "He is the first of the works of God;
>   let him who made him bring near his sword! (Job 40: 15–19 NIV).

Here God is saying that this gigantic animal is the first of his works. This places the animal alongside the time the heavens and the earth were created. Hence, they must have been part of the beings that filled the earth after its creation, before the cataclysm that rendered the earth void and formless. This suggests that these animals roamed the earth long before Adam did. Their disappearance from the earth, and archaeological evidence suggest that they might have died through a sudden cataclysmic event. A large section of the scientific community believes that an asteroid which hit the earth led to their sudden demise[9]. This places them to have occupied the earth alongside the previous occupants of this planet,

---

9. Rannard, "The asteroid", 1

who were destroyed during the war that ensued after the rebellion of Satan.

2.2 SATAN'S COUP D'ÉTAT: THE REBELLION OF SATAN AND HIS ANGELS

It is common knowledge that some time ago, there was a strife in the heaven among the creations of God who inhabit this realm. This ended up in a powerful rebellion that attempted to overthrow God from his seat of power. When the attempted coup failed, Satan, who led the mutiny, alongside other angels loyal to him, lost their place/positions in the highest heaven.

The origin of this strife is usually traced to a point in time when Satan's ambition grew so big, that he aspired to be like God. This was an affront to God, considering that Satan, a created being, contrived in his heart to be like God his maker, so that he can be worshipped as God is:

> [13] You said in your heart,
>   'I will ascend to heaven;
> above the stars of God
>   I will set my throne on high;
> I will sit on the mount of assembly
>   in the far reaches of the north;
> [14] I will ascend above the heights of the clouds;
>   I will make myself like the Most-High.' (Isaiah 14:13-14 ESV).

Ezekiel also hinted at this moment when Satan contrived this plot against God:

> [14] You were an anointed guardian cherub.
>   I placed you; you were on the holy mountain of God;
>   in the midst of the stones of fire you walked.
> [15] You were blameless in your ways
>   from the day you were created,
>   till unrighteousness was found in you. (Ezekiel 28:14-15 ESV).

In these prophesies, God laid bare the cause of fall from grace for the entity/entities, who were once close to God, but did something that turned them into adversaries of God. Considering Satan to be the chief adversary of God, it can be perceived from the passage (Isaiah 14:13-14), that Satan devised this plot from a place that was lower than heaven or where God's throne was. Even though Satan had access to heaven as a

Seraph/Cherub, his throne or phase of influence, was set in a location lower in status than the heaven. Hence, the reason he needed to ascend from where he was to heaven, to establish his throne there. As a guardian cherub (Ezekiel 28:14 ESV) or seraph, it could be inferred that Satan already had a place in heaven, in close proximity to God, so his aspiration for something higher than this position, must be a position that matches or surpasses God's position. As there cannot be two contending thrones or Gods in heaven, this plot of ascension was a direct challenge to the authority of God that cannot be tolerated. It is imperative to note that from the visions in the Ascension of Isaiah, that there was no throne or different groupings of angels in the sixth heaven, as there were in the lower five heavens he was shown:

> 7. And he said: "From the sixth heaven there are no longer angels on the left, nor a throne set in the midst, but (they are directed) by the power of the seventh heaven, where dwelleth He that is not named and the Elect One, whose name has not been made known, and none of the heavens can learn His name.

One may wonder if the reason behind this missing throne was because the original occupant of the throne has been thrown out during the rebellion in heaven, or whether this was originally designed this way.

In addition to his role in heaven, it seems Satan also had an oversight function on the inhabitants of the earth. Hence, it is possible, he may have contrived this plan of ascension into the upper echelons of heaven, while he was on earth. This must be the reason why that earth and any other parts of the universe that were corrupted by Satan and his angels were destroyed.

It is commonly assumed by many Bible scholars that the passages from Isaiah 14 and Ezekiel 28 are God's pronouncements against the same entity (Satan), and allusions to the origin of the strife. However, there is a possibility that Ezekiel's prophesy may be referring to another fallen entity who was a cherub. Satan is usually referred to as a dragon or serpent:

> Then another sign appeared in heaven: an enormous red dragon with seven heads and ten horns and seven crowns on its heads. [4] Its tail swept a third of the stars out of the sky and flung them to the earth. (Revelation 12:3–4 NIV)

> He seized the dragon, that ancient serpent, who is the devil, or Satan, and bound him for a thousand years. (Revelation 20:2 NIV).

This suggests that he was among the Seraphic angelic class (the fiery serpentine beings), whereas the entity in Ezekiel's prophesy was identified as an anointed cherub (the four headed angelic beings that guard the throne of God). The reconciliation of these two descriptions still proves problematic. One guess that may be hazard is that Satan may have been a seraph that also functioned as a cherub, hence the qualification as an *anointed* cherub.

2.3 THE CATACLYSMIC WAR THAT DESTROYED THE EARTH

There are snippets in the Bible that points to a devasting destruction of the entire earth. A passage in Job suggested that God has shaken the earth out of its place before and removed the mountains:

> ⁵ he who removes mountains, and they know it not,
>   when he overturns them in his anger,
> ⁶ who shakes the earth out of its place,
>   and its pillars tremble; (Job 9: 5–6 ESV).

However, since the time of Adam, there is no record of such cataclysmic destruction. Even the flood of Noah was not as destructive (destruction of the entire earth). Noah and his family survived, whereas Jeremiah saw an earth that was devoid of man, vegetation, animals, and cities:

> ²⁵ I looked, and behold, there was no man,
>   and all the birds of the air had fled.
> ²⁶ I looked, and behold, the fruitful land was a desert,
>   and all its cities were laid in ruins
>   before the Lord, before his fierce anger. (Jeremiah 4:23–26 ESV).

Thus, this devastating event must have been because of something else, supporting the view that the earth was destroyed and submerged in the course of the war between the angels of God and those of Satan. The war that ensued from the rebellion of Satan was cataclysm as it destroyed various aspects of the initial creations of God (from the heavens to earth) to warrant a subsequent recreation. The magnitude of this angelic war can only be imagined. There are pointers of several of such cataclysmic events within the scientific community commonly referred to as mass extinction events[10]. Due to the fact that Satan was able to mobilise one-third of angelic beings to fight on his side against God, it can be assumed that this war may have been interplanetary or intergalactic (fought on various fronts across multiple planets and galaxies in the physical and spiritual realms), touching on various spheres of influences of the different beings participating in the battle, including the earth. Jeremiah also saw some aspects of this devastation:

> [23] I looked on the earth, and behold, it was without form and void;
> and to the heavens, and they had no light.
> [24] I looked on the mountains, and behold, they were quaking,
> and all the hills moved to and fro.
> [25] I looked, and behold, there was no man,
> and all the birds of the air had fled.
> [26] I looked, and behold, the fruitful land was a desert,
> and all its cities were laid in ruins
> before the Lord, before his fierce anger. (Jeremiah 4:23–26 ESV).

The passage from Jeremiah is very profound, when processed in depth. It seems to suggest that in the vision he was shown, he initially saw an earth that was teeming with live, but as he looked on, he observed that the earth has become formless and void, and all the people, cities, birds he had seen previously were gone.

Ezekiel also points to this fact that there was a world of old, that was destroyed and waters from the deep covered it:

> [19] "For thus says the Lord God: When I make you a city laid waste, like the cities that are not inhabited, when I bring up the deep over you, and the great waters cover you, [20] then I will make you go down with those who go down to the pit, to the people of old, and I will make you to dwell in the world below, among ruins from of old . . ." (Ezekiel 26:19–20 ESV).

This submerged world of old is most likely the so-called marine kingdom, where mermaids, sirens, and other aquatic humanoid hybrid beings reside. This suggests that part of the beings in this marine world are the remnants of the first generation of beings who inhabited the earth (pre-human beings). These beings may have been made immortal or gained immortality through genetic modification, hence, their ability to

---

10. Cohen, "A Cataclysmic Event", 1; Ritchie, "There have been", 1

survive under the oceans. Or God decided to preserve them till the final Judgement:

> ²⁷ For thus says the Lord, "The whole land shall be a desolation; yet I will not make a full end. (Jeremiah 4:27).

2.4 EXPULSION FROM HEAVEN

A key passage to the expulsion of Satan from the presence of God is the testament of Jesus Christ, who told his disciples that he witnessed the moment Satan fell from heaven:

> ¹⁸ And he said to them, *"I saw Satan fall like lightning from heaven"*. (Luke 10:18 ESV).

Another reference to this moment is contained in Ezekiel 28:

> ¹⁵ You were blameless in your ways
> from the day you were created,
> till unrighteousness was found in you.
> ¹⁶ In the abundance of your trade
> you were filled with violence in your midst, and you sinned;
> so I cast you as a profane thing from the mountain of God,
> and I destroyed you, O guardian cherub,
> from the midst of the stones of fire. (Ezekiel 28:15–16 ESV).

Even though this prophesy was being addressed to the king of Tyre, it seems to be a double prophesy with the king of Tyre, used as a metaphor for Satan. The contents suggest an entity that has lived and walked in the heavens, before being cast out. Hence, it can safely be assumed that when the rebellion of Satan and his angels failed, they were expelled from the mountain of God (the immediate presence of God). Satan lost his position as an anointed cherub. Suffice it to say that they were not chained in prison but rather cast out to another realm in the heavens (Second Heaven), where they presently reside. As a result, there would be the next phase of angelic war in the heavens, during the end time, when Satan and his angels will finally be cast out from the heavens and forced down to the earth:

> 7 Then war broke out in heaven. Michael and his angels fought against the dragon, and the dragon and his angels fought back. 8 But he was not strong enough, and they lost their place in heaven. 9 The great dragon was hurled down—that ancient serpent

called the devil, or Satan, who leads the whole world astray. He was hurled to the earth, and his angels with him. (Revelation 12:7–10 NIV).

Although, many people tend to think that the war in heaven mentioned in the above passage is a reference to the previous war in heaven, this is rather a future war that will happen at the end of ages. Detailed discussion of this was presented in the Final Battle for Earth.[11]

---

11. Anejionu, "The Final Battle", 70.

CHAPTER 3

Cosmic Interregnum and Recreation

3.1 THE INTERREGNUM

After the devastating war in heaven, there seemed to have been an interregnum where the cosmos essentially became dormant and quiet as God takes stock of things. This period could have lasted any length of time, hundreds, thousands, millions of years. This was the state of the universe that was recorded in Genesis 1:2:

> The earth was without form and void, and darkness was over the face of the deep. (Genesis 1:2 ESV).

However, at the end of interregnum, God decided to reactivate things, hence, recreating things that were destroyed during the war:

> And the Spirit of God was hovering over the face of the waters. (Genesis 1:2 ESV).

3.2. LET THERE BE LIGHT!

The next thing God did was to restore cosmic order by separating the good angels from the bad angels. Thus, He called out the Light (the good angels) and after vetting them and found them to be good (possibly a reference to their loyalty during the war), he separated them from the bad angels (Darkness):

> ³ And God said, "Let there be light," and there was light. ⁴ And God saw that the light was good. And God separated the light from the darkness. ⁵ God called the light Day, and the darkness he called Night. And there was evening and there was morning, the first day. (Genesis 1: 3–6 ESV).

It is important to note here that Day and Night in this verse were capitalised, a hint that these are entities with proper names, and different from the 'day' and 'evening' used to mark the different phases of creation. The separation of the good angels from the bad angels, in the second phase (day) of the recreation process points to the barrier between the First Heaven and the Second Heaven. The good angels are placed in the First Heaven, while the bad angels are constrained within the Second Heaven. Subsequently, God created a physical barrier (the firmament) to separate the Third heavens from the Second Heaven and the earth:

> ⁶ And God said, "Let there be an expanse in the midst of the waters, and let it separate the waters from the waters." ⁷ And God made the expanse and separated the waters that were under the expanse from the waters that were above the expanse. And it was so. ⁸ And God called the expanse Heaven. And there was evening and there was morning, the second day. (Genesis 1: 6–8 ESV).

3.3. RECREATION OF THE EARTH

Having separated the Day from the Night, God proceeded to recreate the earth. He did this by making the previously submerged earth to reemerge from the water covering it:

> ⁹ And God said, "Let the waters under the heavens be gathered together into one place, and let the dry land appear." And it was so. ¹⁰ God called the dry land Earth, and the waters that were gathered together he called Seas. And God saw that it was good. Genesis 1: 9–10 ESV

It can be seen from this passage that no creative process, such as laying the foundations of the earth, measuring it, and so on, as God outlined in Job, took place here. The difference between the process God used in creating the earth and what was presented in Genesis 1:9–10 can be gleaned from what God said in Job 38. There were important considerations taken (establishing the foundations and cornerstone of earth;

COSMIC INTERREGNUM AND RECREATION

measuring the dimensions and so on), when God was creating the earth the first time:

> ⁴ Where wast thou when I laid the foundations of the earth? declare, if thou hast understanding.
> ⁵ Who hath laid the measures thereof, if thou knowest? or who hath stretched the line upon it?
> ⁶ Whereupon are the foundations thereof fastened? or who laid the corner stone thereof;
> ⁷ *When the morning stars sang together, and all the sons of God shouted for joy?* (Job 38:4 -7).

These activities that God declared that he used in the creation of the earth, were not reflected in Genesis 1:9. Rather, Genesis stated that God separated the waters so that what it covered could reappear. This is a clear indication that this was not the initial creation, when God created everything from scratch, but a restorative process. What happened here was a re-arrangement and separation of things that already existed (having been created in a different epoch). Note that the land that emerged in this passage was called Earth (note the capitalization). This capitalization of the earth was probably a way to differentiate this new earth from the old one created in the beginning, which was represented with small letter (¹In the beginning, God created the heavens and the earth). From here also it should be noted that although God created heavens (many heaven) in the beginning, during the second day recreation, he did not create the heavens again but merely restored celestial order by separating the entities in heavens into light and darkness, after which the focus shifted to the restoration of the earth. Although, God may have carried out further restoration work in the heavens to repair the impact of the war in heaven, these were not recorded, as the focus was on earth. Hence, the psalmist alluded that God renewed the earth with his spirit (remember the Spirit of God hovered over the waters):

> ³⁰ Thou sendest forth thy spirit, they are created: and thou renewest the face of the earth. (Psalm 104:30 ESV).

This recreation of the earth formed bulk of the descriptions presented in Genesis 1. However, many tend to see this as the description of the initial creation of the earth. It should also be considered that in the process of the recreation and restoration, God may have also created new things that were previously not in existence, as well as choosing not to restore some beings or things that were present in the previous creations.

3.4. RESTORATION OF VEGETATION

During the third day/phase of the recreation process, God restored the vegetative part of the earth. He called them to sprout, which again, suggests that they were already existing within the soil. So, this must not be the first time they were created. They have already been created in various groupings (kinds), hence, the reason they were commanded by God to re-emerge from the soil according to the pre-existing kinds he created them in:

> 11 And God said, "Let the earth sprout vegetation, plants yielding seed, and fruit trees bearing fruit in which is their seed, each according to its kind, on the earth." And it was so. 12 The earth brought forth vegetation, plants yielding seed according to their own kinds, and trees bearing fruit in which is their seed, each according to its kind. And God saw that it was good. 13 And there was evening and there was morning, the third day. (Genesis 1: 11–13 ESV).

3.5. LIGHTS IN THE FIRMAMENT

Following the restoration of the vegetation, God restored the luminaries, to lighten up the earth and support the vegetation, as well as for signs, and for time keeping on earth:

> 14 And God said, "Let there be lights in the expanse of the heavens to separate the day from the night. And let them be for signs and for seasons, and for days and years, 15 and let them be lights in the expanse of the heavens to give light upon the earth." And it was so. 16 And God made the two great lights—the greater light to rule the day and the lesser light to rule the night—and the stars. 17 And God set them in the expanse of the heavens to give light on the earth, 18 to rule over the day and over the night, and to separate the light from the darkness. And God saw that it was good. 19 And there was evening and there was morning, the fourth day. (Genesis 1: 14–19 ESV).

This passage refers to restoration of astronomic bodies to illuminate the newly restored earth, as well as support the vegetation that was sprouting. This is where many normally get confused and run back again to the beginning of the chapter. In Genesis 1: 3–6, we were told that God called out the light and separated it from darkness. We normally associate light

COSMIC INTERREGNUM AND RECREATION

to the sun, moon and stars (the celestial luminaries). However, in this passage God is calling out lights again. So, are these the same light? Or was God creating something new. Again, it can be seen from these passages that creative processes were not taking place. God is calling out what is already existing.

One way to look at these is that God is assigning the lights certain roles to play on earth. We know that angelic beings are usually referred to as beings of light. Behind the physical luminaries (astronomic bodies), there are spirits (celestial beings) that power them. What we perceive as luminaries are physical manifestations of these celestial beings. Here, God was assigning certain duties to them on earth. The primary responsibilities of these angelic beings are to ensure that the separation between the angels of light and angels of darkness is maintained (and to separate the light from the darkness - Genesis 1: 14–18). Here, God was choosing specific sets of angelic beings to be stationed in the heavens to ensure a separation between the light and the darkness. Viewed this way, these are guardian angels at the border between the Third and Second heaven, ensuring the separation is not breached. The secondary responsibility (which is evident in the physical realm) of these entities is to illuminate and support life on earth ([15] and let them be lights in the expanse of the heavens to give light upon the earth). This verse when considered deeply sounds like God was saying let the angelic beings who are primarily separating the day from the night, also, serve as lights in the sky to illuminate the earth. This illumination of the earth by angelic beings is a foreshadow of the future, when God himself will be the one that will illuminate the earth in the new earth that will emerge at the end of age:

> [23] The city does not need the sun or the moon to shine on it, for the glory of God gives it light, and the Lamb is its lamp. [24] The nations will walk by its light ... (Revelation 21: 23-24 NIV).

3.6. RESTORATION OF MARINE LIFE, BIRDS AND TERRESTRIAL ANIMALS

On the fifth day God restored marine, and aerial creatures. He blessed them and commanded them to multiply.

> [20] And God said, "Let the waters swarm with swarms of living creatures, and let birds fly above the earth across the expanse

> of the heavens." ²¹ So God created the great sea creatures and every living creature that moves, with which the waters swarm, according to their kinds, and every winged bird according to its kind. And God saw that it was good. ²² And God blessed them, saying, "Be fruitful and multiply and fill the waters in the seas, and let birds multiply on the earth." ²³ And there was evening and there was morning, the fifth day. (Genesis 1: 20 -23 ESV).

Following the restoration of marine creatures and birds, God restored terrestrial animals on the sixth day:

> ²⁴ And God said, "Let the earth bring forth living creatures according to their kinds—livestock and creeping things and beasts of the earth according to their kinds." And it was so. ²⁵ And God made the beasts of the earth according to their kinds and the livestock according to their kinds, and everything that creeps on the ground according to its kind. And God saw that it was good. (Genesis 1: 24–25 ESV).

Again, God was calling out pre-existing creations of his (Let the earth bring forth living creatures according to their kinds).

3.7. THE CREATION OF HUMANS (MALE AND FEMALE)

Having made the earth conducive for human inhabitation, God proceeded to create humans. This is a special creation that God decided to make. New creatures that would take the image of God. To buttress the importance of this piece of work, God got others involved (*let us make…*). This was remarkably different from the previous acts when God was doing everything by Himself:

> ²⁶ Then God said, "Let us make man in our image, after our likeness. And let them have dominion over the fish of the sea and over the birds of the heavens and over the livestock and over all the earth and over every creeping thing that creeps on the earth." (Genesis 2:26 ESV).

It is important to note that here two beings were created: a male and female.

> ²⁷ So God created man in his own image,
>   in the image of God he created him;
>   male and female he created them. (Genesis 2:27 ESV).

And God gave them dominion over all that he has created on earth:

> [28] And God blessed them. And God said to them, "Be fruitful and multiply and fill the earth and subdue it, and have dominion over the fish of the sea and over the birds of the heavens and over every living thing that moves on the earth." [29] And God said, "Behold, I have given you every plant yielding seed that is on the face of all the earth, and every tree with seed in its fruit. You shall have them for food. [30] And to every beast of the earth and to every bird of the heavens and to everything that creeps on the earth, everything that has the breath of life, I have given every green plant for food." (Genesis 1: 26–31 ESV).

There are key points to note here. These new breeds of beings were created to replace what has been existing on earth prior its destruction. God restored things that used to be on earth, but did not want to restore the previous beings occupying the earth. Hence, the decision to create new beings to take their place. These beings created in the image of God, were created after God had restored every other thing on earth: light, vegetation, marine life, birds, and land animals. This sequence is very critical in understanding subsequent passages, dealing with the creation of Adam and Eve (see Chapter 4).

3.8. THE WHEAT AND TARES (DARNEL)–CORRUPTION OF HUMANS

Jesus Christ told an interesting parable in the gospels that tends to suggest that after God created humans in His image, Satan, created his own set of humans/humanoids on earth:

> [24] He put another parable before them, saying, "The kingdom of heaven may be compared to a man who sowed good seed in his field, [25] but while his men were sleeping, his enemy came and sowed weeds among the wheat and went away. [26] So when the plants came up and bore grain, then the weeds appeared also. [27] And the servants of the master of the house came and said to him, 'Master, did you not sow good seed in your field? How then does it have weeds?' [28] He said to them, 'An enemy has done this.' So the servants said to him, 'Then do you want us to go and gather them?' [29] But he said, 'No, lest in gathering the weeds you root up the wheat along with them. [30] Let both grow together until the harvest, and at harvest time I will tell the

reapers, "Gather the weeds first and bind them in bundles to be burned, but gather the wheat into my barn."' (Mathew 13:24–30 ESV).

[36] Then he left the crowds and went into the house. And his disciples came to him, saying, "Explain to us the parable of the weeds of the field."

He answered and said to them: "He who sows the good seed is the Son of Man. [38] The field is the world, the good seeds are the sons of the kingdom, but the tares are the sons of the wicked one. [39] The enemy who sowed them is the devil, the harvest is the end of the age, and the reapers are the angels. [40] Therefore as the tares are gathered and burned in the fire, so it will be at the end of this age. [41] The Son of Man will send out His angels, and they will gather out of His kingdom all things that offend, and those who practice lawlessness, [42] and will cast them into the furnace of fire. There will be wailing and gnashing of teeth. [43] Then the righteous will shine forth as the sun in the kingdom of their Father. He who has ears to hear, let him hear! (Mathew 13:37–44 ESV).

The agenda of Satan in venturing into this was to corrupt God's creation or to repopulate the newly restored earth with his creations, through the backdoor. There is an allusion of the creation/corruption of humans by Satan and his cohorts presented in the Sumerian creation story such as those presented in the Eridu Genesis[1] and the Epic of Atraḥasis[2]. According to the popular versions of the story, the Annunaki came to earth from a distant planet known as Niburu. They genetically modified humans to become labour force required to mine gold from the earth, which they needed to repair their planet. This version was popularised by Zecharia Sitchin in his book The 12th Planet, published in 1976. This book indicates a tampering of an existing creation by an external force. This line of thinking also aligns with the wheat and tare parable that Christ posited, where the enemy tampered with the creation of God.

The wheat and tares apparently look similar, hence, difficult to differentiate them in their early stages. This suggests that the beings Satan made closely resembled those of God and they mingled with each other. Hence, making it difficult to distinguish at early stages. However,

---

1. Britannica, "Eridu Genesis", 1
2. Mark, "The Atrahasis Epic", 1; US Archives, "The Epic of Atraḥasis",1

at maturity the wheat will produce good grain (fruit) and the tares bad grain (poisonous fruit). This ties up to another passage in the gospel:

> [16] Ye shall know them by their fruits. Do men gather grapes of thorns, or figs of thistles? [17] Even so every good tree bringeth forth good fruit; but a corrupt tree bringeth forth evil fruit. [18] A good tree cannot bring forth evil fruit, neither can a corrupt tree bring forth good fruit. [19] Every tree that bringeth not forth good fruit is hewn down, and cast into the fire. [20] Wherefore by their fruits ye shall know them. (Mathew 7:16–20 AJKV).

This separation will happen at the end of the age and every human will pass through the crucible of the Great Tribulation so as to prove what they are.

CHAPTER 4

The Adamic Era

4.1 THE MAN OF DUST: THE CREATION OF ADAM

Genesis 2:5–7 presents a very curious information about the state of the earth, suggesting that the earth was bare and devoid of vegetation and humans:

> [5] When no bush of the field was yet in the land and no small plant of the field had yet sprung up—for the Lord God had not caused it to rain on the land, and there was no man to work the ground, [6] and a mist was going up from the land and was watering the whole face of the ground— [7] then the Lord God formed the man of dust from the ground and breathed into his nostrils the breath of life, and the man became a living creature. (Genesis 2: 5–7 ESV).

This passage is confusing, considering the fact that back in Genesis 1, God has completed the creation of male and female. So, what is going on here? Is this a flashback to the state of the earth before creation commenced, or is this a different round of creation? The latter appears to be the case, as there are differences in the sequence of creation presented in Genesis 1 and that presented in Genesis 2, as we shall see in this section.

Although, many have been taught to believe that the creation of Adam narrated in Genesis 2 is an expatiation of the creation of humans presented in Genesis 1, there are clear pointers in the passages that suggest otherwise.

THE ADAMIC ERA

The creation and restoration story were concluded on the 7th day, when God rested:

> Thus the heavens and the earth were finished, and all the host of them.
> ² And on the seventh day God ended his work which he had made; and he rested on the seventh day from all his work which he had made. (Genesis 2:1–2 KJV).

Notice here that this passage indicated that the creations of the heavens and earth and their inhabitants (hosts) were completed on the 6th day, before God rested. The writer also reiterated this by stating that the creation of the generations of heavens and earth were completed during this epoch (These are the generations of the heavens and of the earth when they were created, in the day that the LORD God made the earth and the heavens Genesis 2:4 KJV). After this epoch God rested. Pertinent to observe that resting does not imply retirement. God rests, but he does not stop creating. Because what follows next was another epoch of creation.

The creation story subsequently presented in the following passages, strongly suggests a different creation:

> ⁷ And the Lord God formed man of the dust of the ground, and breathed into his nostrils the breath of life; and man became a living soul. ⁸ And the Lord God planted a garden eastward in Eden; and there he put the man whom he had formed.
> 9 And out of the ground made the Lord God to grow every tree that is pleasant to the sight, and good for food; the tree of life also in the midst of the garden, and the tree of knowledge of good and evil. (Genesis 2:7–9 KJV).

Firstly, in Genesis 1 creation story, humans (male and female) were created at the same time (Genesis 1:27), with the mandate to be fruitful, multiply, fill, and subdue the earth (Genesis 1:28). However, in Genesis 2, only a man (man of the dust) was initially created and placed in the garden, with the mandate to maintain the garden:

> ¹⁵ And the Lord God took the man, and put him into the garden of Eden to dress it and to keep it. (Genesis 2:15 KJV).

Clearly this man created here is not the same as the male that was created back in Genesis 1:27. This man that was created from dust is a special breed of mankind, because although he was recognised as a man, he had a distinguishing attribute that was added to him (breath of life) from God that turned him into a living soul (Genesis 2:7). The material used to create the humans of Genesis 1, was not mentioned and there was no indication that they got this breath of life from God. This could be an indication that they were made from a different material other than dust, hence the reason, this new man's material needed to be mentioned.

Secondly, the sequence of creation presented in Genesis 2, was almost completely opposite to that narrated in Genesis 1. Hence, it is either one believes that the Bible was contradicting itself (which I do not believe) or Chapter 1 and Chapter 2 are telling two different stories of different creations). In Genesis 1 creation, the humans were created after God restored every other thing on earth: light, vegetation, marine life, birds, and land animals. They were the last thing God created on the 6th day, before resting. However, in Genesis 2 creation, the man of dust was initially created, even before the vegetation (no bush of the field was yet in the land and no small plant of the field) sprouted (Genesis 2:5), and garden was planted in Eden (Genesis 2: 8–9). After the garden was planted in Eden, trees were subsequently made to grow in the garden (Genesis 2:9), then rivers to water the garden (Genesis 2:10). It is important to note here that in Genesis 1 creation, the earth was commanded to bring forth vegetation comprising of grass, herb, and fruit tree of all kinds (Genesis 1:11), whereas in Genesis 2, only trees of all kinds were made to grow in the garden (Genesis 2:9). This difference might be pointing at something important though not yet clear.

At this point (after the planting of the trees in the garden), the man of dust was still alone in the garden, tending the garden all by himself. His loneliness caused God to create some companions for him:

> [18] Then the Lord God said, "It is not good that the man should be alone; I will make him a helper fit for him." [19] Now out of the ground the Lord God had formed every beast of the field and every bird of the heavens and brought them to the man to see what he would call them. And whatever the man called every living creature, that was its name. [20] The man gave names to all livestock and to the birds of the heavens and to every beast of the field. (Genesis 2:18–20).

Note that at this point the female companion is yet to be created, unlike in the creation of Genesis 1, where man (male and female were created, with the command to be fruitful and multiply almost immediately). Furthermore, here, God created the animals to keep the man company. Note that the animals were created after the man and before

THE ADAMIC ERA

the woman. However, in Genesis 1:24-25, God created the animals before the male and female were created in Genesis 1:26.

Thirdly, another distinctive feature here is that whereas God incorporated others in the creation of the man and woman of Genesis 1 (*Then God said, "Let us make man[h] in our image, after our likeness..."* –Genesis 1: 26 ESV), He solely created Adam without consulting any other being:

> ⁷ then the Lord God formed the man of dust from the ground and breathed into his nostrils the breath of life, and the man became a living creature. (Genesis 2:7 ESV).

Fourthly, in Genesis 4, after Cain was cursed and banished from the land he had occupied with his parents and brother, he was afraid that some people who live outside their immediate vicinity would kill him:

> ¹³ Cain said to the Lord, "My punishment is greater than I can bear. ¹⁴ Behold, you have driven me today away from the ground, and from your face I shall be hidden. I shall be a fugitive and a wanderer on the earth, and whoever finds me will kill me." ¹⁵ Then the Lord said to him, "Not so! If anyone kills Cain, vengeance shall be taken on him sevenfold." And the Lord put a mark on Cain, lest any who found him should attack him. (Genesis 4:13-14).

By making this request to God, Cain was not insinuating that his parents would kill him. He was clearly afraid of others. God told him that "anyone" that attacks or kills him will be punished severely (sevenfold vengeance). This leads to the question of whether Adam, his wife, and children were the only humans/or beings on the earth at this time. Because if they were, why was Cain afraid of being killed by other people? And recall that God did not refute this? This also pops the second question of where Cain got his wife from. His parents at this time did not have any female child. Cain went away after being cursed and settled in the land of Nod, presumably, it was around this vicinity that he got his wife from:

> Then Cain went away from the presence of the Lord and settled in the land of Nod, east of Eden.
> ¹⁷ Cain knew his wife, and she conceived and bore Enoch. When he built a city, he called the name of the city after the name of his son, Enoch. (Genesis 4:13-14).

Judging from the above, it appears that Adam was created after the first generation of humans were created. But why would God create another set of humans after he had already created male and female in day 6 (Genesis 1)? There is strong indication that the first generation of humans (the male and female created on the 6th Day) were corrupted by Satan, thus prompting God to create a new breed of humanity, hence the creation of the man of dust (Adam). Another perspective to look at this is that Adam was created for a different purpose other than the purpose of the previous breed of humans. After he was created, God made a special place for him (the garden in Eden) and took him there to be tending it. Note there was no explicit mandate for Adam to increase and multiply and he was not immediately given any female companion. To support this, only Adam was created, there was no woman, which suggests that God was not planning for Adam to immediately procreate. Even when he got a wife, she was there as a companion/helper. The mandate for Adam to tend the garden might be a euphemism for Adam's purpose, which is to tend the earth, and the humanity created in Day 6 of creation. God was coming to the garden to interact with Adam. It seems that God was training and preparing Adam in the garden to become the ruler of the earth and the rest of humanity. Hence, his primary assignment was not to increase and multiply but to tend the garden. God's regular visit to the Garden of Eden, may be for training and bringing Adam up to speed with the way the universe operates and to govern the earth. The garden was a special place where God can easily communicate with Adam.

In contrast to the above, the humans created in Genesis 1 were identified as male and female and they were immediately charged to increase and multiply (Genesis 2: 1–3 ESV).

Despite the brevity, something profound is captured in this passage. The man was formed by God with the dust of the ground, after which he was activated into a living soul with the breath of God. Subsequently, God constructed/carved out a new garden (Lord God planted a garden) in the east of a place/realm identified as Eden. The use of *'planted'* in this verse suggest that this is a new thing that was not existing. The garden that was planted was a new thing that has not existed before, hence the need for relevant life sustaining resources to be created on it (Genesis 2:9–10 KJV). Although the garden is new, Eden where the garden was planted was already existing. The geographic location of Eden was not provided by the passage, but many readers assume that it is on earth. However, this assumption may be wrong as explored in Section 4.2. Then, God took the man of dust, from the location where he had been created to the newly created garden (⁸ And the Lord God planted a garden eastward in Eden; and there he put the man whom he had formed). Whereas the first humans (man and woman) that were created in Genesis were given the mandate to multiply and fill the earth, Adam was essentially confined within the garden, to preserve him from the corruption outside the garden. Although as a class of human, Adam must have inherently inherited all the attributes (including responsibilities) of the humans of Genesis 1, with additional primary purpose and special attribute of being a *living soul*. This inheritance of the attribute to procreate manifested after the fall, when Adam began to have children with Eve.

To put it clearly, Adam was created as a being of light, to be like the angels (not intended for procreation - mortal beings procreate, immortal beings do not procreate) and was being prepared for immortality (the tree of life, which if eaten will grant him immortality was at the garden–Genesis 3:22). Although, made from dust, the breadth of God turned Adam into something higher. Even though he still had the flesh and human attributes, underneath, he was clothed in light. Here lies Adam's distinguishing character–a special being that has angelic and human attributes. This attribute is an indicator to what his purpose was–a bridge or connector between humans and the celestial realm, which also supports the idea that the garden may have been situated in a realm between earth and the heavens. This attribute enabled him to be in a state where he can easily commune with God. To confirm this, the sons of God that will emerge at the end of age will be like angels and be immortal.

> At the resurrection people will neither marry nor be given in marriage; they will be like the angels in heaven–(Matthew 22:30 NIV).

However, when he lost his superior attribute previously granted to him by God, he became a mortal that can procreate and die, like the Genesis 1 humans. Hence, when they fell, they lost the light that encapsulated them, and at that point, discovered that they were naked. Their covering was gone! Their use of fig leaves to cover the nakedness they felt was an attempt to reconstruct the clothe of light that initially covered them. The core purpose of Christ first and second coming is to transform the descendants of Adam, back to their original state (beings of light–*sons of God*) and return them back to the garden (see Section 14.7 Filli Dei).

Hence, the creation stories of Genesis 1 and 2, are telling different stories of the creation of different entities. It is my strong belief that the first three verses (and possibly the fourth verse) of Genesis 2 belong to Chapter 1:

> Thus the heavens and the earth were finished, and all the host of them. ² And on the seventh day God finished his work that he had done, and he rested on the seventh day from all his work that he had done. ³ So God blessed the seventh day and made it holy, because on it God rested from all his work that he had done in creation.
> These are the generations
> of the heavens and the earth when they were created,
> in the day that the Lord God made the earth and the heavens. (Genesis 2:1–4 ESV).

These verses ought to have been the last verses of Genesis 1 as they easily flow from Genesis 1:31:

> ³¹ And God saw everything that he had made, and behold, it was very good. And there was evening and there was morning, the sixth day (Genesis 1:31 ESV).

I suspect they were erroneously or intentionally moved out of Chapter 1, so as to link the creation of the first man and woman in Chapter 1 to the creation of Adam in Chapter 2; to make it appear as the same creation that were repeated or elaborated on. As usual, the time span between the creation of the first man and woman of Genesis 1 may have taken years (hundreds, thousands, millions etc) before Adam was created. Genesis 2:4 is also a very curious verse as it was referring to generations of heavens and earth created by God:

> These are the generations of the heavens and the earth when they were created, in the day that the Lord God made the earth and the heavens. (Genesis 2:4 ESV).

What generations/cycles was it referring to? This is an indication of the various epochs of creation. It is another pointer to the fact that what was being presented in Genesis 1 was a recreation of the heavens and the earth after they have been originally created by God.

4.2 EDEN-THE GARDEN OF GOD

There is a mystery to the exact location of the Garden of Eden. Many people have suggested different places on earth as where the garden was located, but none of these has ever been objectively confirmed to be the exact location of Eden. The mystery surrounding the location of the garden has become one of the leading topics in biblical studies. Some have argued that the garden is located somewhere on the earth, while others have favored the notion that the garden is on a realm outside the earth.

The Bible did not explicitly say where Eden was located. The manner it was mentioned in the Bible leaves it open for people to interpret it to be located on earth. Interpreted this way, Eden is a part of the earth, that is secluded from the rest of the planet:

> [8] Now the Lord God had planted a garden in the east, in Eden; and there he put the man he had formed. [9] The Lord God made all kinds of trees grow out of the ground—trees that were pleasing to the eye and good for food. In the middle of the garden were the tree of life and the tree of the knowledge of good and evil.
> [10] A river watering the garden flowed from Eden; from there it was separated into four headwaters. [11] The name of the first is the Pishon; it winds through the entire land of Havilah, where there is gold. [12] (The gold of that land is good; aromatic resin and onyx are also there.) [13] The name of the second river is the Gihon; it winds through the entire land of Cush. [14] The name of the third river is the Tigris; it runs along the east side of Ashur. And the fourth river is the Euphrates.
> [15] The LORD God took the man and put him in the Garden of Eden to work it and take care of it. [16] And the LORD God commanded the man, "You are free to eat from any tree in the garden; [17] but you must not eat from the tree of the knowledge of good and evil, for when you eat from it you will certainly die."
> (Genesis 2:8-17 NIV).

However, because Eden was not explicitly stated to be on earth, it can also be interpreted to be located somewhere outside the earth, considering that Eden has also been mentioned elsewhere in Ezekiel, in connection to a location in the heavenlies where Satan had been before his fall. The Eden described by Ezekiel as the garden of God, appears to be a very important place where important things happen in the heavenly realm:

> "You were the signet of perfection,
> full of wisdom and perfect in beauty.
> ¹³ You were in Eden, the garden of God; (Ezekiel 28:12–13 ESV).

Hence, there is an ongoing debate on whether the garden of God mentioned by Ezekiel is the same as the Garden of Eden, where Adam was placed. However, this may not be, considering that the garden in Eden was planted after Adam was made, whereas the garden of God where Satan was, pre-existed Adam. If the Eden, mentioned by Ezekiel as the garden of God, is where God goes to, to relax or communicate with his creations, one way to view the Garden of Eden is that it is a mirror of the heavenly Eden, established around the earth. This would be like the Ark of the Covenant being a mirror of God's temple in Heaven.

This passage from Ezekiel suggests that at some point in the past before his fall, Satan had been at Eden. But we know this was prior to the creation of Adam or even the creation of Earth, because he was still deemed perfect ("You were the signet of perfection, full of wisdom and perfect in beauty). This clearly suggests that the verse was not referring to the time when the Serpent [*nachash*]) came to the Garden of Eden to beguile Eve, but rather to a prior time. Hence, if the garden of God was already existing before the restoration/recreation of Earth (after the chaos caused by the rebellion of Satan), it suggests that the Eden being referred here by Ezekiel is outside the Earth. This leaves one with just two conclusions:

- Eden, the garden of God, is a spiritual realm outside the Earth and is not the same as the garden planted in Eden (Garden of Eden), that is supposedly on Earth, where Adam was placed, or
- the Garden of Eden, where Adam was placed was not on earth (not a physical realm).

Another way to view this is that the Garden of Eden is a realm outside the Earth, where God can freely interact with a special breed of man (the glorified man). This place seems to be a realm where there is direct access between man and God. God comes to Eden at will. Esdras seem to suggest that the Garden of Eden was created before the earth:

> ⁴ "O sovereign Lord, didst thou not speak at the beginning when thou didst form the earth—and that without help—and didst command the dust⁵ and it gave thee Adam, a lifeless body? Yet he was the workmanship of thy hands, and thou didst breathe

into him the breath of life, and he was made alive in thy presence. ⁶ And thou didst lead him into the garden which thy right hand had planted before the earth appeared. (2 Esdras 2: 4–6 RSV).

When God recreated the earth and created the first man and woman, he tasked them to increase and multiply. These sets of humans and their generations would have to be controlled by a leader. Thus, Adam was subsequently created and was placed at Eden, from where he can discharge this duty. Satan who had been expelled from the Eden would not take this lightly. Thus, his plan to undermine Adam, making him to fall from grace so that he can usurp his authority.

Having considered the foregoing, I am more inclined towards the view that the Garden of Eden used to be somewhere on the earth, but with a direct access to the heavenly realm (the garden of God). The nature of the link between the Garden of Eden and the garden of God is comparable to what quantum physicists refer to as quantum entanglement.[1] This view is supported by how the earth would be during and after the Millennial Reign, when Christ will be ruling the entire earth. During this time, Christ will rule the entire world from Jerusalem, which would be comparable to the garden of Eden. Nations outside Jerusalem will be coming over to pay homage to Christ. This was how God planned the earth, before the fall of Adam. The Garden of Eden was intended to be the command-and-control center of the earth, and Adam the king of the earth. However, Satan scuttled this plan, hence, God devised an alternative means to restore this order through Jesus Christ. To buttress this, after the Millennial Reign, when the new earth and new heaven manifests, there would also be a New Jerusalem where the throne of God will be, from where the entire earth and universe will be controlled. This is also sharing similar governance structure as what the Garden of Eden placed on earth was intended for.

4.3 CREATION OF EVE

The creation of Eve is another interesting twist to the Adamic story. With the man of dust having not been satisfied with the initial companions

---

1. Quantum entanglement is when two particles link together in a certain way no matter how far apart they are in space. Their state remains the same; Emspak, "Quantum Entanglement", 1

(animals) that God made for him, God decided to create another entity drawn from his body, that would have almost similar features with the man:

> But for Adam there was not found a helper fit for him. ²¹ So the Lord God caused a deep sleep to fall upon the man, and while he slept took one of his ribs and closed up its place with flesh. ²² And the rib that the Lord God had taken from the man he made into a woman and brought her to the man. ²³ Then the man said,
>
> "This at last is bone of my bones
> and flesh of my flesh;
> she shall be called Woman,
> because she was taken out of Man."
>
> ²⁴ Therefore a man shall leave his father and his mother and hold fast to his wife, and they shall become one flesh. ²⁵ And the man and his wife were both naked and were not ashamed. (Gen 2: 20–25 ESV).

Invariably, God cloned the woman from the man. Clearly, judging from the manner and timing of this event, this woman was not the same woman that was created at the same time with the man of Genesis 1. The Bible did not indicate how long after the creation of Adam that God made the woman. But judging from the fact that after Adam's creation, God planted the garden and the vegetation in it, then he created the animals as Adam's companion, after which he proceeded with the creation of Eve, this might have taken a relatively long time.

However, the creation of Eve completed the emergence of a new breed of humanity, intended by God to rule the earth. This was God's trump card. It was a masterstroke from God against the gimmick of Satan, who had probably corrupted the previous generation of beings created on the 6th day of Genesis 1. With the presence of Adam and Eve, Satan lost any mandate of the earth he might have been clinging unto. Hence, prompting Satan to set in motion actions to bring this new breed down.

4.4 THE FALL - CORRUPTION OF ADAMIC DNA

The story of the fall of man is a very popular one, having been told repeatedly. Literary, we are told that Adam and Eve ate a forbidden fruit and hence, were banished from the garden planted in Eden, because they disobeyed God and listened to Satan (Genesis 3: 1-24 KJV). Although this essentially summarised the story, there was something profound about the story that is not normally revealed to a casual reader about what went down in the garden. Judging from the repercussions of the fall, one can glean that the popular version of the story is merely scratching the surface. The destiny of Adam and his descendants were utterly changed by this event, which goes to say that something deeper happened at the garden.

The fruit story is an allegory that euphemises something far deeper. Firstly, it was so cataclysmic that it uttered the nature or genetic makeup (DNA) of Adam and Eve. Recall, Adam was a special kind of human–man of dust activated with the breath of God (see Section 4.1), which places him above the previous humans made by God. By this, Adam was covered in glory and was able to interact directly with God. After the fall, Adam and Eve lost the glory that covered them, and it was at this point they realised they were naked. Although, it appears they could have continued to live in that garden in their new nature, God did not want them to be immortalised in their fallen state, hence, their expulsion from the garden.

It is my supposition that the eating of the fruit in question was a euphemism for a sexual intercourse that went down at the garden. Simply put, I believe Satan seduced Eve and slept with her. This is a highly controversial aspect of the story, with many against or in favor of it, but there are clues about this even those signposted by Jesus Christ about this.

This will become clearer if one considers the enormity of judgements read out by God for their indiscretion, which seems to be an overkill if a mere fruit was eaten. The judgment meted out to the three actors presented in the chapter could be perceived as a direct correspondence (repercussions/consequences) of their acts and not just God arbitrarily and harshly punishing them for disobedience. That is essentially how God's judgements operate, as could be seen from Deuteronomy when Moses read out the implications of keeping God's laws to the Israelites. Keeping the commandments brings blessings but going against them brings death:

> [26] Behold, I set before you this day a blessing and a curse;
>
> [27] A blessing, if ye obey the commandments of the LORD your God, which I command you this day:

²⁸ And a curse, if ye will not obey the commandments of the LORD your God, but turn aside out of the way which I command you this day, to go after other gods, which ye have not known. (Deuteronomy 11:26–28 KJV).

Hence, for each transgression in the garden, a matching judgment or repercussion was read out to the culprit. To summarise, it is my supposition that Satan seduced (beguiled) Eve and eventually slept with her (The serpent beguiled me, and I did eat. Genesis 3:13 KJV). After this, Eve introduced Adam to the act, and he slept with Eve. I also think that this did not end there, Satan may have also sodomised Adam, to debase him. This was probably the route through which Satan usurped the mandate God had given to Adam. Note that their eyes only opened after Adam ate the fruit and not when Eve ate the fruit first:

> ⁶ And when the woman saw that the tree was good for food, and that it was pleasant to the eyes, and a tree to be desired to make one wise, she took of the fruit thereof, and did eat, and gave also unto her husband with her; and he did eat.
> ⁷ And the eyes of them both were opened, and they knew that they were naked; and they sewed fig leaves together, and made themselves aprons. (Genesis 3:6–7 KJV).

After Eve ate the fruit, there was no apparent change in her, otherwise Adam would have seen the negative impact of the act. There was no obvious danger or adverse effect on Eve after she partook in eating the fruit that would have alarmed Adam. This probably encouraged Adam to oblige Eve.

Hence, Adam eating of the fruit was the critical point that Satan was targeting. As soon as he ate the fruit, the deed was concluded, and their nature changed (their eyes opened). The light that covered them disappeared and they realised they were naked. Adam is the key here because God gave this command to him directly. Eve hasn't been created at the time the command was issued:

> ¹⁶ And the Lord God commanded the man, saying, Of every tree of the garden thou mayest freely eat:
> ¹⁷ But of the tree of the knowledge of good and evil, thou shalt not eat of it: for in the day that thou eatest thereof thou shalt surely die. (Genesis 2: 16–17 KJV).

The fall of Adam marks a pivotal point when the flesh triumphed over the Spirit. Recall that God created Adam from the mud of the earth and breathed his spirit into him. By this act, Adam became a different kind of being from what he had originally been created (man of dust). He became a mixture of spirit and man, with the spirit having the upper hand. Subsequently, he took him away from where he formed him and placed him in the garden. This was an elevation from a lower environment/realm to one much higher. However, at the fall, Adam literally lost his spiritual steam. With the flesh having gained an upper hand, Adam had to fall from the spiritual high moral ground to the level of the flesh. Hence, he had to gravitate to where he was originally formed.

The result of Eve's eating of the fruit was pregnancy, that of Adam was genetic corruption, and the relinquishing of his authority to Satan. If the judgments are reversed engineered, the act/disobedience that led to it would become obvious. The judgement started with God cursing the serpent:

> [14] And the Lord God said unto the serpent, Because thou hast done this, thou art cursed above all cattle, and above every beast of the field; upon thy belly shalt thou go, and dust shalt thou eat all the days of thy life:
> [15] And I will put enmity between thee and the woman, and between thy seed and her seed; it shall bruise thy head, and thou shalt bruise his heel. (Genesis 3:14–15 KJV).

One thing that jumps out here is that God immediately nullified any relationship that may have developed between Satan and Eve (And I will put enmity between thee and the woman). This is very curious considering that if one takes the position of a literal fruit being eaten as the root of the problem, why was God's pronouncement targeting a relation between Eve and Satan? There is a school of thought that believes that Satan's plan was to seduce Eve, debase Adam, and subsequently kill him in order to marry Eve and thus becoming the Lord of the Earth, operating from the garden. Hence, God ensured there was enmity between Eve and Satan, to foil this plot.

The judgement went further to target their seeds, to ensure the enmity continues (and between thy seed and her seed). So where did this jump out from? So, by merely eating a fruit God was already causing enmity between the woman and Satan as well as their offsprings? However, if read from the perspective that a sexual intercourse, which had resulted in a pregnancy had occurred, the judgement being read out by God makes more sense. The relationship had to be invalidated, and the product of that relationship (offsprings of Satan and Eve) cannot be allowed to overshadow subsequent children that Eve would have. And this enmity will lead to future conflict between the seeds of the woman and those of Satan. God is not superfluous with words and if Satan had no seed, God wouldn't have mentioned it. But can Satan, a spirit have offspring? Judging from what happened with the Watchers, angelic beings can impregnate woman and have kids (Nephilim). The contention here is between the seeds of Satan and Eve, one would have to consider these as probably physicals beings and not just spiritual. Hence, Satan appears to have physical offsprings on the earth, who will contend with those of Eve.

God's pronouncement against the woman directly leads one to conclude that sexual encounter happened, and pregnancy resulted. He also reiterated the point that any sensual feelings the woman may have developed for Satan would be invalidated:

> [16] Unto the woman he said, I will greatly multiply thy sorrow and thy conception; in sorrow thou shalt bring forth children; and thy desire shall be to thy husband, and he shall rule over thee. (Genesis 3:16 KJV).

Making her to desire her husband (thy desire shall be to thy husband), suggests that she was already desiring someone else. Who else could that be other than Satan who beguiled her? Hence, God used the curse to force her senses back.

The consequences of Adam's participation in this heinous sin, which defiled the land, was the cursing of the ground. The ground had been pure but desecrated by probably the sexual fluids that emanated from the sexual intercourse with Satan.

> [17] And unto Adam he said, Because thou hast hearkened unto the voice of thy wife, and hast eaten of the tree, of which I commanded thee, saying, Thou shalt not eat of it: cursed is the ground for thy sake; in sorrow shalt thou eat of it all the days of thy life;
> [18] Thorns also and thistles shall it bring forth to thee; and thou shalt eat the herb of the field;
> [19] In the sweat of thy face shalt thou eat bread, till thou return unto the ground; for out of it wast thou taken: for dust thou art, and unto dust shalt thou return. (Genesis 3:17–19 KJV).

At this point, one can begin to understand what was going on in this passage. The contents of verse 20 is also very curious:

> [20] And Adam called his wife's name Eve; because she was the mother of all living. (Genesis 3:20 KJV).

At this point Adam had probably realised that the wife was pregnant hence, the reason he called the wife Eve (the mother of all living). Adam never bothered to call the woman this, until after they had eaten the fruit, hence the name is directly linked to the act of sexual intercourse that has resulted in pregnancy.

The writer captured this entire event in Genesis by masking certain aspects of the details, however, he still left a lot of clues in the passage that will enable a careful reader to decipher what was going on. From the foregoing both Satan and Adam had intercourse with Eve and this resulted in a pregnancy. Cain was the fruit of the intercourse between Satan and Eve, and Abel was the fruit of the intercourse that later occurred between Adam and Eve. To buttress this point, Cain's murderous nature/gene could not have come from Adam, but rather from Satan his father. Adam was created perfect by God, so the murderous DNA must not have been introduced into Cain through Adam. However, it makes perfect sense that the murderous gene in Cain came from Satan, who Jesus Christ described as a murderer from the beginning. John hinted at this when he admonished believers to toe the path of righteousness:

> [12] We should not be like Cain, who was of the evil one and murdered his brother. And why did he murder him? Because his own deeds were evil and his brother's righteous. (1 John 3:12 ESV).

Jesus Christ shined light on this by calling the Pharisees the children of the devil (John 8:44 ESV) as well as brood of vipers (a type of serpent) (Matthew 12:34 ESV):

> [44] You are of your father the devil, and your will is to do your father's desires. He was a murderer from the beginning, and does not stand in the truth, because there is no truth in him. When he lies, he speaks out of his own character, for he is a liar and the father of lies. (John 8:44 ESV).

One thing that jumps out from the command God gave Adam and Eve was that they should not even touch that tree (neither shall ye touch it). So, they were not only admonished not to eat it, but not to even touch it, because God knows that once they touch it, they will be stimulated to the point that they would end up eating it.

More curious is the fact that as soon as Adam and Eve ate the fruit, they immediately covered their genitalia. Why did they do that? The only obvious answer to this is that they had just had sex, having discovered the power of that aspect of their body, and need some level of privacy around the organ they used. Interestingly, Genesis 4 started with Adam knowing his wife and Cain being conceived, then Abel conceived. For all the time they had been in the garden, Adam never thought of knowing the wife until after the eating of the fruit. This is also a pointer that they learnt how to *know* each other from the act of eating the fruit. Another pointer here may be the name of Cain (acquired from the Lord–Genesis 1:4 KJV). Adam is not Lord, so what Lord was being referred to here?

The corruption of Adam's DNA is essentially what the Catholic Catechism allude to as the 'original sin'. This was the event that reduced man to a lower level than he had originally been created to be. The entire redemption story in the Bible was Jesus Christ's efforts to restore man to what he was supposed to be–sons of God (see Chapter 10). This process of rewiring starts with the baptism (man being born again–the old man whose DNA has been corrupted by Satan through Adam will die and a new man born from heaven is raised). This is why any human not born-again cannot be saved, because such a person still has the corrupted gene of Adam (for all have sinned and fall short of the glory of God–Romans 3:23 ESV).

The tree of the knowledge of good and evil maybe a euphemism for Satan. Having been in the presence of God, Satan has knowledge of good, and having fallen, he also has knowledge of evil. Satan also alluded to this when he told Eve that eating the fruit will open her eyes so she will have knowledge of good and evil:

> [4] And the serpent said unto the woman, Ye shall not surely die:
> [5] For God doth know that in the day ye eat thereof, then your eyes shall be opened, and ye shall be as gods, knowing good and evil. (Genesis 3: 4–5 KJV).

What Satan was telling Eve was that once she partakes in eating the fruit, she will essentially be like him, who has knowledge of both good and evil.

4.5. MANDATE TO THE CHILDREN OF MEN OVER THE EARTH

When the earth was initially created (at the point when the *"... morning stars sang together, and all the sons of God shouted for joy"* - *Job 38:4 -7)*, the heavenly entity identified by Isaiah as hê-lêl ben-šā-ḥar, was given charge over the earth. He *laid nations low* (supposedly the nations of the earth) and *made the earth tremble* and *shook kingdoms*. This places this entity in a controlling position over the planet. His throne was somewhere below the heaven because this entity was trying to ascend (from a lower plane to higher one) to heaven above the stars of God (angelic beings) to setup his throne very high (Isaiah 14:12-17 ESV).

So, when this entity rebelled against God, he became an adversary (Satan) and was removed from overseeing the earth. His refusal to relinquish control over the earth probably led to the destruction of the earth and its inhabitants (the pre-adamic people) who were buried in the deep Ezekiel 26:19-20. At the recreation of the earth, God decided to make a new breed (humans), who would have dominion over the earth. He made two: male and female, so they can procreate and fill the earth:

> [26] And God said, Let us make man in our image, after our likeness: and let them have dominion over the fish of the sea, and over the fowl of the air, and over the cattle, *and over all the earth*, and over every creeping thing that creepeth upon the earth. (Genesis 1:26).

This was the purpose and mandate of man, to have dominion over all the earth:

> [16] The heavens are the Lord's heavens,
>   but the earth he has given to the children of man. (Psalm 115:16 ESV).

This mandate to the new creatures of God, was God's way of punishing Satan further, by replacing him with the new beings, *made a little lower than the angels* and placing them in charge of things on earth, where he had previously held sway. This mandate of man over the earth was re-echoed in the Hebrews:

> "What is mankind that you are mindful of them,
>   a son of man that you care for him?
> [7] You made them a little lower than the angels;

> you crowned them with glory and honor
> 8 and put everything under their feet."
>
> In putting everything under them, God left nothing that is not subject to them. Yet at present we do not see everything subject to them. (Hebrews 2:6–8 NIV).

Hence, this set the stage for Satan's attempt to reclaim this mandate. Adam was created to be the leader of mankind, the reason he was targeted by Satan.

CHAPTER 5

Disruption of God's Plan for Man

5.1 SATAN'S USURPING OF ADAM'S AUTHORITY OVER EARTH

After the fall, Adam was forced out of the garden, back to the ground/earth, where he had been made. Even though the expulsion of Adam and Eve from the garden of Eden appears very cruel, it was essentially a protective move by God, to prevent Adam and Eve from remaining eternally in sin–and end up like the rebellious angels or the people of Day 6, whose fate has been sealed. He already has a redemptive plan for Adam; hence, he did not want him to eat from the tree of life, which will enable him to live forever in the fallen state:

> ²² And the Lord God said, Behold, the man is become as one of us, to know good and evil: and now, lest he put forth his hand, and take also of the tree of life, and eat, and live for ever:
> ²³ Therefore the LORD God sent him forth from the garden of Eden, to till the ground from whence he was taken.
> ²⁴ So he drove out the man; and he placed at the east of the garden of Eden Cherubims, and a flaming sword which turned every way, to keep the way of the tree of life. (Genesis 3: 22–24 KJV).

The expulsion of Adam was a demotion from his previous esteemed position in the garden where he was being prepared as the new ruler of the earth, to a mere man who will till the ground. In his place, Satan appropriated the authority over the earth, which Adam had inadvertently relinquished in the process of the fall. This was probably how Satan got the impetus to present himself before God when the sons of God gathered *(Job 1:7)*. One would assume that after Satan has been cast out of heaven (after the rebellion) he would have lost every authority or right to come before God again. But in the passage Satan did appear before God, when the sons of God gathered to report their activities to God (present themselves to God). So how did that happen? He most likely presented himself in the cosmic council in the capacity of the ruler of the earth. In other words, he was there in the stead of Adam. Satan's response to God, also points to this responsibility:

> [7] The Lord said to Satan, "From where have you come?" Satan answered the Lord and said, "From going to and fro on the earth, and from walking up and down on it." (Job 1:7 ESV).

Adam was supposed to be the ruler of the earth. However, the Bible is littered with several passages that declared that Satan was the ruler of the earth. During the temptation of Jesus Christ, Satan emphatically told Jesus that he has authority over the earth. His claim that the authority over the earth has been delivered to him, suggests that originally, he did not have such authority until it was delivered to him:

> [5] And the devil took him up and showed him all the kingdoms of the world in a moment of time, [6] and said to him, "To you I will give all this authority and their glory, for it has been delivered to me, and I give it to whom I will. [7] If you, then, will worship me, it will all be yours." (Luke 4: 5–8).

Interestingly, Jesus did not counter this claim. Rather, Jesus on another occasion, told his disciples about the ruler of the world (a reference to Satan):

> [29] And now I have told you before it takes place, so that when it does take place you may believe. [30] I will no longer talk much with you, for the ruler of this world is coming. He has no claim on me (John 14: 29–30 ESV).

Again, while hinting at the key purpose of his first coming, which is to dethrone Satan from his coveted position as the ruler of the world, Jesus declared:

> [31] Now is the judgment of this world; now will the ruler of this world be cast out. [32] And I, when I am lifted up from the earth, will draw all people to myself." (John 12: 30 ESV).

DISRUPTION OF GOD'S PLAN FOR MAN

Also, in one of his letters to the church in Corinth, Paul wrote:

> ⁴ Satan, who is the god of this world, has blinded the minds of those who don't believe. They are unable to see the glorious light of the Good News. They don't understand this message about the glory of Christ, who is the exact likeness of God. (2 Corinthians 4:4).

The usurpation of Adam's authority over the earth was an aberration, that disrupted God's plan for man and the earth. This disruption inadvertently delayed God's plan of establishing his kingdom on earth. Hence, a contingency plan was activated to remedy the situation. There was a need for the dethronement of Satan from this usurped position of authority over the earth, and to redeem man from his fallen state. The plan to remedy this situation took thousands of years to be accomplished, through the first coming of Christ. Jesus Christ paved the way for the legitimate reclamation of this authority over earth from Satan by his death on the cross and eventual resurrection. Since Satan took the kingship of the earth from a man (Adam), through sin, only a man can legally reclaim this kingship, by overcoming the power of sin. However, no man prior to the coming of Jesus was able to achieve this task of raising man from his fallen state. Therefore, to salvage humanity from its fallen position, and bring it back to its rightful place, originally ordained by God, Jesus Christ had to come as a man to overcome the power of sin and open the gateway for the redemption of humans. In other words, God had to come as a man to defeat Satan. Jesus was very emphatic in referring to himself as the 'Son of Man' because, in line with cosmic legalism (see Section 10.1), only a man can legally defeat Satan and reclaim the authority, which he took from a man.

This reclamation of the authority from Satan was re-echoed by Paul in his first letter to the Corinthians. He hinted that the death of Christ on the cross and his resurrection was essentially a coup to dethrone Satan from being the ruler of this word. This is the reason why the essence of this mission of Christ was hidden in cryptic prophesies, to confound Satan and his cohorts, until it was fully accomplished:

> ⁷ But we impart a secret and hidden wisdom of God, which God decreed before the ages for our glory. ⁸ None of the rulers of this age understood this, for if they had, they would not have crucified the Lord of glory. (1 Corinthians 2:7–8 ESV).

This was also, reiterated in Revelation, where it was stated that Christ redeemed humanity from every tribe for God:

> "You are worthy to take the scroll and to open its seals, because you were slain,
> and with your blood you purchased for God persons from every tribe and language and people and nation.[10] You have made them to be a kingdom and priests to serve our God,
> and they will reign on the earth" (Revelation 5:9–10 ESV).

5.2 THE SEED OF SATAN

Based on the foregoing argument presented in Section 4.4, it could be seen that Satan introduced his seed into the earth via Eve. He may also have introduced his seed among the first generation of humans, judging from the parable of the wheat and the tare. Hence, the pronouncement from God about a perpetual strife between the seed of Satan and that of the woman. The first manifestation of this strife was when Cain murdered his brother Abel. That was a diverging moment when both lineages were separated. Hence, two genealogies were established: Adam's and Cain's. This would be confusing to anyone who believes that Cain was the son of Adam, as it wouldn't make sense that Cain was omitted from Adam's genealogy (presented in Genesis 5), and a separate lineage presented for Cain. The genealogy of Adam's children started with Seth (see summary presented in Table 5.1), as Abel was omitted (because he had no descendants). The verse was also emphatic that Seth was Adam's offspring (his own likeness, and after his image), which also suggests that there might have been a paternity issue with one of Adam's so-called children:

> [3] And Adam lived an hundred and thirty years, and begat a son in his own likeness, and after his image; and called his name Seth. (Genesis 5: 3 KJV).

To hint that Cain was not Adam's son, a separate genealogy was presented for Cain's descendant in Genesis 4:16–22 (see Table 5.1):

> [16] And Cain went out from the presence of the Lord, and dwelt in the land of Nod, on the east of Eden.
> [17] And Cain knew his wife; and she conceived, and bare Enoch: and he builded a city, and called the name of the city, after the name of his son, Enoch.

DISRUPTION OF GOD'S PLAN FOR MAN

[18] And unto Enoch was born Irad: and Irad begat Mehujael: and Mehujael begat Methusael: and Methusael begat Lamech.

[19] And Lamech took unto him two wives: the name of the one was Adah, and the name of the other Zillah.

[20] And Adah bare Jabal: he was the father of such as dwell in tents, and of such as have cattle.

[21] And his brother's name was Jubal: he was the father of all such as handle the harp and organ.

[22] And Zillah, she also bare Tubalcain, an instructer of every artificer in brass and iron: and the sister of Tubalcain was Naamah. (Genesis 4: 16–22 KJV).

Table 5.1: Summary of the genealogies of Adam and Cain (Genesis 4: 25–26, Genesis 5 KJV, Genesis 4: 9–22 KJV) and Book of Jasher (Chapter 2 and 3).

Year	Progenitors				
0	Adam's Lineage			Cain's Lineage	
	Name (Genesis)	Years Lived	Name (Jasher)	Name (Genesis)	Year
130	Seth	130	Seth	Enoch	
235	Enosh	105	Enosh	Irad	
325	Kenan	90	Cainan	Mehujael	
395	Mahalalel	70	**Sons:** Mahlallel, Enan & Mered **Daughters:** Adah & Zillah	Methusael	
460	Jared	65	**From Mahlallel:** Jared	Lamech (2 wives–Adah & Zillah)	
622	Enoch	162	Enoch	**From Ada:** Jabal & Jubal **From Zillah:** Tubal Cain & Naamah	
687	Methuselah	65	**Sons From Enoch:** Methuselah, Elisha, & Elimelech **Daughters From Enoch:** Melca & Nahmah **Daughter from Elisha:** Ashmua		

Year	Progenitors			
0	Adam's Lineage		Cain's Lineage	
874	Lamech	187	**From Methuselah:** Lamech Lamech married *Ashmua*	
1056	Noah	182	Noah (*by his grandfather* Methuselah) and named Menachem (*by his father Lamech*)	
1556	Shem, Ham, and Japheth	500	From Naamah the daughter of Enoch: Japheth & Shem Ham? (Not mentioned until later. Was he from another mother?)	

This separation of the bloodlines of Adam and Cain continued, and conscious efforts were made by the bloodline of Adam not to mix with those of Cain. Although, it seems that the Children of Cain were eager to mix with the bloodline of Adam. The Book of Jasher recorded that Lamech the son of Methusael (from Cain's lineage married two daughters (Adah and Zillah) of Cainan/Kenan (the grandson of Seth) as shown in Table 5.1.

Many would argue that the seed of Satan were crushed by the flood, as only Noah and his immediate family survived the deluge. However, there are also hints in the Bible that suggest that Cain's lineage somewhat survived the flood (Section 6.3). Cain may also have survived the flood. There are various theories focusing on how Cain's bloodline survived. A prominent one being that one of Noah's wives Namaah was from the lineage of Cain (the daughter of Lamech and Zillah and sister to Tubal-Cain). Proving the veracity of these theories are difficult but Jesus Christ seems to allude that there are two separate bloodlines on earth (the children of God via Adam and the children of the devil:

> [37] "I know that you are Abraham's descendants, but you seek to kill Me, because My word has no place in you. [38] I speak what I

DISRUPTION OF GOD'S PLAN FOR MAN

have seen with My Father, and you do what you have seen with your father."

³⁹ They answered and said to Him, "Abraham is our father."

Jesus said to them, "If you were Abraham's children, you would do the works of Abraham. ⁴⁰ But now you seek to kill Me, a Man who has told you the truth which I heard from God. Abraham did not do this. ⁴¹ You do the deeds of your father."

Then they said to Him, "We were not born of fornication; we have one Father—God."

⁴² Jesus said to them, "If God were your Father, you would love Me, for I proceeded forth and came from God; nor have I come of Myself, but He sent Me. ⁴³ Why do you not understand My speech? Because you are not able to listen to My word. ⁴⁴ You are of your father the devil, and the desires of your father you want to do. He was a murderer from the beginning, and does not stand in the truth, because there is no truth in him. When he speaks a lie, he speaks from his own resources, for he is a liar and the father of it." (John 8: 37–44 NKJV).

This dialogue between Jesus Christ and the Pharisees, is quite illuminating. Here the Pharisees claim to be the children of Abraham, but Christ argues that even though they claim to be descendants of Abraham, that does not make them the children of God. He pointedly told them that they were the children of the devil. Although Abraham had many children and descendants only the descendants of Abraham that proceeded from Jacob are regarded as the pure and chosen ones. Abraham ensured that Isaac's lineage was not tainted by the seed of Satan, hence, he made sure he married from a family within his lineage which he was certain have not been tainted by the seed of Satan. The same thing occurred with Jacob. Isaac and Rebecca were infuriated that Esau married from the Canaanite (Section 8.3).

John re-echoed this line of thought in his epistle about the existence of two separate seeds, running parallel on earth:

> ⁷ Little children, let no one deceive you. Whoever practices righteousness is righteous, as he is righteous. ⁸ Whoever makes a practice of sinning is of the devil, for the devil has been sinning from the beginning. The reason the Son of God appeared was to destroy the works of the devil. ⁹ No one born of God makes a practice of sinning, for God's seed abides in him; and he cannot keep on sinning, because he has been born of God. ¹⁰ By this it is evident who are the children of God, and who are the children

of the devil: whoever does not practice righteousness is not of God, nor is the one who does not love his brother.

¹¹ For this is the message that you have heard from the beginning, that we should love one another. ¹² We should not be like Cain, who was of the evil one and murdered his brother. And why did he murder him? Because his own deeds were evil and his brother's righteous. (1 John 3:7–12 ESV).

5.3 CAIN'S CIVILIZATION

The first Biblical record of a city being built on the present earth age was attributed to Cain:

> ¹⁷ Cain knew his wife, and she conceived and bore Enoch; and he built a city, and called the name of the city after the name of his son, Enoch. (Genesis 4:17 RSV).

This giant leap of civilization might be construed as the initial steps in an attempt by Cain to establish a kingdom on earth. The jury is still out on how the idea to build a city came to Cain. One school of thought believes that he was instructed by Satan, who saw him as an opportunity to gain a stronghold on earth. As a matter of fact, many believe that Cain was secretly receiving instructions from Satan right from birth and it may have been Satan who had planted the seed of hatred on Cain to kill his brother Abel. The Writings of Abraham notes that there was secret society among the line of Cain through which sacred knowledge were passed down the line in a secret manner (see Section 6.4):

> WHILE Naamah was yet a child, great consternation fell upon the seed of Cain, for Irad the Son of Enoch, the son of Cain, had become a member of the secret combination and was privy to all it secrets until one night when the Lord appeared to him in a dream saying, Irad, thou hast done evil instead of good and hast followed after Satan rather than God; wherefore, I shall destroy thee and thine house when I send in the floods upon the earth. (Writings of Abraham 12:1).

After the first city, Cain built more cities for his children. Going by the manner Cain was building cities through which he was spreading his dominion over the earth, one could infer that this endeavor by Cain was Satan's first attempt to re-establish an empire/kingdom on the restored earth (re-establishment of the pre-human world). Subsequently, this civilization was expanded by the descendants of Cain who developed other areas of human endeavor : agriculture, music, metallic tools (possibly used for agricultural implements, arts, and weapons).

> [19] And Lamech took two wives; the name of the one was Adah, and the name of the other Zillah. [20] Adah bore Jabal; he was the father of those who dwell in tents and have cattle. [21] His brother's name was Jubal; he was the father of all those who play the lyre and pipe. [22] Zillah bore Tubal-cain; he was the forger of all instruments of bronze and iron. The sister of Tubal-cain was Na'amah. (Genesis 4:17-22 RSV).

Another angle to explore here, is on who the inhabitants of the first city were? A city is built for a large concentration of people. This would make one to wonder if Cain was motivated to build a city only for his immediate family, which at the point would just be Cain, his wife, Enoch, and perhaps Enoch's family? It doesn't make sense that he would be motivated to build a city, which supposedly would have multiple dwellings, just for his immediate family. A logical explanation for the necessity to build a city, would be that Cain was already living among other people (the generations of the first male and female created in Genesis 1)–that is the people he had been afraid might harm him, when God exiled him for killing Abel. It makes more sense to believe that Cain intermingled with these other people and got a wife from among them, hence, solidifying the relationship with those community. Although, the Book of Jubilees, stated that Cain married his sister:

> 9. And Cain took Âwân his sister to be his wife and she bare him Enoch at the close of the fourth jubilee. And in the first year of the first week of the fifth jubilee, houses were built on the earth, and Cain built a city, and called its name after the name of his son Enoch (Book of Jubilees, IV: 9).

This still does not nullify the notion that Cain and wife did not mingle with other pre-existing people, and the motive to build a city was born out of necessity. He probably took a leadership position among these people and decided to reorganize the society into a city. These people were also those who helped him to develop the city, as he couldn't have built a city all by himself at this time.

On the other hand, Adam who was secluded from this people with his family did not build any city until after several generations. While Cain was building these cities, Adam's family were still a very small family compared to the community Cain has embedded himself in, hence, there was no immediate need for a city.

5.4 THE REBELLION OF MEN AGAINST GOD

As the human population began to grow on earth, people started drifting away from the tenets of God. Although this was slightly mentioned in Genesis 6, the Book of Jasher contains more details about the transgressions of this period:

> 4 But in the latter days of Methuselah, the sons of men turned from the Lord, they corrupted the earth, they robbed and plundered each other, and they rebelled against God and they transgressed, and they corrupted their ways, and would not hearken to the voice of Methuselah, but rebelled against him.
>
> 5 And the Lord was exceedingly wroth against them, and the Lord continued to destroy the seed in those days, so that there was neither sowing nor reaping in the earth. (Book of Jasher 4: 4–5).
>
> 16 And all the sons of men departed from the ways of the Lord in those days as they multiplied upon the face of the earth with sons and daughters, and they taught one another their evil practices and they continued sinning against the Lord.
>
> 17 And every man made unto himself a god, and they robbed and plundered every man his neighbor as well as his relative, and they corrupted the earth, and the earth was filled with violence. (Book of Jasher 4:16–21).

The reason for this degradation of character and morals which affected man's relationship with God is not farfetched, considering the fallen state of man. In addition, it could be assumed that with increasing population, the descendants of Adam began to live in proximity with those of the house of Cain, who may have negatively influenced them. Despite this deteriorating level of decadence, there were still few custodians of truth who assiduously worked to correct the ways of men. Prominent among these were Enoch, Methuselah, and Noah at various stages of this period.

This was the situation on earth when the Sons of God (the watchers) took counsel to invade the earth and intermingle with humans.

5.5 THE REBELLION OF THE WATCHERS: THE BRAZEN INCURSION OF THE SONS OF GOD ON EARTH

Genesis 6 briefly mentioned that there was a time that the sons of God became attracted to earthly women and descended from their celestial abode to marry them:

> 6 When man began to multiply on the face of the land and daughters were born to them, ² the sons of God saw that the daughters of man were attractive. And they took as their wives any they chose. ³ Then the Lord said, "My Spirit shall not abide in man forever, for he is flesh: his days shall be 120 years." ⁴ The Nephilim were on the earth in those days, and also afterward, when the sons of God came in to the daughters of man and they bore children to them. These were the mighty men who were of old, the men of renown. (Genesis 6:1–4 ESV).

Although, some people tend to misread and interpret this as the sons of Adam marrying the daughters of Cain, the term '*sons of God*' is consistently used in the Bible to describe beings that were directly created by God. Hence, it is usually used to describe celestial beings, who are direct creations of God. Adam who was directly created by God, is also described as a son of God (see Luke 3:38). However, descendants of Adam are described as sons of men.

The marriage and intercourse between these celestial beings and humans produced a different kind of beings on earth (hybrid of humans and celestial beings known as the Nephilim). The Nephilim are gigantic beings, who lived among men during these times. Details of this event (including the repercussions and punishment of the participants) were extensively captured in the Book of Enoch, which described what led to this and the specific beings who were involved in the incursion. According to Enoch, the class of celestial beings who participated in this egregious act are known as the Watchers.

According to the Book of Jubilees, the descent of the Watchers happened around the time Jared [descent in Hebrew], Enoch's father was born:

> ¹⁵ And in the second week of the tenth jubilee Mahalalel took unto him to wife Dînâh, the daughter of Barâki' êl the daughter of his father's brother, and she bare him a son in the third in the sixth year, and he called his name Jared; for in his days the angels of the Lord descended on the earth, those who are named

the Watchers, that they should instruct the children of men, and that they should do judgment and uprightness on the earth. (Book of Jubilees, 4:15).

To understand the event, it is worth delving into who the Watchers are. These are group of angels assigned to watch over the affairs on earth, hence they are in proximity to humans as they are charged to instruct humans in uprightness and execute judgement on non-adherents (*that they should instruct the children of men, 3 and that they should do judgment and uprightness on the earth - Book of Jubilees, 4:15*). Some Biblical scholars tend to opine that the Watchers were part of the celestial beings who rebelled alongside Satan. However, this belief is flawed, because it tends to suggest that the Watchers were already in a fallen state, before they invaded the earth to take earthly women. Believing this, essentially lessens the gravity of the offence of the Watchers. Biblical passages from many books about the Watchers usually present them as holy angels of God (Daniel 4: 17). No fallen angel is referred to as holy. This group of angels were charged with specific responsibilities by God, which they diligently carried out, before they committed the heinous act. And after they fell, another group of Watchers replaced them so that their duties on earth will continue to be carried out. It may also be that not all the Watchers partook in this act, or the entire gang of Watchers participated and were replaced by other celestial beings. This is evident from the fact that the Watchers were still active in monitoring the affairs on earth and executing judgement on kings of the earth long after the flood (when the rebellious Watchers have already been imprisoned), as shown in Daniel.

The book of Daniel mentioned the Watchers and gave a hint as to what their responsibilities entail. According to Daniel, the Watchers are representatives of God on earth, authorised to make decrees that could affect humanity, such as punishing kings (removing kings from their thrones). They essentially perform oversight functions on earthly affairs. When they see that humanity is going astray, they are permitted to take certain actions to correct such anomalies. This was the case with Nebuchadnezzar, when he became too proud that he stopped recognising the Most-High God, as the power behind his prowess. He saw a vision where a Watcher came to declare to him what the Watchers have decreed would happen to him:

> [13] "I saw in the visions of my head as I lay in bed, and behold, a watcher, a holy one, came down from heaven. [14] He proclaimed

DISRUPTION OF GOD'S PLAN FOR MAN

aloud and said thus: 'Chop down the tree and lop off its branches, strip off its leaves and scatter its fruit. Let the beasts flee from under it and the birds from its branches. [15] But leave the stump of its roots in the earth, bound with a band of iron and bronze, amid the tender grass of the field. Let him be wet with the dew of heaven. Let his portion be with the beasts in the grass of the earth. [16] Let his mind be changed from a man's, and let a beast's mind be given to him; and let seven periods of time pass over him. [17] The sentence is by the decree of the watchers, the decision by the word of the holy ones, to the end that the living may know that the Most-High rules the kingdom of men and gives it to whom he will and sets over it the lowliest of men.'" (Daniel 4:13-17 ESV).

Apparently, the Watchers had judged the actions of Nebuchadnezzar and passed a sentence on him, which was delivered to him in the dream. This eventually came to pass, and Nebuchadnezzar served his terms for the set period. In this light, the Watchers could also serve as judges of men, which corroborates with the job description of the Watchers presented in the *Book of Jubilees, 4:15*. The Book of Jasher, also, referred to them as such:

> [18] And their judges and rulers went to the daughters of men and took their wives by force from their husbands according to their choice (Book of Jasher 4:18).

Hence, the decision of the Watchers to leave their core responsibilities to make incursion into the earth was a grievous abuse of their power and authority, which caused havoc on earth, including a further corruption of man's DNA, with angelic genes. As a result, they were severely punished by God, however, the impact of their actions lingers on earth till date. Even though this event happened before Enoch was born, the facts surrounding it were revealed to him by some angels who God assigned to him to explain certain mysteries to him. According to the Book of Enoch, the Watchers understood that what they were planning to do was a transgression of God's command. They understood there would be consequences for the sin they were about to commit, which confirms that at this point, they had not been in sin or rebellion and had been serving God. Hence, the Watchers at this point were not fallen angels:

> 6.1 And it came to pass, when the sons of men had increased, that in those days there were born to them fair and beautiful daughters. 6.2 And the Angels, the sons of Heaven, saw them

and desired them. And they said to one another: "Come, let us choose for ourselves wives, from the children of men, and let us beget, for ourselves, children." 6.3 And Semyaza, who was their leader, said to them: "I fear that you may not wish this deed to be done and that I alone will pay for this great sin." 6.4 And they all answered him, and said: "Let us all swear an oath, and bind one another with curses, so not to alter this plan, but to carry out this plan effectively." 6.5 Then they all swore together and all bound one another with curses to it. 6.6 And they were, in all, two hundred and they came down on Ardis, which is the summit of Mount Hermon. And they called the mountain Hermon because on it they swore and bound one another with curses. 6.7 And these are the names of their leaders: Semyaza, who was their leader, Urakiba (Araqiel), Rameel, Kokabiel, Tamiel, Ramiel, Daniel, Ezeqiel, Baraqiel, Asael, Armaros, Batariel, Ananel, Zaqiel, Samsiel, Satariel, Turiel, Yomiel, Sariel. (see Ch 8 & Ch 69) 6.8 These are the leaders of the two hundred Angels and of all the others with them. 7.1 And they took wives for themselves and everyone chose for himself one each. And they began to go into them and were promiscuous with them. (The Book of Enoch Chapter 6: 1–8, Chapter 7:1).

Having intermingled with humans, the Watchers began to reveal certain celestial secrets, which they are privy to, to earthly beings. They taught humans how to make: charms and spells (witchcraft), and beautification of bodies, promiscuity, implements of war, astrology, and other secrets (hidden knowledge that were unlawful to be revealed on earth), which humans have been forbidden from having:

> And they taught them charms and spells, and they showed them the cutting of roots and trees. 7.2 And they became pregnant and bore large giants. And their height was three thousand cubits. 7.3 These devoured all the toil of men; until men were unable to sustain them. 7.4 And the giants turned against them in order to devour men. 7.5 And they began to sin against birds, and against animals, and against reptiles, and against fish, and they devoured one another's flesh, and drank the blood from it. 7.6 Then the Earth complained about the lawless ones. 8.1 And Azazel taught men to make swords, and daggers, and shields, and breastplates. And he showed them the things after these, and the art of making them; bracelets, and ornaments, and the art of making up the eyes, and of beautifying the eyelids, and the most precious stones, and all kinds of colored dyes. And the world was changed. 8.2 And there was great impiety, and much

DISRUPTION OF GOD'S PLAN FOR MAN

fornication, and they went astray, and all their ways became corrupt. 8.3 Amezarak taught all those who cast spells and cut roots, Armaros the release of spells, and Baraqiel astrologers, and Kokabiel portents, and Tamiel taught astrology, and Asradel taught the path of the Moon. 8.4 And at the destruction of men they cried out; and their voices reached Heaven (The Book of Enoch Chapter 7:2–6,8:1–3).

Hence, the world entirely changed, and both humans and animals were thoroughly corrupted. This corruption included both genetic (corruption of the DNA of humans and animals) and moral corruption. The Apocalypse of Baruch captured this event as one of the second black water that poured down on the earth following Adam's transgression, which was the first black water:

> 9. And from these black (waters) again were black derived, and the darkness of darkness produced 10. For he became a danger to his own soul, even to the angels became he a danger. 11.For, moreover, at that time when he was created, they enjoyed liberty. 12. And some of them descended, and mingled with women. 13. And then those who did so were tormented in chains. 14. But the rest of the multitude of the angels, of which there is (no) number, restrained themselves. 15. And those who dwelt on the earth perished together (with them) through the waters of the deluge. (Apocalypse of Baruch LVI: 9–15).

The action of the Watchers was also a rebellion and disobedience, that lumped them together with the angels who alongside Satan, rebelled against God. Angels were not created to have children, because they are *spiritual, living an eternal, immortal life*, hence, do not have need for wives to procreate with. Christ alluded to this in (Luke 20:36 and Mark 12:25). Also, God made this abundantly clear to them while passing judgement on them:

> 15.2 And go say to the Watchers of Heaven, who sent you to petition on their behalf: You ought to petition on behalf of men, not men on behalf of you. 15.3 Why have you left the High, Holy and Eternal Heaven, and lain with women, and become unclean with the daughters of men, and taken wives for yourselves, and done as the sons of the earth, and begotten giant sons? 15.4 And you were spiritual, Holy, living an eternal life, but you became unclean upon the women, and begot children through the blood of flesh, and lusted after the blood of men, and produced flesh and blood, as they do, who die and are destroyed. 15.5 And

> for this reason I give men wives; so that they might sow seed in them, and so that children might be born by them, so that deeds might be done on the Earth. *15.6 But you, formerly, were spiritual, living an eternal, immortal life, for all the generations of the world. 15.7 For this reason I did not arrange wives for you; because the dwelling of the spiritual ones is in Heaven.* (Book of Enoch 15:2–7).

The sentences of the Watchers were also alluded to by Peter and Jude:

> [4] For if God spared not the angels that sinned, but cast them down to hell, and delivered them into chains of darkness, to be reserved unto judgment; (2 Peter 2:4 KJV).

> [6] And the angels which kept not their first estate, but left their own habitation, he hath reserved in everlasting chains under darkness unto the judgment of the great day. (Jude 6–7 KJV).

5.6 CONSEQUENCES OF THE FALL OF THE WATCHERS

The grievous act of the Watchers had serious consequences in the order of affairs on earth. Key consequences of the incursion of the Watchers into the earth include the introduction of the Nephilim (the hybrid children of the Watchers and earthly women), further genetic corruption of humans and animals (emergence of chimera), idolatry, and introduction of forbidden knowledge into the earth. The world literally changed, and what followed this incursion was an utterly decadent world, as captured in Genesis 6 and various other extrabiblical texts including, Book of Enoch, Book of Jubilees, and Book of Jasher:

> [5] And God saw that the wickedness of man was great in the earth, and that every imagination of the thoughts of his heart was only evil continually. [6] And it repented the Lord that he had made man on the earth, and it grieved him at his heart. (Genesis 6: 5–6 KJV).

> 23. And everyone sold himself to work iniquity and to shed much blood, and the earth was filled with iniquity. 24. And after this they sinned against the beasts and birds, and all that moves and walks on the earth: and much blood was shed on the earth, and every imagination and desire of men imagined vanity and evil continually. 25. And the Lord destroyed everything from off the face of the earth; because of the wickedness of their deeds,

DISRUPTION OF GOD'S PLAN FOR MAN

and because of the blood which they had shed in the midst of the earth He destroyed everything. 26. (Book of Jubilees, VII, 23–26).

8.2 And there was great impiety, and much fornication, and they went astray, and all their ways became corrupt. (The Book of Enoch 8:2).

18 And their judges and rulers went to the daughters of men and took their wives by force from their husbands according to their choice, and the sons of men in those days took from the cattle of the earth, the beasts of the field and the fowls of the air, and taught the mixture of animals of one species with the other, in order therewith to provoke the Lord; and God saw the whole earth and it was corrupt, for all flesh had corrupted its ways upon earth, all men and all animals. (Book of Jasher 4:18).

The Book of Enoch (19:1) alluded that the fallen Watchers took different shapes (transmogrified/shape-shifted) and made men unclean:

19.1 And Uriel said to me: "The spirits of the Angels who were promiscuous with women will stand here; and they, *assuming many forms, made men unclean and will lead men astray so that they sacrifice to demons as gods.* And they will stand there until the great judgment day, on which they will be judged, so that an end will be made of them (Book of Enoch 19:1).

This change of form alluded to here could mean that the Watchers could have taken the shape of men, to have intercourse with women. It also suggested that they introduced men into worshipping demons and gods (idolatry). This might be pointing to the fact that the Watchers may have introduced themselves to humans as gods. This period most likely marked the beginning of heightening of polytheism across the world.

The import of the incursion of the Watchers into the world was that sin and transgression of the laws of God grew exponentially across the world. All forms of wickedness and immorality including bestiality were rampant (sinning against animals). There were genetic modifications of plants and animals. The Book of Jasher 4:18, seems to suggest that after the Watchers took the wife of men, the men resulted in sleeping with beasts (*And their judges and rulers went to the daughters of men and took their wives by force from their husbands according to their choice, and the sons of men in those days took from the cattle of the earth, the beasts of the field and the fowls of the air*). This was probably the time that chimeras (hybrids of humans and animals such as centaur and Minotaur) were first introduced into this earth age.

The intensity of the sinfulness, corruption, and wickedness of this period was so bad that God decided to flood the earth, to erase all flesh (humans, birds, animals) that have been corrupted by the incursion of the angels. As it turns out only few people living in this period were untouched (their DNA's have not been tampered with) by the sins of the Watchers. It must be recognised that the Nephilim were on earth for long time from Jared's time to Noah's, hence, they had a long time to corrupt humanity. As a result, only Noah and his family were to be preserved:

> 21 And Noah found grace in the sight of the Lord, and the Lord chose him and his children to raise up seed from them upon the face of the whole earth. (The Book of Jasher 4:21).

The few other righteous people living at that time, were allowed to die before the flood arrived:

> 20 And all men who walked in the ways of the Lord, died in those days, before the Lord brought the evil upon man which he had declared, for this was from the Lord, that they should not see the evil which the Lord spoke of concerning the sons of men. (Book of Jasher 4:20).

After God passed the judgment on the Watchers, strife was instigated against the Nephilim, and they fought and killed each other. Part of the judgement of the Watchers was that they will see their offsprings killed and eliminated from the face of the earth. It seems the nature of the angels who fell were different hence the product of their intercourse with humans produced various variants of the Nephilim. The Book of Jubilees identified the following groups: the Giants, the Naphil, and Eljo. There might still be more variants of them. These various groups of Nephilim fought among each other and mankind. And as a result, wickedness, strife, immorality and blood spilling filled the earth at this time:

> 22. And they begat sons the Naphidim, and they were all unlike, and they devoured one another: and the Giants slew the Naphil, and the Naphil slew the Eljo, and the Eljo mankind, and one man another. (Book of Jubilees, VII, 22).

After this, they were rounded up by Archangels: Michael, Gabriel, Raphael, who chained them in the bottomless pit until the time of the final judgement.

DISRUPTION OF GOD'S PLAN FOR MAN

Raphael was given charge over Azazel:

> 10.4 And further the Lord said to Raphael: "Bind Azazel by his hands and his feet and throw him into the darkness. And split open the desert, which is in Dudael, and throw him there. 10.5 And throw on him jagged and sharp stones and cover him with darkness. And let him stay there forever. And cover his face so that he may not see the light. 10.6 And so that, on the Great Day of Judgment, he may be hurled into the fire. (Book of Enoch 10:4-6).

Gabriel was charged to handle the Nephilim:

> *10.9 And the Lord said to Gabriel: "Proceed against the bastards, and the reprobates, and against the sons of the fornicators. And destroy the sons of the fornicators, and the sons of the Watchers, from amongst men. And send them out, and send them against one another, and let them destroy themselves in battle; for they will not have length of days. 10.10 And they will petition you, but the petitioners will gain nothing in respect of them, for they hope for eternal life, and that each of them will live life for five hundred years." (Book of Enoch 10:9-10).*

Michael was tasked to handle Semyaza and the rest of the Watchers:

> 10.11 And the Lord said to Michael: "Go, inform Semyaza, and the others with him, who have associated with the women to corrupt themselves with them in all their uncleanness. 10.12 When all their sons kill each other, and when they see the destruction of their loved ones, bind them for seventy generations, under the hills of the earth, until the day of their judgment and of their consummation, until the judgment, which is for all eternity, is accomplished. 10.13 And in those days, they will lead them to the Abyss of Fire; in torment, and in prison they will be shut up for all eternity. (Book of Enoch 10:11-13).

Another consequence of the incursion of the Watchers was the emergence of demons on earth. Demons are a class of evil spirit that emerged from the disembodied spirits of the Nephilim. When the Nephilim began fighting against themselves, many of them were violently killed. Those who survived were wiped out by the flood[1]. However, because of the abhorrent way they were brought fought to the earth, there was no place prepared in the heavens to receive their souls. Hence, they

---

1. There are indications that some of them were hidden by their fathers to preserve them from the flood.

became demons roaming around the earth (evils spirit trapped within the earthly space):

> 15.8 *And now, the giants who were born from body and flesh will be called Evil Spirits on the Earth, and on the Earth will be their dwelling. 15.9 And evil spirits came out from their flesh, because from above they were created, from the Holy Watchers was their origin and first foundation. Evil spirits they will be on Earth and 'Spirits of the Evil Ones' they will be called. 15.10 And the dwelling of the Spirits of Heaven is Heaven, but the dwelling of the spirits of the Earth, who were born on the Earth, is Earth. 15.11 And the spirits of the giants do wrong, are corrupt, attack, fight, break on the Earth, and cause sorrow. And they eat no food, do not thirst, and are not observed. 15.12 And these spirits will rise against the sons of men, and against the women, because they came out of them during the days of slaughter and destruction.* (Book of Enoch 15:8–12).

Having once experienced life on earth, and without being allocated any spiritual abode, the demons roam the earth, seeking bodies to inhabit so they can continue to experience the life they had been exposed to. Hence, they seduce and possess humans:

> 27. For I see, and behold the demons have begun (their) seductions against you and against your children, and now I fear on your behalf, that after my death ye will shed the blood of men upon the earth, and that ye, too, will be destroyed from the face of the earth. 28. For whoso sheddeth man's blood, and whoso eateth the blood of any flesh, will all be destroyed from the earth. 29. And there will not be left any man that eateth blood, Or that sheddeth the blood of man on the earth. Nor will there be left to him any seed or descendants living under heaven; For into Sheol will they go, And into the place of condemnation will they descend, and into the darkness of the deep will they all be removed by a violent death (Book of Jubilees, VII, 27–29).

5.7 THE NOAH'S FLOOD-THE GREAT RESET

The corruption of the DNA of humans by the Watchers appears to be the last straw that made God to decide to eliminate every human whose gene has been corrupted with those of the Watchers. To God, such creations made up of the genes of angels and humans were an aberration to his creations, that thwarted the purpose God had created man for:

DISRUPTION OF GOD'S PLAN FOR MAN

> ⁵ The Lord saw that the wickedness of man was great in the earth, and that every intention of the thoughts of his heart was only evil continually. ⁶ And the Lord regretted that he had made man on the earth, and it grieved him to his heart. ⁷ So the Lord said, "I will blot out man whom I have created from the face of the land, man and animals and creeping things and birds of the heavens, for I am sorry that I have made them." ⁸ But Noah found favor in the eyes of the Lord. (Genesis 6:5–8 ESV).

In some sense, Noah's Flood was a rectification process, that God used to restore the sanctity of his creation on earth. The flood was essentially a great reset of the world, to remove all the impurities introduced into the world by the Watchers and return it to how it was at the time of Adam. The flood somewhat washed away all their corruption and only Noah and family whose gene has most likely not been tampered with by those of the Watchers and their offspring were spared to repopulate the earth.

However, as we shall see in subsequent chapters, the Nephilim gene somewhat managed to resurface after the flood.

CHAPTER 6

The New Beginning

6.1 THE WORLD AFTER THE FLOOD

With just Noah and his family left after the flood (based on biblical accounts), the task to repopulate the world was enormous and paramount. Hence, God made a new covenant with Noah and blessed them:

> 9 And God blessed Noah and his sons and said to them, "Be fruitful and multiply and fill the earth. (Genesis 9:9 ESV).

This was similar to the charge God gave to the male and female created in Genesis 1. It seems that God was hoping for Noah and descendants to capitalise on this opportunity to restore humanity from its fallen state, brought about by the fall of Adam. However, this was not to be. Soon after the flood Noah's weakness manifested with his getting drunk from the first fruits of his vineyard. Which led to one of his sons sleeping with his wife:

> [20] Noah began to be a man of the soil, and he planted a vineyard. [21] He drank of the wine and became drunk and lay uncovered in his tent. [22] And Ham, the father of Canaan, saw the nakedness of his father and told his two brothers outside. [23] Then Shem and Japheth took a garment, laid it on both their shoulders, and walked backward and covered the nakedness of their father. Their faces were turned backward, and they did not see their father's nakedness. (Genesis 9:20–23 ESV).

The above verse is a very enigmatic passage that hides something quite deep, as to what transpired between Ham and Noah. Although, many read this passage literary to mean that Ham saw the father naked and made fun of him. However, a deeper look into this will reveal the full import of this act, which was carefully masked in the passage. The phrase *seeing the nakedness of someone* was clearly defined in Deuteronomy and Leviticus:

> [30] "A man shall not take his father's wife, so that he does not uncover his father's nakedness. (Deuteronomy 22: 30 ESV).

> [7] You shall not uncover the nakedness of your father, which is the nakedness of your mother; she is your mother, you shall not uncover her nakedness. [8] You shall not uncover the nakedness of your father's wife; it is your father's nakedness. (Leviticus 18: 7–8).

Based on the above, the passage could be interpreted that Ham had sexual intercourse with his father's wife. The pointer to the actual act being depicted here was the curse placed on Cannan (Ham's son), who apparently did no wrong to Noah. It does not make sense that Ham committed an act and Noah cursed Cannan. Ham was the obvious person that ought to have been cursed by Noah, but rather his youngest son was cursed. One could argue that Noah's curse was targeted at Ham's children. However, the curse placed on Cannan seems to be out of place and complicates the matter. If Noah wanted to target Ham's children, he could have cursed Ham's first son, who is the heir of the house of Ham. However, specifically targeting Cannan for this curse points to something else–that is Cannan was connected to the sin Ham committed. The most obvious answer to this enigma would be that Cannan was the product or seed from that sexual intercourse between Ham and Noah's wife:

> [24] When Noah awoke from his wine and knew what his youngest son had done to him, [25] he said,
>
> "Cursed be Canaan;
>   a servant of servants shall he be to his brothers." (Genesis 9:24–25 ESV).

Noah was oblivious of what has been going on between his wife and Ham (*he was drunk*). By the time Noah realised what had transpired,

Canaan was already born. Or he waited after his birth to place the curse on him (see Section 6.3 for further exploration of this topic).

This act soon after the flood apparently opened the path of discord among the descendants of Noah. And it was not long that the earth was once again corrupted with sins and transgressions as the descendants of Noah began to increase and multiply.

6.2 SPIRITUAL INTERFERENCE AND IDOLATRY

The Bible tells the story of the fundamental interaction between man and spirits. The greatest of this spirit is God, who created everything, hence, deserves to be worshipped. However, the Bible portrays that man has not always adhered to this. As a result, man's relationship with his maker has always been suboptimal. This absurd behaviour of man towards God has been linked to spiritual interference in man's choices, which ultimately affects how he relates to God.

Going by various events in the Bible, man has a proclivity not to fully rely on God but leans towards seeking out other gods for help and in turn worship them. This seems to be an innate part of the fallen nature of man and abuse of the privilege of freewill. Possibly a tweak in the DNA that makes man not to totally rely on God. Perhaps the tweak in the DNA of man caused by the fall of Adam opened the doorway for renegade spiritual beings to interfere with man's choices, which end up leading men away from God to worship other beings. As a matter of fact, the various narratives presented in the Bible points toward the wavering allegiance of man to God, and God's desire to redeem man from the clutches of the evil ones, bent on the destroying man:

> [10] The thief comes only to steal and kill and destroy. I came that they may have life and have it abundantly. [11] I am the good shepherd. (John 10:10–11 ESV).

Despite their core differences, every religion in the world, believes in the existence of non-physical entities (spirits) that operate from non-physical realms/dimensions, but with abilities to interact with other physical and non-physical dimensions. The human mind is the interface between the physical and spiritual. Hence, spirits mainly interact or influence humans and their activities on the earth through the mind. Although, they are also capable of physically manifesting their presence on the earth, they rarely do this, as it limits their capabilities (essentially, they will be almost as limited as humans). Spirits could also take habitation within humans or other living physical bodies (animals, trees etc), thus, living side by side with the spirits of the individual.

Spirits also do have their designated places of habitation and might be restricted access to other realms and dimension. Spirits from lower dimensions are not normally allowed access to higher dimensions (unless expressly permitted in certain circumstances), whereas spirits originating from a higher dimension can access other dimensions below their levels. For instance, demons, which are the disembodied spirits of the Nephilim are confined to the earthly realm (Book of Enoch 15.10) and are not permitted to ascend to higher dimensions, beyond the earthly realm. Hence, they wander around the earth and in their restless state seek to live inside humans or animals as was the case with the two demon-possessed men in Gadarenes:

> [30] Some distance from them a large herd of pigs was feeding. [31] The demons begged Jesus, "If you drive us out, send us into the herd of pigs." (Mathew 8:30–31 NIV).

Christ afterwards, also, hinted at this, by suggesting that demons are earth-bound:

> [43] When the unclean spirit is gone out of a man, he walketh through dry places, seeking rest, and findeth none.
> [44] Then he saith, I will return into my house from whence I came out; and when he is come, he findeth it empty, swept, and garnished.
> [45] Then goeth he, and taketh with himself seven other spirits more wicked than himself, and they enter in and dwell there: and the last state of that man is worse than the first. Even so shall it be also unto this wicked generation. (Mathew 12: 43–45 KJV).

Needless to say that not all spirits are bad. Good spirits influence humans to do good things and worship the Most-High God, while bad spirits, who rebelled against God, peel people away from God, by influencing them to do evil things that will hurt God's feelings. The control and enslavement of humans has always been a key target of evil spirits. Hence, they claim to be gods and demand to be worshipped, thus, leading to idolatry.

The origins of idolatry in the current earth age can be traced as far back as to the first generation of Adam's descendants. There is a strong suspicion that this practice may have either been introduced by Cain and his descendants or via the first-generation humans created on Day 6 of Genesis 1. There was a concerted efforts by the descendants of Seth not to intermingle with those of Cain, whose practices were abhorrent to the children of Seth.

One may wonder why humans are attracted to idolatry. One possible reason maybe that there may potentially be some short-term benefits in worshipping other gods/spirits. Spirits tend to reveal to those who worship them certain secrets of the spiritual world, which may give humans some added advantage over other humans. For instance, it was probably through Cain's interaction with these spirits that he was able to build the first city. They may also, offer some level of protection and fortune as their authority permits. However, whatever promises the false spirits/gods offer to their adherents cannot be compared to the innumerable promises of God. The evil spirits understanding the nature of man entrap them with such candyfloss to temporarily satisfy their needs, as a way to draw them away from God.

Thus, from these roots laid as far back as the time of Cain was idolatry spread among humans. Idolatry also continued after the flood, emanating from the sons of Noah. Every culture around the world has different gods they have worshipped in the past or still worship. In doing so, they believe the gods will hear their supplications and cater for their needs, as a reward for their reverence. However, the goal of the gods, is to draw man away from God, to get back at God for expelling them.

The creation of humans drew the ire of some of the spiritual beings who believed God bestowed a lot of favor and capabilities on humans. Hence, their goal is to cause humans to sin against God (going contrary to his will and commandments), and by so doing, draw the anger and judgement of God against them. These entities posing as gods have at one time or the other, rebelled against God, transgressed the laws of God or outrightly disobeyed God (see Section 7.3). Having lost their station in heaven, many of these entities came to earth to coerce man to adore and worship them. This existential struggle of man against negative spiritual influences is captured by Paul in Ephesians:

> 12 For we do not wrestle against flesh and blood, but against the rulers, against the authorities, against the cosmic powers over

this present darkness, against the spiritual forces of evil in the heavenly places.

The strength or the influence of evil spirits could be seen in the reintroduction of idolatry soon after Noah's flood. One would have assumed that after the great reset of the flood and the destruction witnessed, the survivors of the flood must have instructed their descendants to steer clear of evil forces. But this was not to be, because shortly afterwards, man began to worship other gods (see Section 6.5).

One of the key tactics the evil spirits deploy to deceive humans is to pretend they are good spirits. God doesn't remove the powers of the entities, unless those that are chained. Hence, the entities can still bamboozle humans within their capacities to pull off some supernatural stunts. This is why they have been able to mesmerise and deceive humans. With such powers given to them by God, they can appear to be godly or even act as representatives of God:

> 14 And no wonder, for even Satan disguises himself as an angel of light. (2 Corinthians 11:14 ESV).

Hence, the reason John admonishes followers of Christ to test the spirit:

> Beloved, do not believe every spirit, but test the spirits to see whether they are from God, for many false prophets have gone out into the world. (1 John 4:1 ESV).

With this strategy, the false spirits deceived humans in the past and are still using it to deceive the present generation. This is pertinent to modern day followers of Christ, who tend to believe that everything supernatural is from God. Such assumptions made it difficult for people to understand that both good and evil spirits operate in the supernatural, hence, can pull supernatural stunts. Thus, to overcome negative spiritual interference, one must be able to discern the type of spirit they are interacting with.

6.3 POSTDILUVIAN GIANTS

The Bible is littered with references to presence of the Nephilim/giants before and after the flood:

> 4 The Nephilim were on the earth in those days, and also afterward, when the sons of God came into the daughters of man

and they bore children to them. These were the mighty men who were of old, the men of renown. (Genesis 6:4 ESV).

Whereas the origin of pre-flood giants is traced to the incursion of the Watchers, that of the post-flood giants is a bit fuzzy, as there was no explicit explanation of where they came from in any of the existing books of the Bible. There are various records of the bitter encounters between post-flood giants and Israelites in Exodus, Numbers, Deuteronomy, Joshua, and Samuel. Most of these encounters occurred after the departure of Israelites from Egypt, in their bid to take Canaan. David also encountered a descendant of these giants (Goliath).

However, the presence of giants after the flood presents a dilemma to biblical scholars. The flood was supposed to have taken care of them, having destroyed every flesh (humans and other living animals) on earth that was not preserved in Noah's Ark. Furthermore, there was no record in the Bible of a further incursion of another group of Watchers into the earth after the flood. So where did the post-diluvian giants come from? This dilemma once again points to the fact that the Bible as it is today, did not cover everything that may have happened on earth, and important things like these were either deliberately left out or may have been recorded in many sacred books that have been lost through the passage of time.

Despite the challenge this presents, there are four possible ways that the giants may have returned to the earth: another incursion of the Watchers or other group of angels on earth (following the example of the Watchers); through the gene corruption of Noah's children or their spouses prior to the flood; some of the Nephilim hidden or taken to a safe place before the flood hits; and genetic manipulation based on secret knowledge the Watchers taught the children of men.

Although, there is no account of sons of God coming back to the earth to sleep with earthly women, one cannot entirely rule this angle out, because if it has happened before, it could happen again. Furthermore, some of them may also have escaped the flood. Warnings of the coming flood were common knowledge in that era for centuries. Enoch, Methuselah, and Noah told everyone who cared to listen about the impending danger. So, there is a possibility that some of the Nephilim may have taken heed to those warnings and found a suitable hiding place. Arguably, this was not the expected outcome, as God intended to clear them off the earth. However, there is a chance that some of them may

THE NEW BEGINNING

have managed to escape the flood by hiding in underground facilities, or may have been preserved by their fathers, in some secluded parts of the earth or outside of it long before the flood came. Some scholars also, believe that Og, the king of the land of Bashan (a Nephilim) clung unto Noah's ark and was able to survive the flood.[1] The Epic of Gilgamesh (an ancient Mesopotamian odyssey recorded in the Akkadian language[2] tells a story that appears to match the flood story of Noah narrated in the Bible.

In the epic, Gilgamesh, was opportune to speak to a figure known as Utnapishtim, a man who survived a great flood sent by the gods by building a boat at the command of the god Ea. Utnapishtim tells a story very similar to the Genesis Flood narrative.[3] Even though some people believe that the story of the flood, recorded in Genesis was copied from the Akkadian epic, the epic was telling a different story that parallels that of Noah, depicting how some of the Nephilim may have escaped the flood.

Some scholars have suggested that Gilgamesh was used to depict Nimrod.[4] If this supposition is true, on the face of it, it may appear that the Utnapishtim might have been his grandfather Ham or his great-grandfather Noah (who are both survivors of the flood) telling Nimrod about the flood. However, in the light of the passage in the Writings of Abraham, Utnapishtim may have been Cain or any of the Nephilim, who was tipped off by Satan or one of the Watchers to build a boat, to survive the flood:

> Moreover, Nimrod was instructed in all the secrets of the evil combination by his father Cain, for Cain had not perished in the flood. 4. Wherefore, Nimrod became a mighty man among the sons of men and established his kingdom and grew stronger and stronger in wickedness after the order of the secret combination which was from the beginning, for Nimrod spread his dominion over all mankind save those in the city of Shalom. (The Writings of Abrham, 17: 3–4).

It was no secret then that a flood was coming, and that Noah was building a boat. So, some of the Nephilim may have taken steps to preserve their lineage. The main issue then was not knowledge of the coming

---

1. Halickman, "Who Hitched a", 1
2. Britannica, "Epic of Gilgamesh", 1
3. Roat, "7 Facts You", 1
4. Emil et al, "Nimrod", 1; Livingston, "Who Was Nimrod", 1

flood, but people's belief and adherence to the warning. Many thought that Noah was insane building a boat for a flood that will never happen. Others doubted that this event would happen because the warning of a coming flood had been around for generations, that many began to find it ridiculous (similar to the manner many in the contemporarily world are regarding the second coming of Christ and end time tribulations). However, the Watchers who already know how God operates, would not have taken the warnings lightly, and would have taken necessary steps to escape it. Hence, Cain or some Nephilim may have been instructed/commanded to take the warning serious by his spiritual handlers depicted in the Epic of Gilgamesh as a god called Ea. This supposition that Utnapishtim is either Cain or a Nephilim, is supported by what Gilgamesh did next after receiving this knowledge from Utnapishtim. He became angry at God for causing the flood and sets out to kill him (as captured in another part of the Epic of Gilgamesh). This is where the story in the Epic differs from that presented in the Bible. Noah was never angry at God, but grateful that he spared his life, unlike Utnapishtim, who still bore a grudge against God, and transferred this hatred to Gilgamesh.

Another plausible explanation of the origin of the postdiluvian giants is that somehow their DNA survived through one of the sons of Noah. But the identity of the son through which this gene may have been passed down remain arguable. One may also wonder why God allowed this to happen. Was there a purpose for this? The answer to this question may not readily be found in canonised Biblical books. But certain extra Biblical books contain some pointers that may help to answer this.

The Writings of Abraham contains an interesting passage concerning the wives of Noah, his sons, and daughters:

> AND the child grew and waxed strong in wisdom and mighty in the power of the priesthood for he was initiated into the Order of the Ancients in his childhood and learned the rites and ordinances and the powers of the priesthood with the signs and tokens and key words wherewith he could call upon the powers of heaven to combat the forces of the adversary. 2. And when he was come of age, he took twelve wives and begat many sons and daughters who grew up in righteousness and served the Lord all their days and some died and others were caught up unto the city of Enoch. 3. But in the next generation they corrupted themselves, for the daughters of Noah's sons did go forth and lay with the sons of men, which thing was an abomination in the eyes of God. 4. Wherefore, the Lord said unto Noah, Behold,

THE NEW BEGINNING

the daughters of thy sons have sold themselves, for behold, mine anger is kindled against the sons of men, for they will not hearken to my voice; wherefore, all those who go in unto them will be destroyed with them. (The Writings of Abraham 9:1-4).

On the face of it, it seems ludicrous that Noah had twelve wives and gave birth to many sons and daughters prior the birth of the trio Shem, Japheth, and Ham. However, it is more absurd that Genesis recorded that Noah gave birth to the trio at the age of 500:

> 32 After Noah was 500 years old, Noah fathered Shem, Ham, and Japheth. (Genesis 5: 32 ESV).

This absurdity arises from the fact that this did not follow the pattern of his predecessors. Noah seems to be an outlier with respect to this. A curious mind will wonder why it took Noah 500 years before he started having children, whereas his forefathers beginning from Adam had children before clocking 200 years:

> [3] When Adam had lived 130 years, he fathered a son in his own likeness, after his image, and named him Seth. [4] The days of Adam after he fathered Seth were 800 years; and he had other sons and daughters. [5] Thus all the days that Adam lived were 930 years, and he died.
> [6] When Seth had lived 105 years, he fathered Enosh. [7] Seth lived after he fathered Enosh 807 years and had other sons and daughters. [8] Thus all the days of Seth were 912 years, and he died.
> [9] When Enosh had lived 90 years, he fathered Kenan. [10] Enosh lived after he fathered Kenan 815 years and had other sons and daughters. [11] Thus all the days of Enosh were 905 years, and he died.
> [12] When Kenan had lived 70 years, he fathered Mahalalel. [13] Kenan lived after he fathered Mahalalel 840 years and had other sons and daughters. [14] Thus all the days of Kenan were 910 years, and he died.
> [15] When Mahalalel had lived 65 years, he fathered Jared. [16] Mahalalel lived after he fathered Jared 830 years and had other sons and daughters. [17] Thus all the days of Mahalalel were 895 years, and he died.
> [18] When Jared had lived 162 years, he fathered Enoch. [19] Jared lived after he fathered Enoch 800 years and had other sons and daughters. [20] Thus all the days of Jared were 962 years, and he died.

> ²¹ When Enoch had lived 65 years, he fathered Methuselah. ²² Enoch walked with God after he fathered Methuselah 300 years and had other sons and daughters. ²³ Thus all the days of Enoch were 365 years. ²⁴ Enoch walked with God, and he was not, for God took him.
> ²⁵ When Methuselah had lived 187 years, he fathered Lamech. ²⁶ Methuselah lived after he fathered Lamech 782 years and had other sons and daughters. ²⁷ Thus all the days of Methuselah were 969 years, and he died.
> ²⁸ When Lamech had lived 182 years, he fathered a son ²⁹ and called his name Noah, saying, "Out of the ground that the Lord has cursed, this one shall bring us relief from our work and from the painful toil of our hands." ³⁰ Lamech lived after he fathered Noah 595 years and had other sons and daughters. ³¹ Thus all the days of Lamech were 777 years, and he died. Genesis 5:3–31 ESV).

So, it can be seen from the passage above, Noah seems to be the only outlier in this era that waited for 500 years before having children. There is an apparent gap! What has he been doing within those gap period, before he gave birth to the trio of Shem, Japhet and Ham? Or perhaps, he married when he should, like his ancestors and other men of that era, and this was not captured in Genesis.

This conundrum seems to suggest that an attempt was made in the Genesis to mask the fact that Noah had many wives, and that the second generations of his descendants derailed from the righteous pact of Order of the Ancients. Hence, the additional information contained in the Writings of Abraham, seem to account for this gap in Noah's earlier days, that were overlooked in the Genesis account. This buttresses the point that the Writings of Abraham should not easily be dismissed as an unreasonable source of pre-flood information.

Arguably, the most fascinating fact in the Writings of Abraham relative to this topic is the suggestion that one of Noah's wives Naamah was of the seed of Cain:

> AND when Noah was four hundred and fifty years old, he begat a son and he called his name Japheth. 2. Forty two years later he begat another son of her who was the mother of Japheth, and he called his name Shem. 3. Eight years later Noah begat a son of his wife Naamah, who was of the seed of Cain, and he called his name Ham, for he said, Through him will the curse be preserved in the land. (Writings of Abraham 10:1–3).

THE NEW BEGINNING

There are some apparent differences in the account presented here and that presented in Genesis. Genesis records that Noah started having children after he was 500 years and gave birth to Shem, Ham, and Japheth. This passage from Genesis does not necessarily rule out that Noah may have other children before he was 500 years, but that he fathered three sons after this age. Also, the ordering of the sons seems to differ from the account in the Writings of Abraham, which suggests that Japhet was born earlier than Shem, and from the same mother. Again, the presentation in Genesis did not explicitly provide the age of each of the sons. This is also a deviation from the chronological norm previously presented in the chapter for the forefathers of Noah, where the year each of the sons were born was given. By now, it should become clear to the reader that there was something going on with the account of Noah in Genesis. The ordering of the sons of Noah might have been arbitrary, presented by the writer to highlight Shem as the head of the Noah's family to the reader, rather than preserving chronological accuracy. Even so, it is very curious that Genesis 6:9 started with the intention of presenting the generations of Noah, but it abruptly deviated to talk about Noah's instruction to prepare the ark, and ended up, with just one sentence mentioning the three sons of Noah, without delving into any details that normally would have been expected when discussing generations:

> [9] These are the generations of Noah. Noah was a righteous man, blameless in his generation. Noah walked with God. [10] And Noah had three sons, Shem, Ham, and Japheth.
> [11] Now the earth was corrupt in God's sight, and the earth was filled with violence. [12] And God saw the earth, and behold, it was corrupt, for all flesh had corrupted their way on the earth. [13] And God said to Noah, "I have determined to make an end of all flesh, for the earth is filled with violence through them. Behold, I will destroy them with the earth. [14] Make yourself an ark of gopher wood. (Genesis 6:9 -14).

In consideration of the above, one should not quickly dismiss the important fact presented in the Writings of Abraham that Noah married a woman from the line of Cain. It is obviously unimaginable that Noah, a righteous man, who had been trained in the righteous way by his grandfather Methuselah, would have gone to pick a wife from the line of Cain, whom the line of Seth has assiduously avoided. The absurdity of this marriage was obvious to the writer that he had to provide reasons for this oddity:

NOW Noah had taken a wife of the seed of Cain, and she was a righteous woman; nevertheless, the curse remained with her seed according to the word of God. 2. And Noah took her on this wise: For the word of the Lord came unto Noah, saying, Take unto thyself Naamah, the daughter of Lamech, who dwelleth here in the city of thy fathers, for she hath been faithful to my gospel, wherefore I shall preserve through her the seed of Cain through the flood.

3. This Lamech who was the father of Naamah was of the seed of Cain being the son of Methusael, the son of Mahujael, the son of Irad, the son of Enoch, the son of Cain. 4. Lamech had married Adah and Zillah, the daughters of Cainan, the son of Enos, the son of Seth, the son of Adam. Adah bare children unto Lamech, but Zillah was barren until her old age when the Lord opened her womb, and she conceived and bare a son and a daughter. 5. Her son she named Tubal Cain, saying, After I had withered away have I obtained him from the Almighty God. 6. Her daughter she named Naamah, saying, After I had withered away have I obtained pleasure and delight. (Writings of Abraham 11:1–6).

The background story to this is that after Lamech murdered someone (whose identity was not explicitly stated in the Genesis[5]), his wives

5. The death of Cain is a controversial topic with many versions of it. Whereas the Writings of Abraham suggests that Cain survived the flood and stated that the man killed by Lamech was actually Irad who revealed the secrets of the line of Cain to the sons of Seth: *4. Wherefore, Irad went forth and began to reveal the secrets of the sons of Cain unto the sons of Seth. 5. Lamech, being Master Mahan at that time, found Irad sitting in his garden with Joram, the young son of Irad, and slew him. 6. Thus, Lamech slew Irad for the sake of the oath of the secret combination and he slew Irad's son with him. 7. But Tubal Cain, the son of Lamech, had followed him and viewed his evil deed which he had committed and he revealed it unto his mother Zillah and she unto her sister Adah.* (The Writings of Abraham 12:4–7).

The Book of Jubilees suggests that he was killed before the flood shortly after Adam died: *31. At the close of this jubilee Cain was killed after him in the same year; for his house fell upon him and he died in the midst of his house, and he was killed by its stones, for with a stone he had killed Abel, and by a stone was he killed in righteous judgment.* (Book of Jubilees IV: 31). The Book of Jasher however holds that Cain was the man Lamech killed: *26 And Lamech was old and advanced in years, and his eyes were dim that he could not see, and Tubal Cain, his son, was leading him and it was one day that Lamech went into the field and Tubal Cain his son was with him, and whilst they were walking in the field, Cain the son of Adam advanced towards them; for Lamech was very old and could not see much, and Tubal Cain his son was very young. 27 And Tubal Cain told his father to draw his bow, and with the arrows he smote Cain, who was yet far off, and he slew him, for he appeared to them to be an animal. 28 And the arrows entered Cain's body although he was distant from them, and he fell to the ground and died.* (Book of Jasher 2:26–28).

THE NEW BEGINNING

Adah and Zillah, the daughters of Mahalalel from the line of Seth (see Section 5.2, Genesis 4: 25–26, Genesis 5 and Genesis 4: 9–22), left him and returned to their father with their children, among whom was Naamah. It was this same Naamah, who was then living among the house of Seth that Noah eventually married, to preserve the seed of Cain:

> WHILE Naamah was yet a child, great consternation fell upon the seed of Cain, for Irad the Son of Enoch, the son of Cain, had become a member of the secret combination and was privy to all it secrets until one night when the Lord appeared to him in a dream saying, Irad, thou hast done evil instead of good and hast followed after Satan rather than God; wherefore, I shall destroy thee and thine house when I send in the floods upon the earth. 2. But Irad was pricked in his heart and pled with the Lord to show mercy and preserve his seed through the great flood. 3. Seeing that his penitence was true, the Lord said to him, Irad, if thou wilt repent and reveal the evils of the secret combination unto the sons of Seth, I will have mercy upon thee and I will join thy seed unto the seed of Seth that it may be preserved through the great flood. 4. Wherefore, Irad went forth and began to reveal the secrets of the sons of Cain unto the sons of Seth. 5. Lamech, being Master Mahan at that time, found Irad sitting in his garden with Joram, the young son of Irad, and slew him. 6. Thus Lamech slew Irad for the sake of the oath of the secret combination and he slew Irad's son with him. 7. But Tubal Cain, the son of Lamech, had followed him and viewed his evil deed which he had committed and he revealed it unto his mother Zillah and she unto her sister Adah. 8. Wherefore, Adah and Zillah confronted Lamech with his evil and cursed him in the name of the Lord for having slain Irad who had repented of his wickedness from among the sons of men. 9. And Lamech said unto his wives Adah and Zillah, Hear my voice, ye wives of Lamech; hearken unto my speech, for I have slain a man to my wounding and a young man to my hurt. 10. If Cain shall be avenged sevenfold, truly Lamech shall be seventy and seven fold. 11. Lamech's wives, therefore, feared to confront him further, but Lamech repented not of his evil deeds and finding his son Tubal Cain at prayer, he slew him for having revealed his murders. 12. When Adah and Zillah, the wives of Lamech, learned of this, they took their remaining sons and daughters and went unto their father Cainan's city and revealed the remainder of the secrets of this evil combination among the sons of Adam. 13. Thus did Naamah come to dwell among the sons of Adam and she grew up

before the Lord in righteousness and was known for her tender care toward the sick and the unfortunate. 14. Nevertheless, she had not husband because she was of the forbidden race. (Writings of Abraham 12:1–14).

The passage above lays out the full background story to what Genesis captured, regarding why Lamech killed a man. From the passage, it can be deciphered that the line of Seth avoided intermarrying with the line of Cain. Even with her apparent good nature and morals, no one from the line of Seth wanted to have Naamah as a wife. Hence, when Noah got the instruction to marry her, he was baffled and had to make inquiries from his grandfather Methuselah to confirm, he heard right:

> WHEN the word of the Lord came unto Noah, saying, Take unto thyself Naama, the daughter of Lamech who dwelleth here in the city of thy fathers, for she hath been faithful to my gospel, wherefore, I shall preserve through her the seed of Cain through the flood, Noah went unto his father, Methuselah. 2. Methuselah inquired of the Lord and returned this word unto his son Lamech: Verily, thus saith the Lord, Mine handmaiden Naamah have I given unto my son Noah that the seed of Cain might be preserved through the great flood which I will send upon the earth. 3. Wherefore, let not my son Noah fear to take her to wife, for in so doing he shall be blessed for through him will come all nations. 4. Wherefore, say unto him, Noah, my son, I have looked upon the evils of the sons of men which have come up before me, for they have corrupted the whole earth save only this city in which thou dwellest. 5. Therefore, I will send in the floods upon the earth but thou and thy seed will I preserve through the flood, for I will send mine angels to instruct thee in the building of an ark wherein ye shall be saved. 6. Behold, I shall establish thy seed before me forever and I will spread them abroad over the earth as numerous as the sand upon the seashore. 7. Thy seed shall not cease as long as the earth shall stand but through thee and thy priesthood which will be preserved in thy seed shall all nations be blessed. (Writings of Abraham 13:1–7).

Judging from the above, God wanted to retain the two lineages (Seth's and Cain's) till the end. Hence, it is plausible that the DNA of the giants may have been preserved through the seed of Cain via Naamah. When the flood hit, only eight people eventually got into the ark with Noah. Noah's youngest wife, his three sons and their wives. Naamah was

THE NEW BEGINNING

not on the ark. She possibly might have died before the flood, considering she was older than Noah (see Table 5.1):

> THUS did Noah take to wife Naamah, the daughter of Zillah, the wife of Lamech of the seed of Cain, and she bare him a son whom he named Ham, and thus was the curse preserved in the land through the great flood. 2. For when the patience of God was ended in which He did grant a space of time for repentance unto the sons of men, the floods came in upon the earth and destroyed all flesh from off the face of the earth save eight souls only, for Noah and his youngest wife Adah, and his three sons Shem, Japheth, and Ham and one of each of their wives were preserved in the ark which the angels had instructed Noah in building. 3. The remainder of the righteous had died or been caught up into Enoch's city prior to the time of the flood, and these eight were saved. (Writings of Abraham 15:1-3).

Based on the foregoing, Ham had mixture of Cain's and Seth's DNA. With the DNA of Cain's lineage further corrupted by the Watchers, Ham possibly had some Nephilim trait in his DNA. Hence, the act of Ham uncovering the nakedness of his father (sleeping with Noah's youngest wife–see 5.1) may have laid the foundation from which the giants were re-introduced into the world, considering that the Nephilim's DNA was already in Cain's line, who the Watchers actively engaged with. Naamah coming from the union between the seed of Seth (Zillah) and seed of Cain (Lamech), would have had a somewhat diluted gene of Cain (mix of Seth's and Cain's). Hence, Ham, the product of Noah and Naamah, would also have a much more diluted gene of Cain tainted with that of the Nephilim's. Despite the dilution, the DNA was still present. It is plausible to believe that the giant's seed eventually showed up in Canaan, the product of Ham's illicit sex with his father's wife.

Noteworthy is the fact that the giants before the flood were called the Nephilim, whereas those after the flood were referred to as Rephaim. What does this tell us? Are these giants different? Possible, these two sets of giants have some physical differences (smaller in size) as well as diluted DNA. We also know that there are different kinds of antediluvian Nephilim identified in the Book of Jubilees VII: 22 (see Section 5.6). Another pointer to this is the fact that most of the post flood giants were found to live around the land of Canaan.

Another possible route through which the Postdiluvian giants re-emerged is by genetic modification or re-engineering of the genes of the post-flood people. Tabata[6] suggested that it is "likely that (through the use of sorcery and witchcraft) the ancient peoples were able to bring forth the needed changes within themselves and others to make them Nephilim (i.e., giants)". He opined that this may have been the means through which Nimrod became a mighty man (gibbowr/*geborim*), a phrase that is synonymous with the Nephilim in the Genesis. The Book of Jubilee recorded that a great-grandson of Noah (Kâinâm, the son of Arpachshad[7]), stumbled on some secret teachings of the Watchers inscribed on rocks. According to the book, these were codes used by the Watchers to observe the omens of the sun and moon and stars in all the signs of heaven:

> In the twenty-ninth jubilee, in the first week, in the beginning thereof Arpachshad took to himself a wife and her name was Râsû' ĕjâ, the daughter of Sûsân, the daughter of Elam, and she bare him a son in the third year in this week, and he called his name Kâinâm. 2. And the son grew, and his father taught him writing, and he went to seek for himself a place where he might seize for himself a city. 3. And he found a writing which former (generations) had carved on the rock, and he read what was thereon, and he transcribed it and sinned owing to it; for it contained the teaching of the Watchers in accordance with which they used to observe the omens of the sun and moon and stars in all the signs of heaven. 4. And he wrote it down and said nothing regarding it; for he was afraid to speak to Noah about it lest he should be angry with him on account of it. (Jubilees 8:1–4).

Kâinâm was able to decode these secret teachings but what he eventually did with such secret teachings can only be left to imagination. But speculations are rife that the descendants of Noah may have experimented with several ideas and teachings of the Watchers. In the course of these, they may have inadvertently reintroduced the giants to the earth.

In conclusion, despite the attempts made here to trace the origins of the post flood giants, it must be noted that none of these explanations is conclusive. However, it was important to delve into them as there are some elements of truth in them. But fact remains that giants/hybrids of the Watchers and humans existed after the flood and are likely existing till this day among humans–in various variants. This is quite important

---

6. Tabata, "How The Post-Flood", 1
7. Arpachshad is Shem's son born two years after the flood (Jubilees 7:18).

as Christ stated that as it was in the time of Noah, so shall it be during the end of age:

> [26] And as it was in the days of Noah, so it will be also in the days of the Son of Man (Luke 17:26 NKJV).

The days of Noah were characterised by the presence of Nephilim, high level of immorality, and wickedness. Hence, one would expect that for the days of Noah to be replicated in the modern age, all these features will be in our world in the coming years.

6.4 THE ANCIENT ORDERS OF SETH AND CAIN

There are several pointers in the Bible that tend to suggest there were two parallel secret orders through which sacred knowledge was passed down to select members of the blood line of Seth and Cain. Whereas the line of Seth, were towing the righteous path via the Order of the Ancients and assessing such secret knowledge from the angels of God, the line of Cain was gaining theirs from Satan and his agents. Since these blood lines were essentially sworn enemies, the secret knowledge was heavily guarded and only select members of the each of the blood lines, were privy to it. According to the Writings of Abraham, this secret knowledge was highly guarded that Lamech had to kill someone for revealing this secret:

> 6. Thus Lamech slew Irad for the sake of the oath of the secret combination and he slew Irad's son with him. (Writings of Abraham 12:1–6).

· For the line of Seth, the chief custodians of these secrets were the highly regarded patriarchs of these lines who served as both kings and priests to the Most-High God. This order was at some points headed by Seth, Enoch, Methuselah, Noah, Shem, and Abram. It could be seen that not every first son in the line of Seth was qualified to head this order. For instance, Lamech the father of Noah was not found worthy to inherit this top position, rather he was bypassed, and the leadership handed over to his son Noah. Noah then handed this to Shem after the flood:

> SHEM ruled in the city of Shalom and he was called Melchizedek, for the reigned as king under his father Noah, and was a priest of the Most-High God. 2. After the departure of Ham from the presence of his father Noah, Shem and Japheth dwelt

together in peace under the benign rule of Noah; but in time, conflict arose among them and Noah led the seed of Shem to a new land which the Lord showed him where they built a city which they called Shalom, the City of Peace. 3. Noah invested his son Shem with authority to reign as Prince of Peace, and Noah devoted his days to instructing his people after the Order of the Ancients. 4. And his people dwelt in righteousness and worshiped the Lord their God and served Him. 5. They established the order of heaven among them and sought after the City of Enoch and the Lord came among them and ministered to them and those who sought for the gain of this world went out from among them, for they held all things common after the order of Enoch and no man had above his neighbor. (The Writings of Abraham 18:1–5).

Shem subsequently, passed this knowledge down to Abram, Abram in turn handed over to Isaac and Isaac to Jacob. Again, another first son Esau, was bypassed.

6.5 THE RISE OF EVIL AFTER THE FLOOD

One may wonder how evil quickly permeated the earth soon after the flood. The sons of Noah, having witnessed the devastating impact of the flood occasioned by the evils perpetrated by people of that era, would have been very much terrified of the wrath of God. They probably would have passed this down to their children, but this fear soon dissipated, and the descendants of Noah deviated and went back to the old ways. The root of this quick rebound of evil could be linked to spiritual interferences from evil forces (see Section 6.2). The Book of Jubilees noted that soon after the flood, demons (the disembodied spirits of the Nephilim wiped off in the flood), began to torment and lead astray the descendants of Noah. This became a source of worry for Noah and his sons, and he prayed to God to restrain the demons:

> X. And in the third week of this jubilee the unclean demons began to lead astray †the children of the sons of Noah; and to make to err and destroy them. 2. And the sons of Noah came to Noah their father, and they told him concerning the demons which were, leading astray and blinding and slaying his sons› sons. 3. And he prayed before the Lord his God, and said:
> God of the spirits of all flesh, who hast shown mercy unto me,
> And hast saved me and my sons from the waters of the flood,

And hast not caused me to perish as Thou didst the sons of perdition;

> For Thy grace hath been great towards me,
> And great hath been Thy mercy to my soul;
> Let Thy grace be lift up upon my sons,
> And let not wicked spirits rule over them
> Lest they should destroy them from the earth.

> 4. But do Thou bless me and my sons, that we may increase and multiply and replenish the earth. 5. And Thou knowest how Thy Watchers, the fathers of these spirits, acted in my day: and as for these spirits which are living, imprison them and hold them fast in the place of condemnation, and let them not bring destruction on the sons of thy servant, my God; for these are malignant, and created in order to destroy. 6. And let them not rule over the spirits of the living; for Thou alone canst exercise dominion over them. And let them not have power over the sons of the righteous from henceforth and for evermore." (Book of Jubilees, X: 1–6).

After Noah's entreaty to God, angels were sent out by God to restrain the demons, so as to give the descendants of Noah some breathing space:

> 7 And the Lord our God bade us to bind all.
> 8. And the chief of the spirits, Mastêmê, came and said: "Lord, Creator, let some of them remain before me, and let them hearken to my voice, and do all that I shall say unto them; for if some of them are not left to me, I shall not be able to execute the power of my will on the sons of men; for these are for corruption and leading astray before my judgment, for great is the wickedness of the sons of men." 9. And He said: "Let the tenth part of them remain before him and let nine parts descend into the place of condemnation." 10. And one of us He commanded that we should teach Noah all their medicines; for He knew that they would not walk in uprightness, nor strive in righteousness. 11. And we did according to all His words: all the malignant evil ones we bound in the place of condemnation, and a tenth part of them we left that they might be subject before Satan on the earth. 12. And we explained to Noah all the medicines of their diseases, together with their seductions, how he might heal them with herbs of the earth. 13. And Noah wrote down all things in a book as we instructed him concerning every kind of medicine.

> Thus, the evil spirits were precluded from (hurting) the sons of Noah. 14. And he gave all that he had written to Shem, his eldest son; for he loved him exceedingly above all his sons. (Book of Jubilees, X: 7–14).

The account above appears to have been narrated by an angel, who witnessed these events from celestial perspectives. The demons were all to be bound in the underworld prison, probably in the same prison where the Watchers were bound until judgement day (2 Peter 2:4), however, their leader pleaded that some of them should be spared so he can have agents that would tempt (test the loyalty of men to God). Perplexingly, this request was granted and 10% of the demons were left to continue to torment humans who go astray. This seems to suggest that God purposely gave Satan and his angels a free pass to tempt humans (Book of Jubilees, 10: 8), similar to how he allowed Satan to tempt Job. This is all part of the setup to sift out humans who are genuinely loyal to God.

The 10% of the demons that were left were allowed to tempt and overcome the unrighteous, until the final judgement when they will be rounded up and sent into the lake of fire. Hence, these remnants of the demons were left to facilitate the derailment of evil-inclined humans until the last judgement when all shall be judged according to their works. This was probably the reason the demoniacs of Gadarenes were surprised to see Jesus Christ right before them, thinking he had come to send them to the pit they had been spared from by God:

> [28] And when he came to the other side, to the country of the Gadarenes, two demon-possessed men met him, coming out of the tombs, so fierce that no one could pass that way. [29] And behold, they cried out, "What have you to do with us, O Son of God? Have you come here to torment us before the time?" (Matthew 8:28–29).

One may wonder why God will subject man to such a cruel test. The answer to this lies in the fact that the fall of Adam lowered man to a state God had not originally intended. Adam was created to be immortal (he was being groomed to become immortal in the garden), but when he transgressed, death came, hence, he became a mortal being. The destiny of every man is to rise above this fallen state, to ascend to the original state God had created Adam in. For this to happen, God needs to ensure that only the best of humanity who had stripped themselves of all impurities can be promoted to this new level of immortality. He does not want

THE NEW BEGINNING

another Adam scenario, where after being promoted, man falls again at the slightest temptation of Satan. Hence, God has given Satan the free reign to test every man as much as he could, as a way for God to select those who have overcome. The end time trials the (Great Tribulation–see Section 13.6) is the climax of this test, after which those (dead and living) who made it shall be transformed–replacing the mortal body with immortal one. At the final judgement, the scorecard (how every man has performed) will be revealed. Those who did not make it shall be cast into the lake of fire. The second Book of Esdras extensively dealt on this topic across its chapters (see Section 13.5 for further discussion about this regarding the final test).

6.6 NIMROD-ANTICHRIST FORESHADOW

The continued rise of evil after the flood gave rise to another open rebellion against God by humans. This led to the construction of a mighty tower that will enable humanity reach where God was. Arguably, the construction of the Tower of Babel is among the most prominent events recorded in the Holy Bible. However, for such a remarkable story, only few lines of the Genesis were dedicated to the man behind this feat. It seems the writer of Genesis did not wish to draw too much attention to the character of Nimrod. As a matter of fact, Genesis did not directly link Nimrod to the Tower of Babel, as if it wanted to suppress this information. However, conjectures that could be glimpsed from passages in Genesis as well as recordings in other sacred texts, ties Nimrod to the construction of the Tower of Babel.

So, who was Nimrod and how was he able to achieve this feat?

Nimrod was a man that rose to great strength and power in the postdiluvian world to emerge as the first king of the world. He was the great-grandson of Noah from the line of Ham via Cush, who became a very mighty man to the extent that he was able to galvanise the entire world as one force to build a tower that could *reach heaven* (according to the Bible). He built cities after cities in great show of might and strength.

The Bible mentioned Nimrod in 3 books (Genesis 10, 1 Chronicles, and Micah), mostly in passing. Due to the vagueness of the figure of Nimrod in the canonised books of the Bible, it is a bit challenging to fully understand the story behind Nimrod, and how he was able to acquire these extraordinary powers that distinguished him from others in those days. The first mention of Nimrod in the Bible was in the Genesis, where an overview of the descendants of Noah was being presented. The following were said about Nimrod:

> [6] The sons of Ham: Cush, Egypt, Put, and Canaan. [7] The sons of Cush: Seba, Havilah, Sabtah, Raamah, and Sabteca. The sons of Raamah: Sheba and Dedan. [8] Cush fathered Nimrod; he was the first on earth to be a mighty man. [9] He was a mighty hunter before the Lord. Therefore, it is said, "Like Nimrod a mighty hunter before the Lord." [10] The beginning of his kingdom was Babel, Erech, Accad, and Calneh, in the land of Shinar. [11] From that land he went into Assyria and built Nineveh, Rehoboth-Ir, Calah, and [12] Resen between Nineveh and Calah; that is the great city. (Genesis 10: 8–12 ESV).

The second time Nimrod was mentioned in the Bible is in the genealogy of Abraham, presented in 1 Chronicles, where he was briefly mentioned as a descendant of Cush:

> "10 Cush fathered Nimrod. He was the first on earth to be a mighty man." (1 Chronicles 1:10 ESV).

The presentation of Nimrod here mirrors what was written about him in Genesis. Micah also casually mentioned Nimrod:

> "When the Assyrian comes into our land
>   and treads in our palaces,
> then we will raise against him seven shepherds
>   and eight princes of men;
> [6] they shall shepherd the land of Assyria with the sword,
>   and the land of Nimrod at its entrances;
> and he shall deliver us from the Assyrian
>   when he comes into our land
>   and treads within our border." *(Micah 5:5–6 ESV).*

This passage hints that Assyria was still regarded to be connected to the land of Nimrod, at the time of Micah. The Assyrian Empire was a major power in Northern Mesopotamia. At its peak, it covered northern parts of the present-day Iraq and Syria, as well as some parts of Armenia, Iran and southeastern Turkey. Assyria was a dependency of Babylonia and later of the Mitanni kingdom during most of the Second Millennium BCE, before emerging as an independent state in the 14th century BCE.[8] The empire is renowned for its military prowess, conquests and harsh rule.

---

8. The Editors of Encyclopaedia Britannica. "Assyria", 1

THE NEW BEGINNING

Assyrians were known for their formidable military and efficient administrative systems, central to their empire's expansion and control, with their army (the most powerful military force of its time–both doctrinally and technologically advanced) using war chariots and iron weapons, which were the most sophisticated military equipment of the time, far superior to commonly used bronze weapons as at then[9]. The Assyrian empire is distinctively characterised by its centralized government with a strong king ruling over a vast empire–essentially a dictator. This is an archetype of the empire that the antichrist will build, and how this empire will expand, considering the prophecies in Daniel 8: 9–12, Daniel 8: 23–24, Daniel 11). The antichrist will fight many wars that will lead to the expansion of its powers and influence across bulk of the Near East before it pushes into the rest of the world (Daniel 11:14–46). The antichrist will rise as a little horn (someone of not much repute) but through intrigues and military prowess, his powers and influence will spread.

Micah's prophecy suggests that the individual identified as the Assyrian that will lead Assyrians (probably a revived Assyrian empire in the last days) to attack Israel. This individual is a depiction of the final antichrist and a type or descendant of Nimrod (coming in the spirit of Nimrod). Isaiah also hinted at this prospect of an Assyrian final antichrist that would come after Jerusalem, in several prophecies:

> [25] I will crush the Assyrian in my land;
> on my mountains I will trample him down.
> His yoke will be taken from my people,
> and his burden removed from their shoulders." (Isaiah 14:25 NIV).

> "Woe to the Assyrian, the rod of my anger,
> in whose hand is the club of my wrath!
> 6 I send him against a godless nation,
> I dispatch him against a people who anger me,
> to seize loot and snatch plunder,
> and to trample them down like mud in the streets.
> (Isaiah 10: 5–6 NIV).

> [12] When the Lord has finished all his work against Mount Zion and Jerusalem, he will say, "I will punish the king of Assyria for the willful pride of his heart and the haughty look in his eyes. (Isaiah 10: 5–6 NIV).

---

9. History on the net, "Assyrian Empire", 1.

> ²⁴ Therefore this is what the Lord, the Lord Almighty, says:
> "My people who live in Zion,
>   do not be afraid of the Assyrians,
> who beat you with a rod
>   and lift up a club against you, as Egypt did.
> ²⁵ Very soon my anger against you will end
>   and my wrath will be directed to their destruction." (Isaiah 10: 24–25 NIV).

Although, one may be tempted to conclude that these prophecies of Isaiah against the Assyrian, was fulfilled during his time, when Sennacherib, the Assyrian king besieged Jerusalem, under the rule of Hezekiah, it is worthy to note that Sennacherib was not killed in Jerusalem (see 2 Kings 18:17–37). His troops were unable to enter Jerusalem to trample it, as Isaiah prophesied (Isaiah 10:6). He was rather forced to withdrew to his country after the failed invasion of Jerusalem. He only died afterwards at Nineveh. The siege of Jerusalem by Sennacherib is likely a foreshadow of what will happen at the end time when the antichrist and his army will surround and trample Jerusalem (Revelation 11:2, Luke 21:20–24). Daniel holds that the people of the antichrist will be those who destroyed Jerusalem and the temple:

> ²⁶ And after the sixty-two weeks, an anointed one shall be cut off and shall have nothing. And the people of the prince who is to come shall destroy the city and the sanctuary. Its end shall come with a flood, and to the end there shall be war. Desolations are decreed. (Daniel 9:26 ESV).

This prophecy about the destruction of Jerusalem and the temple thereof was fulfilled in 70AD when the Roman armies, led by General Titus, besieged Jerusalem. This has led many to believe that the antichrist will be a Roman or European. However, as have been pointed out by many biblical scholars, the Roman legion that destroyed Jerusalem in 70AD were mainly Syrians. The Siege of Jerusalem was conducted by four main Roman legions, the 5th (Legion V Macedonia, comprising of soldiers and auxiliaries from Judea, Syria and Moesia), 10th (Legion X Fretensis: Syria), 12th (Legion XII Fulminata: Eastern Turkey and Syria) and 15th (Legion XV Apollinaris: Syria, Egypt, Iraq)[10]. This again points to Assyria, which extended to the northern parts of Syria.

---

10. Revelation Now, "The People that", 1; History Tools, "The Destruction of Jerusalem", 1; Richardson, "Daniel 9:26", 1

The above discussion tends to link Nimrod, the Assyrian and antichrist. Even though Genesis did not give out much information about Nimrod, there are some salient facts about him that could be gleaned from the passage. Two things that stand out here is that Nimrod was the first person on earth to become a mighty man after the flood. The Hebrew term used to describe Nimrod was gibbor (a derivative or variant of Gibbowr and Gibborim), the same term used to describe the antediluvian giants (Nephilim). However, even though a human, Nimrod managed to achieve this status without being fathered by a Watcher! The Bible was emphatic about this fact of who the father of Nimrod was, by separating Nimrod from the rest of the sons of Cush in this presentation:

> [6] The sons of Ham: Cush, Egypt, Put, and Canaan. [7] The sons of Cush: Seba, Havilah, Sabtah, Raamah, and Sabteca. The sons of Raamah: Sheba and Dedan. [8] Cush fathered Nimrod (Genesis 10: 8–12 ESV).

Perhaps, this was a way the writer wanted to prevent readers from perceiving or portraying Nimrod as a Nephilim, by clearly stating who his father was. How Nimrod was able to gain this powerful status would be considered further down in this section.

The second thing that stands out is that the passage also hints at Nimrod being a king and perhaps the first postdiluvian king, as it mentioned that he had a kingdom that began from Babel and spread to other parts of the Near East. Only kings have kingdom.

The sentence in Genesis (Therefore it is said, "Like Nimrod a mighty hunter before the Lord." Genesis 10:9 NIV) is a bit confusing considering the context and maybe due to the fact that it is an incomplete sentence. The curious quote suggests that the backdrop of this story about Nimrod might be contained in other books or recordings or in popular sayings/legends. The Book of Jasher, the Writings of Abraham, and Book of Jubilees all contain some of these extra details about Nimrod.

The Book of Jasher links the might of Nimrod to his acquisition of the garments of Adam, which God had made for him at the garden. This garment was imbued with extraordinary powers that enabled Adam to overcome challenges that befell them after their expulsion from the garden of Eden. According to the narrative, Ham had stolen this garment from his father Noah (whom it had been gifted to), after the flood and later handed this garment to Cush, who eventually bequeathed it to Nimrod, his most beloved son.

23 And Cush the son of Ham, the son of Noah, took a wife in those days in his old age, and she bare a son, and they called his name Nimrod, saying, At that time the sons of men again began to rebel and transgress against God, and the child grew up, and his father loved him exceedingly, for he was the son of his old age.

24 And the garments of skin which God made for Adam and his wife, when they went out of the garden, were given to Cush.

25 For after the death of Adam and his wife, the garments were given to Enoch, the son of Jared, and when Enoch was taken up to God, he gave them to Methuselah, his son.

26 And at the death of Methuselah, Noah took them and brought them to the ark, and they were with him until he went out of the ark.

27 And in their going out, Ham stole those garments from Noah his father, and he took them and hid them from his brothers.

28 And when Ham begat his first born Cush, he gave him the garments in secret, and they were with Cush many days.

29 And Cush also concealed them from his sons and brothers, and when Cush had begotten Nimrod, he gave him those garments through his love for him, and Nimrod grew up, and when he was twenty years old he put on those garments.

30 And Nimrod became strong when he put on the garments, and God gave him might and strength, and he was a mighty hunter in the earth, yea, he was a mighty hunter in the field, and he hunted the animals and he built altars, and he offered upon them the animals before the Lord. (The Book of Jasher 7: 23-30).

The above passage presents a more detailed context to that presented in Genesis. Here, it became clear that he was offering the animals he had hunted *"before the Lord"*. This brings in more clarity that presents the right perceptive of what was being conveyed in the passage.

The above passage also portrays that Nimrod began to be great after his father gifted him Adam's garment. The book presents him as someone who slowly became great. He started off as a mighty hunter having been empowered by the garment. Probably, he slowly realised that he could do more with the power emanating from this garment. He started conquering his family's enemies and began to gain more strength and fame:

> 31 And Nimrod strengthened himself, and he rose up from amongst his brethren, and he fought the battles of his brethren against all their enemies round about.
>
> 32 And the Lord delivered all the enemies of his brethren in his hands, and God prospered him from time to time in his battles, and he reigned upon earth.
>
> 33 Therefore it became current in those days, when a man ushered forth those that he had trained up for battle, he would say to them, Like God did to Nimrod, who was a mighty hunter in the earth, and who succeeded in the battles that prevailed against his brethren, that he delivered them from the hands of their enemies, so may God strengthen us and deliver us this day. (The Book of Jasher 7: 31–33).

Then after leading his people to win a decisive battle against their enemies, his kinsmen recognised him as their king:

> 34 And when Nimrod was forty years old, at that time there was a war between his brethren and the children of Japheth, so that they were in the power of their enemies.
>
> 35 And Nimrod went forth at that time, and he assembled all the sons of Cush and their families, about four hundred and sixty men, and he hired also from some of his friends and acquaintances about eighty men, and he gave them their hire, and he went with them to battle, and when he was on the road, Nimrod strengthened the hearts of the people that went with him.
>
> 36 And he said to them, Do not fear, neither be alarmed, for all our enemies will be delivered into our hands, and you may do with them as you please.
>
> 37 And all the men that went were about five hundred, and they fought against their enemies, and they destroyed them, and subdued them, and Nimrod placed standing officers over them in their respective places.
>
> 38 And he took some of their children as security, and they were all servants to Nimrod and to his brethren, and Nimrod and all the people that were with him turned homeward.
>
> 39 And when Nimrod had joyfully returned from battle, after having conquered his enemies, all his brethren, together with those who knew him before, assembled to make him king over them, and they placed the regal crown upon his head.
>
> 40 And he set over his subjects and people, princes, judges, and rulers, as is the custom amongst kings.

41 And he placed Terah the son of Nahor the prince of his host, and he dignified him and elevated him above all his princes. (The Book of Jasher 7: 34–41).

The passage also stated that Nimrod instigated the building of his first city in Shinar. This is where the Tower of Babel was built. So, this might be a reference to the initiation of the construction of the Tower of Babel and the first direct link of Nimrod to the tower:

42 And whilst he was reigning according to his heart's desire, after having conquered all his enemies around, he advised with his counselors to build a city for his palace, and they did so.
43 And they found a large valley opposite to the east, and they built him a large and extensive city, and Nimrod called the name of the city that he built Shinar, for the Lord had vehemently shaken his enemies and destroyed them. (The Book of Jasher 7: 42–43).

Nimrod crushed more enemies, and his kingdom became very great. Subsequently, other nations also recognised him as their king as they were probably afraid of being crushed by Nimrod. Hence, he unified all the nations under his control (*and Nimrod reigned in the earth over all the sons of Noah, and they were all under his power and counsel*). This unification was the first time such confederation of nations was forged under one ruler in postdiluvian era, and seems to be a foreshadow of the one world government the antichrist will form at the end of age:

44 And Nimrod dwelt in Shinar, and he reigned securely, and he fought with his enemies and he subdued them, and he prospered in all his battles, and his kingdom became very great.
45 And all nations and tongues heard of his fame, and they gathered themselves to him, and they bowed down to the earth, and they brought him offerings, and he became their lord and king, and they all dwelt with him in the city at Shinar, and Nimrod reigned in the earth over all the sons of Noah, and they were all under his power and counsel. (The Book of Jasher 7: 42–45).

Although Genesis stated that Nimrod's kingdom began from Babel, this must have been a reference to Shinar. Because the name Babel was assigned to the place after the disruption of the construction of the tower:

[8] So the Lord dispersed them from there over the face of all the earth, and they left off building the city. [9] Therefore its name was called Babel, because there the Lord confused the language of

all the earth. And from there the Lord dispersed them over the face of all the earth. (Genesis 11:1-9 ESV).

There is no doubt the following passages in Genesis and Book of Jasher are both referring to the same event when the city of Shinar and the tower in it were being built under the instructions of Nimrod:

> 11 Now the whole earth had one language and the same words. ² And as people migrated from the east, they found a plain in the land of Shinar and settled there. ³ And they said to one another, "Come, let us make bricks, and burn them thoroughly." And they had brick for stone, and bitumen for mortar. ⁴ Then they said, "Come, let us build ourselves a city and a tower with its top in the heavens, and let us make a name for ourselves, lest we be dispersed over the face of the whole earth." (Genesis 11:1-4 ESV).

> 43 And they found a large valley opposite to the east, and they built him a large and extensive city, and Nimrod called the name of the city that he built Shinar, for the Lord had vehemently shaken his enemies and destroyed them. (The Book of Jasher 7: 43).

The trajectory of Nimrod's rise to power presented in the Book of Jasher seems to be a foreshadow of the trajectory that would be taken by the antichrist to rise to power. Daniel 11 also hinted at several battles the antichrist will have to fight with various nations, which he would win. He would be crushing his enemies as he rises to global prominence. Finally, at the peak of this, Revelation 17 informs that there would be 10 last kings on earth who will eventually handover their power to the antichrist and he would become the overall ruler of the world:

> ¹¹ As for the beast that was and is not, it is an eighth but it belongs to the seven, and it goes to destruction. ¹² And the ten horns that you saw are ten kings who have not yet received royal power, but they are to receive authority as kings for one hour, together with the beast. ¹³ These are of one mind, and they hand over their power and authority to the beast. ¹⁴ They will make war on the Lamb, and the Lamb will conquer them, for he is Lord of lords and King of kings, and those with him are called and chosen and faithful." (Revelation 17:11-14 ESV).

The Writings of Abraham also presented a similar story to that contained in the Book of Jasher, with few more extra details added at different parts of the story. According to the Writings of Abraham, Ham stole the garment from Noah, having been aware of the powers it has and knowing that he will not make it to the top of the Order of the Ancients in the line of Seth, having the blood of Cain in him:

> 2. And when the grape harvest was come in, Noah made wine and drank of the new wine in his tent and his heart was made glad and he rejoiced before the lord for the bounty which the Lord had given him. 3. And it was upon the Feast of Pentecost when Noah drank of the new wine before the Lord and lay down naked in his tent to sleep. 4. When Ham, the son of Noah, entered the tent he saw his father sleeping naked upon his bed with the sacred garments which had been given to Adam in the garden of Eden laying nearby.
>
> 5. Ham knew that he and his posterity could not bear the priesthood because of the curse of Cain which was upon them and knowing there was great power in the sacred garments, he stole them from his Father Noah and hurried to his tents. 6. Rousing his family, Ham instructed them to strike their tents and led them away to the plain of Shinar where he dwelt and where Ham died. 7. Now Ham's wife was named Zeptah and she was also of the seed of Cain and they had a daughter named Zeptah. 8. This daughter, after the death of Ham, led a body of his people westward until they reached a body of water in the land of Zeptah, which is Egypt, where they settled and as the waters receded from off the land, they spread out and build many cities and temples. (The Writings of Abraham 16: 2–8).
>
> BEFORE the death of Ham, the sacred garments were given secretly by him to his son Cush 2. Cush also kept them hidden and in his old age gave them unto his son Nimrod and when Nimrod was twenty years of age, he put on the garments and he derived great strength and power from them. 3. Moreover, Nimrod was instructed in all the secrets of the evil combination by his father Cain, for Cain had not perished in the flood. 4. Wherefore, Nimrod became a mighty man among the sons of men and established his kingdom and grew stronger and stronger in wickedness after the order of the secret combination which was from the beginning, for Nimrod spread his dominion over all mankind save those in the city of Shalom (The Writings of Abraham 17: 1–4).

From the above, it could be seen that the Writings of Abraham links the stealing of this garment from Noah to the uncovering of Noah's nakedness. Considering the earlier position of this book on what the "uncovering of Noah's nakedness was" (see Section 6.3), it could mean that these two events happened at the same time. A hypothesis that could be presented here is that after Noah became drunk and left this precious garment unguarded, Ham came upon this incident and stole the powerful garment from his father, to become more powerful than his siblings. After this, he may have been emboldened and when he came across Noah's youngest wife, who was probably in the tent with Noah, he slept with her. Perhaps she was also as drunk as Noah, when this happened.

It is also worth examining whether this act by Ham was just a sexual rascality or a calculated intent, to pass off one of his seeds as Noah's. In the light of the fact that he intentionally stole this garment from his father, it could be presumed that sleeping with his father's wife (his step mum) was premeditated. Having realised that he was not going to be considered as being part of the line of Seth, he might have plotted to get one of his descendants regarded as a direct son of Noah? In this regard, this act was not immediately discovered. At least Canaan must have been born before Noah discovered this. Otherwise, he wouldn't have cursed an unborn baby that has not been given a name. This discovery may have been made because Ham may have bragged about his plot to his brothers. It may be that this plot worked for some time and Canaan was perhaps considered the direct son of Noah before the discovery of the heinous act was uncovered. This could be seen from the nature of the curse Noah placed upon Canaan where he considered him as the brother of Shem and Japhet and not their nephew:

> Cursed be Canaan;
> a servant of servants shall he be to his brothers." (Genesis 9: 25 ESV).
>
> [26] He also said,
> "Blessed be the LORD, the God of Shem;
> and let Canaan be his servant.
> [27] May God enlarge Japheth,
> and let him dwell in the tents of Shem,
> and let Canaan be his servant." (Genesis 9: 25-27 ESV).

Note here that Noah first of all cursed Canaan that he would be the servant of his brothers. After this he identified who those brothers, he was referring to Shem and Japhet. On both occasions, where he blessed Shem and Japhet he ended the blessing by saying "let Canaan be his servant".

Before this incident, this garment seems to have been passed on through the line of Seth to only the heads of this line: Adam, Enoch, Methuselah, and Noah. It must be understood that both the lines of Seth and Cain had well-guarded secret knowledge gained from spiritual beings, which are passed down separately along each line (see Section 6.4). This garment of Adam might have been among the highest symbols of authority in the line Seth.

Hence, when it fell into the hands of the line of Cain through Ham, Nimrod was eventually able to galvanise the secret knowledge and powers of both blood lines, which he used to stimulate extraordinary powers that he projected across his kingdom. The most extraordinary claim in this passage was that Nimrod was exposed to the secret knowledge by Cain, who somehow survived the flood. Although, it may sound outlandish that Cain survived the flood, one cannot entirely rule out this possibility, especially when the Bible is silent on when or how Cain died. For such a prominent figure, it raises a lot of doubt why the Bible did not cover this aspect of Cain's life.

In the Epic of Gilgamesh, Gilgamesh, was depicted as a great warrior king of the Mesopotamian city-state Uruk (Erech), that was ruthless and depraved. At some point Gilgamesh encountered Utnapishtim, while seeking to learn immortality from him. The similarities between the figure of Nimrod and Gilgamesh have made many to believe that the characters are the same[11]. They were both great and seem to have a common enemy–God. Gilgamesh became angry at God for causing the flood and sets out to kill him, after his meeting with Utnapishtim. This is similar to what Nimrod did. According to the Writings of Abraham, after receiving secret instructions from Cain, Nimrod began to be a mighty man and turned against God:

> 3. Moreover, Nimrod was instructed in all the secrets of the evil combination by his father Cain, for Cain had not perished in the flood. 4. Wherefore, Nimrod became a mighty man among the sons of men and established his kingdom and grew stronger and stronger in wickedness after the order of the secret combination which was from the beginning, for Nimrod spread his dominion over all mankind save those in the city of Shalom (The Writings of Abraham 17: 3–4).

---

11. Livingston, "Who Was Nimrod", 1

THE NEW BEGINNING

The construction of the Tower of Babel embarked upon by Nimrod might have been Nimrod's attempt to get to God to avenge the flood. Mostly likely he was building the tower as a staging post for his intended attack on God. The evil purpose of the construction of the tower was alluded to in the Book of Jubilee and Book of Jasher, which hinted at the reason that Peleg named his son Reu:

> [18.] And in the three and thirtieth jubilee, in the first year in the second week, Peleg took to himself a wife, whose name was Lômnâ the daughter of Sînâ'ar, and she bare him a son in the fourth year of this week, and he called his name Reu; for he said: "Behold the children of men have become evil through the wicked purpose of building for themselves a city and a tower in the land of Shinar." (Book of Jubilees, 10:18–27).

In Jasher 9, three reasons for the construction of the tower were proffered:

> [25] And the building of the tower was unto them a transgression and a sin, and they began to build it, and whilst they were building against the Lord God of heaven, they imagined in their hearts to war against him and to ascend into heaven.
>
> [26] And all these people and all the families divided themselves in three parts; the first said We will ascend into heaven and fight against him; the second said, We will ascend to heaven and place our own gods there and serve them; and the third part said, We will ascend to heaven and smite him with bows and spears; and God knew all their works and all their evil thoughts, and he saw the city and the tower which they were building. (Book of Jasher: 9: 25 - 26).

This also points to what the antichrist would attempt to do during the end times. Daniel 8 reveals that at some point during the end times, the antichrist will attempt to reach the throne of God:

> [9] Out of one of them came a little horn, which grew exceedingly great toward the south, toward the east, and toward the glorious land. [10] It grew great, even to the host of heaven. And some of the host and some of the stars it threw down to the ground and trampled on them. [11] It became great, even as great as the Prince of the host. And the regular burnt offering was taken away from him, and the place of his sanctuary was overthrown. (Daniel 8:9–11 ESV).
>
> [23] And at the latter end of their kingdom, when the transgressors have reached their limit, a king of bold face, one who

> understands riddles, shall arise. ²⁴ His power shall be great—but not by his own power; and he shall cause fearful destruction and shall succeed in what he does, and destroy mighty men and the people who are the saints. ²⁵ By his cunning he shall make deceit prosper under his hand, and in his own mind he shall become great. Without warning he shall destroy many. And he shall even rise up against the Prince of princes, and he shall be broken—but by no human hand. (Daniel 8: 23-25 ESV).

From the foregoing, it could be proposed that Nimrod was able to achieve greatness through the combination of secret power imbued in the lines of Seth and Cain, through the instructions Cain or other spiritual guides.

6.7 TOWER OF BABEL

The story of the construction of the Tower of Babel (Genesis 11:1-9), centers around a controversial physical structure that was most likely commissioned by Nimrod to be built in Shinar, the first city of his kingdom (which later became Babylon in modern day Iraq). It is a story of how humans galvanised force to build a tower that could reach heaven. Although Genesis did not explicitly connect Nimrod to this tower, the Book of Jasher somewhat did, by connecting Nimrod to the individual who commissioned the construction of the city of Shinar, the same city where the tower was built:

> 42 And whilst he was reigning according to his heart's desire, after having conquered all his enemies around, he advised with his counselors to build a city for his palace, and they did so. 43 And they found a large valley opposite to the east, and they built him a large and extensive city, and Nimrod called the name of the city that he built Shinar, for the Lord had vehemently shaken his enemies and destroyed them. (The Book of Jasher 7: 42-43).

The Book of Jubilees also provided additional details about this event, especially on what happened after the confusion of tongues, information on the dimension of the tower and how long it took them to build it. According to the book, it took about 43 years of construction before God decided to stop the project. After the confusion of tongues, God sent a wind that reduced the tower to the ground. The book also indicated that the construction of the tower commenced (about the time Reu, the son

THE NEW BEGINNING

of Peleg[12] was born). The account in the Book of Jubilees, like some of the other stories in the book, seem to have been narrated by an angel, who witnessed the entire action and narrating it from the heavenly point of view:

> 18. And in the three and thirtieth jubilee, in the first year in the second week, Peleg took to himself a wife, whose name was Lômnâ the daughter of Sînâ'ar, and she bare him a son in the fourth year of this week, and he called his name Reu; for he said: "Behold the children of men have become evil through the wicked purpose of building for themselves a city and a tower in the land of Shinar." 19. For they departed from the land of Ararat eastward to Shinar; for in his days they built the city and the tower, saying, "Go to, let us ascend thereby into heaven." 20. And they began to build, and in the fourth week they made brick with fire, and the bricks served them for stone, and the clay with which they cemented them together was asphalt which cometh out of the sea, and out of the fountains of water in the land of Shinar. 21. And they built it: forty and three years were they building it; its breadth was 203 bricks, and the height (of a brick) was the third of one; its height amounted to 5433 cubits and 2 palms, and (the extent of one wall was) thirteen stades (and of the other thirty stades). 22. And the Lord our God said unto us: "Behold, they are one people, and (this) they begin to do, and now nothing will be withholden from them. Go to, let us go down and confound their language, that they may not understand one another's speech, and they may be dispersed into cities and nations, and one purpose will no longer abide with them till the day of judgment." 23. And the Lord descended, and we descended with Him to see the city and the tower which the children of men had built. 24. And He confounded their language, and they no longer understood one another's speech, and they ceased then to build the city and the tower. 25. For this reason the whole land of Shinar is called Babel, because the Lord did there confound all the language of the children of men, and from thence they were dispersed into their cities, each according to his language and his nation. 26. And the Lord sent a mighty wind against the tower and overthrew it upon the earth, and behold it was between Asshur and Babylon in the land of Shinar, and they called its name «Overthrow.» 27. In the fourth week in the first year in the beginning thereof in the four and

---

12. Peleg was the son of Eber, the son of Salah, the son of Arphaxad, the son of Shem

thirtieth jubilee, were they dispersed from the land of Shinar. (Book of Jubilees, 10:18–27).

This story is among the outstanding stories in the Bible. The tower was a massive structure. The height of 5433 cubits and 2 palms is about 2.4 kilometers. It is also important to note that the name "babel" only became attributed to the tower after the languages of the people were confused. The story itself is a highly controversial one, as many contend that considering how far heaven is from earth, it is inconceivable that a physical structure on earth can be built to reach heaven. Whereas many, especially non-believers dismiss this outrightly as an outlandish claim or a myth used to justify the origins of diverse languages in the world, many accept this story literary, without digging deeper to have a better understanding of it. Due to the controversies this story has generated, many theories have sprung up to offer some kind of explanation about this.

To tackle this, certain questions become pertinent to ask. Why were the people building a tall tower? What was the purpose for the tower? Were they building a structure that could reach heaven or were they building a tall structure that could save some people from another event of flood? Some historians such as Josephus hold this view that the tower was meant to serve as a refuge in a case of another episode of flooding[13]. Or was the tower some form of interdimensional technology that could transcend from the physical to the spiritual? If this tower was going to house such a technology for interdimensional portal opening, were they trying to place it at a location where the next episode of flood could not reach? Or could it be that for the technology to be effective, it must be activated at a certain point above the ground? All these mysteries surrounding the tower are so difficult to unravel. Attempt will be made in the following section to explore some of these further.

6.7.1 Tower of Babel and the CERN Connection

The entire story about the Tower of Babel, with the capability to reach heaven might be an allegory used to portray the tower as having the potential to enable humans to access/approach heaven at will. This tower may be a metaphor for an ancient technology of some sort that was being constructed, which could open interdimensional portal/gateway. This maybe an attempt by the people to create something with similar nature

---

13. Josephus, *Antiquities of the Jews Book* 14:2

like the garden of Eden for accessing heaven. Such portal could be used by man to easily access the spiritual realm where the heaven is. One thing that was clear from the passage was that the tower posed a real threat to the order of things that God had to destroy it. Many have suggested that the tower, might have been a Ziggurat[14]. Heiser stated that *"Ziggurats were divine abodes, places where Mesopotamians believed heaven and earth intersected. The nature of this structure makes evident the purpose in building it—to bring the divine down to earth."*

Others suggest it might have been a stargate that allows humans access to the spiritual dimensions[15]. Portals to other realms and gateways to star systems are common knowledge to many ancient cultures who believed that was where their "creators" reside.[16] The Bible is littered with stories of angelic beings visiting the earth, and it is believed they enter via portals strategically placed around the earth. In 2012, National Aeronautics and Space Administration (NASA) confirmed the existence of such portals within the Earth's magnetic field.[17] They called these X-points, which are *"places where the magnetic field of Earth connects to the magnetic field of the Sun, creating an uninterrupted path leading from our own planet to the sun's atmosphere 93 million miles away"*

The tower could have been both: built as ziggurat, but functions as a stargate that could open interdimensional portal. Despite what this tower might have been, it had real capabilities or potentials that threatened the order of things, which God had established, that made God decide to disrupt the project. God hardly interferes with the affairs of humans, unless the activity in question threatens the order of things, which God had established for the earth. God gave man the freedom and ability to develop the earth, however, that freedom is obviously limited to the earth, and man is not allowed to undertake activities that could destabilise the already established cosmic order or affect other planets and creations of God. The Tower of Babel seems to have been a project that had real potential to disrupt this order. Hence, it was stopped.

I lean towards the opinion that the Tower of Babel may not really be a mighty tower that was being built to reach to the heavens (or sky in the least), but a powerful structure with the capabilities that could open interdimensional portals, which could be utilised by humans to

14. Heiser, "The Tower of Babel", 1; Rohl, "Was the Tower", 1
15. Hamp, "Tower of Babel", 1; Ramos, "Nimrod", 1
16. Lowth, "10 Ancient Sites", 1
17. NASA, "Hidden Portals", 1

illegally access the heavens (other realms, dimensions) at will. The phrase a tower with its top in the heavens, could imply that the tower will make a connection between the earth and the heavens:

> ⁶ And the Lord said, "Behold, they are one people, and they have all one language, and this is only the beginning of what they will do. And nothing that they propose to do will now be impossible for them. (Genesis 11:6 ESV).

This sort of technology pursued by Nimrod, may be like what the European Council for Nuclear Research (Conseil Européen pour la Recherche Nucléaire–CERN) is hoping to achieve, with their Large Hadron Collider (LHC). The LHC is a powerful subterranean scientific instrument, which lies in circular tunnel constructed beneath the France–Switzerland border near Geneva, with circumference of 27kilometers[18]. On the surface, CERN is conducting experiments with LHC to understand the nature of the universe and what it is made of. The LHC is currently the world's largest and most powerful particle accelerator, used to speed up and increase the energy of a beam of particles by generating electric fields that accelerate the particles, and magnetic fields that steer and focus them. The LHC consists of a 27-kilometer ring of superconducting magnets with several accelerating structures to boost the energy of the particles that passes through it. Inside the accelerator, two high-energy particle beams travelling at close to the speed of light in opposite directions are made to collide. What happens after this collision is what scientist at CERN are apparently investigating. Essentially, they are looking at generating antimatter, that is, the opposite counterpart of the matter we can see in the material world. This is different from the dark matter,[19] which is more or less the invisible part of the universe that humans have not been able to observe but know exists (essentially the spiritual realm). In a July 2012 experiment, scientist at CERN trapped some antimatter and for the first time discovered the Higgs boson, the so called "god particle". The Higgs boson is the fundamental force-carrying particle of the Higgs field, which is responsible for granting other particles their mass. The researchers at CERN are hoping that through the entrapment of antimatter, they would unlock the secrets of how the universe was created

---

18. CERN, "The Large Hadron", 1
19. Riess, dark matter, 1

THE NEW BEGINNING

and support the Big Bang theory of how an invisible, universe-wide field gave mass to all matter right after the Big Bang.[20]

Despite the apparent innocuous experiments going on at CERN, many observers, including renowned scientists have warned of the dangers of the activities going on at CERN. A curious incident occurred on June 26, 2016, 10 days after the center commenced the Advanced WAKEfield Experiment (AWAKE)[21] project, to accelerate charged particles. Christophe Suarez, a photographer observed and captured some strange and ominous clouds on the skies hanging above CERN[22]. The photos he published on Twitter showed a strange cloud formation and electrical activities above the CERN complex, which prompted many to fear that CERN might open some black holes that would devastate the earth. As a matter of fact, the LHC has already detected mini black holes while smashing the particles. As far back as 2014, Stephen Hawking, a renowned British physicist warned in his book, Starmus, that the Higgs boson particle could destroy the universe, through the creation of microscopic black holes, which could grow and eventually lead to the implosion of the earth. Other scientists have also re-echoed this fear.

However, many followers of Christ fear that CERN's real intent is to open an interdimensional portal to the spiritual realm. Precisely, many fear that CERN is aiming at opening the portal to the bottomless pit (Abyss), to release and harness the dark energy (entities) locked up there. This fear largely emanates from the fact that scientists refer to black holes as "bottomless pits" of gravity. It is uncanny that the exact same words appear in the Bible and in the scientific community. This is the first giveaway of the real intent of CERN. Conducting experiments to unravel the origins of the universe is akin to getting to God, or unmasking what or who God is. This is essentially the same aim of the Tower of Babel. The bottomless pit is the prison where hardened rebellious angelic beings are locked up until the end time when they will be released to play their last role before they are finally judged and destroyed:

> [4] For if God did not spare angels when they sinned, but cast them into hell and committed them to chains of gloomy darkness to be kept until the judgment (2 Peter 2:4 ESV).

20. Lin, "CERN—looking for God", 1

21 A project investigating the use of protons to drive plasma wakefields for accelerating electrons to higher energies than can be achieved using conventional technologies; Rao, "AWAKE successfully", 1

22. Suarez, "Christophe Suarez on X", 1

⁶ And the angels which kept not their first estate, but left their own habitation, he hath reserved in everlasting chains under darkness unto the judgment of the great day (Jude 1:6 KJV).

Interestingly, CERN is located in a place that was once called Appolliacum (Apollo's temple). Apollo (Apollyon) in Greek means destruction). The Greeks and Romans traditionally considered Apollo's temple to be the entrance to the bottomless pit or the gateway to the underworld (Lin. 2020). The historical Apolliacum, is now the modern-day Saint-Genus-Poilly[23], where CERN is located.[24] It is eerie that Apollyon/Abaddon was directly referred to in the Revelation as the chief fallen angel that would be released from the bottomless pit, where he is locked up, to cause serious destruction on the earth and torment the people with his hordes:

> 9 And the fifth angel blew his trumpet, and I saw a star fallen from heaven to earth, and he was given the key to the shaft of the bottomless pit. ² He opened the shaft of the bottomless pit, and from the shaft rose smoke like the smoke of a great furnace, and the sun and the air were darkened with the smoke from the shaft. ³ Then from the smoke came locusts on the earth, and they were given power like the power of scorpions of the earth. ⁴ They were told not to harm the grass of the earth or any green plant or any tree, but only those people who do not have the seal of God on their foreheads. ⁵ They were allowed to torment them for five months, but not to kill them, and their torment was like the torment of a scorpion when it stings someone. ⁶ And in those days people will seek death and will not find it. They will long to die, but death will flee from them.
> ⁷ In appearance the locusts were like horses prepared for battle: on their heads were what looked like crowns of gold; their faces were like human faces, ⁸ their hair like women's hair, and their teeth like lions' teeth; ⁹ they had breastplates like breastplates of iron, and the noise of their wings was like the noise of many chariots with horses rushing into battle. ¹⁰ They have tails and stings like scorpions, and their power to hurt people for five months is in their tails. ¹¹ They have as king over them the angel of the bottomless pit. His name in Hebrew is Abaddon, and in Greek he is called Apollyon. (Revelation 9:1–11 ESV).

---

23. "Poilly" is the same word as Apollyon/Apollo
24. Patton, "Is CERN Trying", 1

THE NEW BEGINNING

From the passage above, a fallen angel was given the key that was used to open the bottomless pit. There was no indication what this key is, however, the endeavor will succeed during the end times as part of God's plan for the times. The bottomless pit is not just a prison for some fallen angels but also of 90% of demonic spirits who were removed from the earth and locked up until the end time (Book of Jubilees, 10:1–17) after Noah prayed for God to intervene (see Section 6.5).

Putting all these breadcrumbs together, a logical conclusion to draw from them is that CERN is trying to open the portal into another dimension, to allow Apollyon to enter the earth. This satanic intent of CERN is made manifest by the connection it is trying to make with the Hindu goddess of destruction. Curiously, CERN has the statue of the Hindu goddess of destruction Shiva emerging through a portal, prominently mounted at its entrance. One would normally wonder what the goddess of destruction was doing at an innocuous scientific center, or the connection whatsoever, other than CERN was openly declaring to the public what its real intent is–open the bottomless pit to allow the angel of destruction to enter. In addition, their logo contains the 666 (the number of the beast) looped into a ring. Some commentators have also linked the controversial video of the opening ceremony[25] of Gotthard Tunnel in Switzerland,[26] which showed the opening of a portal that let satanic creature into the world, to CERN's real intent.

In the past, God truncated this plan of opening interdimensional portal during the time of Nimrod, by disrupting the construction of the Tower of Babel, but during the end time, God will allow man to achieve this feat through CERN or similar scientific endeavors, as part of the end time judgement. By the time God allows CERN to succeed in ripping open the protective shields preventing the wicked entities from other dimensions from reaching the earth, the entire earth will be flooded with such wicked entities that would harm man. These entities are the locust of Revelation 11 alongside their leader Apollyon (Revelation 9:1–11).

6.7.2 Nimrod and Ancient One World Government

Another motivation for the building of the city and tower in Shinar by Nimrod was the unification of the world. Soon after the flood Noah's

---

25. https://www.youtube.com/watch?v=ikDpJZRSqzo
26. Littman, "Switzerland", 1

children began to quarrel among themselves to the extent that they secretly divided the land among themselves. In competition with each other, they started building cities on their apportioned lands (Book of Jubilee VIII: 8–10). It got to a point that Noah had to admonish them:

> 26. " And we were left, I and you, my sons, and everything that entered with us into the ark, and behold I see your works before me that ye do not walk in righteousness ; for in the path of destruction ye have begun to walk, and ye are parting one from another, and are envious one of another, and (so it comes) that ye are not in harmony, my sons, each with his brother. 27. For I see, and behold the demons have begun (their) seductions against you and against your children, and now I fear on your behalf, that after my death ye will shed the blood of men upon the earth, and that ye, too, will be destroyed from the face of the earth. 28. For whoso sheddeth man's blood, and whoso eateth the blood of any flesh, will all be destroyed from the earth. (Book of Jubilee VII: 26–28).

This bickering among the descendants of Noah continued and they kept fighting among themselves, until Nimrod decided to unify them via a series of battles he fought. He initially became a king over all his brethren and slowly subdued other nations, who came under his authority:

> 44 And Nimrod dwelt in Shinar, and he reigned securely, and he fought with his enemies and he subdued them, and he prospered in all his battles, and his kingdom became very great.
>
> 45 And all nations and tongues heard of his fame, and they gathered themselves to him, and they bowed down to the earth, and they brought him offerings, and he became their lord and king, and they all dwelt with him in the city at Shinar, and Nimrod reigned in the earth over all the sons of Noah, and they were all under his power and counsel.
>
> 46 And all the earth was of one tongue and words of union, but Nimrod did not go in the ways of the Lord, and he was more wicked than all the men that were before him, from the days of the flood until those days.
>
> 47 And he made gods of wood and stone, and he bowed down to them, and he rebelled against the Lord, and taught all his subjects and the people of the earth his wicked ways; and Mardon his son was more wicked than his father. (The Book of Jasher 7:42–47).

Hence, at this point, Nimrod turned the entire world into one mind, soul, and purpose. This was a civilization without God as Nimrod openly rebelled against God and compelled others to do same. This was the world order of Nimrod, similar to the world that the antichrist will build in the future (the beast empire).

The idea behind the building of the city in Shinar was to provide an area where all the people will dwell in, such that there would not be need for them to be spread out. The people apparently believed that there was more strength in a unified force than a scattered one:

> Then all they that had been divided and dwelt upon the earth gathered together thereafter, and dwelt together; and they set forth from the East and found a plain in the land of Babylon: and there they dwelt, and they said every man to his neighbour: Behold, it will come to pass that we shall be scattered every man from his brother, and in the latter days we shall be fighting one against another. Now, therefore, come and let us build for ourselves a tower the head whereof shall reach into heaven, and we shall make us a name and a renown upon the earth. (Antiquities of Philo 6:1).

One thing that stands out in the story of the Tower of Babel was that the people were of one mind, while building the structure. Nimrod was able to galvanise the people into a one world system. And part of the stated goal of construction of the city of Shinar, was to prevent the people from straying away from the control of the king. Essentially, Nimrod was building a one world government that he can easily control:

> [4] Then they said, "Come, let us build ourselves a city and a tower with its top in the heavens, and let us make a name for ourselves, lest we be dispersed over the face of the whole earth." (Genesis 11:1–9 ESV).

This is a precursor to what the antichrist would attempt to achieve in the end times. As a matter of fact, Nimrod and the antichrist have a lot in common. In many rights, the antichrist will behave in the same rebellious manner that Nimrod did towards God. Like Nimrod the antichrist would be a human who would later become a mighty man (gibbor) after being inhabited and empowered by the spirit of Satan:

> The dragon gave the beast his power and his throne and great authority. [3] One of the heads of the beast seemed to have had a fatal wound, but the fatal wound had been healed. The whole

world was filled with wonder and followed the beast. ⁴ People worshiped the dragon because he had given authority to the beast, and they also worshiped the beast and asked, "Who is like the beast? Who can wage war against it?" (Revelation 13: 2–4 NIV).

Hence, the confusion of tongues was a master stroke God used to disrupt the plans of Nimrod, as it did not only lead to the stoppage of the construction of the tower, but also the dispersal of humans across the world, the exact opposite of what Nimrod had hoped to achieve:

> "⁸ So the Lord dispersed them from there over the face of all the earth, and they left off building the city. (Gen 11:8 ESV).

Regarding the confusion of languages, presumably only the people participating in the construction of the tower were affected. These are people considered to be within the kingdom Nimrod had established. But not everyone was under the power of Nimrod. This is because the progenies of the line of Seth were under the control of Shem in the city of Peace (*city of Shalom*), which was like a parallel kingdom to the one Nimrod oversaw (see Section 5.4). This was made evident in the Writings of Abraham:

> 4. Wherefore, Nimrod became a mighty man among the sons of men and established his kingdom and grew stronger and stronger in wickedness after the order of the secret combination which was from the beginning, for Nimrod spread his dominion over all mankind *save those in the city of Shalom* (The Writings of Abraham 17:4).

This raises the question of whether Shem and his people somewhat retained their original language after the event at the tower or whether every human was affected? This also points to the fact that at every generation there are few individuals (the remnants), who are not swayed by the corruption of the world at their time. Before the flood, only Noah and his family were found to be worthy to escape the flood, whereas the rest of the world were compromised and their DNAs tainted with those of the Nephilim. At the time of Nimrod, even when the Bible says the whole world were under him, there was still the remnant under the authority of Shem, who were holding on to the truth, while working on the sidelines or in the underground. This same pattern is expected when the antichrist shows up on earth. Virtually all humans would be corrupted and swayed to worship Satan. Only a remnant will refuse to do this, even at the point of death. Hence, even though it may be reported that the antichrist was ruling over the entire earth, there will still be some people who will not subject themselves to his authority.

CHAPTER 7

Reordering of the World–Emergence of a New World Order

7.1 THE DIVISION OF THE EARTH AMONG THE SONS OF GOD

After the event at the Tower of Babel, God re-ordered the world. This was to smash the one-world order that Nimrod was previously pursuing. Moses, in Deuteronomy alluded to a point in history, when God divided the people on earth, and allotted different portions of the earth to them:

> [7] Remember the days of old;
>   consider the years of many generations;
> ask your father, and he will show you,
>   your elders, and they will tell you.
> [8] When the Most-High gave to the nations their inheritance,
>   when he divided mankind,
> he fixed the borders of the peoples
>   according to the number of the sons of God.
> [9] But the Lord's portion is his people,
>   Jacob his allotted heritage. (Deuteronomy 32:7–9 ESV).

The only logical point in history when this could have happened is at the dispersal of the people at Babel. The nations that came out of this process were the 70 nations listed in the table of nations in Genesis 10, which emanated from the three sons of Noah. This was made clear by the last verse which stated that:

REORDERING OF THE WORLD – EMERGENCE OF A NEW WORLD ORDER

³² These are the clans of the sons of Noah, according to their genealogies, in their nations, and from these the nations spread abroad on the earth after the flood. (Genesis 10:32 ESV).

The nations had their specific lands and languages, suggesting that this separation was after the dispersal from Babel and not before when they all had one language.

The full list is enumerated below:

10 These are the generations of the sons of Noah, Shem, Ham, and Japheth. Sons were born to them after the flood. ² The sons of Japheth: Gomer, Magog, Madai, Javan, Tubal, Meshech, and Tiras. ³ The sons of Gomer: Ashkenaz, Riphath, and Togarmah. ⁴ The sons of Javan: Elishah, Tarshish, Kittim, and Dodanim. ⁵ From these the coastland peoples spread in their lands, each with his own language, by their clans, in their nations.

⁶ The sons of Ham: Cush, Egypt, Put, and Canaan. ⁷ The sons of Cush: Seba, Havilah, Sabtah, Raamah, and Sabteca. The sons of Raamah: Sheba and Dedan. ⁸ Cush fathered Nimrod; he was the first on earth to be a mighty man. ⁹ He was a mighty hunter before the LORD. Therefore it is said, "Like Nimrod a mighty hunter before the LORD." ¹⁰ The beginning of his kingdom was Babel, Erech, Accad, and Calneh, in the land of Shinar. ¹¹ From that land he went into Assyria and built Nineveh, Rehoboth-Ir, Calah, and ¹² Resen between Nineveh and Calah; that is the great city. ¹³ Egypt fathered Ludim, Anamim, Lehabim, Naphtuhim, ¹⁴ Pathrusim, Casluhim (from whom the Philistines came), and Caphtorim.

¹⁵ Canaan fathered Sidon his firstborn and Heth, ¹⁶ and the Jebusites, the Amorites, the Girgashites, ¹⁷ the Hivites, the Arkites, the Sinites, ¹⁸ the Arvadites, the Zemarites, and the Hamathites. Afterward the clans of the Canaanites dispersed. ¹⁹ And the territory of the Canaanites extended from Sidon in the direction of Gerar as far as Gaza, and in the direction of Sodom, Gomorrah, Admah, and Zeboiim, as far as Lasha. ²⁰ These are the sons of Ham, by their clans, their languages, their lands, and their nations.

²¹ To Shem also, the father of all the children of Eber, the elder brother of Japheth, children were born. ²² The sons of Shem: Elam, Asshur, Arpachshad, Lud, and Aram. ²³ The sons of Aram: Uz, Hul, Gether, and Mash. ²⁴ Arpachshad fathered Shelah; and Shelah fathered Eber. ²⁵ To Eber were born two sons: the name of the one was Peleg, for in his days the earth was divided, and

his brother's name was Joktan. ²⁶ Joktan fathered Almodad, Sheleph, Hazarmaveth, Jerah, ²⁷ Hadoram, Uzal, Diklah, ²⁸ Obal, Abimael, Sheba, ²⁹ Ophir, Havilah, and Jobab; all these were the sons of Joktan. ³⁰ The territory in which they lived extended from Mesha in the direction of Sephar to the hill country of the east. ³¹ These are the sons of Shem, by their clans, their languages, their lands, and their nations.

³² These are the clans of the sons of Noah, according to their genealogies, in their nations, and from these the nations spread abroad on the earth after the flood. (Genesis 10:1–32 ESV).

Thus, after the confusion of their languages, which ultimately led the people to abandoning the construction of the Tower at Babel, God allocated the newly dispersed nations to certain sons of God to oversee. The sons of God, being referred to here are high-level celestial beings who were part of the divine council of God (see Section 1.3.3). They were among the contingent of the sons of God who came down with God to see the ongoing construction of the tower at Shinar:

> 32 And God said to the seventy angels who stood foremost before him, to those who were near to him, saying, Come let us descend and confuse their tongues, that one man shall not understand the language of his neighbour, and they did so unto them. (Book of Jasher 9:32).

Hence, after they descended, God decided to apportion a certain part of the earth under their control. These sons of God had the responsibilities of taking care of the various nations. Psalm 82 gave a snippet of what these responsibilities were:

> 82 God has taken his place in the divine council;
>   in the midst of the gods he holds judgment:
> ² "How long will you judge unjustly
>   and show partiality to the wicked? Selah
> ³ Give justice to the weak and the fatherless;
>   maintain the right of the afflicted and the destitute.
> ⁴ Rescue the weak and the needy;
>   deliver them from the hand of the wicked."
>
> ⁵ They have neither knowledge nor understanding,
>   they walk about in darkness;
>   all the foundations of the earth are shaken.
>
> (Psalm 82: 1–5 ESV).

These sons of God were to oversee(judge) the nations to ensure that the people did not unify again and that they behaved accordingly. After the Babel event, God was probably worried that humans have still not learnt their lessons and probably needed some shepherding by divine beings. This is because, barely few centuries after the devastating deluge that wiped off humanity, the descendants of Noah were embarking on a project that could have seriously affected the order of things in the cosmic or even destroy humanity. Hence, by having the sons of God as divine beings over the nations, God was hoping that humanity will maintain order.

Prior to this event, God was directly ruling every part of the earth. He was directly communicating with Adam and his descendants. He even communicated with Cain before and after he killed his brother. Hence, that era was God and humans and no intermediaries. This communication line continued with descendants of Adam (e.g. Enoch and Noah).

According to Moses, after the separation of the nations, he introduced the sons of God as intermediaries, so he does not have to deal with humans directly. However, he reserved a portion for himself:

> [9] But the Lord's portion is his people,
> Jacob his allotted heritage. (Deuteronomy 32:7–9 ESV).

This portion of the earth covers most parts of the Levant. He eventually showed it to Abraham as his inheritance, which his descendants will occupy[1]:

> The Lord had said to Abram, "Go from your country, your people and your father's household to the land I will show you. (Genesis 12:1 NIV).

God also clearly defined the boundaries of this land, which incorporates Cannan, and other nations:

> [18] On that day the Lord made a covenant with Abram and said, "To your descendants I give this land, from the Wadi of Egypt to the great river, the Euphrates— [19] the land of the Kenites, Kenizzites, Kadmonites, [20] Hittites, Perizzites, Rephaites, [21] Amorites, Canaanites, Girgashites and Jebusites." (Genesis 15: 18–21 NIV).

---

1. This promise was eventually fulfilled when the children of Israel left Egypt and resettled at Canaan (the land flowing with milk and honey). However, they did not take all the lands that had been assigned to them.

Thus, with the division of the earth to the 70 nations, each of the nations had a son of God (prince/chief angel) overseeing affairs there. The concept of spiritual or cosmic rulers controlling affairs of nation is contained in certain passages in the Bible. Isaiah hinted about the host of nations:

> For the Lord is enraged against all the nations,
> and furious against all their host;
> he has devoted them to destruction,[a] has given them over for slaughter. (Isaiah 34:2 ESV).

The *host* is a term usually used for angelic beings. To confirm this, the passage went ahead to provide further detail about where these host are:

> All the host of heaven shall rot away,
>   and the skies roll up like a scroll.
> All their host shall fall,
>   as leaves fall from the vine,
>   like leaves falling from the fig tree.
>
> ⁵ For my sword has drunk its fill in the heavens;
>   behold, it descends for judgment upon Edom,
>   upon the people I have devoted to destruction. (Isaiah 34:4–5 ESV).

In Daniel, we were given a snippet of the happenings in the heavens/spiritual realm, regarding the influence of these angelic beings over the territories they oversee. The passage provided an account of a struggle between the Archangel Gabriel and an entity who he identified as the prince of Persia. This entity was preventing Gabriel from entering his territory and a serious fight ensued, which lasted for 21 days. This passage portrays the prince of Persia as one of the rebellious sons of God, who reneged on their duties over the nations (see Section 7.2). Gabriel was able to win because Archangel Michael came to the rescue. Within that passage, another prince (the prince of Greece) was introduced:

> ¹² Then he said to me, "Fear not, Daniel, for from the first day that you set your heart to understand and humbled yourself before your God, your words have been heard, and I have come because of your words. ¹³ The prince of the kingdom of Persia withstood me twenty-one days, but Michael, one of the chief princes, came to help me, for I was left there with the kings of Persia, ¹⁴ and came to make you understand what is to happen

to your people in the latter days. For the vision is for days yet to come." (Daniel 10:12-14 ESV).

[20] Then he said, "Do you know why I have come to you? But now I will return to fight against the prince of Persia; and when I go out, behold, the prince of Greece will come. [21] But I will tell you what is inscribed in the book of truth: there is none who contends by my side against these except Michael, your prince. (Daniel 10:20-21 ESV).

This passage identified three princes of three nations/kingdoms: Persia, Greece and Israel. Hence, if there is a prince of Persia, prince of Greece, and prince of Israel, it could be extrapolated that there is also a prince of India, Egypt and so on. These princes have so much power and authority that they can detain powerful angels as well as kings:

[13] The prince of the kingdom of Persia withstood me twenty-one days, but Michael, one of the chief princes, came to help me, for I was left there with the kings of Persia. (Daniel 10:12-14 ESV).

This prince refused Gabriel passage to his territory. Notice the passage mentioned that Gabriel was detained with the kings of Persia, which suggests that the prince of Persia had some form of authority over the territory to legally detain Gabriel. From this passage, it could be inferred that every nation has a prince/principality/ruler that is controlling affairs in the territory from the spiritual realm.

Here, Gabriel identified Archangel Michael as one of the chief princes (confirming there were other chief princes). He further provided the detail that Michael's jurisdiction is over Israel (Michael, your prince). Thus, he is the principality/prince that God placed in charge of the land of Israel. Yet, he was still doing the will of God and has not rebelled.

From the interference of Michael in this struggle, it could also be seen that not all the sons of Most-High who were given authority over the nations misbehaved and were judged. Most likely, Michael might be the only one among the princes standing upright based on the hint provided by Gabriel ([21] But I will tell you what is inscribed in the book of truth: there is none who contends by my side against these except Michael, your prince. (Daniel 10:20-21 ESV)).

Supposedly, these princes have other lower-level entities working under them in a hierarchical order. Paul gave insight to this in Ephesians, where he identified some levels of cosmic authorities that humans are wrestling against:

> For we do not wrestle against flesh and blood, but against the rulers, against the authorities, against the cosmic powers over this present darkness, against the spiritual forces of evil in the heavenly places. (Ephesians 6:11–12 ESV).

In the fight described in the preceding paragraph, Michael had the impetus to join this fight because he is the prince in charge of Israel, hence he had the legal duty to ensure that the message which Gabriel was bringing from the throne of God to the children of Israel exiled in Persia, got to them.

7.2 REBELLION OF THE SONS OF GOD

Unfortunately, some years down the line, the sons of God who were assigned these tasks of overseeing the affairs of the nations derailed and started abusing their powers. These rebellious sons of God appropriated the position of God among their subjects and made humans to worship them as such. They instituted wicked norms and rules that were abhorrent to God within the nations where their spheres of influence span. The Bible is littered with instances of these gods of different nations, which led people they were supposed to guide towards God, away from God. There also appears to be some form of battle of supremacy among these gods, as the various nations they were ruling fought against each other to increase their territories beyond the boundaries God had originally allocated to them. Their atrocities were led bare in the snippet presented in Psalm 82, where they were being judged. The following passage from the psalm appear to show a snippet of the Divine Council in action:

> God has taken his place in the divine council;
>   in the midst of the gods he holds judgment:
> [2] "How long will you judge unjustly
>   and show partiality to the wicked? Selah
> [3] Give justice to the weak and the fatherless;
>   maintain the right of the afflicted and the destitute.
> [4] Rescue the weak and the needy;
>   deliver them from the hand of the wicked."

> [5] They have neither knowledge nor understanding,
> they walk about in darkness;
> all the foundations of the earth are shaken.
>
> [6] I said, "You are gods,
> sons of the Most-High, all of you;
> [7] nevertheless, like men you shall die,
> and fall like any prince." (Psalm 82:1 -7 ESV).

Although there are alternate interpretations to what this psalm portrays, the setting of this council is clear, and the facts point to a meeting of superior beings and not men. God was sitting among other beings identified as gods (sons of the Most-High). He had a special throne (God has taken his place in the divine council), and was the one with the highest authority, since he has a special position in the council (his place) and was the one pronouncing the judgement. These entities God was judging are not humans and actually had a far higher status than humans. This is made evident by the fact that part of their punishment was that they will die like men. This implies a denigration or demotion from their rank. A key passage that is consistently quoted to present an alternate interpretation to what was captured in Psalm 82 is John 10:34:

> [34] Jesus answered them, "Is it not written in your Law, 'I said, you are gods'?
> [35] If he called them gods to whom the word of God came—and Scripture cannot be broken— [36] do you say of him whom the Father consecrated and sent into the world, 'You are blaspheming,' because I said, 'I am the Son of God'?..." (John 10:34–36 ESV).

Among many followers of Christ and especially Biblical scholars, there are those scared to confront the truth being presented in the Bible. Hence, they either try to avoid this truth by ignoring it or attempt to twist the facts to fit their perspectives of what they believe the Bible is saying. Despite how hilarious this appears; some scholars believe that those temporarily sitting on the throne of God to judge the rulers of the nations are humans. The danger in this is that by taking this position, they are essentially blaspheming, by granting the position of God to humans. The verse in question *(John 10:34–38)*, has Jesus Christ quoting Psalm 82:6 ([6] "You are gods, sons of the Most-High, all of you) to the Jews, when they challenged him on why he was making himself equal to God. What he was saying essentially was, if God addressed those entities, he was speaking to (*who the words came to*) in Psalm 82 as gods, why is it a problem that the one God himself consecrated and sent into the world, should not be referred to as a god/son of God? The phrase *If he called them gods to whom the word of God came* was not a reference to the Jews listening to Jesus, but rather the beings who God was addressing in that divine council. Hence, Jesus was not comparing himself to the Jews right before him at that time but rather comparing himself to the *sons of God* that were being judged at the Divine Council, who God referred to as gods. It was not a direct speech as many construe it to be. He was essentially quoting a verse and not directly speaking to the Jews by saying '*I said, you are gods.*' This misinterpretation has also led many Christians to believe that they can become gods (hence, falling into the entrapment of Satan promising humans of the capability to be like God).

There are also those who take it to the extreme by using this as strong evidence of polytheism. However, the facts are clear. None of the gods being judged were of equal rank or status with God. They were subjects to God, the reason he was judging them. It was more like a president upbraiding his defaulting cabinet members. There is no nation on earth that has equated a cabinet member to be of equal rank with the president or prime minister. So why would the gods be equated to God?

The gods erred and were judged by their boss. Judging from the passage, these gods in charge of these nations were possibly instilling fear on humans, punishing them severely to assert their positions and make them to be worshipped. These directives of the gods probably ran contrary to the briefs God had initially given them. They were to stick to the standards of heaven, in ruling the people. Variants of these standards can be found in many cultures as laws and commandments (see Section 10.1 for a discussion on cosmic legalism). So, the gods were handed over this template to implement in the nations they were overseeing. God having recognised the weakness of humans (^{5} They have neither knowledge nor understanding, they walk about in darkness; all the foundations of the earth are shaken), apparently gave them the nations to oversee using the commandments as a template, while still reporting back to him as the God. However, during their rulership, the gods began to tinker with these laws, removing some and adding new ones that diminish the position of God among their subjects. The sons of God were charged to help the people return to God after their rebellion at Babel. However, they drove them further away from God and infuriating God by this.

Hence, as this wickedness of the sons of God continued, God had to convene the Divine Council, where these gods were to be judged. Perhaps a petition was brought against them by other sons of God (just like they did with the case of the Watchers), and the case has to be looked into.

Asaph, the psalmist did not capture what happened afterwards, rather he concurred with the judgement and urged God to arise and judge the earth, so as to take back these nations from the gods:

> [8] Arise, O God, judge the earth;
> for you shall inherit all the nations!
> (Psalm 82:1–8 ESV).

However, from the subsequent actions of these renegade sons of God, all or most of them did not accept the judgement. Thus, they rebelled and refused to relinquish their authorities over these nations. Many are still holding on to power over these nations waiting for enforcement of the judgement. An example is the prince of Persia. Despite knowing that Gabriel carried a message from God to Daniel, he refused him entry into his territory. This shows that this is a rebellious angel, defiant to the orders of God. However, he was still operating in the heavenly realm. This suggests that those gods, who have been judged have not lost their positions in the heavens (many of them are still holding their grounds, in defiance, I must add, in the Second Heaven). It seemed that these new sets of rebellious sons of God, subsequently joined forces with the other sons of God that previously rebelled against God alongside Satan.

7.3 FALLEN ONES AND THE RENEGADE GODS

There seems to be some level of misconception of who the fallen angels are. Many only associate them with the Sons of God (the Watchers) who came down to earth to sleep with women (see Section 5.5 for the rebellion of the Watchers). Also, others consider them to be the angels who rebelled against God alongside Satan. However, considering that both the Watchers and the sons of God who rebelled with Satan all fell from grace, the term fallen angels should be regarded as a broad term used to describe all heavenly beings that have at one point or the other fallen out of favor with God. From various passages in the Bible, we are made to understand that there were three (there may even be more occasions that were probably not captured in the sacred books available to us) separate occasions when the sons of God disobeyed or rebelled against him. The original fallen angels are all the angels or heavenly beings who rebelled against God alongside Halel/Lucifer. This group were subsequently joined by the watchers who came down to earth to grab and mate with earthly women to produce the Nephilim. The titans in Greek mythology are most likely the Watchers who fell. Later, this group was later joined by the sons of God who reigned over the earth after the flood and were judged in Psalm 82 for maltreating humans who God handed over to them to rule. These are the third sets of rebellious angels captured in the Bible.

The key argument in this section, is that some of the celestial beings who were once referred to as gods, did not remain loyal to God's authority[2], and at some point, rebelled against God's authority and fell out of favor with God. Hence, they were judged severely for that and condemned. Despite having been judged, these entities did not relinquish their positions but held onto it while waiting for the final battle with the angels of God. These gods are renegade supernatural beings, commonly referred to as fallen angels. They are renegades because at some point in their lifetime they were servants of God, doing his bidding while working for him in certain parts of the universe before they went astray and rebelled against his orders.

The proliferations of gods and deities in all the cultures around the world is linked to these entities, because on coming down to earth, they claimed to be gods and assert their authorities over the nations, instead of sticking to their positions as servants of the Most-High God. Some of them told the people distorted stories about having a fight or fallout with their father as contained in ancient myths of the Greeks and other cultures. Hence, they drew the worship of the people away from God to themselves and in so doing irked God.

There is no culture or nation that do not have stories/myth or connection to supernatural beings who they consider their gods. Some cultures claim their gods fell from the sky in ancient times. There is a plethora of gods across the continents, even till this day where many traditional religions cling to the patronage and protection of these gods. Bulk of the passages in the Old Testament essentially centered on the continual struggle of Israelites to overcome the temptation of worshipping these other gods. The Israelites were exposed to some of the gods of the various nations they encountered and hence, were drawn to them.

---

2. It also has to be noted that not all them rebelled against. Many them have continued to give God the glory everyday.

REORDERING OF THE WORLD – EMERGENCE OF A NEW WORLD ORDER

Throughout the Old Testament, God was using the prophets to draw Israel away from these gods and back to himself:

> 19 And lest thou lift up thine eyes unto heaven, and when thou seest the sun, and the moon, and the stars, even all the host of heaven, shouldest be driven to worship them, and serve them, *which the LORD thy God hath divided unto all nations* under the whole heaven. (Deuteronomy 4: 14–49 KJV).

Severally God accused Israel of harlotry, as they abandoned him (their husband) to go to these other gods. Seen from this perspective, the enormity of the offence of the Israelites becomes clearer. God was emphatic about Israelites not worshipping the other gods by centring the first two of the Ten Commandments on this topic:

> ² I am the Lord thy God, which have brought thee out of the land of Egypt, out of the house of bondage.
> ³ Thou shalt have no other gods before me.
> ⁴ Thou shalt not make unto thee any graven image, or any likeness of anything that is in heaven above, or that is in the earth beneath, or that is in the water under the earth.
> ⁵ Thou shalt not bow down thyself to them, nor serve them: for I the LORD thy God am a jealous God, visiting the iniquity of the fathers upon the children unto the third and fourth generation of them that hate me; (Exodus 20: 2–5 KJV).

God punished them severely whenever they go after these gods, culminating in their final conquering and captivity by other nations.

This was not just an Israeli issue. The influence of the gods was global. These gods held sway all over the world before the coming of Jesus Christ. People of various nations worshipped them and did all their biddings, even sacrificing humans to them:

> ⁵ They have built the high places of Baal to burn their children in the fire as offerings to Baal—something I did not command or mention, nor did it enter my mind. (Jeremiah 19:5 NIV).

Such practices were not limited to the Mesopotamia but have been well documented to have occurred in various other cultures such as the Mayans, Incas, Aztecs, Nahuas, Greeks, Celts, Chinese, and Egyptians[3]. This human sacrifice practice was so rampant across the world in those days that God cautioned the Israelites in Leviticus not to indulge in it:

3. Britannica, "Human sacrifice", 1; Daley, "Did the Ancient", 1; Jarus, "25 cultures", 1; Leigh, "Blood for the Gods", 1

> [21] "You are not to present any of your children to Molech as a sacrifice. That way, you won't defile the name of your God." (Leviticus 18:21–23 ISV).

This was the darkness and imprisonment that Jesus Christ came to untangle humans from. God's loving kindness was kindled, and he prepared a way through which humans can be liberated from the clutches of these gods. In 1 Corinthians, Paul mentioned rulers of this world, who would have thwarted the plans of redemption of man through the death of Christ, had they been aware of the secret plot by God:

> [7] But we impart a secret and hidden wisdom of God, which God decreed before the ages for our glory. [8] None of the rulers of this age understood this, for if they had, they would not have crucified the Lord of glory. (1 Corinthians 2:7–8).

The rulers of this world that Paul referred to were certainly not the Roman Emperor who was ruling a large chunk of the earth at this time. And there was no other earthly ruler who would have been interested in such matters concerning the redemption of man from sin at that time. So, Paul must have been referring to some other forms of rulers, who will lose something great if humans were redeemed. These are the rebellious sons of God, who fear that humans might stop worshipping them and go back to God. These gods were also afraid that if humans were redeemed from their sins, they might eventually take their place in the heavenly realm.

The coming of Jesus Christ and his preaching of the arrival of the Kingdom of God, was essentially an announcement to these gods that their time was up, and God was coming to take over all the nations. The spread of Christianity across the world whittled down the worship and devotion to these gods, pushing them into the background, with their followers worshipping them in secret. As Christianity spread, loyalty to these gods and their worship declined.

However, the influence of Christianity over these gods appears to be waning as we approach the end times, and the influence of these gods are resurging across the nations. This is expected as the time of their punishment approaches, they will put up their last fight, to retain the grounds.

7.4 THE SUPREMACY OF GOD

For anyone who has carefully studied the Bible, especially the Old Testament books, one conclusion that would come to mind is that although, there are many lesser supernatural beings (gods, deities), who people interact with (see Section 1.3.2), there is only one God, who created everything. He is the ultimate Supreme Being, besides whom there is no other:

> ³⁵ Unto thee it was shewed, that thou mightest know that the Lord he is God; there is none else beside him. (Deuteronomy 4:35 KJV).

These does not however, contradict the fact that these lesser beings exist, as some biblical scholars tend to suggest. These scholars in their bid to project their views on monotheism, dismiss the existence of these deities, whose influence on humans are well documented in various books in the Bible. However, in reality, monotheism portrays that God is the only supreme God, with other lesser entities under him. The existence of God does not in any way nullify the existence of lesser gods. The Bible is very clear on this. What the Bible projects is the supremacy of God over these other entities.

Many biblical passages alluded to God's supremacy through his actions of judging and punishing the gods. Hence, if these entities referred to as gods do not exist, why would God waste his time judging and punishing them? Time after time, God demonstrated his supremacy by judging and punishing these gods, whenever they get out of line. Jeremiah while speaking about the defeat of Egypt by Nebuchadnezzar, at the Battle of Carchemish, also made pronouncements against Amon, the Egyptian god:

> ²⁵ The Lord of hosts, the God of Israel, said: "Behold, I am bringing punishment upon Amon of Thebes, and Pharaoh and Egypt and her gods and her kings, upon Pharaoh and those who trust in him. ²⁶ I will deliver them into the hand of those who seek their life, into the hand of Nebuchadnezzar king of Babylon and his officers. Afterward Egypt shall be inhabited as in the days of old, declares the Lord. (Jeremiah 46:25–26, ESV).

Amon referred here was one of the greatest deities in Egypt then, who they revered as king of the gods[4] But here he was being judged by God.

---

4. Britannica, "Amon summary", 1

Throughout the Old Testament there was a constant struggle of Israelites to stay true to God. They were often swayed by influences of the gods of neighbouring countries such as Baal, Asherah/Ashotoreth, Marduk/Moloch. To demonstrate his power over these gods, swaying the Israelites, God punished them in several ways that will make the people to recognise that their gods were being dealt with. The encounter between Elijah and the prophets of Baal was a classic example of this, where the supremacy of God was demonstrated (1 Kings 18:25–29). Baal, regarded as the storm god was at some point, the supreme god in ancient Canaan and Phoenicia. The goddess, Asherah/Ashtoreth, the chief female deity was his consort, hence, they (Baal and Asherah) were often mentioned together in the Bible. They were revered as fertility gods, and their worship rites involved sexual perversion. Hence, when Baal was unable to consume the sacrifice by his prophets, it was a clear demonstration to the people who the Supreme Being was–the God that answered the call of Elijah with the fire that consumed the sacrifice prepared for him. The supremacy of God was also reflected in the story of Shadrach, Meshach, and Abednego (Daniel 3:16–28). Leading Nebuchadnezzar to declare that God was the Most High:

> [26] Nebuchadnezzar then approached the opening of the blazing furnace and shouted, "Shadrach, Meshach and Abednego, servants of the Most High God, come out! Come here!" (Daniel 3: 26 NIV).

He further acknowledged the supremacy of God by proclaiming that no other god could save his servants from the fire:

> [29] Therefore I decree that the people of any nation or language who say anything against the God of Shadrach, Meshach and Abednego be cut into pieces and their houses be turned into piles of rubble, *for no other god can save in this way.*" (Daniel 3: 29 NIV).

Arguably, the most profound illustration of the supremacy of God over these gods is contained in 1 Samuel in the interesting encounter between the Ark of God and Dagon:

> And the Philistines took the ark of God, and brought it from Ebenezer unto Ashdod.
> [2] When the Philistines took the ark of God, they brought it into the house of Dagon, and set it by Dagon.

³ And when they of Ashdod arose early on the morrow, behold, Dagon was fallen upon his face to the earth before the ark of the Lord. And they took Dagon, and set him in his place again.

⁴ And when they arose early on the morrow morning, behold, Dagon was fallen upon his face to the ground before the ark of the Lord; and the head of Dagon and both the palms of his hands were cut off upon the threshold; only the stump of Dagon was left to him.

⁵ Therefore neither the priests of Dagon, nor any that come into Dagon's house, tread on the threshold of Dagon in Ashdod unto this day.

⁶ But the hand of the Lord was heavy upon them of Ashdod, and he destroyed them, and smote them with emerods, even Ashdod and the coasts thereof.

⁷ And when the men of Ashdod saw that it was so, they said, The ark of the God of Israel shall not abide with us: for his hand is sore upon us, and upon Dagon our god.

⁸ They sent therefore and gathered all the lords of the Philistines unto them, and said, What shall we do with the ark of the God of Israel? And they answered, Let the ark of the God of Israel be carried about unto Gath. And they carried the ark of the God of Israel about thither.

⁹ And it was so, that, after they had carried it about, the hand of the Lord was against the city with a very great destruction: and he smote the men of the city, both small and great, and they had emerods in their secret parts.

¹⁰ Therefore they sent the ark of God to Ekron. And it came to pass, as the ark of God came to Ekron, that the Ekronites cried out, saying, They have brought about the ark of the God of Israel to us, to slay us and our people.

¹¹ So they sent and gathered together all the lords of the Philistines, and said, Send away the ark of the God of Israel, and let it go again to his own place, that it slay us not, and our people: for there was a deadly destruction throughout all the city; the hand of God was very heavy there.

¹² And the men that died not were smitten with the emerods: and the cry of the city went up to heaven. (1 Samuel 5:1–12 KJV).

Dagon (fish god) was one of the oldest deities in Mesopotamia (worshipped in ancient Syria across the middle of the Euphrates), and the chief deity of the Philistines. He is primarily associated with fertility, abundant crop harvests, and anointing kings and leaders. The idol of Dagon was crafted in the likeness of a half man and half fish hybrid–a large man with a fish-like lower body. Going by this he has the nature of a merman, (male counterpart of a mermaid). The Philistines worshipped Dagon through sacrifices and feasts. The worship of this pagan god dates to the third millennium BC. According to ancient mythology, Dagon was the father of Baal. In certain parts of the upper Euphrates, he was regarded as the "father of gods" like the Mesopotamian Enlil or Hurrian Kumarbi, as well as a lord of the land, a god of prosperity, and a source of royal legitimacy[5]. In Mesopotamia, where many rulers regarded him as the god capable of granting them kingship over the western areas.

In Philistines, the temples of Dagon were located at Ashdod and Gaza. Hence, when the Philistines captured the Ark of the Covenant from the Israelites, they brought the ark to the temple of Dagon in Ashdod, where the idol of Dagon was prominently placed. In their mind, they have captured the god of Israelites and by placing him by the side of Dagon, they were equating God to the same level as Dagon or even lower.

This was the height of insult and God was not taking it and decided to teach them a historic lesson. The next morning the idol of Dagon was prostrating before the ark. A curious mind would ask at this point, what is really going on? This is supposedly an inanimate idol that was made by the hands of man, with no power or entity behind it. So why was it prostrating (*Dagon was fallen upon his face to the earth before the ark of the* LORD) in reverence to the God that is present in the ark? This would not make sense, unless one recognises that there was an entity behind the statue of Dagon, and that entity knows his position before God or has been forced to bow.

Unfortunately, the priests of Dagon, did not recognise this at first, and possibly thought it was a fluke that brought down their most revered god before the ark. So, they repeated the mistake by setting him on his previous position. But this time, God made the message clearer to them by decapitating the statue of Dagon. Simply put, Dagon cannot stand beside God ("*there is no other God besides Him*").

To make the message loud and clear, God went further to punish the people of Ashdod for their errors. They immediately, realised that it was not a fluke, but that God was judging them and their revered god:

---

5. Archi, "Translation of Gods", 319–336; Schwemer, "The Storm-Gods", 1

⁷ And when the men of Ashdod saw that it was so, they said, The ark of the God of Israel shall not abide with us: for his hand is sore upon us, and upon Dagon our god. (1 Samuel 5:7 KJV).

7.5 THE INHERITANCE AND NATION OF GOD

One might wonder why God gives Israel special treatment or why he seems so fixated on Israel. To understand the relationship between God and Israel, one would have to consider Israel as a sample set God uses to work with the world. God wants to show the nations of the world his nature through his relationship with Israel. By this he can claw back the rest of the nations who have gone astray. Based on Moses's account, when God divided the earth into separate nations according to the descendants of Noah, he reserved a portion to himself (see Section 7.1). Moses implied that this land, which God reserved for himself, was Canaan, and the descendants of Jacob, were the bloodline that will eventually occupy this nation of God.

Asaph, the psalmist[6], also hinted at this in Psalm 79, where he stated that God's inheritance (referring to Jerusalem) has been taken over by other nations:

> O God, the nations have come into your inheritance;
>   they have defiled your holy temple;
>   they have laid Jerusalem in ruins. (Psalm 79: 1 ESV).

Asaph clearly understood this idea of cosmic dynamics at play at his time. He demonstrated this through his psalms especially Psalm 82. He understood that God was angry at Israel for turning to other gods, hence the punishment from God. As a matter of fact, the themes of his psalms centerd around this concept, with Psalm 82, (where the gods were being judged, and Asaph urging God to take all the nations), being the climax of his thesis. The onus of Psalm 79 was to plead for God's mercy and to beckon on him to turn his anger on the nations who have defiled his inheritance:

> How long, O Lord? Will you be angry forever?
>   Will your jealousy burn like fire?
> ⁶ Pour out your anger on the nations
>   that do not know you,
>   and on the kingdoms

---

6. A worship leader assigned by David for the tabernacle choir

> that do not call upon your name!
> ⁷ For they have devoured Jacob
>   and laid waste his habitation. (Psalm 79: 5–7 ESV).

God's intention for taking Israel as his inheritance, was to rule, nurture and turn them into a model for other nations to emulate. This was why God was displeased when Israelites demanded that Samuel anoint a king for them like the other nations. He told Samuel the implication of Israelites' request:

> And the Lord told him: "Listen to all that the people are saying to you; it is not you they have rejected, but they have rejected me as their king. ⁸ As they have done from the day I brought them up out of Egypt until this day, forsaking me and serving other gods, so they are doing to you. (1 Samuel 8:7–8 NIV).

Viewed from this perspective the enormity of the action of the Israelites was mind-blowing. Here was God planning to make Israel a role model for other nations, while Israel was desiring to be like the other nations. On top of that, they rejected God as their king. This shows how far the people had fallen at that point from their forefathers. Moses understood the cosmic dynamics at play and took time to explain all the details to them in Deuteronomy 32, while warning them about the implication of rejecting God. Yet, they went ahead to reject God.

The rejection of God by Israel essentially commenced from the time they requested for a king over them. It came to a head during the time Jeremiah was prophesying and churning out tons of warning on the implication of Israel not understanding their relationship with God and abusing his mercy, that he decided to ruin them and send them into exile:

> 'In the same way I will ruin the pride of Judah and the great pride of Jerusalem. ¹⁰ These wicked people, who refuse to listen to my words, who follow the stubbornness of their hearts and go after other gods to serve and worship them, will be like this belt—completely useless! ¹¹ For as a belt is bound around the waist, so I bound all the people of Israel and all the people of Judah to me,' declares the Lord, 'to be my people for my renown and praise and honor. But they have not listened.'

The derailment of Israel is disheartening, considering that God took time to select the seed through which he will establish his nation. After the division of the earth, there was no immediate move by God to establish this nation. He bid his time to get the perfect individual through

REORDERING OF THE WORLD – EMERGENCE OF A NEW WORLD ORDER

which he would establish this nation. This individual has to come from the line of Shem, which had remained undefiled and keeping to the righteous paths of God, according to the Order of the Ancients (see Section 6.4). Abraham became the chosen man, set aside by God to be used to establish this nation.

However, Noah, and Shem and some of their descendants (following the righteous path) were already residing in a portion of this land known as the City of Shalom, even before Abraham. It appears they moved to this land around the time that Nimrod was rising in power and spreading his influence across the lands:

> SHEM ruled in the city of Shalom and he was called Melchizedek, for he reigned as king under his father Noah, and was a priest of the Most-High God. 2. After the departure of Ham from the presence of his father Noah, Shem and Japheth dwelt together in peace under the benign rule of Noah; but in time, conflict arose among them and Noah led the seed of Shem to a new land which the Lord showed him where they built a city which they called Shalom, the City of Peace. (The Writings of Abraham 18:1–2).

> 3. Noah invested his son Shem with authority to reign as Prince of Peace, and Noah devoted his days to instructing his people after the Order of the Ancients. 4. And his people dwelt in righteousness and worshiped the Lord their God and served Him. 5. They established the order of heaven among them and sought after the City of Enoch and the Lord came among them and ministered to them and those who sought for the gain of this world went out from among them, for they held all things common after the order of Enoch and no man had above his neighbor. (The Writings of Abraham 18:1–5).

Hence, they did not participate in the construction of the Tower of Babel and Nimrod's dominion did not reach this land:

> Nimrod spread his dominion over all mankind save those in the city of Shalom. *(The Writings of Abraham 17:4).*

CHAPTER 8

Establishment of the Nation of God

8.1 THE PATRIARCH: THE MISSING EARLY LIFE OF ABRAM

Abraham is a key figure in the Bible, considering the role he played in the establishment of the nation of God. However, for such a prominent figure, much of his early life was not captured in Genesis. The writer of Genesis rather focused on his adult age, when he received the call from God to go to Canaan from Haran. Based on the account recorded in Genesis 11:27–32, we can glean that his father was Terah. Genesis 11: 1- 26 traced the genealogy of Terah from Shem, hence linking Abraham to the line of Shem. He had two brothers (Nahor and Haran). Haran who is the father of Lot died early; hence, Abram became Lot's guardian. At some point in his life, Terah took Abram, Sarai and Lot and left Ur, where they had been residing with the aim to reach Canaan. However, he aborted his journey at Haran, without reaching Canaan (Genesis 11: 31). This account did not say why Nahor was not taken on this journey or what prompted Terah to make this journey from a place he had an established network of friends to a new location.

Despite the little detail provided in Genesis about Abram's early life, there is a strong indication that he was groomed from an early age to be the father of nations. He had absolute faith in God, which shows that he had a good understanding of God and his ways and has built a good relationship with God. Such qualities don't come easy and usually require

ESTABLISHMENT OF THE NATION OF GOD

a long period of training and obedience. Simply put he was not a novice by the time the call for him to set out to Canaan came.

Due to this obvious lacuna in Genesis, several accounts have emerged about the early life of Abraham. One of such is the account in Chapter VI of the Biblical Antiquities of Pseudo-Philo,[1] which tend to purport that Abraham witnessed the construction of the Tower of Babel and refused to participate alongside 11 others (Antiquities of Pseudo-Philo 6: 1–4).

Although this event may have occurred but wrongfully attributed to Abraham. This is based on the fact that judging from the genealogy of Terah presented in Genesis 11:1–26 and summarised in Table 8.1, Abraham could not have witnessed the construction of the Tower of Babel. According to the Book of Jubilees, Reu was born to Peleg around the time the tower was being built:

> and she bare him a son in the fourth year of this week, and he called his name Reu; for he said: "Behold the children of men have become evil through the wicked purpose of building for themselves a city and a tower in the land of Shinar." (Book of Jubilees, 10:1–3).

Abram was born about 292 years after the flood and about 118 after the disruption of the tower construction (see Table 8.1). The ancestors of Abraham who may have witnessed the tower construction include Shem, Arpachshad, Shelah, Eber, and Peleg.

Table 8.1. Summary of Abraham's genealogy based on Genesis 11: 10–26 timelines

Event	Father	Age	Son	Year # After the Flood
Birth of Shem	Noah		Shem	
The Great Flood		0		0
When Shem was 100 years old, he fathered Arpachshad two years after the flood	Shem	100	Arpach-shad	2
Arpachshad had lived 35 years, he fathered Shelah	Arpachshad	35	Shelah	37
Shelah had lived 30 years, he fathered Eber	Shelah	30	Eber	67

1. James, "The Biblical Antiquities", 1

Event	Father	Age	Son	Year # After the Flood
When Eber had lived 34 years, he fathered Peleg	Eber	34	Peleg	101
When Peleg had lived 30 years, he fathered Reu/ Tower of Babel Commencement (Book of Jubilees, 10:1–3)	Peleg	30	Reu	131
When Reu had lived 32 years, he fathered Serug	Reu	32	Serug	163
Disruption of the Babel (43 years after Reu's birth–(Book of Jubilees, 10:21)		43		174
When Serug had lived 30 years, he fathered Nahor	Serug	30	Nahor	193
When Nahor had lived 29 years, he fathered Terah	Nahor	29	Terah	222
When Terah had lived 70 years, he fathered Abram, Nahor, and Haran	Terah	70	Abram	292
Peleg's Death		209		340
Nahor's Death		119		341
After the flood Noah lived 350 years. 29 All the days of Noah were 950 years, and he died	Noah's Death	350		350
Reu's Death		207		370
Serug's Death		200		393
Arpachshad's Death		403		440
Shelah's Death		403		470
Shem's Death		500		502
Eber's Death		430		531

A more credible story on the early life of Abram is contained in the Writings of Abraham. According to the account, Abraham was groomed by Shem, who was also known as Melchizedek because he reigned as king and priest of the Most-High God. According to the account (chapters 18 and 19 of the Writings of Abraham), Abraham's forefathers starting from Serug abandoned the righteous path of their parents and sojourned into the kingdom controlled by Nimrod. This kingdom was a very wicked and

ESTABLISHMENT OF THE NATION OF GOD

rebellious kingdom; hence, it was an oddity that the line of Shem and by extension, the line of Seth were mingling with the descendants of the line of Ham (postdiluvian extension of line of Cain). Serug was subsequently initiated into the ways of Nimrod's followers. It was there he gave birth to Nahor, who subsequently fathered Terah (Abram's father). Down the line, Terah became great in Nimrod's kingdom, possibly one of the king's advisers. Both the Book of Jasher and the Writings of Abraham noted the prominence of Terah in the kingdom of Nimrod, which gives some credence to the veracity of the account:

> 49 And Terah the son of Nahor, prince of Nimrod's host, was in those days very great in the sight of the king and his subjects, and the king and princes loved him, and they elevated him very high.
>
> 50 And Terah took a wife and her name was Amthelo the daughter of Cornebo; and the wife of Terah conceived and bare him a son in those days.
>
> 51 Terah was seventy years old when he begat him, and Terah called the name of his son that was born to him Abram, because the king had raised him in those days, and dignified him above all his princes that were with him. (The Book of Jasher 7: 49–51).
>
> AMONG those who went forth from the city of Shalom was Peleg, who travelled to the northwest and established a city after the order of his father Noah, for Peleg was the son of Eber, the son of Salah, the son of Arphaxad, the son of Shem; and his people sought after the heavenly order and obtained it for they were caught up like the City of Enoch. 2. But Serug, the son of Reu, the son of Peleg, followed not after the way of his fathers, for he sought after gain for himself; wherefore, he led those who were of a like mind with himself out from the City of Peleg and they journeyed even unto the land of Shinar and became confederate with Nimrod. 3. Under the direction of Nimrod, Serug and his companions entered into the secret combination and became men of power and wealth in Nimrod's kingdom. 4. In the land of Shinar, Serug begat Nahor, and Nahor begat Terah, my father. 5. And Terah became great in the eyes of Nimrod, and Nimrod elevated him over all his people to stand at his right hand and advise him on all matters. (The Writings of Abraham, 19:1–5).

The highlight of the account was Nimrod's attempt to eliminate Abram soon after his birth because he was warned that the newborn will displace him. However, Terah prevented this by hiding Abram and the mother in a secret cave. According to the account Abram first encountered God in a dream at the age of three, while dwelling in the cave. Abram was in this cave for 10 years, before being guided to the city of Shalom where Noah and Shem lived, by an angel:

> WHEN I was ten years of age, I departed from the cave by night while my mother and my nurse slept and the angel of God met me and led me to the city of Shalom where Noah and his son Shem dwelt, and no man knew where I was. (The Writings of Abraham, 24:1).

He was subsequently tutored in the ways of God by Shem for 39 years. Both the Book of Jasher (Chapter 8) and the Writings of Abraham (Chapter 19–Chapter 25) covered these details.

This account seems a bit credible because it is quite plausible that Abraham met Noah, Shem and Nimrod. Based on the account presented in Genesis 11 Noah died 350 years after the flood, Shem died about 502 years after the flood, while Abram was born 292 years after the flood. Nimrod also might have lived more than 400 years after the flood, considering the ages of his contemporaries such as Shelah (the grandson of Shem). who died 470 years after the flood. Book of Jasher noted that the lifespan of humans was shortened, after the birth of Yoktan (the younger brother of Peleg):

> 19 These are the generations of Shem; Shem begat Arpachshad and Arpachshad begat Shelach, and Shelach begat Eber and to Eber were born two children, the name of one was Peleg, for in his days the sons of men were divided, and in the latter days, the earth was divided.
> 20 And the name of the second was Yoktan, meaning that in his day the lives of the sons of men were diminished and lessened. (Book of Jasher 7: 19–20).

This is also evident from Table 8.1 considering that the ages reduced by almost 50% starting from Peleg.

Hence, Abraham was groomed by Shem (Melchizedek) and Noah, to make him fit to build the nation of God. He was instructed in the ways of the ancients which Noah and Shem were the custodians:

> I received, under the direction of Noah and Shem, those instructions whereby I might enter into the Order of the ancients and I became a rightful heir and high priest, holding the right

belonging to the Fathers. For I was ushered into the Church of the Firstborn and tasted of the fruits of heavenly life. (The Writings of Abraham, 24:3).

The mere fact that Abraham received direct instructions in this regard from both Noah and Shem is very significant, because it implies that he must have been told about many things of the past that have been handed over from Adam through Seth, Enoch, Methuselah, and Noah. Thus, he learned all the details about the Flood from the very men who built the ark and survived the flood.[2] It has to be considered that Noah knew Methuselah for many hundreds of years, Methuselah knew Enoch and Adam for hundreds of years, which means that Abraham received reliable information about everything that happened since the creation of Adam.

After his training by Shem and Noah, Abram was sent back to Shinar, the kingdom of Nimrod, where his father and the rest of his family (the descendants of Serug who left the city of Peleg to join forces with Nimrod) have been; to bring them back into the righteous path. Hence, he reunited with his family and commenced his evangelistic work:

> In my fiftieth year, Father Shem called me into his presence and instructed me to return to the house of my father, for there were many there now who were seeking after light and truth for they had seen the foolishness of worshiping idols of wood and stone, but they knew not where to find the true God. (The Writings of Abraham 25:1).

The encounter between Abraham and Melchizedek recorded in Genesis, makes more sense under this light. According to the account Abraham was met by Melchizedek, introduced as king of Salem and priest of God Most-High. This meeting happened after Abraham won an important battle. Based only on the account in Genesis, there was a lot of mystery surrounding this encounter, starting from Melchizedek, who seemed to have appeared from nowhere. However, viewed from the account in the Writings of Abraham, this meeting was more like an endorsement of a teacher to a protege who has demonstrated he understood what he has been thought:

> [17] After his return from the defeat of Chedorlaomer and the kings who were with him, the king of Sodom went out to meet him at the Valley of Shaveh (that is, the King's

---

2. Mindel, "Abraham's Early", 1

Valley). ¹⁸ And Melchizedek king of Salem brought out bread and wine. (He was priest of God Most-High.) ¹⁹ And he blessed him and said,

> "Blessed be Abram by God Most-High,
>   Possessor of heaven and earth;
> ²⁰ and blessed be God Most-High,
>   who has delivered your enemies into your hand!"

And Abram gave him a tenth of everything. (Genesis 14: 17–20 ESV).

8.2 ABRAM'S EVANGELISM IN SHINAR AND ENCOUNTER WITH NIMROD

On reaching Shinar, Abraham met a highly developed and wealthy city in contrast to the City of Shalom, where he had come from. However, underneath this development and wealth lies dark and sinful practices (The Writings of Abraham, Chapter 28). The residents were practicing all sorts of wickedness to enrich themselves and to prosper. They were idolaters worshiping many gods, while forsaking the only true God. These gods claimed to be the creators of mankind and the universe:

> 2. And when he would hear me, I said unto him, Father, where is the God who created heaven and earth and all the hosts of them? 3. My father Terah answered me and said, Behold, my son, those gods who created all things are here with us in the house. (The Writings of Abraham, 32:2–3).

> 6. And my father said unto me, Behold, my son, these twelve great ones are rulers among the gods and this largest one is ruler above all and these others were their assistants in creating all things. (The Writings of Abraham, 32:6).

These claims of the gods align with the popular Sumerian creation story which claims that the Annunakis ("Those who came from the heavens to Earth") created humans.[3] These claims have been repeated across cultures and history by these gods. They will also be evoked in the last days when the antichrist and his cohorts will claim to be the creators.

Thus, when Abram got to Ur in Shinar, he began to evangelise and inform the few people in the city who have realised that the gods were not the true creator, about the Most-High God. He instructed them in

---

3. Goswami, "Did the Anunnaki", 1

the ways of the ancients and the righteous paths. However, he ran into serious trouble when he destroyed his father's idols. This escalated and Abram was brought to the court of Nimrod to be judged. On seeing Nimrod, Abram railed against him, denouncing him and his ways, and calling him the son of Perdition:

> 3. Why wilt thou not serve the Most-High God who created all things in heaven and on earth, who hath created these and holdeth the power to sustain thy life or to destroy thee? 4. O foolish, ignorant, wicked king, woe shall be unto thee forever and ever for thou art the son of Perdition for it is he who is thy father. 5. Thou hast corrupted the earth with thy sins and with the sins of thy people who follow thee. 6. It was for entering into this wicked combination to get gain that you ancestors were destroyed in the flood when only eight souls were saved. (The Writings of Abraham, 39:2–6).

The term 'son of Perdition used here against Nimrod is the same words Christ used to describe Judas (John 17:12) and Paul used for the antichrist (2 Thessalonians 2:3 KJV). Here, again Abraham alluded to the fact that Nimrod somehow had the gene of Satan running through him (*for thou art the son of Perdition for it is he who is thy father*). This is another allusion that Nimrod is of the line of Cain and was toeing the same line that his ancestors toed which led to the corruption of the previous world in the flood (*It was for entering into this wicked combination to get gain that your ancestors were destroyed in the flood*).

Abraham's utterances riled Nimrod and his princes that they decided that Abram must be burned alive in a furnace for reviling him and their gods. However, a twist emerged when Nimrod's astrologers recognised Abram as the child, they had advised the king to eliminate 50 years earlier, to forestall his overthrow. While investigating the matter, Terah was implicated. To extricate himself from the charge, Terah in turn fingered his other son Haran, as the main culprit who advised him to deceive the king. Hence, both Abram and Haran were thrown into the fire. Haran died in the process, because despite being a believer in the Most-High God, he had little faith in God. Genesis did record that Haran died prematurely *in the presence of his father*, but nothing was said of how he died in the book (*Haran died in the presence of his father Terah in the land of his kindred, in Ur of the Chaldeans–Genesis 11:28 ESV*). However, Abram was miraculously rescued from the fire, despite spending three days there. He was rather surrounded by angels who continued to instruct him while the fire raged, as God protected him to enable him to continue to preach the gospel across other lands and to establish the nation of God:

> 2. Nevertheless, while I was in the prison the Lord sent His angels to minister unto me and to comfort me and they said unto me, Fear not, Abram, for thy work is not yet finished for thou shalt yet become the father of many nations and thou shalt preach the gospel in far places, even in the land of Egypt shalt thou declare the mysteries of thy God. (The Writings of Abraham, 42:2).

According to the account, this singular event helped the evangelical work Abram was undertaking in Nimrod's kingdom, as having survived the flames, Nimrod gave him the opportunity to present the gospel of the Most-High God to his princes and subjects. Although Nimrod did not repent, many in his kingdom repented and joined Abram. Similar accounts of Abram's early age were captured in the Book of Jasher, thus, lending more credence to this story.

This story about the early life of Abraham recounted in the Book of Jasher and Writings of Abraham appears to be as credible as that told in Genesis. They filled the gaps that were missing in Genesis and gave insight into the foundations of the faith of Abraham in God. It does make sense that God would put the individual he wants to use to establish his nation through trials and difficult situation to build up his faith.

8.3 THE CUSTODIANS OF GOD'S TRUTH

The house of Noah, which later became the house of Shem and Eber, was like a learning center for the spreading of the undiluted truth of God. Only selected few were sent to this house to learn. Abraham, Isaac, and Jacob who were the chosen line to establish the nation of God, underwent training in this house.

> 17. And when the days of their mourning passed by Abraham sent away his son Isaac, and he went to the house of Shem and Eber, to learn the ways of the Lord and his instructions, and Abraham remained there three years. (Book of Jasher 24:17).

Isaac also, did the same with Jacob and sent him off to learn the ways of God from Shem. Esau declined the tutelage, preferring to stay at home:

> 18. At that time Isaac sent his younger son Jacob to the house of Shem and Eber, and he learned the instructions of the Lord, and Jacob remained in the house of Shem and Eber for thirty-two years, and Esau his brother did not go, for he was not willing to go, and he remained in his father's house in the land of Canaan (Book of Jasher 28:18).

8.4 GOD'S COVENANT WITH ABRAHAM

To establish his nation in the land he has reserved for himself after the division at Babel, God just needed one man through which he can build this nation. From the time the division occurred, God was sifting through the descendants of Seth, to make his selection. He finally zeroed in on Abraham, who was sent on a course from an early age to learn the ways of God in the House of Noah and Seth (see Section 8.1). After his training, Abraham was sent back to his father's house to evangelise about the kingdom of God and confront Nimrod (see Section 8.2). These were supposedly part of the preparation for Abraham to be able to be used for the establishment of the nation of God.

Another test Abraham underwent that proved his worthiness to be used by God was his battle with Chedorlaomer king of Elam. In this story briefly presented in Genesis 14 and Book of Jasher 13, the kings of the various tribes in Canaan (Bera the king of Sodom, Birsha the king of Gomorrah, Shinab the king of Admah, Shemeber the king of Zeboiim, and the king of Bela (that is, Zoar)) where Abram had been sojourning, had been subjects to Chedorlaomer, the king of Elam for twelve years. In the thirteenth year, they revolted against Chedorlaomer:

> In the days of Amraphel king of Shinar, Arioch king of Ellasar, Chedorlaomer king of Elam, and Tidal king of Goiim, ² these kings made war with Bera king of Sodom, Birsha king of Gomorrah, Shinab king of Admah, Shemeber king of Zeboiim, and the king of Bela (that is, Zoar). Genesis 14:1–2 ESV).

Hence, Chedorlaomer coopted other kings in league with him (Amraphel–aka Nimrod) king of Shinar, Arioch king of Ellasar) to deal a crushing blow on the rebellious kings of Canaan. What was not obvious from the account in Genesis was that Nimrod participated in this battle. However, Amraphel, king of Shinar is Nimrod. The Book of Jasher provided this insight by identifying Nimrod as Amraphel, and providing the reason for that:

> 6 And Nimrod dwelt in Babel, and he there renewed his reign over the rest of his subjects, and he reigned securely, and the subjects and princes of Nimrod called his name Amraphel, saying that at the tower his princes and men fell through his means (Book of Jasher 11:6).

At this time, Nimrod was already in his decline and was under the influence of Chedorlaomer. Chedorlaomer had defeated Nimrod in a battle couple of years before the battle with the kings of Canaan (Book of Jasher 13: 12–16). Hence, Nimrod was coopted by Chedorlaomer to join his war against the Canaan kings who had revolted against him (Book of Jasher 13: 12–16). The participation of Nimrod in this battle demonstrates the significance of this battle, where Abram has to confront Nimrod once again.

Needless to say that this battle of Chedorlaomer and kings of Canaan was a highly significant one with spiritual connotations. This was a war against Canaan (the land God wants to give Abram). The kings of Canaan were roundly defeated by Chedorlaomer. At this time Abram was residing in this land a stranger, so he did not participate initially. But when they took Lot his nephew and his properties, he was drawn into the battle. Hence, Abram who was the rightful owner of Canaan came to the rescue by launching a surprise attack on Chedorlaomer and his army. Abram with very little army comprising of his servants defeated Chedorlaomer and rescued the people and goods captured from Canaan (including Lot). By landing this decisive defeat on these four kings, Abram demonstrated he could defend the land God intends to give him, better than the usurper kings.

Thus, when Melchizedek met Abram after he defeated the armies of Chedorlaomer (the king of Elam) and the other three kings, it was more like a spiritual endorsement to highlight the fact that Abram has demonstrated his abilities to defeat the enemies of God and defend God's nation (Canaan).

> [18] And Melchizedek king of Salem brought out bread and wine. (He was priest of God Most-High.) [19] And he blessed him and said,

> "Blessed be Abram by God Most-High,
> Possessor of heaven and earth;
> [20] and blessed be God Most-High,
> who has delivered your enemies into your hand!"
>
> (Genesis 14:18–20 ESV).

Soon after this battle, God decided to enter a covenant with Abraham, to concretise his intention to use Abraham to establish his nation:

> 18 On that day the Lord made a covenant with Abram and said, "To your descendants I give this land, from the Wadi of Egypt to the great river, the Euphrates— 19 the land of the Kenites, Kenizzites, Kadmonites, 20 Hittites, Perizzites, Rephaites, 21 Amorites, Canaanites, Girgashites and Jebusites." (Genesis 15: 18 NIV).

He revealed to Abraham how this nation would be established and when it would happen. Part of this revelation was that his descendants would be sojourners in a foreign land from where they would be rescued after 400 years to take possession of the land God reserved for himself.

8.5 ISRAEL'S RESCUE FROM EGYPT

Before establishing his nation, God allowed the chosen bloodline to sojourn in different lands as strangers. Abraham, Isaac, and Jacob during their lives, lived among Canaanites, and Egyptians. But God never stopped to reiterate that he will give them the land of Cannan in due time. It was as if God was bidding his time, to allow the Israelites to grow in strength and number to be able to take the land, which was not empty but already occupied by other powerful nations. Also, as a just and righteous God, he was also waiting for the sins of those nations occupying the land to get to the critical point that would tip the balance against them (legally justify the reason for their eviction from the land), else it would appear they were unjustly treated:

> [13] Then the Lord said to Abram, "Know for certain that your offspring will be sojourners in a land that is not theirs and will be servants there, and they will be afflicted for four hundred years. [14] But I will bring judgment on the nation that they serve, and afterward they shall come out with great possessions. [15] As for you, you shall go to your fathers in peace; you shall be buried in a good old age. [16] And they shall come back here in the fourth

generation, for the iniquity of the Amorites is not yet complete."
(Genesis 15: 13–16 ESV).

The final lap of their tutelage was in Egypt where they ended up as slaves placed under harsh conditions. This condition was probably orchestrated by God to build both resilience and motivation to take on the inhabitants of the promised land. There was also another purpose for the sojourning of Israelites in Egypt. At that time, Egypt was about the leading nation, and supposedly had powerful gods as backups. God demonstrated the supremacy of his power in Egypt through the rescue of the children of Israel from Egypt. Egypt was a nation under other gods. And to rescue them God has to destroy or whittle down the powers of these gods. Moses harped on this:

> [34] Has any god ever tried to take for himself one nation out of another nation, by testings, by signs and wonders, by war, by a mighty hand and an outstretched arm, or by great and awesome deeds, like all the things the Lord your God did for you in Egypt before your very eyes? 35 You were shown these things so that you might know that the Lord is God; besides him there is no other. (Deuteronomy 4:34–35 NIV).

God deliberately subjected Israel and his descendants under the Egyptians and wrenched them out from the hands of the fallen gods, to demonstrate his might and power. This move was a way God demonstrated that in the future, he was going to rescue the rest of humanity (the nations that were subjected under the control of the fallen gods) and bring them back into his kingdom, the same way he brought the Israelites into the promised land.

Hence the rescue of Israel from Egypt was a precursor of what God was going to do for the rest of humanity through Jesus Christ–rescuing humans from the clutches of the gods and Satan (see Section 9.3). The Israelites were in slavery in Egypt for four hundred years before they were rescued by God through Moses, just like the world/humanity were slaves to sin for four thousand years from the time of Adam, till when Christ came to rescue man from the captivity of sin and Satan. But in the meantime, God was going to start with Israel and then bring the rest of humanity back into his fold. Egypt represents the fallen world that has entrapped humanity, from where God is calling out his sons:

> When Israel was a child, I loved him,
>   and out of Egypt I called my son. (Hosea 11:1 ESV).

8.6 THE BATTLE OF THE BLOODLINES

> I will put enmity between you and the woman,
>   and between your offspring and her offspring;
> he shall bruise your head,
>   and you shall bruise his heel." (Genesis 3:15 ESV).

There appear to be broadly two separate groups of people on earth: the righteous and the wicked, the true humans and the tainted humans (hybrids), the sheep and the goat, the list goes on and on. This division has caused strife from the time of the sons of Adam till date. There are suggestions from many biblical passages and supported by extrabiblical passages that indicate two distinct bloodlines of humans emanating from the sons of Adam (via Seth) and those of Cain.

Within this mix are the first generations of humans who occupied the earth before Adam was created. There is no record in the Bible that these beings who were commissioned by God to increase and multiply disappeared after the creation of Adam. A key indication of their existence on earth during the time of Adam was presented after Cain killed Abel. Cain was worried that these people would harm him, if he was exiled from the camp of Adam (Genesis 4: 13 -15 ESV).

One interesting thing from this passage is that God did not refute Cain's claim or reassure him that that there was no one to fear because they were the only ones inhabiting the earth at that moment. Rather, as a loving father who understands Cain's fear, he went ahead to put a mark on Cain's forehead. Note that at this point, it was just Adam, Eve, and Cain, and Cain could not have been afraid that his parents would harm him, after all he has been exiled from their camp. This proves that Cain's fear of other beings harming him was not frivolous, but a valid one.

After his exile from the house of Adam, Cain appears to have settled among these early humans, having been reassured by God that he would be protected. He ended up marrying their daughter:

> [16] Then Cain went away from the presence of the Lord and settled in the land of Nod, east of Eden. 17 Cain knew his wife, and she conceived and bore Enoch. When he built a city, he called the name of the city after the name of his son, Enoch. *(Genesis 4: 13–15 ESV).*

Hence, the corruption of Cain's DNA continued with genes of these people. These sets of beings were also most likely corrupted by Satan.

Or within this mix were beings created by Satan and his cohorts. Christ alluded to this in the parable of the wheat and the tare (Matthew 13:24–13:30), where he indicated that after God created humans, Satan also made a replica of the humans God created (see Section 3.9):

These sets of beings who apparently had been on the earth longer than Adam and his children had garnered more knowledge about the earth than them. Satan may also have contributed to giving them this knowledge as a way to enable them overcome Adam and his family. They eventually exposed Cain to various ancient knowledge enabling him to quickly build cities before Adam and Seth did (see Section 5.3).

So, within the bloodline of Cain was the seed of Satan (see Section–5.2), mixed with the gene of the pre-adamic races. Then there was the bloodline of Seth, which were not tainted with the genes of the pre-adamic people nor those of Satan. These two bloodlines coexisted before the flood. However, there was clear distinction between these two bloodlines noted in the Bible. It was so important for these two bloodlines to be separated that the Holy Bible excluded Cain from the genealogy of Adam (Genesis 5) and presented a separate genealogy for Cain (Genesis 4: 17–22).

Reading Genesis carefully, one will easily understand the two bloodlines running parallel to each other and only on rare occasions mixed up via marriage, before the flood. The sons of Seth were very careful not to mix with the bloodline of Cain, whereas the sons of Cain were eager to mix the two bloodlines. Lamech the son of Methushael from the line of Cain was the first recorded in Genesis to have succeeded to cross these paths by marrying the daughters of Mahalalel, from the line of Seth (see Table 5.1), hence introducing the bloodline of Seth into those of Cain. Then Noah ended up marrying Naamah, the daughter of Lamech (albeit reluctantly), whose mum brought them back to the camp of Seth after they discovered Lamech had committed a heinous act of killing someone (see sections 5.2 and 6.3). It was suggested that the purpose of God letting Noah to marry Naamah was to preserve the two bloodlines to the end, when they will be finally separated.

Hence, the two bloodlines survived the flood and has continued to live side by side on the earth. The distinction between the two bloodlines seemed to have been muddled up after the flood. And with time it became difficult to separate the two. One would wonder, why Abraham stressed on getting a wife for his son Isaac from his father's line:

ESTABLISHMENT OF THE NATION OF GOD

> ² And Abraham said to his servant, the oldest of his household, who had charge of all that he had, "Put your hand under my thigh, ³ that I may make you swear by the Lord, the God of heaven and God of the earth, that you will not take a wife for my son from the daughters of the Canaanites, among whom I dwell, ⁴ but will go to my country and to my kindred, and take a wife for my son Isaac." (Genesis 24: 2–4 ESV).

He was certain that their gene pool has not been tampered with, unlike those of the Canaanites. The same thing happened with Jacob. Isaac also made sure he went to get a wife from their kindred:

> "You must not take a wife from the Canaanite women. ² Arise, go to Paddan-aram to the house of Bethuel your mother's father, and take as your wife from there one of the daughters of Laban your mother's brother. ³ God Almighty bless you and make you fruitful and multiply you, that you may become a company of peoples. ⁴ May he give the blessing of Abraham to you and to your offspring with you, that you may take possession of the land of your sojournings that God gave to Abraham!" (Genesis 28: 1–4 ESV).

Isaac and Rebekah were not happy with Esau that he took wives from the Canaanite community:

> ³⁴ And Esau was forty years old when he took to wife Judith the daughter of Beeri the Hittite, and Bashemath the daughter of Elon the Hittite:
> ³⁵ Which were a grief of mind unto Isaac and to Rebekah. (Genesis 26:34–35).
> ² Esau took his wives of the daughters of Canaan; Adah the daughter of Elon the Hittite, and Aholibamah the daughter of Anah the daughter of Zibeon the Hivite; (Genesis 36:2 KJV).

If what is going on here is still not obvious one has to go back to Abraham's choice of wife. He was also specifically asked to go to his father's household to get a wife:

> 4. Behold, in thy father's house dwelleth she to whom the promises belong, for she is a princess in the house of the Most-High and shall reign as a queen over thy posterity forever.
> 5. Seek after her and take her to wife for she will be the mother of the promised seed. (The Writings of Abraham 25: 4–5).

As a matter of fact, Sarah was Abraham's niece:

> 44 And at that time Nahor and Abram took unto themselves wives, the daughters of their brother Haran; the wife of Nahor was Milca and the name of Abram's wife was Sarai. And Sarai, wife of Abram, was barren; she had no offspring in those days. (The Book of Jasher, 12:44).

Isaac married the granddaughter of his uncle Nahor:

> [15] Before he had finished speaking, behold, Rebekah, who was born to Bethuel the son of Milcah, the wife of Nahor, Abraham's brother, came out with her water jar on her shoulder. (Genesis 24: 15 ESV).

Likewise, Jacob was made to marry his cousin, the daughter of his uncle Laban. Based on the foregoing, it has become apparent that a conscious effort was made by Abraham not to contaminate his bloodline with those of others. This was especially important, because that is the bloodline God was planning to use to establish his chosen nation. Ordinarily, Ishmael, Abraham's first son ought to have inherited his things and the promise, however he was denied this, because he was not from the preserved bloodline.

The sons of Jacob most likely did not keep this tenet, hence the two bloodlines were further mixed up, making it extremely difficult to distinguish them. Although the strife between these two bloodlines appears to have largely gone underground, where one bloodline (the line of Cain) has continued to hoodwink and control the other (the line of Seth), who are largely oblivious of who they are. Fragments of these information have been communicated among the line of Cain through various secret societies in the world. Hence, they are far ahead in this game than those from the line of Seth. Christ alluded to this when he stated that the children of the light are unwise:

> [8] And the lord commended the unjust steward, because he had done wisely: for the children of this world are in their generation wiser than the children of light. (Luke 16:8 KJV).

As a matter of fact, many prominent secret societies in the world try to claim their origin from the anti-diluvian era, many tracing their roots to Nimrod[4].

---

4. Huss, *Secret Societies*, 1

Prior the flood, the secret knowledge was communicated to select few in both bloodlines (see Section 8.3). Despite the fact that the Flood nearly wiped out the line of Cain, the seed of Cain preserved through Ham (see Section 6.3) or through another son of Noah, has largely remained well informed.

The final separation of these bloodlines will eventually take place towards the end, when the angels of Christ would come to harvest the earth (see *Matthew 13:24–13:30 ESV, Rev 14: 14–20*). A key purpose of the Great Tribulation is to facilitate the sifting of the bloodlines (see Section 13.5). The children of light will be crystalised through the tribulation, whereas the children of darkness will gravitate towards the antichrist. At this point the separation between the wheat and the tare will be easier for the angels.

8.7 GENOCIDAL WAR AGAINST THE POST-DILUVIAN GIANTS

One of the key questions that many objective Bible readers and non-Christians tend to pose is: why would a loving God direct Israelites through Moses to unleash onslaught on the inhabitants of Canaan after their Exodus from Egypt? Many of these cities were "devoted to destruction". In modern parlance, *devotion of a city or nation to destruction* is essentially genocide–complete wipeout of that city and its inhabitants. So why would God allow this to happen? What did the Israelites have that these people did not have? Were the Israelites more superior than those inhabitants of Canaan? What was the offence of these people that made them to be routed from the land they were occupying?

To answer these questions, one would have to understand who the inhabitants of those lands were. Recall that soon after the disruption of the construction of Tower of Babel, God put in place a new world order, whereby the entire world was apportioned to 70 sons of God, who were to oversee affairs in their respective lands (see Section 7.1). God reserved Canaan (bulk of the Levant) for himself, where his chosen lot will reside and placed Archangel Michael in charge of it (see Section 7.5). However, prior to this division, Noah has already divided the earth among his sons. This formal division was triggered by the actions of the sons of Noah, who secretly divided the earth among the three of them. And when Noah got a wind of this, he decided to formally divide the earth by casting lots among his three sons. Shem got the middle portion of the earth, Japhet got the northern part (cold and temperate regions) and Ham the southern part (hot and tropical). Details of this division are contained in the Book of Jubilees, VIII, 8–30. Subsequently, the sons of Noah sub divided their portions to their children (Book of Jubilees, IX: 1–15). This subsequent division was ratified by Noah who bound them with an oath not to trespass into lands not allocated to them:

> And thus the sons of Noah divided unto their sons in the presence of Noah their father, and he bound them all by an oath, imprecating a curse on every one that sought to seize the portion which had not fallen (to him) by his lot (Book of Jubilees, IX: 18).

So, it is curious how Canaan and his children ended up in the Levant when they were supposed to go to the South, with the other sons of Ham. When Ham divided his portion of land among his children, he gave Canaan the westernmost part of his land, beyond the portion allocated to Put (present day Libya). So, Cannan was to take the land west of Put (this is supposedly comprising of today's Algeria, possibly Tunisia, Morocco, Western Sahara, Mali, Mauritania and beyond (the sea–Atlantic Ocean):

> And Ham divided amongst his sons, and the first portion came forth for Cush towards the east, and to the west of him for Mizraim, and to the west of him for Put, and to the west of him [and to the west thereof] on the sea for Canaan. (Book of Jubilees, IX: 1).

After the dispersal from Babel, Ham and his children left Shinar to take possession of the land allocated to them, however, when Canaan saw the Levant, he fell in love with it and decided to settle there with his children. His father and brothers frowned at this, aware that he was trespassing into the portion allocated to Shem and his children:

> 27. In the fourth week in the first year in the beginning thereof in the four and thirtieth jubilee, were they dispersed from the land of Shinar.28. And Ham and his sons went into the land which he was to occupy, which he acquired as his portion in the land of the south. 29. And Canaan saw the land of Lebanon to the river of Egypt that it was very good, and he went not into the land of his inheritance to the west (that is to) the sea, and he dwelt in the land of Lebanon, eastward and westward from the border of Jordan and from the border of the sea. 30. And Ham, his father, and Cush and Mizraim, his brothers, said unto him: «Thou hast

ESTABLISHMENT OF THE NATION OF GOD

settled in a land which. is not thine, and which did not fall to us by lot: do not do so; for if thou dost do so, thou and thy sons will fall in the land and (be) accursed through sedition; for by sedition ye have settled, and by sedition will thy children fall, and thou shalt be rooted out for ever. 31. Dwell not in the dwelling of Shem; for to Shem and to his sons did it come by their lot. 32. Cursed art thou, and cursed shalt thou be beyond all the sons of Noah, by the curse by which we bound ourselves by an oath in the presence of the holy judge, and in the presence of Noah our father." 33. But he did not hearken unto them, and dwelt in the land of Lebanon from Hamath to the entering of Egypt, he and his sons until this day. 34. And for this reason that land is named Canaan. (Book of Jubilees, X: 27–34).

However, the Levant, the land Canaan occupied is the same piece of Land that God reserved for himself, during the subsequent division of the lands among the sons of God, after the dispersal. So as the sons of Noah and their children were taking possession of the lands allocated to them, God was assigning those lands to the sons of God to supervise affairs in these lands.

The descendants of Canaan (at least some of them) occupied this land until the Israelites returned from Egypt:

> [15] Canaan fathered Sidon his firstborn and Heth, [16] and the Jebusites, the Amorites, the Girgashites, [17] the Hivites, the Arkites, the Sinites, [18] the Arvadites, the Zemarites, and the Hamathites. Afterward the clans of the Canaanites dispersed. [19] And the territory of the Canaanites extended from Sidon in the direction of Gerar as far as Gaza, and in the direction of Sodom, Gomorrah, Admah, and Zeboiim, as far as Lasha. (Genesis 10:16–19 ESV).

The land of Canaan was also a hotspot for postdiluvian giants. Why the giants decided to settle in Canaan is a matter of opinion. It seems that giants who were being eradicated from other lands finally settled in Canaan and lived among the descendants of Canaan. Perhaps there was something going on among the Canaanites that was attractive to these beings. Some of the renegade sons of God may even have been the progenitors of the post-diluvian giants, by mating with Canaanites (a post-diluvian repetition of Genesis 6). Although, there is little evidence to support this, this is a plausible angle that needs to be seriously considered, while trying to decipher the origin of the post-diluvian giants. The Bible records that there were giants living among the children of Canaan and may have interbred with them. Amos indicates that the Amorites (descendants of Canaan) were gigantic in nature, by comparing their heights to be like cedar and their strength like an oak:

> ⁹ "Yet it was I who destroyed the Amorite before them,
> whose height was like the height of the cedars
> and who was as strong as the oaks;
> I destroyed his fruit above
> and his roots beneath. (Amos 2:9 NIV).

It may also be that when the sons of God went rogue, they inspired the people under their control to trespass into the land God allocated to himself, as a way to spite God. It can be assumed that part of the derailment of the sons of God in charge of different lands/nations was that the nations they oversaw started encroaching into other nations, through wars. One nation would fight another nation for their lands and take control of it and by so doing, the sons of God would expand their influence over other territories that fell under the control of the nation they oversee. So even the land God reserved for himself was not spared and they encroached upon it. Thus, it can be construed that all the people living in Canaan at the time the Israelites came to the land after their exodus from Egypt were trespassers and usurpers, with no legitimate claim to it. By the time the children of Jacob/Israel made their way out of Egypt, large chunks of the land of Canaan were already occupied by post diluvian giants such as the Anakim and the Raphaim[5] (see Section 6.3), living among the sons of Canaan.

The emergence of giants after the flood was an aberration to the post-diluvian order, God had established. Eventually, it became a problem to the descendants of Noah, that God had to compel the descendants of Abraham and other pure races to wipe them all out and dispossess them of the lands they had settled in, whenever the opportunity arose. Many non-believers have accused Israelites of carrying out wholesome genocide of various races they encountered after their exodus from Egypt, and God sanctioning such atrocities. However, such criticisms are due to apparent ignorance of the origins of these races and their abhorrent history, which warrants their elimination. Simply put, they are not humans, and the earth was made for humans. The earth is not made as

---

5. It appears that collectively, the post flood giants may have been referred to as the Rephaim: 10 *The Emim formerly lived there, a people great and many, and tall as the Anakim. 11 Like the Anakim they are also counted as Rephaim, but the Moabites call them Emim.* (Deuteronomy 2:10–11 ESV).

an abode for celestial or hybrids emanating from them. Any human-like being that is not human living on the earth is an illegitimate occupier. Hence, the apparent genocidal wars by Israelites against the various nations they encountered in Canaan were essentially an attempt to rid the earth of the post-diluvian giants.

This eradication of the giants began long before the Israelites came into Canaan. Chedorlaomer king of Elam, defeated various groups of the Rephaim during the time of Abraham:

> 5 In the fourteenth year Chedorlaomer and the kings who were with him came and defeated the Rephaim in Ashteroth-karnaim, the Zuzim in Ham, the Emim in Shaveh-kiriathaim, 6 and the Horites in their hill country of Seir as far as El-paran on the border of the wilderness. 7 Then they turned back and came to En-mishpat (that is, Kadesh) and defeated all the country of the Amalekites, and also the Amorites who were dwelling in Hazazon-tamar. (Genesis 14:5–7 ESV).

Long before the Israelites came into the land, other descendants and relatives of Abraham contended with the giants and took over their land after destroying them. The Edomites (descendants of Esau), the Moabites and the Ammonites (descendants of Lot fought with the giants. The Emites were defeated and chased out of Ar by Moabites (Deuteronomy 2:9–11), the Zamzummim were defeated and dispossessed by the Ammonites (Deuteronomy 2:20–21), the Horites, were chased out of Seir by descendants of Esau, and the Avvim, who lived in villages as far as Gaza, were defeated and dispossessed by the Caphtorim (descendants of Egypt - Genesis 10:13):

> 20 (That too was considered a land of the Rephaites, who used to live there; but the Ammonites called them Zamzummites. 21 They were a people strong and numerous, and as tall as the Anakites. The Lord destroyed them from before the Ammonites, who drove them out and settled in their place. 22 The Lord had done the same for the descendants of Esau, who lived in Seir, when he destroyed the Horites from before them. They drove them out and have lived in their place to this day. 23 And as for the Avvites who lived in villages as far as Gaza, the Caphtorites coming out from Caphtor destroyed them and settled in their place.) (Deuteronomy 2:20–23 NIV).

Hence, the Exodus was the time for the children of Jacob to take a stab at the post-diluvian giants as their cousins had done before them.

Moses led Israelites to annihilate most of the giant tribes on their way to Canaan. Prominent among these were two Amorite kings, King Og of Bashan and King Sihon of Heshbon whom Moses devoted to destruction. Shihon and his army were roundly defeated at the Battle of Jahaz and all inhabitants were killed by the Israeli army:

> [32] *When Sihon and all his army came out to meet us in battle at Jahaz,* [33] *the Lord our God delivered him over to us and we struck him down, together with his sons and his whole army.* [34] *At that time we took all his towns and completely destroyed them—men, women and children. We left no survivors. (Deuteronomy 2: 32-34 NIV).*

King Og was the last of the Rephaites and was defeated at the Battle of Edrei:

> *Next we turned and went up along the road toward Bashan, and Og king of Bashan with his whole army marched out to meet us in battle at Edrei.* [2] *The Lord said to me, "Do not be afraid of him, for I have delivered him into your hands, along with his whole army and his land. Do to him what you did to Sihon king of the Amorites, who reigned in Heshbon."*
> [3] *So the Lord our God also gave into our hands Og king of Bashan and all his army. We struck them down, leaving no survivors.* [4] *At that time we took all his cities. There was not one of the sixty cities that we did not take from them—the whole region of Argob, Og's kingdom in Bashan. (Deuteronomy 3:1-4 NIV).*

> [11] *(Og king of Bashan was the last of the Rephaites. His bed was decorated with iron and was more than nine cubits long and four cubits wide. It is still in Rabbah of the Ammonites.) (Deuteronomy 3:11 NIV).*

Under Joshua, the Israelites contended mainly with the Anakim in Canaan. The Anakims were identified in Numbers 13 as Nephilim of great height (giants):

> "The land, through which we have gone to spy it out, is a land that devours its inhabitants, and all the people that we saw in it are of great height. [33] And there we saw the Nephilim (the sons of Anak, who come from the Nephilim), and we seemed to ourselves like grasshoppers, and so we seemed to them." *(Numbers 13:32-33 ESV).*

ESTABLISHMENT OF THE NATION OF GOD

Moses had charged Joshua to annihilate all the giants and take possession of the promise land. Despite the frightening reports of the spies, Joshua launched a devastating campaign against many Anakim nations:

> [21] *And at that time came Joshua, and cut off the Anakims from the mountains, from Hebron, from Debir, from Anab, and from all the mountains of Judah, and from all the mountains of Israel: Joshua destroyed them utterly with their cities.*
>
> [22] *There was none of the Anakims left in the land of the children of Israel: only in Gaza, in Gath, and in Ashdod, there remained.*
>
> [23] *So Joshua took the whole land, according to all that the Lord said unto Moses; and Joshua gave it for an inheritance unto Israel according to their divisions by their tribes. And the land rested from war. (Joshua 11:21–23 KJV).*

As the passage informs, Joshua almost destroyed all the Anakim except for a few that remained in Gaza, in Gath, and in Ashdod (*Joshua 11: 21–22*). Incidentally, it is from these parts of Gaza that Goliath, who David encountered, and his brother giants came from. So, David continued from where Joshua left it. After the encounter with Goliath, David and his men encountered and killed other giants in Philistines among whom were Goliath's brother:

> [4] And after this there arose war with the Philistines at Gezer. Then Sibbecai the Hushathite struck down Sippai, who was one of the descendants of the giants, and the Philistines were subdued. [5] And there was again war with the Philistines, and Elhanan the son of Jair struck down Lahmi the brother of Goliath the Gittite, the shaft of whose spear was like a weaver's beam. *(1 Chronicles 20:4–5 ESV).*

> [15] There was war again between the Philistines and Israel, and David went down together with his servants, and they fought against the Philistines. And David grew weary. [16] And Ishbi-benob, one of the descendants of the giants, whose spear weighed three hundred shekels of bronze, and who was armed with a new sword, thought to kill David. [17] But Abishai the son of Zeruiah came to his aid and attacked the Philistine and killed him. Then David's men swore to him, "You shall no longer go out with us to battle, lest you quench the lamp of Israel."

> [18] After this there was again war with the Philistines at Gob. Then Sibbecai the Hushathite struck down Saph, who was one of the descendants of the giants. [19] And there was again war with

the Philistines at Gob, and Elhanan the son of Jaare-oregim, the Bethlehemite, struck down Goliath the Gittite, the shaft of whose spear was like a weaver's beam. ²⁰ And there was again war at Gath, where there was a man of great stature, who had six fingers on each hand, and six toes on each foot, twenty-four in number, and he also was descended from the giants. ²¹ And when he taunted Israel, Jonathan the son of Shimei, David's brother, struck him down. ²² These four were descended from the giants in Gath, and they fell by the hand of David and by the hand of his servants. *(2 Samuel 21: 15–21 ESV).*

Despite all the attempts made to eradicate the giants from the earth, it is obvious that some of them escaped destruction and ran to safety beyond the reach of the children of Israel. The skeletons of giants have been found around the world such as in the Islands of Sardinia and Paracas[6]. Some of them may still be hiding in certain remote parts of the world such as the giant of Kandahar, allegedly killed by US special forces in 2002, at the height of Operation Enduring Freedom in 2002 launched against the Taliban in Afghanistan[7]. Numerous stories about the "Big foot" and Yetis might be pointing towards the existence of these giants till date. Importantly, some of them with diluted genes may have mingled with the pure blood humans over several generations, to produce Nephilim with apparent normal human appearance. They will re-emerge once again towards the end time to join forces with Satan and the antichrist to subjugate humans and takeover control of the earth from humans (see Section 12.4):

> [37] *As it was in the days of Noah, so it will be at the coming of the Son of Man (Matthew 24:37 NIV).*

---

6. Gillian, "How DNA Testing", 1
7. Giacomazzo, "The Real Story", 1

CHAPTER 9

The World Under Dark Forces

9.1 THE WORLD UNDER THE CAPTIVITY OF SATAN

Before the coming of Christ, Satan held sway as the ruler of the world, having almost cornered the world and all its rulers, except for a few minorities keeping the righteous ordinances of God. In this regard, he was controlling all the kingdoms of the world who were inadvertently doing his bidding. When Christ appeared on the scene, Satan brazenly told him that he was in charge of the world. While tempting Christ, Satan showed him the kingdoms of the world and asserted his lordship over them:

> [8] Again, the devil took him to a very high mountain and showed him all the kingdoms of the world and their glory. [9] And he said to him, "All these I will give you, if you will fall down and worship me." (Matthew 4: 8–9 ESV).

Satan could not have offered to give the kingdoms of the world to Christ, if they don't already belong to him. This was also buttressed with the illuminating story in Job when the Sons of God came to present themselves before God:

> [6] Now there was a day when the sons of God came to present themselves before the Lord, and Satan also came among them. [7] The Lord said to Satan, "From where have you come?" Satan answered the Lord and said, "From going to and fro on the earth, and from walking up and down on it." [8] And the Lord said to Satan, "Have you considered my servant Job, that there is none like him on the earth, a blameless and upright man, who

fears God and turns away from evil?" ⁹ Then Satan answered the Lord and said, "Does Job fear God for no reason? ¹⁰ Have you not put a hedge around him and his house and all that he has, on every side? You have blessed the work of his hands, and his possessions have increased in the land. ¹¹ But stretch out your hand and touch all that he has, and he will curse you to your face." ¹² And the Lord said to Satan, "Behold, all that he has is in your hand. Only against him do not stretch out your hand." So Satan went out from the presence of the Lord. (Job 1: 6–12 ESV).

Supposedly, this was a routine gathering where the Sons of God are given the opportunity to report back on their activities and what they had been up to. It must be factored in that God delegates authority to the heavenly beings to oversee various aspects of His creations, hence, the need for them to report back. This was the backdrop of the occasion.

Surprisingly, despite being an adversary of God, Satan attended this event. One may ask what for? Was he not cast out of heaven? What gave him the impetus to appear where the Sons of God were appearing? To illuminate on this a bit, it should be considered that Satan still regards himself as a Son of God, hence, the reason he presented himself at this gathering. But which aspect of God's creation was he in charge of that he came to present a report on during that assembly? Well, Satan himself provided the answer. When asked by God where he had come from, which is a way of God asking him to render his account. Satan responded by stating that he has been walking to and fro the earth and up and down it. On the face of it, this may appear that Satan was saying he was aimlessly perambulating around the earth. However, there is a much deeper meaning to what he was saying. Although, it may not be obvious, this was Satan's way of asserting that he was in total control of all parts of the earth (*to and fro the earth and up and down it*), and to insinuate that virtually all humans were under his control. God understanding this, threw a jibe at him with Job, by asking if he had noticed that Job had been very faithful to God and not under Satan's rule. Infuriated by this, Satan, while indirectly acknowledging that Job was not under his control, claimed it was because of the extra help Job was receiving from God, which makes it difficult for Satan to get across to him.

This appearance of Satan among the gathering of the sons of God, was not a one-off thing, because he appeared again in another gathering of the sons of God, and God brought up the case of Job once again:

THE WORLD UNDER DARK FORCES

2 Again there was a day when the sons of God came to present themselves before the Lord, and Satan also came among them to present himself before the Lord. ² And the Lord said to Satan, "From where have you come?" Satan answered the Lord and said, "From going to and fro on the earth, and from walking up and down on it." ³ And the Lord said to Satan, "Have you considered my servant Job, that there is none like him on the earth, a blameless and upright man, who fears God and turns away from evil? He still holds fast his integrity, although you incited me against him to destroy him without reason." ⁴ Then Satan answered the Lord and said, "Skin for skin! All that a man has he will give for his life. ⁵ But stretch out your hand and touch his bone and his flesh, and he will curse you to your face." ⁶ And the Lord said to Satan, "Behold, he is in your hand; only spare his life." (Job 2:2-6 ESV).

This encounter with Job was a confirmation that the world was virtually in the pocket of Satan, and he was the entity representing the earth in the gathering of the sons of God. However, the world under Satan was a dark world filled with all sorts of wickedness and immorality. Hence, Christ came to the world to liberate humans from the captivity of Satan:

> ¹³ Who hath delivered us from the power of darkness, and hath translated us into the kingdom of his dear Son:
> ¹⁴ In whom we have redemption through his blood, even the forgiveness of sins: (Colossians 1:13-14 KJV).

This is at the core of the redemptive story surrounding his first coming. He made this clear when he was given the scroll to read at the synagogue and he read from the book of Isaiah, setting out the objectives of his first coming:

> ¹⁷ And the scroll of the prophet Isaiah was given to him. He unrolled the scroll and found the place where it was written,
>
> ¹⁸ "The Spirit of the Lord is upon me,
>   because he has anointed me
>   to proclaim good news to the poor.
> He has sent me to proclaim liberty to the captives
>   and recovering of sight to the blind,
>   to set at liberty those who are oppressed,
>   ¹⁹ to proclaim the year of the Lord's favor."
>
> ²⁰ And he rolled up the scroll and gave it back to the attendant and sat down. (Luke 4:17-4:21 ESV).

Even though Satan controls the world (kingdoms of the world), he doesn't necessarily control the earth. The Bible says that the earth is the Lord's:

> The earth is the Lord's and the fullness thereof,
>   the world and those who dwell therein,
> ² for he has founded it upon the seas
>   and established it upon the rivers. (Psalm 24: 1–2 KJV).

While Satan lays claim to the kingdoms of the world, he doesn't necessarily claim the ownership of the earth. Hence, Satan's critical goal is to control every aspect of the earth. To achieve this, Satan plans to control every human, render them completely useless to God, and destroy them, so that he and his cohorts can inherit the earth:

> ¹⁰ The thief comes only to steal and kill and destroy. I came that they may have life and have it abundantly. (John 10: 10 ESV).

9.2 THE STRUCTURE OF SATAN'S GOVERNMENT OVER THE WORLD

One may wonder if Satan controls the kingdoms of the world, how does he do it? Well, Satan has a hierarchical governance structure, that involves a lot of celestial and human entities. The structure resembles a pyramid with Satan at the peak of the pyramid, followed by fallen angels who masquerade as gods. Below the fallen angels are the demons and their human agents that control various aspects of the world. Under this hierarchical structure, the earth is subdivided into many territories and a prince is assigned over each territory. This territory could be an entire continent or a country. Each prince has other lower level fallen angels and demons working for him, who in turn control partitions of this territory and their human agents. Depending on the spiritual atmosphere pervading the space, more than one prince can be assigned over a country. Hence, a country may be split into multiple territories than another, with fallen angels assigned to each territory. The central idea is to assign enough satanic forces over an area to bring the area under the full authority of Satan.

The principalities and their minions essentially work behind the scenes, while manipulating and using their human agents to physically manifest their powers. As spiritual beings they are not permitted to directly change things on the earth, and going against the cosmic laws has severe consequences. This is not to say they cannot physically manifest on earth, but when they do, their powers are whittled down greatly to those of humans, hence, their preferred mode of operation is to hide behind their human agents to carry out their plans. Hence, the core strategy they adopt is subterfuge, where they use human agents to carry out their nefarious work on earth.

The main interface between the human agents and the satanic forces are through witchcraft and occultism. This has been the modus operandi from time immemorial. There has been a widespread occultism and witchcraft practices in various forms throughout human history, through which humans contact and interact with satanic beings. These practices have not abated among the modern generation but as a matter of fact, have proliferated. Although many of these cults, masquerade with benevolent façade, deep down lies their nefarious nature. The beings are contacted at different levels, some of the interfaces such as witchcraft practices can only contact beings at a particular level, whereas others can go higher in the hierarchy of beings they are in contact with. Hence, a low-level witch/wizard or warlock may be interacting with low level demons and elemental spirits, whereas a grand master of a cult group could be dealing with a territorial prince or even with Satan. Despite the level of interaction, the aim is to hijack a nation and everything in it to bring it under the authority of Satan.

9.2.1 Principalities and their Modus Operandi

The princes who work with Satan are mainly the rebellious sons of God who reneged on their duties to oversee the nations. Prior to their denouncement, God gave them authority to oversee the nations, but they later deviated from their missions and were judged and condemned (see sections 7.1 and 7.3). These renegade sons of God, who he referred to as gods in Psalm 82:6 are sitting at the top hierarchy of the dark forces– among the top echelon of Satan's council. At this level sits gods like Baal, Moloch, Marduk, Dagon etc.

This is in addition to the celestial beings who participated with Satan during the rebellion in heaven. Many of the angels who fell with Satan after their rebellion was squashed, settled within the Second Heaven. The Watchers who came to earth to procreate with earthly women, were captured and imprisoned in the bottomless pit (2 Peter 2:4, Jude 1:6). So, it is safe to assume that they are not part of the princes working with Satan. Rather the spirits of their offspring work with Satan as demonic forces unleashed against humans. These demonic forces roam the earth, as no place was found for them anywhere outside the earth, because they are aberrations to God's creative plan. Because they have been disembodied, they seek to hijack human bodies so they can continue to experience and satiate their desires through those individuals (see Section 6.5). Worthy to note here that the demons operating with Satan are only one-tenth, with the remaining locked up in the bottomless pit (Book of Jubilees, 10: 8–9).

The governance structure Satan implemented is an attempt to mirror God's divine council. It is this structure that humans battle against. The dark council of Satan orchestrate things on earth from the spiritual abode in the Second Heaven. Paul cautioned about this, declaring that we wrestle *against principalities, against powers, against the rulers of the darkness of this world, against spiritual wickedness in high places* (Ephesians 6:12). This statement sheds a light into the key hierarchy of the satanic kingdom. This stratification of the beings in satanic kingdom is probably because Satan rebelled with celestial beings from various ranks, who probably maintained their ranks and powers in the dark kingdom.

The process of hijacking a nation starts in a very subtle way both at individual and territorial levels. The demons act like foot soldiers for the dark kingdom. They mainly work on individuals, slowly hijacking their minds and actions. When most individuals in a particular community or territory have been demonised, the entire community is technically demonised and will become malleable to the influences of demonic forces. At territorial levels, the demons and principalities work on the leaders of the territory to manipulate the policies and laws that are used to regulate the territory. This is the reason many prominent influencers, politicians and leaders of various nations belong to one cult or the other. The cult serves as an interface through which the individuals can communicate with the celestial entities of darkness. They receive their instructions from their spiritual masters and execute them on earth. In return they are made wealthy, powerful, and influential. One can hardly ascend to these levels without taking certain oaths of allegiance to these satanic forces through the cults they are coerced to join. When the laws and policies are implemented or changed to align with the objectives of Satan, the territory aligns with Satanic rule. The moves are very gradual and subtle and may take many years before a particular objective is achieved. But once achieved, it permeates through every fabric of that territory and becomes normalised. This will then become part of the existing culture and practice in such an area. Hence, a certain practice or behaviour that was once considered abhorrent in a particular area for a while, would become an accepted norm after a couple of years after satanic influence has pervaded the space. From the cultural level, these will make their way into the economy and commerce of the area. At this point, the livelihood of the residents of the area are tied to these demonic cultures and practices. When it gets to this point it is usually extremely difficult to push away the territorial spirits as the people benefiting from those practices will be the vanguards of attack on anyone who wishes to change these. The territorial spirits can literally go to sleep at this point as they have gained complete control of the area. And it would be an uphill task to dislodge such a norm or practice. The climax of the hijacking of a territory is the rejection of God and open worship of demons and gods. This was the case in Nimrod's Babylonian kingdom and other instances in the Bible such as Sodom and Gomorrah.

Apart from working through human elements, in rare occasions, they spirits could also influence the physical elements such as water, fire and air to achieve a particular purpose. Such attacks were launched at Christ and Paul when they embarked on critical missions that could dislodge the influence of Satan over an area. On several occasions Christ came under severe storms aimed at preventing Him and the apostles from arriving at a particular territory. A prominent example is the storm that Christ and his apostles encountered while trying to enter the territory of the Gerasenes (Mark 4: 35–41). Following this passage was the encounter with the demoniac, as soon as they landed on the territory of the Gerasenes (Mark: 5). A careful read of these two passages would reveal that the purpose of the storm was to stop Christ from entering that territory. The principalities and demonic influences over the area having seen what Christ had done in other areas he had preached the gospel, were bent on preventing Him from entering their territory. As soon as Christ and his apostles came into the Gerasenes, having calmed the storm, they were confronted by the dangerous demoniac. The story narrated in the passage is so enlightening and profound, showing the inner workings in the dark kingdom. It revealed that the demons knew who Christ was, were terrified of him, and knew he was coming into the territory:

> They came to the other side of the sea, to the country of the Gerasenes. ² And when Jesus had stepped out of the boat, immediately there met him out of the tombs a man with an unclean spirit. ³ He lived among the tombs. And no one could bind him anymore, not even with a chain, ⁴ for he had often been bound with shackles and chains, but he wrenched the chains apart, and he broke the shackles in pieces. No one had the strength to subdue him. ⁵ Night and day among the tombs and on the mountains he was always crying out and cutting himself with stones. ⁶ And when he saw Jesus from afar, he ran and fell down before him. ⁷ And crying out with a loud voice, he said, "What have you to do with me, Jesus, Son of the Most-High God? I adjure you by God, do not torment me." ⁸ For he was saying to him, "Come out of the man, you unclean spirit!" ⁹ And Jesus asked him, "What is your name?" He replied, "My name is Legion, for we are many." ¹⁰ And he begged him earnestly not to send them out of the country. ¹¹ Now a great herd of pigs was feeding there on the hillside, ¹² and they begged him, saying, "Send us to the pigs; let us enter them." ¹³ So he gave them permission. And the unclean spirits came out and entered the pigs; and the herd, numbering about two thousand, rushed down the steep bank into the sea and drowned in the sea. (Mark 4: 1–13 ESV).

Very instructive to note here is that the residents of the territory, having heard what Jesus had done and the economic loss of the herds that had drowned in the river, begged Jesus to leave their territory:

> ¹⁴ The herdsmen fled and told it in the city and in the country. And people came to see what it was that had happened. ¹⁵ And they came to Jesus and saw the demon-possessed man, the one who had had the legion, sitting there, clothed and in his right mind, and they were afraid. ¹⁶ And those who had seen it described to them what had happened to the demon-possessed man and to the pigs. ¹⁷ And they began to beg Jesus to depart from their region. (Mark 4: 14–17 ESV).

What happened here is quite illuminating in understanding what goes on in a territory completely under the control of evil spirits. The people asked Jesus to leave their area, because they were worried that judging from what He had done to the herds as he just stepped into their territory, if allowed in, he may wreck their entire economy. They were not confrontational as they were truly terrified of Christ, so they begged. The controlling territorial spirits in that area essentially changed tactics from their earlier confrontational stance to a diplomatic one. The area and the people have completely been influenced by the satanic forces that they were more comfortable living with demoniacs than to allow Jesus to enter their territory to eradicate the demons in their town. The situation in this town reflects the situation in most places that have been wrapped under the influence of Satanic forces, even to this day.

9.2.2 Demons and Modus Operandi

Demons on the other hand do not hold territories. They rather go after human beings or animals to possess them. This is due to their nature as disembodied spirits who have no place prepared for them to live. Hence, they sought other bodies to reside in to continue to live on earth and experience all their desires. So, they are like foot soldiers to the principalities. They hijack human bodies and make them malleable to manipulations so that they could do the will of the principalities.

The process of demonic possession takes different forms and stages, but fundamentally the human target would have to do certain things that would open them up for possession. Usually it starts with demonic influence, which is essentially a battle of the mind where the demons suggest various ideas to their intended victims. Adhering to these suggestions and carrying them out opens the victim up for possession. The individual will continue to be influenced so that more demons may enter the person, until they take full control of the body. The human body is a temple capable of housing spirits–holy or evil spirits. A body not filled with the holy spirit is a target for the demons. Christ made this clear in Mathew, while describing how evil spirits return to their prey:

> [43] "When an evil spirit goes out of a person, it travels over dry country looking for a place to rest. If it can't find one, [44] it says to itself, 'I will go back to my house.' So it goes back and finds the house empty, clean, and all fixed up. [45] Then it goes out and brings along seven other spirits even worse than itself, and they come and live there. So when it is all over, that person is in worse shape than at the beginning. This is what will happen to the evil people of this day." (Matthew 12:43–45 GNT).

Possession can occur through sinful and amorous behaviours, as well as making contact or using physical objects linked to evil forces; dabbling into witchcraft and occultism, using substances (psychedelic/

hallucinogenic drugs), foods entangled with evil spirits (rituals, sacrifices). Certain psychedelic drugs and food can shift human consciousness, hence, making the minds of those individuals consuming them susceptible to demonic influences, attacks and eventual possession[1]. The battle usually starts from the mind and if an individual is captured at that level, it would only be a matter of time before the body also succumbs.

9.2.3 Mind Control

The mind is the spiritual battleground for the forces of good and evil. This is because the mind is an interface between the spirit and the physical. It functions like an antenna that receives signals from the spiritual realm and passes it on to the physical world and vice versa. The dreamworld gives an idea of how the physical meshes with the spiritual–all done in the mind.

The mind is capable of receiving both negative and positive signals. The positive signals/messages emanate from the kingdom of light whereas the negative comes from the kingdom of darkness. The positive signals usually come from God and Christ, when they directly speak to man, through the holy spirit, and the good angels. The mind was essentially made to enable God and man to communicate. When one prays, the thoughts go through the mind to the spiritual. Hence, the disruption of this direct communication between God and humans, is a key strategic objective of Satan and his cohorts.

To disrupt this communication, evil forces send out their own signals which interfere with the signals coming from God to man or from man to God. These signals from the evil forces can emanate from both physical and spiritual sources. Hence, at any point in time, the human mind is bombarded by several signals, which come in the form of thoughts, ideas, intuition, and inspiration. So, the mind struggles to sift through these. The mind is thus the main ground where the spiritual battle is fought, because whichever thought captures the mind, is what would be manifested through the body of the individual to the physical. This concept has also been revealed in some scientific studies. In 1994, Japanese researcher, Masaru Emoto finds that human consciousness directly shapes the physical matter[2]. The battle starts from the subcon-

---

1. Charles, "The Six Types of", 1
2. Emoto, "The Hidden Messages", 1; Radin et al., "Double-blind", 408–11

scious mind and if accepted makes its way to the conscious mind from where it can be vocalised or acted upon. James hinted at this:

> ¹⁴ But each person is tempted when he is lured and enticed by his own desire. ¹⁵ Then desire when it has conceived gives birth to sin, and sin when it is fully grown brings forth death. (James 1: 14–15 ESV).

It is often difficult to distinguish which thought came from the individual or was suggested to it by a spirit. At times the individual may think a thought came from him, but this may have been suggested by a spirit. This was demonstrated in Mathew 16 when Christ asked his disciples who they think he was, and Peter answered that he was the Messiah. While giving this answer, Peter most likely thought that the idea came from him, until he was corrected by Jesus who told him exactly where the thought had emanated from:

> ¹⁷ And Jesus answered and said unto him, Blessed art thou, Simon Barjona: for flesh and blood hath not revealed it unto thee, but my Father which is in heaven. (Matthew 16:17 KJV).

To further demonstrate that the human mind is capable of processing multiple thoughts from different sources, after vocalising the good thought that emanated from God, the next moment, Peter was vocalising an opposing thought from Satan to dissuade Jesus from going to the cross. Having discerned what was going on with Peter, Christ rebuked Satan, which He recognised as the originator of the thought that Peter was vocalising:

> ²² Then Peter took him, and began to rebuke him, saying, Be it far from thee, Lord: this shall not be unto thee.

> ²³ But he turned, and said unto Peter, Get thee behind me, Satan: thou art an offence unto me: for thou savorest not the things that be of God, but those that be of men. (Matthew 16: 22 - 23 KJV).

Continuing from the foregoing, when a thought permeates the mind, it takes root and becomes a stronghold, that determines how a person thinks and acts. Once these strongholds take root, they will start to influence the viewpoint, values, ideologies, or philosophies of the individual. As more strongholds are introduced into the mind of an individual, such a person will gradually begin to change, behaving in a way that matches those strongholds. The negative actions of this individual will subsequently become the gateway through which the demons enter the body of such persons. At this stage, the individual is being influenced by the demons. As this continues, the strongholds will be the anchors that will hold the demons within the individual, thus making it difficult for such individuals to extricate themselves from the demons. With time the lives of such individuals will be in sync with the desires of the demons and to such individuals everything seems normal, even though a careful observer would be able to discern that something had terribly gone wrong with the individual. At this point the individual has been possessed by the demons.

These are the strongholds Paul was referring to that needs to be pulled down and brought under captivity and obedient to Christ:

> [3] For though we walk in the flesh, we do not wage war according to the flesh. [4] For the weapons of our warfare are not fleshly but powerful through God for the tearing down of strongholds. We are tearing down false arguments [5] and every high-minded thing that exalts itself against the knowledge of God. We are taking every thought captive to the obedience of Messiah— [6] ready to punish all disobedience, whenever your obedience is complete. (2 Corinthians 10: 1–18 TLV).

9.2.4 Dislodging Principalities and demons - Christ's Encounter with Territorial Spirits

To dislodge territorial spirits, one needs to start from the root to uproot them. The roots are the people–specifically the minds of the people. Hence, working at individual level to rewire their minds (renewal of mind), to enable them to refocus their attention towards Christ. Renewal of the mind is a key aspect of the repentance process. Preaching to the people, turning their minds away from evil and casting out demons that are holding the people hostage are the various ways the powers of principalities over an area is defeated. Direct confrontation with territorial spirit were hardly deployed by the apostles. When more righteous people rise in an area, the powers of darkness are whittled down. And if this momentum is sustained and righteousness pervades the territory, the influence of evil forces dwindles and, in their place, the good spirits take over. Light attracts light and darkness attracts darkness.

Christ while on earth was constantly doing these things. Wherever he went to preach the good news to the people, key elements that featured were the good news about the kingdom of God, casting out of demons and unclean spirits, healing the people and calling them to repentance and not to return to sin. These are essential ingredients used in dethroning principalities controlling a territory. The disciples of Christ also adopted this strategy.

When the principalities controlling an area feel threatened by effects of the gospel, they usually incite the masses in their territory into a frenzy to fight or attack the individual/s through whom the threat is emanating from. Such individuals can be attacked for superficial reasons, that the people can easily relate to, such as being accused of breaking the law of the land, destroying the community's businesses, lifestyle, values, cultures and so on. This is the point where the greatest spiritual fight ensues. This could be gleaned from various encounters Christ had with evil spirits in different areas he preached, as well as the experiences of the apostles during their evangelistic missions, especially Paul. For instance, when the evil forces sensed that Christ was whittling down their influence across Judea and surrounding areas, they incited the people to kill him. On several occasions the Jews made attempts to kill him. But because they had no authority to do that, they failed. They only succeeded in the final attempt when Christ purposely allowed them to have power over him for a moment, so that the will of God could be accomplished:

> [17] The reason my Father loves me is that I lay down my life— only to take it up again. [18] No one takes it from me, but I lay it down of my own accord. I have authority to lay it down and authority to take it up again. This command I received from my Father." (John 10: 17–18 NIV).

> [11] Jesus answered him, "You would have no authority over me at all unless it had been given you from above. Therefore, he who delivered me over to you has the greater sin." (John 19:11 ESV).

Paul also encountered many of this type of incitement of the people against him, when his gospels began to threaten the territorial spirits in the territories, he was spreading the gospel in. One of such encounters is the one at Philippi, with the slave girl who had the spirit of divination in her, which she used to rake in a lot of money for her master. This led to Paul and his companion being beaten and sent to prison:

> ¹⁶ As we were going to the place of prayer, we were met by a slave girl who had a spirit of divination and brought her owners much gain by fortune-telling. ¹⁷ She followed Paul and us, crying out, "These men are servants of the Most High God, who proclaim to you the way of salvation." ¹⁸ And this she kept doing for many days. Paul, having become greatly annoyed, turned and said to the spirit, "I command you in the name of Jesus Christ to come out of her." And it came out that very hour.
> ¹⁹ But when her owners saw that their hope of gain was gone, they seized Paul and Silas and dragged them into the marketplace before the rulers. ²⁰ And when they had brought them to the magistrates, they said, "These men are Jews, and they are disturbing our city. ²¹ They advocate customs that are not lawful for us as Romans to accept or practice." ²² The crowd joined in attacking them, and the magistrates tore the garments off them and gave orders to beat them with rods. ²³ And when they had inflicted many blows upon them, they threw them into prison, ordering the jailer to keep them safely. ²⁴ Having received this order, he put them into the inner prison and fastened their feet in the stocks. (Acts 16:16–24 ESV).

Paul had several of such attacks inspired by supernatural forces that he became a veteran in this sort of spiritual warfare and hence his advice on how to go about this sort of battle:

> Finally, be strong in the Lord and in the strength of his might. ¹¹ Put on the whole armor of God, that you may be able to stand against the schemes of the devil. ¹² For we do not wrestle against flesh and blood, but against the rulers, against the authorities, against the cosmic powers over this present darkness, against the spiritual forces of evil in the heavenly places. ¹³ Therefore take up the whole armor of God, that you may be able to withstand in the evil day, and having done all, to stand firm. ¹⁴ Stand therefore, having fastened on the belt of truth, and having put on the breastplate of righteousness, ¹⁵ and, as shoes for your feet, having put on the readiness given by the gospel of peace. ¹⁶ In all circumstances take up the shield of faith, with which you can extinguish all the flaming darts of the evil one; ¹⁷ and take the helmet of salvation, and the sword of the Spirit, which is the word of God, ¹⁸ praying at all times in the Spirit, with all prayer and supplication. To that end, keep alert with all perseverance, making supplication for all the saints, (Ephesians 6:10–18 ESV).

Many early Christians were martyred in this guise in several places where they took the gospel to. The highlight being the martyrdom in Rome, where Emperor Nero used trump up charges to launch a brutal massacre of many Christians using various cruel and horrific means.

For an individual to resist or dislodge demons, one must guard against negative suggestions and thoughts that bombard the mind, so that such thoughts do not become strongholds. One of the easiest ways to accomplish this is to consciously fill the mind with positive/holy thoughts as suggested by Paul:

> [8] Finally, brothers, whatever is true, whatever is honorable, whatever is just, whatever is pure, whatever is lovely, whatever is commendable, if there is any excellence, if there is anything worthy of praise, think about these things. (Philippians 4: 8).

This aligns with age long saying, which holds that *"as a man thinketh, so is he"*. What one fills his mind with is what will control him.

9.3 ANCIENT EGYPT: THE EPITOME OF THE WORLD UNDER SATANIC INFLUENCE

Egypt is a prominent country mentioned severally in the Bible from the Old to the New Testament. There was an active relationship between Egypt and Israel. The ancient Egypt was about the greatest civilization the contemporary world has witnessed. Many artifacts of this civilization such as the pyramid are still present. Contrary to general opinion in the scientific community, this civilization was arguably, built after the flood, for the following reasons. Firstly, Egypt did not exist as a nation before the flood, because the progenitor of the nation of Egypt/Mizraim was the grandson of Noah, according to the table of nations:

> [6] The sons of Ham:
> Cush, Egypt, Put and Canaan. (Genesis 10: 6 NIV).

Secondly, there is no significant water damage in prominent landmarks of the Egyptian civilization such as the Great Pyramid of Giza.[3] If the pyramids were already in place before the flood, there would have been evidence of the devastating impact of the flood on the pyramid. Thirdly, the pyramids were built on sedimentary rock layer (fossil-bearing

---

3. Hodge, "Were the Pyramids", 1

rock layers) from the Flood[4]. Supposedly, the original god of Egypt was one of the sons of God given charge over the nation. This god eventually fell like the others and became a renegade. Supposedly, he teamed up with other forces and began to build a civilization possibly similar to the Atlantean civilization, to rival God. This god may have teamed up with other fallen gods in this endeavor that Egypt eventually became a melting pot of the fallen ones.

One thing that is not readily obvious was that in ancient Egypt, humans and spirits were actively interacting. Many Gods of the Egyptians were represented as hybrids of humans and animals. The power of the gods and other angelic beings were made manifest in this civilization. These gods were practically living amongst men. This continued until God judged the gods of Egypt before the exodus of Israelites from the land:

> [12] For I will pass through the land of Egypt this night, and will smite all the firstborn in the land of Egypt, both man and beast; and against all the gods of Egypt I will execute judgment: I am the Lord. (Exodus 12:12 KJV).

The exodus of Hebrews from Egypt was a clear demonstration of God's power over the renegade sons of God (gods) and his plan to rescue the nations from the grip of the false gods. God is calling out his true sons from nations under the clutches of Satan and renegade gods. Hence the declaration that "out of Egypt I called my son" (Hosea 11:1 ESV). This is the purpose of the gospel, to bring light to the people under dark forces.

The events in ancient Egypt, with all its key characteristics will be played out again during the end time. The whole world will once again come under the influence of dark forces, when the fallen ones fall from heaven (Matthew 24:29, Revelation 6:13), after they lose the battle there. Satan will replicate conditions like in the ancient Egypt across the world. This is one of Satan's key targets during the end time. The Beast System that will be headed by the antichrist will be a mirror of the ancient Egypt but supercharged with more wicked and evil ones and activities than the Egyptian one as Satan and all the fallen ones, who have been chased down from the Second Heaven and those from the underworld (bottomless pit) will be present on earth at this time. These evil entities will be allowed a short time to exercise their authority over all nations on earth alongside the beast:

4. Cosner and Carter, "Were the Egyptian", 1

[5] The beast was given a mouth to utter proud words and blasphemies and to exercise its authority for forty-two months. [6] It opened its mouth to blaspheme God, and to slander his name and his dwelling place and those who live in heaven. [7] It was given power to wage war against God's holy people and to conquer them. And it was given authority over every tribe, people, language and nation. (Revelation 13: 5 NIV).

CHAPTER 10

The First Coming of Christ–Redemption of Man from Darkness

10.1 COSMIC LEGALISM

The laws of God are immutable and irrevocable principles that govern every aspect of God's creation. For anything God created such as planets, luminaries, fire, air, water, and beings (angels and humans), there are always laws they must obey to continue functioning in the established order. Physicists and mathematicians have managed to discover some of the laws governing the physical world, and some of the spiritual laws (under quantum physics). Despite the efforts of man to unravel God, there are yet many other laws yet to be discovered.

The breach of any of the laws established by God by the respective creatures will cause an imbalance that would affect the functioning of that creature, and indirect impact on others. Hence, any breach of these laws has severe consequences, including death:

> [32] Though they know God's righteous decree that those who practice such things deserve to die, they not only do them but give approval to those who practice them. (Romans 1:32 ESV).

For some of the laws, any breach of them will cause instant repercussions. For instance, if someone jumps from a cliff or high-rise building, he will surely land on the ground because the law of gravity will kick in. In the same vein, when Uzzah touched the Ark of the Covenant, while trying to prevent it from falling, he died instantly (2 Samuel 6:1-7 and 1 Chronicles 13:9-12), because he was in breach of the law given to Moses about who could touch or go near the ark. Similarly, when the sons of Aaron (Nadab and Abihu), made attempt to offer a sacrifice (burning incense) to God, which they were not authorised to, they died instantly (consumed by fire-Leviticus 10).

Some other laws, when breached can be argued out in a trial in the court of God. For instance, before God judged the Watchers, they were brought before him to plead their cases, and their sentences read directly to them (*Book of Enoch 15:4-7*). Psalm 82 also illustrates this with a snippet of the judgement of the renegade Gods.

When God sits in judgement, He considers the breaches of the laws and applies the relevant judgement/punishment. For instance, when Adam sinned, the law that states a soul that sinneth shall die was applied. Adam who God created to be immortal was brought down to level of a mortal who shall die.

Satan was called an accuser of the brethren, who accused them before God, day and night (Revelation 12:10), which suggests that he brings cases to God, against anyone (humans and angels), whom he believed has breached the laws of God. Having been in close proximity to God, he is probably well versed in the laws of God and their nuances. He can easily sniff out when any of these laws are being broken. Having been kicked out of heaven for breaking God's laws, while attempting to overthrow God, he plans to get as many humans and angels as possible to break the laws, so that they can face similar consequences. Or perhaps if he can prove that all have sinned and contravened one law of God or the other, he may make God to change his mind and forgive him or face the anguish of seeing His creatures languishing in hell. Hence, one of his key strategies is to deploy subtlety to make his targets to breach the laws of God, and he would use this to bring a case against them before God. A classic example of this was what he did to Adam and Eve. Adam was his ultimate target. He wanted to make Adam to break the law of God governing his original nature. To get to Adam, he worked through his wife. And as soon as Adam failed, the consequences kicked in instantly as something happened to Adam and Eve transforming them from beings of light to beings of flesh-they changed, lost their glory and their eyes opened - Genesis 3:7 (see Section 4.4). Notice that this transformation had already taken place, even before God came to check on them and read out the rest of the consequences of their actions. Also, with the fall of Adam and their transformation, a new form of law kicked in. They must be stopped from becoming immortal in that fleshy and fallen state:

> ²² And the Lord God said, Behold, the man is become as one of us, to know good and evil: and now, lest he put forth his hand, and take also of the tree of life, and eat, and live for ever (Genesis 3: 22 KJV).

Observe that this was not an issue in their former state. God was not worried that they can reach out to the tree of life. As a matter of fact, they were not prohibited from reaching out their hands and eating from the tree of life before their fall. It can also be safely assumed that other laws governing mortal beings were activated after the fall. These were the laws Adam, and his descendants must keep, to continue to function as mortal human beings.

Hence, the laws that were eventually codified by Moses, transcended from Adam to his descendants. These are the cosmic laws established by God for humans to comply with while living on earth. Long before the commandments were given through Moses to Israelites, the law for mortal beings was already in place. The universal laws established by God has been around long before Moses. The line of Seth has been guided by such laws, whereas those of Cain have been violators of the laws. Sodom and Gomorrah were destroyed (long before Moses gave the laws to the Israelites) because they sinned against this universal canon. Sin cannot exist where there is no law. The antediluvian world was destroyed because of sin. So, there was a law already in place during that period. Sin came into this world through Adam, who transgressed the commands of God, and this was sustained by his descendants:

> ¹² Therefore, just as sin came into the world through one man, and death through sin, and so death spread to all men because all sinned— ¹³ for sin indeed was in the world before the law was given, but sin is not counted where there is no law. ¹⁴ Yet death reigned from Adam to Moses, even over those whose sinning was not like the transgression of Adam, who was a type of the one who was to come. (Romans 5:12 -14 ESV).

Many modern-day Christians tend not to recognise that the laws of God have been observed by the righteous ones even before Moses gave the 10 commandments. Although, these laws may not have been codified, there were guiding principles that the ante-diluvian world were living by. If there were not, God would not have judged that world

THE FIRST COMING OF CHRIST—REDEMPTION OF MAN FROM DARKNESS

through the flood. It was through the standards of these ante-diluvian laws that the righteous and wicked were able to be separated. Many of them were judged for idolatry, sexual immorality, and other forms of sins/wickedness:

> 8.2 And there was great impiety, and much fornication, and they went astray, and all their ways became corrupt. (The Book of Enoch 8:2).

> 18 And their judges and rulers went to the daughters of men and took their wives by force from their husbands according to their choice, and the sons of men in those days took from the cattle of the earth, the beasts of the field and the fowls of the air, and taught the mixture of animals of one species with the other, in order therewith to provoke the Lord; and God saw the whole earth and it was corrupt, for all flesh had corrupted its ways upon earth, all men and all animals. (Book of Jasher 4:18).

> ⁵ The LORD saw that the wickedness of man was great in the earth, and that every intention of the thoughts of his heart was only evil continually. ⁶ And the LORD regretted that he had made man on the earth, and it grieved him to his heart. ⁷ So the LORD said, "I will blot out man whom I have created from the face of the land, man and animals and creeping things and birds of the heavens, for I am sorry that I have made them." ⁸ But Noah found favor in the eyes of the LORD. (Genesis 6:5-8 ESV).

In addition to the judgement of Sodom and Gomorrah, there are other key instances where people were judged based on these laws, even before Moses came into the scene. Back in the days of Abraham, God was already taking note of the sins of the Amorites:

> ¹⁶ But in the fourth generation they shall come hither again: for the iniquity of the Amorites is not yet full. (Genesis 15-16 KJV).

The Amorites were eventually judged after the Israelites departed Egypt because of their iniquities:

> ¹⁶ However, in the cities of the nations the Lord your God is giving you as an inheritance, do not leave alive anything that breathes. ¹⁷ Completely destroy them—the Hittites, Amorites, Canaanites, Perizzites, Hivites and Jebusites—as the Lord your God has commanded you. ¹⁸ Otherwise, they will teach you to follow all the detestable things they do in worshiping their

gods, and you will sin against the Lord your God. (Deuteronomy 20: 16–18 NIV).

²⁴ "'Do not defile yourselves in any of these ways, because this is how the nations that I am going to drive out before you became defiled. ²⁵ Even the land was defiled; so I punished it for its sin, and the land vomited out its inhabitants'". (Leviticus 18: 24–25 NIV).

As a matter of fact, God referenced the transgressions of these laws by both the Egyptians and the Canaanites, while giving them the laws through Moses:

> The Lord said to Moses, ² "Speak to the Israelites and say to them: 'I am the Lord your God. ³ You must not do as they do in Egypt, where you used to live, and you must not do as they do in the land of Canaan, where I am bringing you. Do not follow their practices. ⁴ You must obey my laws and be careful to follow my decrees. I am the Lord your God. ⁵ Keep my decrees and laws, for the person who obeys them will live by them. I am the Lord. (Leviticus 18: 1–5 NIV).

Cain was judged for killing Abel his brother. This is a breach of the 6th Commandment given to Moses (*Thou shalt not murder*–Exodus 20:13). Ham was condemned for sleeping with his father's wife and the offspring from this intercourse (Canaan), was cursed for it. This was a breach of the law against uncovering the nakedness of one's father:

> ⁷ The nakedness of thy father, or the nakedness of thy mother, shalt thou not uncover: she is thy mother; thou shalt not uncover her nakedness.
> ⁸ The nakedness of thy father's wife shalt thou not uncover: it is thy father's nakedness. (Leviticus 18:7–8 KJV).

Sodom and Gomorrah were judged for their wickedness and atrocious lifestyle, which profaned God. One would ask, which laws were their judgement based on, since Moses was not in the scene then? These were the laws written deep in the hearts of men. Every human being knows when he contravenes these laws, even without being told. The conscience is always there to pull a tug on humans, to remind them when they are contravening these laws.

Some of the ancients such as Seth, Enoch, Noah, Shem, Abraham are examples of patriarchs recognised for keeping the laws of God or for their righteousness. These people lived before Moses codified the laws.

At this point, it is worth noting that similarities have been drawn between the Ten Commandments and other laws such as the Hammurabi's code, making some to conclude that Moses copied these laws from other Mesopotamian cultures, that predates the Exodus of Israelites from Egypt. Many non-believers have actually accused Moses of plagiarising Sumerian laws and claiming they have been given to him by God. However, the similarities are due to the fact that the source of these laws is the same source–from God. Even though some of them have been tainted by evil forces and their human collaborators in an elaborate scheme of deception. In the light of the foregoing, it could be seen that God has made these laws known to man from the beginning. It also must be recognised that at one point humanity was unified, before various nations emerged. With each nation going with some narrative of these laws and events of the period. Even Jethro, the father in-law of Moses, recognised as a Midianite priest kept the laws of God[1], even before Moses was given the 10 commandments. He mentored Moses and was probably the one who introduced Moses into the ways of God when he fled Egypt. Moses was brought up as an Egyptian prince, hence, was trained to know the gods of Egypt. However, after his sojourn in the house of Jethro, he essentially became aware of the ways of God, that he was able to recognise the presence of God in the burning bush.

Based on the foregoing, when humanity transgressed the immutable laws of God, there is bound to be consequences. And to liberate itself from the consequences of transgressing God's laws, humanity is expected to redeem itself, in accordance with cosmic legalism.

10.2 MAN OUGHT TO REDEEM HIMSELF

Prior to the coming of Christ, the world was in darkness–under the influence and control of Satan and his hosts of evil spirits:

> [2] The people that walked in darkness have seen a great light: they that dwell in the land of the shadow of death, upon them hath the light shined (Isaiah 9:2 KJV).

---

1. As a confirmation that Jethro was a priest of God, he led a sacrifice to God at the mountain of God, when he brought Moses's wife and kids after the Exodus. (Exodus 18).

¹³ Who hath delivered us from the power of darkness, and hath translated us into the kingdom of his dear Son (Colossians 1:13 KJV).

Various levels of wickedness were being perpetrated on the earth. This darkness entered the world because Adam transgressed the commands of God and essentially handed his authority to rule the world to Satan. Hence, allowing Satan and his minions unrestrained access to the world. Figuratively, the darkness emanating from Satan enveloped the world. From that point on, it became extremely difficult for man to recover his status. Esdras summarised this:

> ⁷ And thou didst lay upon him one commandment of thine; but he transgressed it, and immediately thou didst appoint death for him and for his descendants. From him there sprang nations and tribes, peoples and clans, without number. ⁸ And every nation walked after its own will and did ungodly things before thee and scorned thee, and thou didst not hinder them. ⁹ But again, in its time thou didst bring the flood upon the inhabitants of the world and destroy them. ¹⁰ And the same fate befell them: as death came upon Adam, so the flood upon them.
>
> ²¹ For the first Adam, burdened with an evil heart, transgressed and was overcome, as were also all who descended from him. ²² Thus the disease became permanent; the law was in the people's heart along with the evil root, but what was good departed, and the evil remained. (2 Esdras 3: 7–10, 21–22).

Thus, man transgressed the law of God–through Adam who disobeyed God, causing him to lose his place and glory. This sin transcended down the lines of his descendants. Thus, man was in sin and darkness, because Satan's influence was over the world. This was the state of the world before Christ came into the scene (Isaiah 9:2).

Christ came into the picture because man was unable to redeem himself from son. Unlike the rebellious angels that fell out with God, God was gracious enough to give man the opportunity to restore his lost glory and rise to the original intent he had created him for. But in accordance with cosmic legalism, man would have to redeem himself, because it was him that defaulted, so only man can fix it. For years no man from Adam through Enoch, Noah, Abraham, Isaac, Jacob, Moses, David and so on, was able to redeem man from the captivity he had fallen into.

THE FIRST COMING OF CHRIST—REDEMPTION OF MAN FROM DARKNESS

Hence, God had to send His son into the world to redeem man. This was the highest act of love of God to man:

> [16] For God so loved the world, that he gave his only begotten Son, that whosoever believeth in him should not perish, but have everlasting life.
> [17] For God sent not his Son into the world to condemn the world; but that the world through him might be saved. (John 3:16–17 KJV).

However, this presents a cosmic dilemma. Christ cannot come into the world as God to redeem man, because only a man can legally redeem man from his fallen state. Therefore, for this to be accomplished, Christ must shed his divine nature to enter the world as a common man. It was a pure demonstration of love by Christ to leave his high-ranking position in heaven to become a man, to redeem man, who has failed to redeem himself. The import of this is captured in Philippians:

> [6] who, though he was in the form of God, did not count equality with God a thing to be grasped, [7] but emptied himself, by taking the form of a servant, being born in the likeness of men. [8] And being found in human form, he humbled himself by becoming obedient to the point of death, even death on a cross. (Philippians 2: 5–8 ESV).

This act confounded Satan and his cohort who did not understand why God would do this. Even the entire operation was a top-level secret as was presented in the Ascension of Isaiah Chapter 10 and Chapter 11).

10.3 INTRIGUES SURROUNDING THE FIRST COMING OF CHRIST

When Jesus Christ showed up on earth, Satan and his cohorts recognised who he was, but they were not exactly clear on what his mission was. The first impulse was instant elimination, so that he does not rise to oppose them. A prominent attempt to kill Christ was through Herod. Supposedly, Satan made further attempts at the life of Christ during his infancy. There were further attempts to kill Jesus recorded in the gospels.

When these failed, they began to watch him closely and scope out exactly what his mission was about. At any given opportunity, Satan and his agents would try to inquire on what Jesus's mission on earth was about. The most prominent scoping job was conducted by Satan himself, while tempting Jesus in the wilderness. Two of the temptations Satan presented to Jesus were to truly ascertain his identity and gain an insight into what his mission was:

> "*If You are the Son of God,* command that these stones become bread." (Matthew 4: 3 NKJV)

> "If You are the Son of God, throw Yourself down. For it is written:
> 'He shall give His angels charge over you,'
> and,
> 'In their hands they shall bear you up,
> Lest you dash your foot against a stone.'" (Matthew 4: 5–6 NKJV).

Note that each of these questions were aimed at ascertaining if Christ was truly the son of God (If You are the Son of God). It seems that even though, Satan and his agents had initially recognised him as the son of God, Jesus's lifestyle, which was not matching with their expectation of how the son of God should behave confused them, and they needed some hard proof to confirm that he was truly the son of God. The greatest confusion for them would have been them watching Christ subjecting himself under John the Baptist to be baptised. Baptism was meant for sinners, but here was Christ getting baptised by a man. This was an obvious paradox, and they needed to ascertain this. Recall that the temptation happened soon after the baptism of Christ.

The encounter with the two demoniacs was also a scoping job. Apparently, the appearance of the son of God on earth was a source of worry to the dark world that virtually every one of them may have been tasked to source out any relevant information that could be useful by Satan for countering Christ's mission:

> "What have you to do with us, O Son of God? Have you come here to torment us before the time?" (Matthew 8:29 RSV).

The demoniacs asked him point-blank, *what have you to do with us? Have you come to judge us before the time?* Three things jump out here. Firstly, the demoniacs knew exactly who he was even when some of his followers and Jews were still struggling to believe he is the son of God. Secondly, the demoniacs knew there is a time of judgment when they will be judged and punished accordingly. Thirdly, from their calculations based on the information they have, the time of judgement had not yet

THE FIRST COMING OF CHRIST–REDEMPTION OF MAN FROM DARKNESS

arrived, hence, their perplexity in wondering what Christ was doing on earth, if not to judge them?

Christ's response to this seemingly innocuous question of the demoniacs was telling–nothing! He did not bother to respond to their question, because doing so, may have revealed certain aspects of the top-secret assignment he was sent to earth for.

To underlie how critical this information was to the dark world, this same question was posed to Christ by the man with an unclean spirit in the synagogue:

> [24] "What have you to do with us, Jesus of Nazareth? Have you come to destroy us? I know who you are—the Holy One of God." [25] But Jesus rebuked him, saying, "Be silent, and come out of him!" (Mark 1: 24–25 ESV).

Throughout his mission, Satan and his minions continued to watch Jesus closely. Towards the end of His mission, when it seems from Christ's utterances that he was about to launch a war against the dark kingdom, they become highly threatened. A prominent one was the proclamation by Jesus against the gates of hell made in the district of Caesarea Philippi:

> [18] And I tell you, you are Peter, and on this rock, I will build my church, and the gates of hell shall not prevail against it. [19] I will give you the keys of the kingdom of heaven, and whatever you bind on earth shall be bound in heaven, and whatever you loose on earth shall be loosed in heaven." (Matthew 16: 18–19 NIV).

It is instructive to note that Caesarea Philippi, where this pronouncement was made is located at the base of Mount Hermon, the same mount where the watchers descended on to earth to mate with women. This was a highly notorious place at the time of Christ, literary known as the gates of hell. The area was originally known as Panias in honour of Pan (the half-goat, half-man Greek god) before being renamed by Herod to Caesarea Philippi. It was under satanic influence (dotted with shrines and temples dedicated to many gods), even at the time of Christ. In addition, it was home to a cave known as the gate to the underworld. Pagan worshippers in the land believed that their city was literally the gate of hell. Expectedly, for a place under satanic influence, the area was steep high in immorality, with inhabitants engaging in horrific, immoral acts such as prostitution and sexual interaction between humans and goats[2].

---

2. Rager, "What Are the", 1

This was the exact place Christ chose to take his disciples to reveal himself to the dark kingdom. To cap it all, he declares that the dark world cannot prevail against his mission. This was a direct challenge to the dark world, in what seem to appear that God was telling the dark world that he was coming for them. In hindsight, we now know that Christ was intentionally goading them to make the wrong move.

The final straw was when he rode into Jerusalem as a king, after having literally declared that the gates of hell shall not prevail against his church. At this point, Satan and his minions decided to act before things get out of hand. They had to incite the Jewish leaders to bay for the blood of Christ, before he destroys them. Again, the dark forces were working behind the scenes to inspire the people to carryout their actions. The Jewish religious and political class were threatened by the emerging prominence of Christ. They were also afraid he could upturn existing relationship between them and their Roman rulers. Furthermore, they were worried that he would wreck their economy with the messages he was preaching, especially after flogging out the merchants from the temple. These were all physical justifications the dark forces deployed to inspire the people to move against Christ. Unknown to the dark forces, Christ's pronouncement and actions were finely calibrated tactics designed to draw the dark forces into action. It was the trap of the century, set to catch Satan and his minions off-guard as God conducts the greatest surgical operation to redeem man from Satan's enslavement:

> [7] But we speak the wisdom of God in a mystery, even the hidden wisdom, which God ordained before the world unto our glory:
> [8] Which none of the princes of this world knew: for had they known it, they would not have crucified the Lord of glory. (1 Corinthians 2: 7-8 KJV).

Basically, Christ pulled a classic psyop on Satan and his agents. He made them believe he had come to take the nations away from them at that time, so they can react. Thus, when he rode into Jerusalem on the donkey, with the people proclaiming him as king, the dark forces perceived that his next move would be to start reclaiming the nations. They decided to strike first before he gets to them. Unknown to them, Christ was only after the first aspect of his agenda–redemption of men from Satan's influence. He thus, blindsided them, as they focused on killing him, he was focused on redeeming man, in his first mission. The second aspect of his mission (the total destruction of the dark forces) was left to be accomplished during his second coming.

10.4 THE AUTHORITY OF CHRIST

One of the things that usually sticks out for unbelievers is the authority of Jesus Christ. Often times they question the level of authority he has that places him above other spiritual leaders who once walked upon the earth. At different occasions in the gospels, the Jews questioned Christ's authority (Mark 11:27-28). Muslims acknowledge him as a great prophet but can never accept that he is the Son of God. Others question why it must only be through him that one can access God? Many agents of Satan masquerading in the world usually attack his authority or try to erode it. However, Christ was unequivocal in making his authority known. Whereas other spiritual leaders or founders of various religious groups around the world never claimed to be the Son of God, Christ clearly made it known that God is his father:

> [19] Jesus gave them this answer: "Very truly I tell you, the Son can do nothing by himself; he can do only what he sees his Father doing, because whatever the Father does the Son also does. [20] For the Father loves the Son and shows him all he does. Yes, and he will show him even greater works than these, so that you will be amazed. [21] For just as the Father raises the dead and gives them life, even so the Son gives life to whom he is pleased to give it. (John 5: 19-20 NIV).

He also stated that he was the only way that leads to God and any other way will lead to destruction:

> [6] Jesus answered, "I am the way and the truth and the life. No one comes to the Father except through me. (John 14:6 NIV).

He stated that those before him were thieves, whereas he is the good shepherd:

> [7] Therefore Jesus said again, "Very truly I tell you, I am the gate for the sheep. [8] All who have come before me are thieves and robbers, but the sheep have not listened to them. [9] I am the gate; whoever enters through me will be saved. They will come in and go out, and find pasture. [10] The thief comes only to steal and kill and destroy; I have come that they may have life, and have it to the full. (John 10: 7-10 NIV).

After his resurrection and shortly before he ascended, Christ affirmed to his apostles that he has been given tremendous authority over the heaven and on earth:

> [18] Then Jesus came to them and said, *"All authority in heaven and on earth has been given to me.* [19] *Therefore go and make disciples of all nations, baptizing them in the name of the Father and of the Son and of the Holy Spirit,* [20] *and teaching them to obey everything I have commanded you. And surely I am with you always, to the very end of the age." (Matthew 28:16-20 ESV).*

This was the reward of his sacrifice and achievement in defeating Satan and his cohorts on the cross and tallies with vision Daniel was shown long before the first coming of Christ:

> [13] I saw in the night visions, and, behold, one like the Son of man came with the clouds of heaven, and came to the Ancient of days, and they brought him near before him.
> [14] And there was given him dominion, and glory, and a kingdom, that all people, nations, and languages, should serve him: his dominion is an everlasting dominion, which shall not pass away, and his kingdom that which shall not be destroyed. (Daniel 7: 13-14 KJV).

Paul re-echoed this in Ephesians:

> [19] And what is the exceeding greatness of his power to us-ward who believe, according to the working of his mighty power,
> [20] Which he wrought in Christ, when he raised him from the dead, and set him at his own right hand in the heavenly places,
> [21] Far above all principality, and power, and might, and dominion, and every name that is named, not only in this world, but also in that which is to come:
> [22] And hath put all things under his feet, and gave him to be the head over all things to the church,
> [23] Which is his body, the fulness of him that filleth all in all. (Ephesians 1:19-23 KJV).

Christ has authority to teach, to heal, to forgive sins, to cast out demons, and authority over physical and natural forces[3]. Evidence of the level of authority that Christ has is littered through the Bible. There were several instances where evil forces trembled before him. His authority

---

3. Jarrett, "What Kind of", 1

was also manifesting through his disciples who used his name to do wonders:

> ¹⁷ And the seventy returned again with joy, saying, Lord, even the devils are subject unto us through thy name.
> ¹⁸ And he said unto them, I beheld Satan as lightning fall from heaven.
> ¹⁹ Behold, I give unto you power to tread on serpents and scorpions, and over all the power of the enemy: and nothing shall by any means hurt you. (Luke 10:17–19 KJV).

One of the authorities God bestowed on Christ is the authority to forgive sins. This authority was a hard nut for the Jews to crack that Christ had to demonstrate it to them. Christ demonstrated this earlier on in his ministry when he healed the paralytic, to the astonishment of the scribes who questioned this:

> ⁶ But I want you to know that the Son of Man has authority on earth to forgive sins." So he said to the paralyzed man, "Get up, take your mat and go home." (Matthew 9:6 NKJV).

The Jews were aghast at Christ for saying he can forgive sin, because they understood clearly that only God can forgive sins. This is because sin is the contravention of God's laws. And every sin has a relevant consequence attached to it. When a sin is forgiven, God is basically wiping off the consequences of that sin and making amends for any disruption in the cosmic order, arising on the occasion of the sin.

This authority to forgive sins is a precursor to the redemptive mission of Christ first coming. Redemption of man was the core mission of Christ to earth. In addition to redeeming humanity from the sins of Adam and clutches of Satan, Christ also needed to redeem the nations that have been under the influence of false gods. As was discussed in Section 7.1, after the Tower of Babel event, God gave authority over the nations to certain sons of God. These eventually became the gods of the various nations. However, when they went rogue, God had to summarily discharged them from their duties (Psalm 82) and withdrew the authority they initially had over the nations. Hence, when Christ showed up on earth, he had the authority to take back the nations for God and establish the kingdom of God on earth. The nations were no longer subject to the gods as they have gone rogue. The essence of the gospel is to announce to the people under captivity of these rogue gods that God had taken back the authority to oversee the nations through Christ. All the nations are being called into the light of Christ from the darkness of the evil forces they have previously been subject to. Hence, anyone still worshipping these gods, based on the fact that the nations were previously given to them does not have the latest memo, which Christ brought. Such a person is deceived or ignorant of the good news that Christ brought. This is why the gospel must reach the ends of the world before the second coming of Christ, so that no one can claim ignorance of this fact, during the final judgement. Bringing the nations under the authority of God through Christ were preparatory steps toward the establishment of the kingdom of God on earth.

Christ also had great authority over evil forces as was echoed by Paul in Philippians:

> [9] Therefore God has highly exalted him and bestowed on him the name that is above every name, [10] so that at the name of Jesus every knee should bow, in heaven and on earth and under the earth, [11] and every tongue confess that Jesus Christ is Lord, to the glory of God the Father. (Philippians 2: 9–11 ESV).

The name God gave him is akin to a rank that surpasses other ranks in the whole universe, that wherever and whenever that name is invoked every other entity must bow and obey. Christ had tremendous powers over the forces of darkness, who prior to his coming, held sway in the world. He demonstrated his authority over the renegade gods in several ways in the Bible. One of the prominent ones was his calming of the storm and walking on the water. This was his simple way of demonstrating his powers and authority over the gods of the sea such as Baal, regarded as the god of storm:

> [37] A furious squall came up, and the waves broke over the boat, so that it was nearly swamped. [38] Jesus was in the stern, sleeping on a cushion. The disciples woke him and said to him, "Teacher, don't you care if we drown?"
> [39] He got up, rebuked the wind and said to the waves, "Quiet! Be still!" Then the wind died down and it was completely calm.
> [40] He said to his disciples, "Why are you so afraid? Do you still have no faith?"
> [41] They were terrified and asked each other, "Who is this? Even the wind and the waves obey him!" (Mark 4:35–41 NIV).

The storm had been orchestrated by the evil forces to kill Christ and his apostles, thus, truncating his mission. The forces of darkness perceiving that Christ was tired and weak at that point, decided to strike. However, in calming the storm, Christ literary told Baal and his minions to shut up and obey! Having seen what had taken place in the spiritual realm (how Christ had subdued the gods they fear), the two demoniacs were on their knees begging Christ for mercy when he stepped out of the vessel:

> [28] And when he came to the other side, to the country of the Gadarenes, two demoniacs met him, coming out of the tombs, so fierce that no one could pass that way. [29] And behold, they cried out, "What have you to do with us, O Son of God? Have you come here to torment us before the time?" (Matthew 8:28–29 RSV).

On another occasion, he deliberately walked on top of water (Matthew 14:22–33), as a way to literally stamp his authority over the gods of the sea. It was essentially a challenge to them to try and get him if they could. He simply walked over them! His disciples who witnessed this recognised the import of this and acknowledged that he *was truly* the Son of God. (14:33):

> Now when evening came, He was alone there. [24] But the boat was now in the middle of the sea, tossed by the waves, for the wind was contrary.
> [25] Now in the fourth watch of the night Jesus went to them, walking on the sea. [26] And when the disciples saw Him walking on the sea, they were troubled, saying, "It is a ghost!" And they cried out for fear.
> [27] But immediately Jesus spoke to them, saying, "Be of good cheer! It is I; do not be afraid."
> [28] And Peter answered Him and said, "Lord, if it is You, command me to come to You on the water."
> [29] So He said, "Come." And when Peter had come down out of the boat, he walked on the water to go to Jesus. [30] But when he saw that the wind was boisterous, he was afraid; and beginning to sink he cried out, saying, "Lord, save me!"
> [31] And immediately Jesus stretched out His hand and caught him, and said to him, "O you of little faith, why did you doubt?" [32] And when they got into the boat, the wind ceased.
> [33] Then those who were in the boat came and worshiped Him, saying, "Truly You are the Son of God." (Matthew 14:22–33 NKJV).

Casting out of demons was another way Christ demonstrated his powers over dark forces. When he cast out unclean spirits from the man in Synagogue in Capernaum, those present recognised how powerful his authority over evil spirits is:

> [27] And they were all amazed, so that they questioned among themselves, saying, "What is this? A new teaching with authority! He commands even the unclean spirits, and they obey him." [28] And at once his fame spread everywhere throughout all the surrounding region of Galilee. (Mark 1:21-28 ESV).

Also, when he declared at Caesarea that the gates of hell cannot prevail against the movement/church he was establishing, he directly poked the gods in their eyes, as he was literally standing in their domain of influence, while making that declaration.

Finally, his death and descent into the Hades, and eventual resurrection confirms he conquered Hades and other gods in the underworld, to be able to escape from their clutches to re-emerge on earth (see Section 10.7).

10.5 THE GOSPEL

The gospel is the good news brought to the people by Christ that God has come to take back all the nations from the renegade gods. It is good news because God has decided to liberate the people from the wickedness of the fallen gods. Christ re-echoed this when he read the scroll of Isaiah and asserted that he has come to set the captives who were oppressed free and to open the sights of the people blinded by the forces of darkness:

> [18] "The Spirit of the Lord is upon me,
>   because he has anointed me
>   to proclaim good news to the poor.
> He has sent me to proclaim liberty to the captives
>   and recovering of sight to the blind,
>   to set at liberty those who are oppressed,
> [19] to proclaim the year of the Lord's favor."

Wherever Christ went he proclaimed to the people that the kingdom of God was at hand. This proclamation was not only aimed at the people but also targeted at the renegade gods who had continued to clinch unto the territories. He was essentially telling them that their time was up, because God has come to take back the nations from them. No other person prior Christ brought this memo of the kingdom of God to the people. This was an essential part of his mission:

> [16] "The Law and the Prophets were until John; since then the good news of the kingdom of God is preached, and everyone forces his way into it. (Luke 16: 16 ESV).

To spread this gospel, he delegated his 12 apostles to initially proclaim this good news to several towns in Israel (12 here symbolises the 12 tribes of Israel, who needs to be brought into the kingdom first), and equipped them with necessary authority over the forces of darkness:

> When Jesus had called the Twelve together, he gave them power and authority to drive out all demons and to cure diseases, [2] and he sent them out to proclaim the kingdom of God and to heal the sick. [3] He told them: "Take nothing for the journey—no staff, no bag, no bread, no money, no extra shirt. [4] Whatever house you enter, stay there until you leave that town. [5] If people do not welcome you, leave their town and shake the dust off your feet as a testimony against them." [6] So they set out and went from village to village, proclaiming the good news and healing people everywhere. (Luke 9: 1–6 NIV).

The 12 apostles were sent only to the lost sheep of Israel with Christ specifically asking them not to enter any gentile or Samaritan town. The choice of the 12 apostles was symbolic of the 12 tribes of Israel. The good news must be first preached to Israel before it goes to the rest of the nations:

> [5] These twelve Jesus sent out, instructing them, "Go nowhere among the Gentiles and enter no town of the Samaritans, [6] but go rather to the lost sheep of the house of Israel. [7] And proclaim as you go, saying, 'The kingdom of heaven is at hand.' [8] Heal the sick, raise the dead, cleanse lepers, cast out demons. (Mathew 10: 5–8 ESV).

The impact of the work of the apostles resounded across the land that even Herod got wind of it and was perplexed at what was happening:

> 7 Now Herod the tetrarch heard about all that was going on. And he was perplexed because some were saying that John had been raised from the dead, 8 others that Elijah had appeared, and still others that one of the prophets of long ago had come back to life. 9 But Herod said, "I beheaded John. Who, then, is this I

hear such things about?" And he tried to see him. (Luke 9: 7–9 NIV).

This demonstrates how powerful their message to the cities they had visited rattled the dark forces. Subsequently, Christ sent out 70 disciples to go and proclaim the good news to other towns beyond Israel. There was no restriction this time for them not to enter gentile or Samaritan town (Luke 10:1–11). The number of disciples chosen was also instructive as it tries to tally with the 70[4] nations that the world was divided into (Genesis 10). Christ's sending out 70 disciples to proclaim the gospels of the kingdom–was essentially an announcement to the principalities that their time over these nations was up and God is about to take the nations away from them:

> After this the Lord appointed seventy-two[a] others and sent them on ahead of him, two by two, into every town and place where he himself was about to go. 2 And he said to them, "The harvest is plentiful, but the laborers are few (Luke 10:1–2 ESV).

There is also suggestion that the world was shared among the 72 sons of God. Hence, in the gospels some manuscript says 70 disciples and others 72, were sent to proclaim the gospel to the people:

> After this the Lord appointed seventy-two[a] others and sent them on ahead of him, two by two, into every town and place where he himself was about to go. (Luke 10: 1 ESV).

This was a symbolic move by Christ to notify the gods originally handed the lands that he was coming to reclaim all the lands for God.

It is amply clear from the foregoing that Christ came to reclaim these nations–bringing all of them into the kingdom of God. He was not shy about this. Paul also alluded to this, while addressing the Greeks at Lystra who had wanted to offer sacrifice to Barnabas and Paul, assuming them to be "Zeus" and "Hermes," respectively:

> [16] In past generations he allowed all Gentiles to go their own ways; [17] yet, in bestowing his goodness, he did not leave himself without witness, for he gave you rains from heaven and fruitful seasons, and filled you with nourishment and gladness for your hearts." Acts 14: 16–17 NABRE).

---

4. The discrepancies in the number (70 or 72) come from differences found in approximately half of the ancient scrolls used in translation. https://www.gotquestions.org/70-or-72-disciples.html

Surprisingly, during the temptation in the wilderness, Satan offered to give Christ all the kingdoms of the earth with the catch that Christ must worship him:

> [8] Again, the devil took him to a very high mountain and showed him all the kingdoms of the world and their splendor. [9] "All this I will give you," he said, "if you will bow down and worship me." (Matthew 4:8–9 NIV).

These kingdoms of the earth were essentially what Christ came to reclaim. Satan must have suspected that Christ had come to take back the nations, so he decided to offer them to him with one hand and reclaim them with another. This was a clever move by Satan, because had Christ fallen for it, it would have scandalised his mission on earth, and Satan would still have the authority he usurped and the kingdoms of the world intact. Had Jesus accepted the offer from Satan, he would have been in charge of the kingdoms of the world without going to the cross, but since he must have bowed down to worship Satan, that would have negated the purpose, because Satan would have still been on top of him and those kingdoms.

Christ saw through this chicane, and rejected the offer, and proceeded in spreading the good news of the Kingdom of God. To buttress the importance of the gospel, before his ascension, Christ also commissioned his disciples to go into the world and spread the good news of the Kingdom of God to all nations (Section 11.4.6). And once again during the Pentecost, the apostles had the opportunity to spread the gospel to people from different nations.

10.6 THE KINGDOM OF GOD

Often, when the kingdom of God is mentioned, people tend to focus only on the spiritual connotation of this. However, the kingdom of God that Christ preached is literally the physical manifestation of the rule of God over all the nations of the earth. At the full manifestation of this, the throne of God would be present on earth:

> Then I saw "a new heaven and a new earth," for the first heaven and the first earth had passed away, and there was no longer any sea. [2] I saw the Holy City, the new Jerusalem, coming down out of heaven from God, prepared as a bride beautifully dressed for her husband. [3] And I heard a loud voice from the throne saying,

"Look! God's dwelling place is now among the people, and he will dwell with them. They will be his people, and God himself will be with them and be their God. (Revelation 21:1–3 NIV).

The import of this is mind-blowing. With the throne of God brought to earth and God dwelling on earth, the entire universe will be ruled from earth. Thus, making the earth the center of the whole universe. Technically speaking this is a new dispensation (a new earth and new heaven), contrasting the old dispensation, when the throne of God was in heaven and the earth his footstool:

This is what the Lord says:
"Heaven is my throne,
 and the earth is my footstool.
Where is the house you will build for me?
Where will my resting place be? (Isaiah 66:1 NIV).

The process of establishing the Kingdom of God started with the first coming of Christ when he brought the gospel of the Kingdom of God and declared to the gods of the nations that their time was up. This will be culminated during his second coming, when he would utterly defeat the forces of darkness and establish his rule here on earth (see Section 13.9). This was hinted at in Revelation 11 after the 7th Trumpet was blown and loud voices in heaven proclaimed that the kingdom of the world has become part of the kingdom of God:

15 Then the seventh angel blew his trumpet, and there were loud voices in heaven, saying, "The kingdom of the world has become the kingdom of our Lord and of his Christ, and he shall reign forever and ever." 16 And the twenty-four elders who sit on their thrones before God fell on their faces and worshiped God, 17 saying,

"We give thanks to you, Lord God Almighty,
 who is and who was,
for you have taken your great power
 and begun to reign.

(Revelation 11: 15–17 ESV).

The purpose of Christ's second coming is to eradicate evil in the world and establish this kingdom. This kingdom will be headquartered in Jerusalem and every other nation would be coming to pay homage to Christ. Detailed discussion of this is presented in Chapter 14.

10.7 THE MYSTERY OF THE CROSS

Many have long wondered on the mystery of the cross. Why was it necessary that Christ needed to die for God to forgive the sins of men? Was there no other way God could have done it than subjecting his son under such an excruciating pain. After all, he is God and can do whatever he wants? These are all legitimate and logical questions. However, a lot of the mystery surrounding the death of Christ on the cross has to do with cosmic legalism (Section 10.1). God is holy and righteous and cannot break his own laws. God has already decreed that *a soul that sinneth shall die*. When Adam fell, humanity, which he embodied also fell. Hence, man ought to die because he had sinned:

> [12] Therefore, just as sin came into the world through one man, and death through sin, and so death spread to all men because all sinned— [13] for sin indeed was in the world before the law was given, but sin is not counted where there is no law. [14] Yet death reigned from Adam to Moses, even over those whose sinning was not like the transgression of Adam, who was a type of the one who was to come. (Romans 5: 12–14 ESV).

For thousands of years after Adam, man was subject to death–eternal death, I must add. However, because God had a soft spot for man, and did not want man to perish, he sent his son to redeem man from the captivity of death. For this to be accomplished the son of God had to die for man:

> [6] For while we were still weak, at the right time Christ died for the ungodly. [7] For one will scarcely die for a righteous person—though perhaps for a good person one would dare even to die— [8] but God shows his love for us in that while we were still sinners, Christ died for us. [9] Since, therefore, we have now been justified by his blood, much more shall we be saved by him from the wrath of God. [10] For if while we were enemies we were reconciled to God by the death of his Son, much more, now that we are reconciled, shall we be saved by his life. [11] More than that, we also rejoice in God through our Lord Jesus Christ, through whom we have now received reconciliation. (Romans 5: 6–11 ESV).

The shedding of blood was required for this, because it is the life force of man and is required for the remission of sin:

> [22] And almost all things are by the law purged with blood; and without shedding of blood is no remission. (Hebrews 9:22 KJV).

Hence, by shedding his blood on the cross, Christ (symbolically embodying humanity) died and with that the old man (the Adamic man) died. Thus, the requirement of the cosmic law about sin fulfilled. The foreshadow of this ultimate sacrifice by Christ was instituted in Levitus:

> [11] For the life of the flesh is in the blood: and I have given it to you upon the altar to make an atonement for your souls: for it is the blood that maketh an atonement for the soul. (Leviticus 17:11 KJV).

Another way to look at this is to consider that Adam was created as a being of light, but when he fell, he became a being of flesh. What powers a being of flesh is blood (*For it is the life of all flesh; the blood of it is for the life thereof - Leviticus 17:14*). Hence, to transform man from a being of flesh back to a being of light, the blood that was acquired when Adam fell, which powered the flesh had to be completely shed.

The crucifixion of Jesus Christ on the cross could be likened to a painful spiritual surgery required to remove the bad blood and genetic materials that were introduced into Adam and subsequently his lineage, when he fell at the garden. At the fall, Adam was recoded–his nature drastically changed. This recoding of his gene transformed him from an immortal being of light to a mortal fleshly being. Hence, to turn man back to what he was before, some spiritual procedure had to be performed on man. Surgeries are usually very painful process, but the result is always good. This surgery was extremely painful because every strand of evil that was introduced into the gene pool of man through Adam was removed by the excruciating pains Christ experienced on the cross and throughout the passion. It seems Satan embedded the virus/malware deep into the human code, where he felt would be impossible to get to. The operation he carried out on Adam was a well calculated plan to doom man forever. However, when Christ subjected himself under the pains of the cross, he allowed God to conduct the surgery to conclusion:

> [30] When Jesus therefore had received the vinegar, he said, It is finished: and he bowed his head, and gave up the ghost. (John 19: 30 KJV).

Note that vinegar is used in wound treatment. When the vinegar was offered to Christ it signified that the surgery has been completed,

THE FIRST COMING OF CHRIST—REDEMPTION OF MAN FROM DARKNESS

and the healing process commencing. Hence, the declaration from Christ that it is finished. By his death and resurrection, the entire process was completed, and a new brand of humans was created, with Jesus Christ as the first fruit of this elevated form of humans:

> [20] But now is Christ risen from the dead, and become the firstfruits of them that slept.
> [21] For since by man came death, by man came also the resurrection of the dead.
> [22] For as in Adam all die, even so in Christ shall all be made alive.
> [23] But every man in his own order: Christ the firstfruits; afterward they that are Christ's at his coming. (1 Corinthians 15:20–23 KJV).

Thus, whatever Satan did to humanity was reversed on the cross and through Christ's death:

> [18] Therefore, as one trespass led to condemnation for all men, so one act of righteousness leads to justification and life for all men. [19] For as by the one man's disobedience the many were made sinners, so by the one man's obedience the many will be made righteous. (Romans 5: 18–19 ESV).

The import of this is so great when considered in detail. Satan may have presented the case before the court of God, after the fall of Adam, that since Adam has fallen, all beings coming from Adam, should be adjudged as fallen. Having established this precedence, God reversed the argument to hold that through the death of Christ, all humans have died for that sin. Hence, no man can be held liable to that sin any longer. Then by the resurrection of Christ a new man was born through Christ. Thus, humans only have to believe in Jesus Christ for them to begin the process of this transformation back to the original form in which Adam was created–a being of light. Christ alluded to the transformation when he introduced the concept of *"being born again"* (see Section 11.4.2). Every human who diligently followed the footsteps of Christ will at the end be transformed into this form of new beings:

> [51] But let me reveal to you a wonderful secret. We will not all die, but we will all be transformed! [52] It will happen in a moment, in the blink of an eye, when the last trumpet is blown. For when the trumpet sounds, those who have died will be raised to live forever. And we who are living will also be transformed. [53] For

our dying bodies must be transformed into bodies that will never die; our mortal bodies must be transformed into immortal bodies. (Corinthians 15:51 - 53 NLT).

This form of new beings is commonly referred to as the sons of God. This is the ultimate destination of man. The earth is a testing ground that would be used to sift man so that only the best of the best can be promoted into this new form of beings, which creation awaits:

> [19] *For the earnest expectation of the creature waiteth for the manifestation of the sons of God. (Romans 8: 19 KJV).*

This transformation will happen during the end times. Revelation 20 captured this moment and termed it the First Resurrection). These are the people that will eventually enter the Kingdom of God. Natural bodies are not fit to enter this kingdom:

> [50] What I am saying, dear brothers and sisters, is that our physical bodies cannot inherit the Kingdom of God. These dying bodies cannot inherit what will last forever. (Corinthians 15:50 NLT).

Paul opined in Romans that man can have some level of temporary experience of this new life even before the final transformation that will happen at end time, if filled with the Spirit of God:

> [11] But if the Spirit of him that raised up Jesus from the dead dwell in you, he that raised up Christ from the dead shall also quicken your mortal bodies by his Spirit that dwelleth in you. (Romans 8: 11 KJV).

> 14 For as many as are led by the Spirit of God, they are the sons of God. (Romans 8: 14 KJV).

10.7.1 Descent into underworld

When Christ died, his soul did not immediately go to heaven but went to the underworld, where the dead go (sheol and Abraham's bosom). Christ also went to paradise. We know this by his response to one of the insurgents crucified alongside him, while hanging on the cross:

> [39] One of the criminals who hung there hurled insults at him: "Aren't you the Messiah? Save yourself and us!"

> ⁴⁰ But the other criminal rebuked him. "Don't you fear God," he said, "since you are under the same sentence? ⁴¹ We are punished justly, for we are getting what our deeds deserve. But this man has done nothing wrong."
> ⁴² Then he said, "Jesus, remember me when you come into your kingdom.
> ⁴³ Jesus answered him, "Truly I tell you, today you will be with me in paradise." (Luke 23: 39–43 NIV).

This event narrated in Luke's gospel shows that both insurgents have heard about Christ and even the gospel. One of them had urged Christ to save himself and them at the cross as he was the Messiah. The other begged Christ to remember him when he comes into his Kingdom. They probably have listened to Christ preaching at some point but stopped following him and went the wrong way. While the first criminal recognised that Christ was the Messiah, the second criminal not only recognised this fact but also knew that the kingdom of Christ was yet to come, hence his plea for Christ to remember him, when the kingdom emerges. This was a powerful conclusion to arrive at, considering that Christ was hanging helplessly on the cross at this point, yet this criminal still knew he was a king! He was instantly rewarded with forgiveness of sin and an invitation into paradise where Christ was headed to on that day (*"Truly I tell you, today you will be with me in paradise"*).

Curiously, Christ did not say he was going to heaven that day, but we know he went somewhere–paradise. So, what is paradise and where is it? One thing any careful reader will be clear about is that the paradise Christ went to was not Heaven (where God's throne is), because Christ only went to Heaven soon after he resurrected (when he went to present himself to God), and not before. Many also confuses paradise with Abraham's side. However, these three places (Heaven, paradise and Abraham's side) are different places.

The word paradise was sparingly used in the Bible. Its etymology is traced to an Akkadian (pardesu) and Old Persian (paridayda) word for garden (DailyHistory.org, 2024). Hence, for the ancients, there was no ambiguity of what paradise was. They knew it was the Garden of Eden, a place of bliss, harmony and peace, where God and Adam interacted without any barrier.

Its first occurrence in the New Testament was introduced by Jesus Christ at his crucifixion, when he told one of the thieves that was crucified with him that he shall be with him in paradise on that day. The second time paradise was used in the New Testament was in 2 Corinthians, where Paul was describing how a man (most likely himself) was caught up in a realm, he called the third heaven as well as paradise, and heard unspeakable things:

> ² I knew a man in Christ above fourteen years ago, (whether in the body, I cannot tell; or whether out of the body, I cannot tell: God knoweth;) such an one caught up to the third heaven.
> ³ And I knew such a man, (whether in the body, or out of the body, I cannot tell: God knoweth;)
> ⁴ How that he was caught up into paradise, and heard unspeakable words, which it is not lawful for a man to utter. (2 Corinthians 12: 2–4 KJV).

The third and last time the word paradise was used was in Revelation, while Christ was admonishing the church of Ephesus:

> ⁷ To him that overcometh will I give to eat of the tree of life, which is in the midst of the paradise of God. (Revelation 2:17 KJV).

Putting all these together, points to the fact that paradise is the Garden of Eden. This was why Christ was heading off there on the day he was crucified, to reopen the door of the Garden of Eden to readmit humans. Remember, access to the garden was blocked off for the first Adam after his fall, and Christ the second Adam came to repair the broken relationship between God and man and to reopen the door to the garden. The tree of life was found in the Garden of Eden; this is the same tree that Christ is promising that he would give the *sons of God* to eat from in the Kingdom of God.

In addition to going to paradise, various Biblical passages suggest that Christ also went to sheol and Abraham's bosom. Abraham's bosom is a temporary place where the righteous souls go to rest, while awaiting resurrection and the final judgement. Unrighteous souls, also have a temporary holding place commonly known as hell (Hades, Shoel). According to Peter, the gospel was also preached to the dead:

> 6 For this is why the gospel was preached even to those who are dead, that though judged in the flesh the way people are, they might live in the spirit the way God does. (1 Peter 4:2 ESV).

It is important to differentiate hell from Gehena (the lake of fire), which is the destination of the unrighteous after the final judgement.

There is also Tartarus (deep abyss/ bottomless pit), which is a prison in a section hell, where hardened spirits (where Abaddon and other wicked fallen ones) are detained.

Continuing from the foregoing, after death, the righteous proceeds to Abraham's bosom and the unrighteous to hell (Hades). Christ hinted at this in the parable of the rich man and Lazarus, which he used to give an insight into what happens when humans die:

> [22] And it came to pass, that the beggar died, and was carried by the angels into Abraham's bosom: the rich man also died, and was buried;
>
> [23] And in hell he lift up his eyes, being in torments, and seeth Abraham afar off, and Lazarus in his bosom.
>
> [24] And he cried and said, Father Abraham, have mercy on me, and send Lazarus, that he may dip the tip of his finger in water, and cool my tongue; for I am tormented in this flame.
>
> [25] But Abraham said, Son, remember that thou in thy lifetime receivedst thy good things, and likewise Lazarus evil things: but now he is comforted, and thou art tormented.
>
> [26] And beside all this, between us and you there is a great gulf fixed: so that they which would pass from hence to you cannot; neither can they pass to us, that would come from thence. (Luke 16: 22–26 KJV).

From the above passage one can glean that both the righteous and unrighteous go to a place where they can see each other literarily. From the parable, it appears that Abraham's bosom and hell are geolocated and souls would have been able to cross from side to the other if not for a wide impassable gulf, that separates the two sides The righteous are in a better place than the unrighteous, which was the message the passage was conveying.

It is safe to assume that after Christ died, he went to all these places: Sheol/Hades, Tartarus, paradise, and Abraham's side. For each of these places there are important tasks he needed to accomplish. He spent three days in the grave before resurrecting, which enabled him to cover all the grounds, he needed to. There have been several conjectures on what Christ did while his soul was in the underworld, because details about this were not presented in the Bible. Despite the diverse theory, one thing that was clear was that he was not idle there. He did some important work, that culminated in the redemption of man, and his resurrection from that place. Peter did allude that after he was made alive in this place by the Spirit, he proceeded to preach to the unrighteous spirits imprisoned there:

> He was put to death in the body but made alive in the Spirit. [19] After being made alive, he went and made proclamation to the imprisoned spirits— [20] to those who were disobedient long ago when God waited patiently in the days of Noah while the ark was being built. (1 Peter 3: 18 -20 NIV).

This passage indicates that Christ went to Tartarus, to proclaim his victory to the fallen ones imprisoned there. Many have interpreted this to mean that Christ preached to the souls of the Nephilim or even their fathers (the Watchers imprisoned in the Abyss), who corrupted the world during the time of Noah. This was a clear demonstration of what Christ stated at Caesarea Philippi (Matthew 16:18) before his death that the gates of hell shall not prevail against his church. Psalm 24 also alluded to the moment when Christ was descending into the underworld and the angels commanding the gates of hell to be opened:

> [7] Lift up your heads, O ye gates; and be ye lift up, ye everlasting doors; and the King of glory shall come in.
> [8] Who is this King of glory? The Lord strong and mighty, the Lord mighty in battle.
> [9] Lift up your heads, O ye gates; even lift them up, ye everlasting doors; and the King of glory shall come in.
> [10] Who is this King of glory? The Lord of hosts, he is the King of glory. Selah. (Psalm 24:7–10 KJV).

He went to where these spirits were chained without any hindrance, to proclaim to them that he has won and accomplished the task God set before him. This must be a gruelling moment for the forces of darkness who had previously thought just moments earlier that they have aborted Christ's mission by nailing him on the cross, only for them to realise that by that singular act, they had undone what they had held unto for generations.

There have also been other suggestions such as those that claim that it was also at this point that God rescued Adam from Satan's clutches (the Gospel of Bartholomew extensively covered this in Chapter 2). Although, the veracity of this interpretation cannot be confirmed, one thing that can be taken from Peter's sermon was that Christ was doing some work while in that place, which culminated in the redemption of man.

It maybe that Christ first went to Hades to overcome Satan's power over the sinful man and convict the unrighteous with his proclamation. David prophesied about Christ going to Sheol in one of his Psalms:

> ¹⁰ For you will not abandon my soul to Sheol,
>   or let your holy one see corruption. (Psalm 16:10 ESV).

Peter also referenced this in his sermon at the Pentecost, confirming that this prophesy from David was pointing to Christ and his journey into the underworld:

> ²⁴ God raised him up, loosing the pangs of death, because it was not possible for him to be held by it. ²⁵ For David says concerning him,
>
> "'I saw the Lord always before me,
>   for he is at my right hand that I may not be shaken;
> ²⁶ therefore my heart was glad, and my tongue rejoiced;
>   my flesh also will dwell in hope.
> ²⁷ For you will not abandon my soul to Hades,
>   or let your Holy One see corruption.
> ²⁸ You have made known to me the paths of life;
>   you will make me full of gladness with your presence.'(Acts 2:24-27 ESV).

It does makes sense that since Christ embodied the sins of humanity on the cross ("*He himself bore our sins*" *in his body on the cross, so that we might die to sins and live for righteousness;–1 Peter 2:24 NIV*); to fulfil all righteousness, he must also descend to the place where the sinful go after their death. It was from this rock-bottom place, which the sinful man has fallen to that he resurrected from, having conquered all forces holding humanity captive for his sins. Subsequently, he went to paradise to reopen access to the garden for man, and then to Abraham's bosom to interact with souls there.

10.8 RESURRECTION OF CHRIST

The resurrection of Christ was a marvellous mystery. All previous resurrections have been done by someone on another person, such as Christ raising Lazarus and others from the dead, or those performed by Elijah (1 Kings 17:17–24), Elisha (2 Kings 4:18–37), Peter (Acts 9:36–42), and Paul (Acts 20:7–12). No man has ever raised himself from the dead before. So, when this happened as Christ had earlier prophesied, it disrupted a lot of things physically and spiritually. Even till date many still dispute that this event happened. The dispute started from the Jewish leaders who saw this as a threat to their authority over the people, hence, they harshly contested this and did all in their power to suppress this good news.

However, the resurrection of Christ is the fulcrum on which his mission on earth rests. Without him resurrecting from the dead, his mission would not have been accomplished, and humanity would have remained unredeemed. The core mystery of the death and resurrection of Jesus Christ was that he reclaimed Adam's lost authority to rule over the earth, from Satan, and gave man the opportunity to be reborn into a new creature. This authority which Satan stole at the fall of Adam, gave Satan tremendous authority and power over human race. He wielded this power over humans to ensure that they will not be redeemed. Hence, when Christ reclaimed this authority, he re-opened the way for the fallen man to once again re-enter the Garden of Eden and be able to ascend to become sons of God.

Despite having lost his authority, Satan did not lose his power, hence, he has continued to operate in an illegal manner, truncating God's plans. Hence, at the second coming of Christ, he would be defeated in a physical battle that will be fought on earth.

10.8.1 Presentation of the blood at the Heavenly Altar

Soon after his resurrection Christ went to heaven to present his blood at the heavenly altar of God. He indicated this when he told Mary not to cling unto him, because he has yet to ascend to his Father:

> [17] Jesus saith unto her, Touch me not; for I am not yet ascended to my Father: but go to my brethren, and say unto them, I ascend unto my Father, and your Father; and to my God, and your God. (John 20:17 KJV).

Although, many may interpret that the ascension Christ was alluding to here (while conversing with Mary) was his final ascension to heaven, which his disciples witnessed, this *ascension to the father* hinted at here, was an imminent one, judging from the statement. Christ was essentially telling Mary, do not touch me, I need to ascend to heaven first, to present myself to my father; let my disciples know where I am going. Christ was ascending to heaven as a high priest to present his blood at the heavenly altar of God. This was the final phase of the salvation process, which comprises of the following: shedding of blood on the cross, death, descent into the netherworld, resurrection, and the presentation of his sacrificial blood to the father. This presentation at the altar of God in heaven was captured in Hebrews:

> [11] But when Christ came as high priest of the good things that are now already here, he went through the greater and more perfect tabernacle that is not made with human hands, that is to say, is not a part of this creation. [12] He did not enter by means of the blood of goats and calves; but he entered the Most Holy Place once for all by his own blood, thus obtaining eternal redemption. [13] The blood of goats and bulls and the ashes of a heifer sprinkled on those who are ceremonially unclean sanctify them so that they are outwardly clean. [14] How much more, then, will the blood of Christ, who through the eternal Spirit offered himself unblemished to God, cleanse our consciences from acts that lead to death, so that we may serve the living God! (Hebrews 9:11-14 NIV).

This was a ritual he needed to accomplish before coming back to earth to appear before his disciples. After accomplishing this, he came back to earth, and began to appear before his disciples, eating with them and even allowing them to touch him (unlike when he previously told Mary not to hold on to him).

10.9 SALVATION: THE RECTIFICATION PROCESS

One thing that is clear to any reader of the Bible is that humanity is not at the state it was designed to be. Simply put, man is not operating in his full capacity. Something corrupted man and hence, limiting it from reaching its originally designed state and potentials. In other words, humanity is at a fallen state. This corruption of humanity can be viewed exoterically or esoterically. Exoterically man fell due to sin. This is the most popularly presented view that can easily be gleaned from the Bible. But below this level, there is a hidden (esoteric) message that holds the entire truth. Esoterically, man fell due to the infusion of Satan's gene with that of man, hence, the spirit of Satan works in man. By this infusion, every man has been tainted and vulnerable to the influence of Satan:

> [23] For all have sinned, and come short of the glory of God (Romans 3:23 KJV).

Whichever way this is viewed, the human race required a saviour to restore it to its original state. This saviour of humans is Jesus Christ:

> ⁷ Then Jesus said to them again, "Most assuredly, I say to you, I am the door of the sheep. ⁸ All who ever came before Me are thieves and robbers, but the sheep did not hear them. ⁹ I am the door. If anyone enters by Me, he will be saved, and will go in and out and find pasture. ¹⁰ The thief does not come except to steal, and to kill, and to destroy. I have come that they may have life, and that they may have it more abundantly.
>
> ¹¹ "I am the good shepherd. The good shepherd gives His life for the sheep. (John 10: 7 -11 NKJV).

Humanity was tainted by Satan and to fully reunite man with God, every element of Satan in man must be extricated. This was what Christ came to do for man. Hence, salvation is a rectification process. It was designed to rectify a defect that was introduced into man, to bring it back to its default state. It functions like factory-resetting of man.

To be fully restored to his original nature, man must be reborn, so he can acquire a fresh set of gene (his corrupt gene repaired or transformed to its original state). This is the basis of the concept of being born-again. The old man must die for the new man to be born. This is symbolised in baptism. When a man repents from his unrighteous ways, he demonstrates his willingness to die and be restored by undergoing the ritual of baptism. Immersion into the water symbolises the death of the old self and the re-emergence from the water symbolises the transformation.

The death of Jesus Christ on the cross was the surgery that rectified the problem with man. As Jesus bled to death, every element of Satan introduced into man was completely drained out of him and the fallen nature of man eventually died in Christ. Hence, when Christ rose again, a new form of human was born! *Oh the wisdom of God, which confounds all!* Ordinarily, every man ought to have gone through the same excruciating process that Christ underwent. But God being so magnanimous, accepted Christ's death as the death of humanity who descended from Adam and accepted that anyone born of Christ will be adjudged as saved. In essence, this was a reversal of the logic/legal argument presented by Satan against humans, which led to the condemnation of all descendants of Adam. Satan had claimed that since Adam has sinned (been corrupted) every seed proceeding from Adam should be adjudged as corrupted and condemned to death. Thus, after Christ died and resurrected, God allowed the acceptance of the death of Christ (one man) to be representative of the death of all humans who come through Christ. Since Christ overcame sin, all his descendants should also be considered as free of sin. This is the mystery of being born again. Humans who hope to benefit from the sacrifice of Christ and the salvation offered must be born again through Christ, so they can claim inheritance from Christ. Hence, all humans who cling to Christ are acquitted of all sins:

> [25] Therefore he is able to save completely those who come to God through him, because he always lives to intercede for them. (Hebrews 7: 25 NIV).

Isaiah prophesied about this design of God, regarding the deliverance of the descendants of Christ:

> [10] The Lord says,
>
> "It was my will that he should suffer;
> his death was a sacrifice to bring forgiveness.
> And so he will see his descendants;
> he will live a long life,
> and through him my purpose will succeed.
> [11] After a life of suffering, he will again have joy;
> he will know that he did not suffer in vain.
> My devoted servant, with whom I am pleased,
> will bear the punishment of many
> and for his sake I will forgive them. (Isaiah 53: 10–11 GNB).

God planned that the salvation of humans can only be accomplished through Christ. No other entity is qualified to deliver man from the prison of sin:

> [12] And there is salvation in no one else, for there is no other name under heaven given among men by which we must be saved." (Acts 4:12 ESV).

It is pertinent to point out that the salvation of humans is essentially free, made available through God's grace (benevolence). It is free because Jesus Christ did all the work concerning salvation ("...*it is finished*" - John 19:30). The promise of salvation is like a *get-out-of-jail-free* card that Christ has promised to hand out to any descendant of Adam who wishes to accept it:

> [4] But God, being rich in mercy, because of the great love with which he loved us, [5] even when we were dead in our trespasses, made us alive together with Christ—by grace you have been

saved— ⁶ and raised us up with him and seated us with him in the heavenly places in Christ Jesus, ⁷ so that in the coming ages he might show the immeasurable riches of his grace in kindness toward us in Christ Jesus. ⁸ For by grace you have been saved through faith. And this is not your own doing; it is the gift of God, ⁹ not a result of works, so that no one may boast. (Ephesians 2: 4–8 ESV).

However, despite receiving salvation free of charge through grace, followers of Christ are also expected to do good works. Salvation is like a promissory note offered to the followers of Christ. If they continue to abide in him, he will surely apply the salvation on them at the end of ages. It is through the good works they have performed will they be rewarded at the final judgement. Jesus Christ made this amply clear in the gospels and enumerated what some of those good works are:

> ³¹ "When the Son of Man comes in his glory, and all the angels with him, then he will sit on his glorious throne. ³² Before him will be gathered all the nations, and he will separate people one from another as a shepherd separates the sheep from the goats. ³³ And he will place the sheep on his right, but the goats on the left. ³⁴ Then the King will say to those on his right, 'Come, you who are blessed by my Father, inherit the kingdom prepared for you from the foundation of the world. ³⁵ For I was hungry and you gave me food, I was thirsty and you gave me drink, I was a stranger and you welcomed me, ³⁶ I was naked and you clothed me, I was sick and you visited me, I was in prison and you came to me.' ³⁷ Then the righteous will answer him, saying, 'Lord, when did we see you hungry and feed you, or thirsty and give you drink? ³⁸ And when did we see you a stranger and welcome you, or naked and clothe you? ³⁹ And when did we see you sick or in prison and visit you?' ⁴⁰ And the King will answer them, 'Truly, I say to you, as you did it to one of the least of these my brothers, you did it to me.' (Mathew 25: 31–40 ESV).

Note that these good works was counted to them as righteousness (*Then the righteous will answer him, saying, 'Lord, when did we see you hungry and feed you, or thirsty and give you drink?*). Also, in the Parable of the Talent (Mathew 25: 14 -30), Jesus Christ alluded to this idea of work, vis-à-vis putting into practice and of good use what one has received freely from God. Jesus Christ expects his followers not to misappropriate the gift of salvation but to put it in good use and do the necessary work

THE FIRST COMING OF CHRIST—REDEMPTION OF MAN FROM DARKNESS

they have been called to do in this world, to become the light/salt of the world:

> [13] "You are the salt of the earth, but if salt has lost its taste, how shall its saltiness be restored? It is no longer good for anything except to be thrown out and trampled under people's feet.
> [14] "You are the light of the world. A city set on a hill cannot be hidden. [15] Nor do people light a lamp and put it under a basket, but on a stand, and it gives light to all in the house. [16] In the same way, let your light shine before others, so that they may see your good works and give glory to your Father who is in heaven. (Matthew 5:13–5:16 ESV).

There would be severe punishment for anyone who did not put his talent in good use/good work. This theme of *"doing good work"* is replete across the Bible. While describing the White Throne Judgement that would occur at the end of the ages, John saw that people were judged according to what they had done. Books where the deeds of the people have been recorded would be used as evidence against them. It turns out that anyone who did good work would have his name written in another book (the Book of Life). The Book of Life contains a list of those destined to inherit eternal life. The qualification of person's name to be written and maintained in Book of Life is based on what has been written against their names in the other books:

> [12] And I saw the dead, great and small, standing before the throne, and books were opened. Then another book was opened, which is the book of life. And the dead were judged by what was written in the books, according to what they had done. (Revelation 20: 12 ESV).

There are other snippets of this in the Bible:

> 27 For the Son of Man is going to come with his angels in the glory of his Father, and then he will repay each person according to what he has done. (Matthew 16: 27 ESV).
> 12 and that to you, O Lord, belongs steadfast love. For you will render to a man according to his work. (Psalm 62:12 ESV).
>
> If you say, "Behold, we did not know this,"
>   does not he who weighs the heart perceive it?
> Does not he who keeps watch over your soul know it,
>   and will he not repay man according to his work?
> (Proverbs 24:12 ESV)

> "I the Lord search the heart
> and test the mind,
> to give every man according to his ways,
> according to the fruit of his deeds." (Jeremiah 17:10)

> [19] great in counsel and mighty in deed, whose eyes are open to all the ways of the children of man, rewarding each one according to his ways and according to the fruit of his deeds. (Jeremiah 32: 19 ESV).

> [23] and I will strike her children dead. And all the churches will know that I am he who searches mind and heart, and I will give to each of you according to your works. (Revelation 2:23 ESV).

> 5 But because of your hard and impenitent heart you are storing up wrath for yourself on the day of wrath when God's righteous judgment will be revealed.
> 6 He will render to each one according to his works: 7 to those who by patience in well-doing seek for glory and honor and immortality, he will give eternal life; 8 but for those who are self-seeking[a] and do not obey the truth, but obey unrighteousness, there will be wrath and fury. (Romans 2:5–8).

> [12] "Behold, I am coming soon, bringing my recompense with me, to repay each one for what he has done. (Revelation 22:12 ESV).

It can be seen from the foregoing that salvation and good works go together. They complement each other. Without salvation, all good works will be in vain. That is to say that any human who has not been born again through Christ (has not become a descendant/seed of Christ) can never be saved and rewarded as a son of God, no matter the good works he has done. This is an immutable legal requirement (which cannot be toiled with) that all must become the offsprings of Christ (through the Holy Spirit) for them to benefit from the salvation he has earned on the cross. Conversely, without good works, the purpose of salvation will amount to nothing, because anyone found wanting or coming short of the expected target, will not be rewarded with salvation at the end of age:

> [14] What does it profit, my brethren, if someone says he has faith but does not have works? Can faith save him? [15] If a brother or sister is naked and destitute of daily food, [16] and one of you says to them, "Depart in peace, be warmed and filled," but you

do not give them the things which are needed for the body, what does it profit? [17] Thus also faith by itself, if it does not have works, is dead.

[18] But someone will say, "You have faith, and I have works." Show me your faith without your works, and I will show you my faith by my works. [19] You believe that there is one God. You do well. Even the demons believe—and tremble! [20] But do you want to know, O foolish man, that faith without works is dead? [21] Was not Abraham our father justified by works when he offered Isaac his son on the altar? [22] Do you see that faith was working together with his works, and by works faith was made perfect? [23] And the Scripture was fulfilled which says, "Abraham believed God, and it was accounted to him for righteousness." And he was called the friend of God. [24] You see then that a man is justified by works, and not by faith only.

[25] Likewise, was not Rahab the harlot also justified by works when she received the messengers and sent them out another way?

[26] For as the body without the spirit is dead, so faith without works is dead also. (James 2:14-26 NKJV).

Simply put, man was originally created to do certain work/s on the earth. However, this purpose was temporally derailed (disrupted) when Adam failed at the garden, and man became inadequate to undertake this work effectively. So, salvation was required to restore man to his original state so he can carry out the purpose he had originally been created for. Hence, it is pointless or even an abuse of grace, for a man who has been saved to not do the work he had originally been created for. In this regard, a cardinal responsibility of man is to obey God's command. A man that disobeys God's command is not worthy to be saved, and if already saved will lose the salvation. Consider what happened to Adam. He was created and placed on a high standing, but as soon as he disobeyed God's command, he lost his status. An analogy to this would be a person who went to prison and stopped discharging his parental duties adequately. When he eventually gets out of prison, he is expected to continue to discharge his parental duties. That is his main responsibility, and even though getting out of prison was important for him to adequately discharge his duties, he will be assessed on how well he discharged his parental duties. Likewise, the transgression of Adam got man into prison. The salvation by Christ rescued man from this prison, so that man can do the actual work he has been created for. At the end, man would be assessed based on this scorecard to determine whether he can be promoted to the next level of humans that God has planned for man:

> Beloved, now we are children of God; and it has not yet been revealed what we shall be, but we know that when He is revealed, we shall be like Him, for we shall see Him as He is. (1 John 3:2 NKJV)

> But as it is written, Eye hath not seen, nor ear heard, neither have entered into the heart of man, the things which God hath prepared for them that love him. (1 Corinthians 2:9 KJV).

10.9.1 The Mystery of Salvation

Redemption is only for the children of Adam and not for the beings who were before Adam, who had already been corrupted by Satan and his angels. It is also not extended to Nephilim and their offspring. So, Jesus Christ came to redeem only pure humans who came from Adam.

What does this mean really? Christ came to rectify the sins of Adam, which has cascaded down to his descendants. Hence, only Adam and his descendants can benefit from the salvation of Christ. Other humanoid beings (pre-adamic beings, Nephilim, etc) who have somewhat found some kind of footing on earth are excluded from this, because they had not originally been designed as beings of light.

To fully understand this, let's consider what happened at the garden, Adam was created as a special breed of human–a being of light. Before Adam, there was the first generation of humans created on the 6th day. These beings somehow offended God or did not satisfy his desire, hence, the need to create Adam, imbued with better qualities (see Section 4.1). However, Adam transgressed, and fell to a lower level than he was originally created to function in. He became flesh and blood. As a triune being, Adam had light, flesh and blood. However, when he fell, he lost the light and became only flesh and blood. Having become a fleshly being, he must die!

But due to the immense love of God towards Adam and his descendants, he wanted to reconstruct man and bring him back to the original status he had designed the new breed of humans to be. Ordinarily, man ought to have redeemed himself from this lower level. However, for many generations no man was able to this. Thus, Jesus Christ (a being of light) had to descend to earth (a lower level) to become flesh and blood (mimicking the fall of Adam), to redeem man from this quagmire.

At the end of his mission, Jesus Christ had to shed every blood in him. This signifies the draining of the human blood, which has been corrupted at the garden. The blood had to be completely shed through a painful process, so that man can ascend and regain his rightful position as a being of light through him. At the crucifixion, the fleshly man, which Adam became after the fall, died, so that the *being of light*, which Adam had originally been designed to be, would re-emerge:

> 17 Therefore, if anyone is in Christ, he is a new creation.[a] The old has passed away; behold, the new has come. 18 All this is from God, who through Christ reconciled us to himself and gave us the ministry of reconciliation; 19 that is, in Christ God was reconciling[b] the world to himself, not counting their trespasses against them, and entrusting to us the message of reconciliation. 20 Therefore, we are ambassadors for Christ, God making his appeal through us. We implore you on behalf of Christ, be reconciled to God. 21 For our sake he made him to be sin who knew no sin, so that in him we might become the righteousness of God. (2 Corinthians 5:17–21 ESV).

The re-emergence of the new breed of light was symbolised by the resurrection of Christ. Hence, Christ is referred to as the first fruit of this new creature/being:

> [20] But now is Christ risen from the dead, and become the firstfruits of them that slept.
> [21] For since by man came death, by man came also the resurrection of the dead.
> [22] For as in Adam all die, even so in Christ shall all be made alive.
> [23] But every man in his own order: Christ the firstfruits; afterward they that are Christ's at his coming. (1 Corinthians 15:20–23 KJV).

This new breed of humans, which Jesus Christ has opened the way for is what is referred to as the sons of God. This is the destination of humans–to be transformed into sons of God, a class of humans that will end up being like angels. This is the glorious plan of God for man, which Paul exclaimed on realization:

> [6] Yet among the mature we do impart wisdom, although it is not a wisdom of this age or of the rulers of this age, who are

doomed to pass away. ⁷ But we impart a secret and hidden wisdom of God, which God decreed before the ages for our glory. ⁸ None of the rulers of this age understood this, for if they had, they would not have crucified the Lord of glory. ⁹ But, as it is written,

"What no eye has seen, nor ear heard,
   nor the heart of man imagined,
what God has prepared for those who love him"—

¹⁰ these things God has revealed to us through the Spirit. (1 Corinthians 2: 6–10 ESV).

This transformation is tied to the salvation which Christ is offering. Only those that are saved will be transformed. The salvation of humans will be applied at the end of ages. Any follower of Christ is currently undergoing probationary period and not fully saved. This was alluded to in Hebrews:

²⁴ For Christ has entered, not into holy places made with hands, which are copies of the true things, but into heaven itself, now to appear in the presence of God on our behalf. ²⁵ Nor was it to offer himself repeatedly, as the high priest enters the holy places every year with blood not his own, ²⁶ for then he would have had to suffer repeatedly since the foundation of the world. But as it is, he has appeared once for all at the end of the ages to put away sin by the sacrifice of himself. ²⁷ And just as it is appointed for man to die once, and after that comes judgment, ²⁸ so Christ, having been offered once to bear the sins of many, will appear a second time, not to deal with sin but to save those who are eagerly waiting for him. (Hebrews 9:24–28 ESV).

Notice that the passage above is saying that Christ is coming a second time to save those who are waiting for him. This means that no one has yet been saved, but rather followers of Christ have been offered a promise of salvation if they remained in Christ till the end. Salvation happens at the end of age (¹³ *But he that shall endure unto the end, the same shall be saved Mathew 24: 13 KJV*). That's when the blood of Christ is applied to save all those who had believed in him and assiduously worked to become sons of God (But as it is, he has appeared once for all at the end of the ages to put away sin by the sacrifice of himself - *Hebrews 9:26 ESV*). Without Christ, no human being can ascend to become a son of God–no matter how hard he tries. This is the mystery of salvation.

As usual, Satan who now understands this is mystery (after the fact), is selling humanity a fake version of this new breed of humans in the form of transhumanism/posthumanism (Section 12.5). Through transhumanism, Satan is promising to elevate man to higher capabilities through the merger of man with machines and artificial intelligence, that would make man overcome his existential challenges. However, Satan's true intension is to further corrupt humans such that they will not attain the sons of God status. This concept of transhumanism is explored further in Chapter 12.

CHAPTER 11

The Way–Becoming a Follower of Christ

11.1 LAW AND GRACE CONUNDRUM

There is a raging debate among Christians on the relevance of laws of God in the life of Christians. The laws of God in question are those codified by Moses. Moses gave the Israelites the 10 commandments (Deuteronomy 5 and 6), and other laws they were to keep (Leviticus) soon after their exodus from Egypt. He also told them that there are both blessings and curses associated with the laws. If they kept the laws they will reap the blessings, but if they transgress the laws, they will face severe consequences. And he instilled in them that keeping the laws is a path to righteousness:

> 25 And it will be righteousness for us, if we are careful to do all this commandment before the Lord our God, as he has commanded us. (Deuteronomy 6:25 ESV).

While some argue that the laws have been relegated to the background by grace, after the resurrection of Christ, others believe that the laws are still relevant, and Christians should keep them.

Jesus Christ kept the laws and did not break any aspect of it. Several times he insisted that he came to fulfil the laws. This is understandable, considering that he came to repair the relationship between God and man to restore man to his former state. For this to happen, man would have to obey all the laws and commands of God set out to retrain humans. At the accomplishment of these, man can be promoted to the level of a being of light–the sons of God.

Christ also stated that no aspect (iota and dot) of the law can be removed from it, until the end of age (until heaven and earth pass away):

> [17] "Do not think that I have come to abolish the Law or the Prophets; I have not come to abolish them but to fulfill them. [18] For truly, I say to you, until heaven and earth pass away, not an iota, not a dot, will pass from the Law until all is accomplished. (Matthew 5:17–18 ESV).

> [17] But it is easier for heaven and earth to pass away than for one dot of the Law to become void. (Luke 16:17 ESV).

This is a clear confirmation that the laws will continue to exist and be relevant till the end. The 'relevance' of the law is an aspect of it and, if Christ says no aspect of it shall be removed from it, the 'relevance' of the laws cannot be relegated or ignored.

The argument commonly put forward is that after the death and resurrection of Christ, Christ has fulfilled every aspect of the law, so there is no requirement for Christians to continue to keep the laws. Those who believe that keeping the law and commandments is no longer relevant for the New Testament believers (post-resurrection followers of Christs), hinges their argument on the basis that Christ has done all the work, and his followers only have to be plugged to him, to inherit the benefits of it via grace. This idea is surprising, considering that Christ held the laws in high esteem. He made clear the importance of keeping the laws of God. For all those he healed and forgave, he always charged them not to sin again (essentially, not to transgress the laws of God again). He clearly stated that the law will continue to be in force till the end of ages. Notice that in the passage in *Luke 16:17*, Christ clearly stated that no aspect of the law will become irrelevant until heaven and earth pass away. He did not say "*not until after my death and resurrection*", but after this heaven and earth has stopped to exist. Hence, until the new heaven and earth are established to replace the existing one, the laws will continue to be relevant to humans. This is because the law is for humans and humans will continue to exist until the end, when humans would be changed into a superior state–sons of God state. At this point, a new law that would be obeyed by the sons of God would kick in, in accordance with established cosmic protocols of God (see Section 10.1). As a matter of fact, the final judgement that will be used to determine those that will enter the Kingdom of God will be based on the laws. Only those adjudged to have kept the laws will be considered worthy to receive the salvation that will be applied at the end of ages, and subsequent entrance into the Kingdom of God and eternal life.

When once asked by an intended follower what he ought to do to have eternal life, Christ reeled out the entire commandment, as a prerequisite and added something else on top (some level of personal sacrifice-disposing ones wealth):

> [17] As Jesus started on his way, a man ran up to him and fell on his knees before him. "Good teacher," he asked, "what must I do to inherit eternal life?"
> [18] "Why do you call me good?" Jesus answered. "No one is good—except God alone. [19] You know the commandments: 'You shall not murder, you shall not commit adultery, you shall not steal, you shall not give false testimony, you shall not defraud, honor your father and mother.'
> [20] "Teacher," he declared, "all these I have kept since I was a boy."
> [21] Jesus looked at him and loved him. "One thing you lack," he said. "Go, sell everything you have and give to the poor, and you will have treasure in heaven. Then come, follow me." (Mark 10:17–21 KJV).

When pressed further on this by his disciples, Christ did not mince words in letting them know how difficult it is for one to enter the kingdom of God:

> "Children, how hard it is to enter the kingdom of God! [25] It is easier for a camel to go through the eye of a needle than for someone who is rich to enter the kingdom of God." (Mark 10:24–25 KJV).

To make this even simpler, Christ warned that the level of standard of keeping these laws for his followers should exceed those of the scribes and Pharisees:

> [20] For I tell you, unless your righteousness exceeds that of the scribes and Pharisees, you will never enter the kingdom of heaven. (Matthew 5: 20 ESV).

He used the righteousness of the scribes and Pharisees as a base standard, because at that time, they were among the main sects that were zealous in adhering to the laws. He went further to give examples of the level of righteousness expected of his followers, who wish to enter the kingdom of God (Matthew 5: 21–48). For instance, whereas the Pharisees keep the laws of not committing murder, Christ expects his followers not to even be angry, as that would be equated to murder:

> [21] "You have heard that it was said to those of old, 'You shall not murder; and whoever murders will be liable to judgment.' [22] But I say to you that everyone who is angry with his brother will be liable to judgment; whoever insults his brother will be liable to the council; and whoever says, 'You fool!' will be liable to the hell of fire. (Matthew 5: 21–22 ESV).

There was also a similar one about adultery, where he stated that "anyone who looks at a woman lustfully has already committed adultery with her in his heart" (Matthew 5:27 NIV), as well as loving one's enemies, turning the cheek, not swearing and taking oaths, in the same passage. Christ also warned against trivialising the laws or any aspects of it:

> [19] Therefore whoever relaxes one of the least of these commandments and teaches others to do the same will be called least in the kingdom of heaven, but whoever does them and teaches them will be called great in the kingdom of heaven (Matthew 5:17–19 ESV).

This instruction was not limited to only his followers at that point, but also for future believers, who would come into the faith after he has left the earth. Hence, that command is still relevant in the present. If these commands were not going to be relevant after Christ's resurrection, why would he have bothered to instruct his followers about them? He would have said: *"don't bother about them, because I will take care of them"*. Worthy to note that the rich man in Mark 10:17, specifically asked Jesus what he must do to inherit eternal life. Eternal life was what Christ came to open the door for man, yet he told him to start by keeping the commandments, before even following him.

Snippets from the Bible also suggest that the disciples of Christ kept the laws even after the ascension of Christ. In Acts 10:9–16, Peter was presented with all sorts of unclean food to eat in a vision, which he declined to eat and asserted that he has never eaten anything unclean before:

> [14] But Peter said, "By no means, Lord; for I have never eaten anything that is common or unclean." (Acts 10: 14 ESV).

This statement confirms that while Peter was with Christ, he did not break this law about unclean food, and he continued to keep this law even after Christ has left the world. Another instance was when Peter returned to Jerusalem from the house of Cornelius, the disciples at Jerusalem were livid and pounced on him for going into the house of a Gentile. This also suggests that they were also adherents of the laws:

> Now the apostles and the brothers who were throughout Judea heard that the Gentiles also had received the word of God. ² So when Peter went up to Jerusalem, the circumcision party criticized him, saying, ³ "You went to uncircumcised men and ate with them." (Acts 11:1–3 ESV).

However, they were assuaged after Peter narrated his vision to them. Note that it did not come to them as a surprise that Peter initially avoided eating the unclean food presented to him in the vision. Furthermore, the essence of the vision was to persuade him to go to the house of a Gentile. Jews are prohibited from entering the houses of Gentiles, hence the vision to persuade him to do this:

> ²⁸ And he said to them, "You yourselves know how unlawful it is for a Jew to associate with or to visit anyone of another nation, but God has shown me that I should not call any person common or unclean. ²⁹ So when I was sent for, I came without objection." (Acts 10: 28–29 ESV).

The vision was like a special permission granted to Peter, to overlook this specific law to bring the Gentile into the fold. This also confirms that he was adhering to this law, prohibiting Jews from entering the house of a Gentile prior this vision. Even after the Cornelius incident, Peter continued to avoid eating with Gentiles, until he was rebuked by Paul.

Although some may argue that because Cornelius was not a Jew, he was not keeping the laws; yet, Christ opened the door of salvation to him, which may suggest that keeping the law was not necessary. However, Cornelius was described as a devout man who feared God, which somehow suggests that he was adhering to the laws of God, even though he was a Gentile:

> At Caesarea there was a man named Cornelius, a centurion of what was known as the Italian Cohort, ² a devout man who feared God with all his household, gave alms generously to the people, and prayed continually to God. ³ About the ninth hour of the day he saw clearly in a vision an angel of God come in and say to him, "Cornelius." ⁴ And he stared at him in terror and said, "What is it, Lord?" And he said to him, "Your prayers and

THE WAY-BECOMING A FOLLOWER OF CHRIST

your alms have ascended as a memorial before God. (Acts 10: 1-4 ESV).

So, what endeared him to God was his righteousness, and even at that he still needed Peter an apostle to graft him into the fold. Peter also emphasised on this while addressing Cornelius, stating the righteous from all nations are acceptable to God:

> [34] So Peter opened his mouth and said: "Truly I understand that God shows no partiality, [35] but in every nation anyone who fears him and does what is right is acceptable to him. (Acts 10: 34-35 ESV).

If righteousness and adhering to the laws of God, were not important Peter ought to have been sent to other Gentiles littered all over Jerusalem at that time. What Peter did was in line with the Great Commission which mandated them to go out to the nations and make disciples from there and bringing them into the fold through baptism:

> "[19] Therefore go and make disciples of all nations, baptizing them in the name of the Father and of the Son and of the Holy Spirit, [20] and teaching them to obey everything I have commanded you. And surely I am with you always, to the very end of the age." (Matthew 28:19-20 ESV).

Again, the importance of obeying the laws and commandments were reiterated by Christ in this passage *(teaching them to obey everything I have commanded you)*. After this, it was obvious from many passages in the Bible, that the disciples of Christ continued to keep the laws and were zealous about it. James hinted that the disciples in Jerusalem were *"all zealous for the law"* (Acts 21:20). Paul described Ananias who baptised him as an adherent of the law:

> [12] "And one Ananias, a devout man according to the law, well spoken of by all the Jews who lived there, [13] came to me, and standing by me said to me, 'Brother Saul, receive your sight.' (Acts 22: 12-13 ESV).

So, from where did the raging debate about law and grace emanate from? Paul!

Paul introduced a radical concept among the followers of Christ in his zeal to reach out to the Gentile nations. He posited that believers are justified through faith and not by works of the law:

> [28] *For we hold that one is justified by faith apart from works of the law.* (Romans 3:28 ESV).

He hinted this concept in most of his epistles but expounded on it mainly in Romans, and Galatians. In Romans, Paul argues that the main purpose of the law is to expose the unrighteousness of men:

> [20] For by works of the law no human being will be justified in his sight, since through the law comes knowledge of sin. (Romans 3: 20 ESV).

And the unrighteousness of man on the other hand, reveals the righteousness of God:

> [5] But if our unrighteousness serves to show the righteousness of God, what shall we say? That God is unrighteous to inflict wrath on us? (I speak in a human way.) [6] By no means! For then how could God judge the world? (Romans 3: 20 ESV).

This leads him to present a new teaching of righteousness of God outside of the law but gained through faith. Essentially that God does not need the law to show how righteous he is:

> [21] But now the righteousness of God has been manifested apart from the law, although the Law and the Prophets bear witness to it— [22] the righteousness of God through faith in Jesus Christ for all who believe. (Romans 3:21–22 ESV).

He further argues that God adopted this strategy because all have sinned–both those under the law and those outside of the law. Hence, God provided man an avenue to be justified–his grace through the redemption made possible by Jesus Christ:

> For there is no distinction: [23] for all have sinned and fall short of the glory of God, [24] and are justified by his grace as a gift, through the redemption that is in Christ Jesus, [25] whom God put forward as a propitiation by his blood, to be received by faith. (Romans 3:23–25 ESV).

The context of grace used here by Paul is akin to an act of kindness to allow his son to die, so as to redeem man from his fallen nature. To benefit from this redemption, man would have sufficient faith to believe that this is so. That is the faith to abandon other beliefs and false gods and believe that Christ death absolved man from the original sin, which separated man from God. He emphasised that this was to demonstrate the righteousness of God to those who may accuse God of being unrighteous for judging man who he knows is incapable of keeping the law:

> This was to show God's righteousness, because in his divine forbearance he had passed over former sins. 26 It was to show his righteousness at the present time, so that he might be just and the justifier of the one who has faith in Jesus. (Romans 3:25-26 ESV).

Despite presenting the foregoing argument, Paul still upheld the relevance of the law:

> [31] Do we then overthrow the law by this faith? By no means! On the contrary, we uphold the law. (Romans 3:31 ESV).

Paul's key argument is that access to this redemptive grace is obtained through faith. One must first believe in the redemptive purpose of Christ to inherit this grace:

> Therefore, since we have been justified by faith, we have peace with God through our Lord Jesus Christ. [2] Through him we have also obtained access by faith into this grace in which we stand, and we rejoice in hope of the glory of God. (Romans 5: 1-2 ESV).

This grace Paul is referring to does not necessarily cover sin, but enables humans to have power over sin:

> [12] Let not sin therefore reign in your mortal body, to make you obey its passions. [13] Do not present your members to sin as instruments for unrighteousness but present yourselves to God as those who have been brought from death to life, and your members to God as instruments for righteousness. [14] For sin will have no dominion over you, since you are not under law but under grace. (Romans 6:12-14 ESV).

Here, Paul was urging people to not let sin reign over them. This suggests that humans have a role to play in avoiding sin and sinful lifestyle. The grace that is given does not mean humans will not make any effort to avoid sinning; however, grace provides the strength that will enable humans to overcome the pressure to sin. Grace is sort of an enabler, but will not block humans from sinning, but rather can provide the strength and escape route to flee from sin:

> [11] For the grace of God has appeared, bringing salvation for all people, [12] training us to renounce ungodliness and worldly passions, and to live self-controlled, upright, and godly lives in the present age, (Titus 2:11–12 ESV).

Basically, Paul is of the view that without this grace, it would be almost impossible to overcome sin, but with the grace, overcoming sin is made far easier (For sin will have no dominion over you, since you are not under law but under grace).

Humans can wilfully sin, even where grace abounds. By doing this, they will wilfully be presenting themselves as slaves of sin, hence coming under the dominion of sin instead of the dominion of righteousness:

> [15] What then? Are we to sin because we are not under law but under grace? By no means! [16] Do you not know that if you present yourselves to anyone as obedient slaves, you are slaves of the one whom you obey, either of sin, which leads to death, or of obedience, which leads to righteousness? [17] But thanks be to God, that you who were once slaves of sin have become obedient from the heart to the standard of teaching to which you were committed, [18] and, having been set free from sin, have become slaves of righteousness. [19] I am speaking in human terms, because of your natural limitations. For just as you once presented your members as slaves to impurity and to lawlessness leading to more lawlessness, so now present your members as slaves to righteousness leading to sanctification. (Romans 6: 15–19 ESV).

Viewed from this lens, grace seems to act like an Automated Lane Keeping System (ALKS) in modern cars. When activated, the ALKS will keep the car going in a particular lane, and whenever the driver tries to steer away from the lane, he feels a sort of restraint, however, this function can be overridden when the driver ignores the restraining prompt and keeps going into the other lane. Same way, this grace will restrain a believer from sinning, but a believer can wilfully ignore this and present himself to sin.

Based on the above passage, there are two opposites: sin and righteousness. The goal of humans is to become righteous (to become slaves of righteousness). According to Paul, grace enables followers of Christ to be obedient to the *standard of teaching* (Romans 6:17). This *standard of teaching* is essentially the laws of God. What Paul is trying to say is that ordinarily, it is extremely difficult for humans to keep to the laws of God (standards of God, which were in place before Moses was giving the commandments), but through the power of grace keeping to the laws become effortless. This counters the widespread weird view of many followers of Christ that tends to suggest that grace is a licence to sin, which goes directly against Paul's admonition: Are we to sin because we are not under law but under grace? By no means!

Paul went ahead to introduce the concept of two laws: The law of the Spirit of God and the Law of sin and death that are constantly at play in human life. According to him, humans are trapped in the interplay of these two opposing laws. In his mind he is obedient to the law of God, whilst his body which is weak is still subject to the law of sin:

> [14] For we know that the law is spiritual, but I am of the flesh, sold under sin. [15] For I do not understand my own actions. For I do not do what I want, but I do the very thing I hate. [16] Now if I do what I do not want, I agree with the law, that it is good. [17] So now it is no longer I who do it, but sin that dwells within me. [18] For I know that nothing good dwells in me, that is, in my flesh. For I have the desire to do what is right, but not the ability to carry it out. [19] For I do not do the good I want, but the evil I do not want is what I keep on doing. [20] Now if I do what I do not want, it is no longer I who do it, but sin that dwells within me.
>
> [21] So I find it to be a law that when I want to do right, evil lies close at hand. [22] For I delight in the law of God, in my inner being, [23] but I see in my members another law waging war against the law of my mind and making me captive to the law of sin that dwells in my members. [24] Wretched man that I am! Who will deliver me from this body of death? [25] Thanks be to God through Jesus Christ our Lord! So then, I myself serve the law of God with my mind, but with my flesh I serve the law of sin. (Romans 7: 14–25 ESV).

Thus, he suggests that to overcome the laws of sin, one must be subject to the law of the Spirit through Jesus Christ. One must walk according to the Spirit to benefit from this:

> There is therefore now no condemnation for those who are in Christ Jesus [2] For the law of the Spirit of life has set you free in Christ Jesus from the law of sin and death. [3] For God has done what the law, weakened by the flesh, could not do. By sending his own Son in the likeness of sinful flesh and for sin, he condemned sin in the flesh, [4] in order that the righteous requirement of the law might be fulfilled in us, who walk not according to the flesh but according to the Spirit. [5] For those who live

according to the flesh set their minds on the things of the flesh, but those who live according to the Spirit set their minds on the things of the Spirit. ⁶ For to set the mind on the flesh is death, but to set the mind on the Spirit is life and peace. ⁷ For the mind that is set on the flesh is hostile to God, for it does not submit to God's law; indeed, it cannot. ⁸ Those, who are in the flesh, cannot please God.

⁹ You, however, are not in the flesh but in the Spirit, if in fact the Spirit of God dwells in you. Anyone who does not have the Spirit of Christ does not belong to him. ¹⁰ But if Christ is in you, although the body is dead because of sin, the Spirit is life because of righteousness. ¹¹ If the Spirit of him who raised Jesus from the dead dwells in you, he who raised Christ Jesus from the dead will also give life to your mortal bodies through his Spirit who dwells in you.

12 So then, brothers, we are debtors, not to the flesh, to live according to the flesh. 13 For if you live according to the flesh you will die, but if by the Spirit you put to death the deeds of the body, you will live. 14 For all who are led by the Spirit of God are sons[f] of God. 15 For you did not receive the spirit of slavery to fall back into fear, but you have received the Spirit of adoption as sons, by whom we cry, "Abba! Father!" 16 The Spirit himself bears witness with our spirit that we are children of God, 17 and if children, then heirs—heirs of God and fellow heirs with Christ, provided we suffer with him in order that we may also be glorified with him. (Romans 8:1–17 ESV).

What Paul is essentially saying here is that the commandments and laws are physical manifestation that transcended from pre-existing spiritual laws that were governing all things. Even prior the laws were given on earth; they were already in place in the cosmic realm. And since humans have been incapable of keeping the physical laws in flesh, the only chance they have is to try to fulfil this through the spirit. Ordinarily, this would have been impossible for humans to do, but Jesus Christ opened the doors for humans through his obedience to all the laws in flesh and his death and resurrection. By his death, he gave humans access to this grace and the Holy Spirit through which they can keep the Spiritual laws, which are superior to the earthly laws that transcended from it. Hence, the key here is for believers to abide in Christ, so as to be plugged into this grace he has made available. To abide in Christ entails that one must strive to kill the desires of the flesh (provided we suffer with him in order

THE WAY—BECOMING A FOLLOWER OF CHRIST

that we may also be glorified with him - Romans 8:17 ESV). Many snippets in other passages in the Bible point to this:

> [15] Do not love the world or the things in the world. If anyone loves the world, the love of the Father is not in him. [16] For all that is in the world—the desires of the flesh and the desires of the eyes and pride of life—is not from the Father but is from the world. [17] And the world is passing away along with its desires, but whoever does the will of God abides forever. (1 John 2: 15–17 ESV).

> [28] And now, little children, abide in him, so that when he appears we may have confidence and not shrink from him in shame at his coming. [29] If you know that he is righteous, you may be sure that everyone who practices righteousness has been born of him. (1 John 2: 28–29 ESV).

> [3] And everyone who thus hopes in him purifies himself as he is pure.
> [4] Everyone who makes a practice of sinning also practices lawlessness; sin is lawlessness. [5] You know that he appeared in order to take away sins, and in him there is no sin. [6] No one who abides in him keeps on sinning; no one who keeps on sinning has either seen him or known him. [7] Little children, let no one deceive you. Whoever practices righteousness is righteous, as he is righteous. [8] Whoever makes a practice of sinning is of the devil, for the devil has been sinning from the beginning. The reason the Son of God appeared was to destroy the works of the devil. [9] No one born of God makes a practice of sinning, for God's seed abides in him; and he cannot keep on sinning, because he has been born of God. [10] By this it is evident who are the children of God, and who are the children of the devil: whoever does not practice righteousness is not of God, nor is the one who does not love his brother. (1 John 3: 3–10 ESV).

> [12] Therefore, my beloved, as you have always obeyed, so now, not only as in my presence but much more in my absence, work out your own salvation with fear and trembling, [13] for it is God who works in you, both to will and to work for his good pleasure. (Philippians 2: 12–13 ESV).

11.2 FAITH VS WORKS: THE JAMES VS PAUL DEBATE

For many Bible scholars, one of the fascinating discourses in the Bible is the apparent opposing views presented by Paul and James with regards to the role of faith and work in the life of a Christian. James is of the view that work/action is a demonstration of faith. It complements faith, and without it, faith is fruitless (You see that a person is justified by works and not by faith alone–*James 2:24*). However, Paul seems to suggest that faith supersedes work:

> [5] And to the one who does not work but believes in him who justifies the ungodly, his faith is counted as righteousness (Romans 4: 5 ESV).

These two views seem to be diametrically opposed to each other. What even makes it more interesting is that both used Abraham as a test case to prove their points, yet, arrived at conclusions that seem to oppose each other.

James opines that Abraham's willingness (works/actions) to sacrifice his only son was accounted to him as righteousness (because it demonstrated his faith):

> [20] Do you want to be shown, you foolish person, that faith apart from works is useless? [21] Was not Abraham our father justified by works when he offered up his son Isaac on the altar? [22] You see that faith was active along with his works, and faith was completed by his works; [23] and the Scripture was fulfilled that says, "Abraham believed God, and it was counted to him as righteousness"—and he was called a friend of God. [24] You see that a person is justified by works and not by faith alone. (James 2: 20–24 ESV).

But Paul argues that it was because Abraham believed God, that he was regarded as righteous. In this regard, it is the faith that is counted as righteousness and not the work:

> 4 What then shall we say was gained by Abraham, our forefather according to the flesh? [2] For if Abraham was justified by works, he has something to boast about, but not before God. [3] For what does the Scripture say? "Abraham believed God, and it was counted to him as righteousness." [4] Now to the one who works, his wages are not counted as a gift but as his due. [5] And to the one who does not work but believes in him who justifies the ungodly, his faith is counted as righteousness, [6] just as David

also speaks of the blessing of the one to whom God counts righteousness apart from works:

> [7] "Blessed are those whose lawless deeds are forgiven,
> and whose sins are covered;
> [8] blessed is the man against whom the Lord will not count his sin." (Romans 4:1-8 ESV).

To reconcile these two, one must realise that even though Abraham was used as an example, two different events in his life were used to support each view. Whereas James's work was focused on the action Abraham made to demonstrate his faith by his willingness to sacrifice his son, Paul was focusing on Abraham's circumcision. According to Paul, Abraham was not justified because he circumcised himself, but was justified as soon as he believed in what God has told him about the circumcision:

> [9] Is this blessing then only for the circumcised, or also for the uncircumcised? For we say that faith was counted to Abraham as righteousness. [10] How then was it counted to him? Was it before or after he had been circumcised? It was not after, but before he was circumcised. [11] He received the sign of circumcision as a seal of the righteousness that he had by faith while he was still uncircumcised. The purpose was to make him the father of all who believe without being circumcised, so that righteousness would be counted to them as well, [12] and to make him the father of the circumcised who are not merely circumcised but who also walk in the footsteps of the faith that our father Abraham had before he was circumcised. (Romans 4: 9-12 ESV).

The introduction of circumcision is a pointer to where Paul was headed–that circumcision was not a key part of salvation. It is more like a superficial marker for the heirs of Abraham. Placing James's and Paul's discourses side-by-side, it appears that the distinguishing factor between their views is the audience they were addressing in their respective epistle. Whereas James's letter was addressing the 12 tribes of Israel, Paul's appears to be targeting Gentile nations. Based on this, it seems the rules/standards are different for the two groups. The Israelites who are direct descendants of Abraham are expected to keep all the laws given to Moses (including circumcision), whereas Gentiles are not expected to keep all the laws. This was obvious from the resolution of the Jerusalem council:

> [19] Therefore my judgment is that we should not trouble those of the Gentiles who turn to God, [20] but should write to them to abstain from the things polluted by idols, and from sexual immorality, and from what has been strangled, and from blood. (Acts 15: 19 -20 ESV).

Furthermore, there was no mention in the Bible that neither Cornelius nor his guests at that event were circumcised before they received the gift of the Holy Spirit. He was a righteous man and even received the Holy Spirit before being baptised (Acts 10:44–48). This seems to suggest that the law may have been relaxed for Gentiles. But why would this be, since Christ taught that every iota of the law will continue to be in force till this earth and heavens have passed away. This may be traced back to the separation of nations, where God chose Israel for himself and allowed the other nations to fall under the control of the sons of God (see Section 7.1). Hence, Gentile nations are technically not under the direct control of God, until God judged the gods (Psalm 82). Thus, whereas a Jew who converts to Christianity is expected to continue to keep to the laws prescribed to them by Moses, for a Gentile, the core requirements for them to be grafted in is to abandon their worship of these false gods and accept Jesus as their Lord and master. This was essentially what Paul was preaching. Furthermore, the circumcision may not be considered as a cosmic law but rather a marker God placed on Abraham and his descendants after the deal (covenant) he had with Abraham. Hence, Gentiles who are not direct descendants of Abraham are not under any obligation to keep this.

Although it may not appear so, Paul recognised that it was a very difficult requirement for someone entrenched in the worship of other gods or religion to abandon these entities, to embrace another God, especially one that is being brought to them by foreigners. All they have was faith in what has been preached to them that Christ is their saviour, and only through him would they be delivered. Thus, accepting the good news that was being brought to them is already an arduous task. This may be likened to getting a modern-day Muslim in Saudi Arabia to openly accept Christianity. This is not only a difficult decision, but very dangerous. Paul alluded to this by recognising the sufferings of the Gentile converts in his second letter to the church in Thessalonica where he encouraged them to endure the suffering emanating from their choice of following Christ:

THE WAY—BECOMING A FOLLOWER OF CHRIST

> ⁴ So that we ourselves glory in you in the churches of God for your patience and faith in all your persecutions and tribulations that ye endure:
>
> ⁵ Which is a manifest token of the righteous judgment of God, that ye may be counted worthy of the kingdom of God, for which ye also suffer:
>
> ⁶ Seeing it is a righteous thing with God to recompense tribulation to them that trouble you;
>
> ⁷ And to you who are troubled rest with us, when the Lord Jesus shall be revealed from heaven with his mighty angels, (2 Thessalonians 1: 4–7 KJV).

This level of faith to switch from one's previous beliefs to a new one is akin to the level of faith Abraham had, which was accounted to him as righteousness. This level of faith is also expected during the end times when to openly proclaim Christ under the antichrist rule will be met with severe punishment including death and imprisonment. Hence, anyone brave enough to have faith in Jesus and call on his name or declare that he is Lord shall be saved:

> ⁹ If you declare with your mouth, "Jesus is Lord," and believe in your heart that God raised him from the dead, you will be saved. (Romans 10:9 ESV).

> And everyone who calls on the name of the LORD will be saved; for on Mount Zion and in Jerusalem there will be deliverance, as the LORD has said, even among the survivors whom the LORD calls. (Joel 2:32 NIV).

Hence, whereas it might seem that Paul was trivialising the requirements for keeping the law, in reality, he simply understood that the Gentiles were taking a giant leap of faith to abandon gods they have known and worshipped for generations, to accept Jesus as their Messiah. Thus, the desire not to add additional burden to them, since even the Jews who were circumcised, were not all regarded as righteous on account of that, because they were breaking other laws of God, and do not even have faith in Jesus Christ, who brought the redemptive grace.

One thing that may not easily be obvious in this, is that Paul also knew that by accepting Christ, the Gentiles will surely abandon their old ways (lifestyles), and accept the righteous path taught by Christ. He expected them to have a new lifestyle that reflects their new belief. Paul made this clear in his letter to Ephesians, where he posited that the lives they lived while under darkness must change to reflect the light they have now embraced:

> Therefore, be imitators of God, as beloved children. ² And walk in love, as Christ loved us and gave himself up for us, a fragrant offering and sacrifice to God.
>
> ³ But sexual immorality and all impurity or covetousness must not even be named among you, as is proper among saints. ⁴ Let there be no filthiness nor foolish talk nor crude joking, which are out of place, but instead let there be thanksgiving. ⁵ For you may be sure of this, that everyone who is sexually immoral or impure, or who is covetous (that is, an idolater), has no inheritance in the kingdom of Christ and God. ⁶ Let no one deceive you with empty words, for because of these things the wrath of God comes upon the sons of disobedience. ⁷ Therefore do not become partners with them; ⁸ for at one time you were darkness, but now you are light in the Lord. Walk as children of light ⁹ (for the fruit of light is found in all that is good and right and true), ¹⁰ and try to discern what is pleasing to the Lord. ¹¹ Take no part in the unfruitful works of darkness, but instead expose them. ¹² For it is shameful even to speak of the things that they do in secret. ¹³ But when anything is exposed by the light, it becomes visible, ¹⁴ for anything that becomes visible is light. (Ephesians 5: 1–14 ESV).

This expectation can be gleaned from his disappointment when he learnt that there were Gentile converts who were still indulging in their old ways. He scolded them and urged the church in Corinth to expel such people from their midst:

> It is actually reported that there is sexual immorality among you, and of a kind that is not tolerated even among pagans, for a man has his father's wife. ² And you are arrogant! Ought you not rather to mourn? Let him who has done this be removed from among you.
>
> 3 For though absent in body, I am present in spirit; and as if present, I have already pronounced judgment on the one who did such a thing. 4 When you are assembled in the name of the Lord Jesus and my spirit is present, with the power of our Lord Jesus, 5 you are to deliver this man to Satan for the destruction of the flesh, so that his spirit may be saved in the day of the Lord. (1 Corinthians 5: 1–5 ESV).

He reiterated this in Romans, where he urged them to emulate his ways:

> ⁹ Those things, which ye have both learned, and received, and heard, and seen in me, do: and the God of peace shall be with you. (Phillipians 4:9 KJV).

When it appeared that Paul was extending this teaching about circumcision not being a necessity to diaspora Jews living among the Gentiles, James was concerned and drew Paul's attention to this, when he came to Jerusalem:

> ²¹ And they are informed of thee, that thou teachest all the Jews which are among the Gentiles to forsake Moses, saying that they ought not to circumcise their children, neither to walk after the customs. (Acts 21:21 KJV).

Consequently, he urged Paul to clear this out by demonstrating to the believers in Jerusalem that he was still observing the laws:

> ²² What then is to be done? They will certainly hear that you have come. ²³ Do therefore what we tell you. We have four men who are under a vow; ²⁴ take these men and purify yourself along with them and pay their expenses, so that they may shave their heads. Thus, all will know that there is nothing in what they have been told about you, but that you yourself also live in observance of the law. ²⁵ But as for the Gentiles who have believed, we have sent a letter with our judgment that they should abstain from what has been sacrificed to idols, and from blood, and from what has been strangled, and from sexual immorality." ²⁶ Then Paul took the men, and the next day he purified himself along with them and went into the temple, giving notice when the days of purification would be fulfilled and the offering presented for each one of them. (Acts 21: 22- 26 ESV).

Paul believed that circumcision is of value if the circumcised person keeps the law. This was probably to correct the error among Jews that because they were circumcised, they have been justified. Paul posited that an uncircumcised Gentile who keeps the law is better than a circumcised Jew who breaks the law. In this vein he seems to equate circumcision as a custom for direct descendants of Abraham and not a law that is binding on Gentiles:

> ²⁵ For circumcision indeed is of value if you obey the law, but if you break the law, your circumcision becomes uncircumcision. ²⁶ So, if a man who is uncircumcised keeps the precepts of the law, will not his uncircumcision be regarded as

> circumcision? ²⁷ Then he who is physically uncircumcised but keeps the law will condemn you who have the written code and circumcision but break the law. ²⁸ For no one is a Jew who is merely one outwardly, nor is circumcision outward and physical. ²⁹ But a Jew is one inwardly, and circumcision is a matter of the heart, by the Spirit, not by the letter. His praise is not from man but from God. (Romans 2: 25–28 ESV).

> ¹² For all who have sinned without the law will also perish without the law, and all who have sinned under the law will be judged by the law. ¹³ For it is not the hearers of the law who are righteous before God, but the doers of the law who will be justified. ¹⁴ For when Gentiles, who do not have the law, by nature do what the law requires, they are a law to themselves, even though they do not have the law. ¹⁵ They show that the work of the law is written on their hearts, while their conscience also bears witness, and their conflicting thoughts accuse or even excuse them ¹⁶ on that day when, according to my gospel, God judges the secrets of men by Christ Jesus. (Romans 2: 12–16 ESV).

Paul's core argument is that the Gentile nations (previously under the influence of false gods), who has never known the law are unrighteous. But this did not stop God from providing a way through which they can be justified outside of the law. They only have to believe in the true God through Jesus Christ to be justified. This believe as presented earlier, is not an easy one, because it requires them to reject the gods, they have known all their lives, to accept another God, who they can only interact with through faith; just the same way Abraham rejected the gods his father had worshipped (see Section 8.2) to believe in the true God. He hinged this on the fact that faith was already counted as righteousness for Abraham even before he was circumcised, hence, being circumcised was not a prerequisite to being considered righteous, but merely a physical/cosmetic sign to seal this faith:

> ¹¹ He received the sign of circumcision as a seal of the righteousness that he had by faith while he was still uncircumcised. The purpose was to make him the father of all who believe without being circumcised, so that righteousness would be counted to them as well. (Romans 4: 11 ESV).

He further argues that physical circumcision alone is not sufficient, because one will still have the same level of faith that Abraham had to reject other gods and believe in the one true God, to be considered righteous:

> [12] and to make him the father of the circumcised *who are not merely circumcised but who also walk in the footsteps of the faith that our father Abraham had before he was circumcised.* (Romans 4: 12 ESV).

Paul essentially believes that inward circumcision of the heart is what really matters, and not its physical manifestation. As far as Paul was concerned once the individual believes in his heart to worship the true God, he has inwardly been circumcised, and there is no longer a necessity for the physical circumcision.

The key here is *"walking in the footsteps of the faith that our father Abraham had before he was circumcised" (Romans 4: 12).* This points to the fact that Abraham did have faith but also walked in certain ways that demonstrated his faith and belief. If a circumcised or uncircumcised person does not walk in this right way, the faith is useless. This tallies with what James opined. This is where the apparent divergent views of both converge:

> 18 But someone will say, "You have faith, and I have works." Show me your faith without [a]your works, and I will show you my faith by [b]my works. (James 2:18 NKJV).

Similarly, for the gentiles who have known other gods and have been in darkness, if they turn around to believe in the only true God and in the redemption of man through Jesus Christ, it would be counted to them as righteousness:

> It will be counted to us who believe in him who raised from the dead Jesus our Lord, [25] who was delivered up for our trespasses and raised for our justification. (Romans 4: 12 ESV).

This is because such faith comes with a lot of risk and consequences, and accompanied by a demonstration that they have rejected those gods through the new way they walk in. Such faith comes from an inward belief in the salvation made possible by Christ, which when confessed openly, unequivocally demonstrates the person's allegiance:

> [9] because, if you confess with your mouth that Jesus is Lord and believe in your heart that God raised him from the dead, you will be saved. [10] For with the heart one believes and is justified, and with the mouth one confesses and is saved. [11] For the

Scripture says, "Everyone who believes in him will not be put to shame." [12] For there is no distinction between Jew and Greek; for the same Lord is Lord of all, bestowing his riches on all who call on him. [13] For "everyone who calls on the name of the Lord will be saved." (Romans 10: 9–13 ESV).

This is almost similar to the same faith Abraham had that comes with inbuilt work. For a person who has such faith, sin must not reign over him. Such a person would not be an instrument of sin:

> [11] So you also must consider yourselves dead to sin and alive to God in Christ Jesus.
> [12] Let not sin therefore reign in your mortal body, to make you obey its passions. [13] Do not present your members to sin as instruments for unrighteousness, but present yourselves to God as those who have been brought from death to life, and your members to God as instruments for righteousness. [14] For sin will have no dominion over you, since you are not under law but under grace. (Romans 6: 11–3 ESV).

What shall we say then? Are we to continue in sin that grace may abound? [2] By no means! How can we who died to sin still live in it? [3] Do you not know that all of us who have been baptized into Christ Jesus were baptized into his death? (Romans 6: 1–3 ESV).

A careful reading of the passages above will see some action words in them: *'consider', 'let not', 'do not'*. All these point to the fact that the followers of Christ are expected to act in certain ways or do certain things that demonstrate their faith. All of these are works of faith that James presented as the demonstrators of one's faith (James 2: 18 ESV).

While acknowledging the zeal of Jews for God, he was pained that while the Gentiles have keyed into the salvation brought by Christ, the Jews are yet to benefit from this, because of their ignorance of the righteousness of God. Again, just as it is very difficult for a Gentile to reject the gods he has been worshipping to believe in Christ, it is also difficult for a Jew who do not believe and confess that Jesus Christ is the Son of God. This kind of believe and confession comes with demonstration of faith. While mainly focusing on converting the Gentiles into the faith, Paul was also desirous to see the Jews saved. As a matter of fact, he seems to be taunting the Jews with the Gentiles, so he can make them to get their acts together and benefit from the redemptive power of Christ.

Ultimately, Paul recognises that the law is still in force, however he believes that grace can enable Christians to fulfil the requirements of the law. In warning against sin and immorality, Paul urged believers to be transformed from their former lifestyle to a righteous lifestyle, and present their bodies as a living sacrifice for God:

> I appeal to you therefore, brothers, by the mercies of God, to present your bodies as a living sacrifice, holy and acceptable to God, which is your spiritual worship. ² Do not be conformed to this world, but be transformed by the renewal of your mind, that by testing you may discern what is the will of God, what is good and acceptable and perfect. (Romans 12: 1–2 ESV).

He further gave a guideline to believers on what their new way of life should consists of, which essentially touches on all Christ has asked his followers to be doing such as loving one another, being good to all (both friends and enemies, avoiding evil deeds, enduring persecutions/tribulation:

> ⁹ Let love be genuine. Abhor what is evil; hold fast to what is good. ¹⁰ Love one another with brotherly affection. Outdo one another in showing honor. ¹¹ Do not be slothful in zeal, be fervent in spirit, serve the Lord. ¹² Rejoice in hope, be patient in tribulation, be constant in prayer. ¹³ Contribute to the needs of the saints and seek to show hospitality.
>
> ¹⁴ Bless those who persecute you; bless and do not curse them. ¹⁵ Rejoice with those who rejoice, weep with those who weep. ¹⁶ Live in harmony with one another. Do not be haughty, but associate with the lowly. Never be wise in your own sight. ¹⁷ Repay no one evil for evil, but give thought to do what is honorable in the sight of all. ¹⁸ If possible, so far as it depends on you, live peaceably with all. ¹⁹ Beloved, never avenge yourselves, but leave it to the wrath of God, for it is written, "Vengeance is mine, I will repay, says the Lord." ²⁰ To the contrary, "if your enemy is hungry, feed him; if he is thirsty, give him something to drink; for by so doing you will heap burning coals on his head." ²¹ Do not be overcome by evil, but overcome evil with good. (Romans 12: 9–21 ESV).

To make this clearer, he re-echoed Jesus's command to his followers to love their neighbours:

> ⁸ Owe no one anything, except to love each other, for the one who loves another has fulfilled the law. ⁹ For the commandments, "You shall not commit adultery, You shall not murder, You shall not steal, You shall not covet," and any other

commandment, are summed up in this word: "You shall love your neighbor as yourself." ¹⁰ Love does no wrong to a neighbor; therefore love is the fulfilling of the law. (Romans 13: 8–10 ESV).

So then let us cast off the works of darkness and put on the armor of light. 13 Let us walk properly as in the daytime, not in orgies and drunkenness, not in sexual immorality and sensuality, not in quarreling and jealousy. 14 But put on the Lord Jesus Christ, and make no provision for the flesh, to gratify its desires. (Romans 13: 12–14 ESV).

11.3 WALKING THE RIGHTEOUS PATH

To be righteous is to do what is right before God and man. In practical terms, this is mostly accomplished by keeping the instructions, laws, and commandments of God. To be unrighteous, on the other hand, is to do things that are not right (transgressing God's laws and commandment) or harmful to another person. Essentially, keeping the commandments of God is a key aspect of being righteous, followed by one's attitude and actions towards other people. This is summed up by Christ in the following way:

> ³⁰ And you shall love the Lord your God with all your heart and with all your soul and with all your mind and with all your strength.' ³¹ The second is this: 'You shall love your neighbor as yourself.' There is no other commandment greater than these." (Mark 12:30–31 ESV).

> ¹² "So whatever you wish that others would do to you, do also to them, for this is the Law and the Prophets. (Matthew 7:12 ESV).

Transgression of the laws and commandments of God is a breach of faith/disobedience that is commonly referred to as sin against God. Literally sin in Hebrew (chata/khata) and in Greek (hamartia) means to fall short or to miss the mark. Based on this definition, it implies there is a target that has been missed, when someone is said to have sinned. This target is usually tied to an expectation from a relationship. There is always an expectation from every relationship. Hence, when one of the parties in a relationship fails to meet their terms of the relationship, he sins. One can sin against a fellow human being, as well as sin against God:

> 15 "If your brother sins against you, go and tell him his fault, between you and him alone. (Matthew 18:15 ESV).

> 14 For if you forgive other people when they sin against you, your heavenly Father will also forgive you. 15 But if you do not forgive others their sins, your Father will not forgive your sins. (Matthew 6:14 ESV).

Human relationship with others is considered very important by God that he attaches it as a condition in our relationship with him. The above passage is simply saying that if we are not in good terms with our fellow human beings, we cannot be in good terms with God. We are obliged to forgive others, when they sin against us, so as to maintain a good relationship with them. But if we fail to forgive others who sinned against us, God will also not forgive us when we sin against him. This was also reflected in the Lord's prayer (*and forgive us our debts, as we forgive our debtors. - Matthew 6:12 KJV*).

Despite the importance of our relationship with others as has been presented above, generally, the focus of most Christians is on sin against God, which is considered a mortal sin, because it leads to death (*the soul that sinneth shall die*). Every human being by default has a relationship with God, and as part of that relationship, God expects humans to do certain things or adhere to the terms of the relationship, the same way humans expect some things from God. God is faithful and keeps his own side of the deal. Hence, the breach is usually on the side of humans. They fail to hit the mark; hence they sin against God. Every human being has at one point or the other missed this mark (*for all have sinned and fall short of the glory of God–Romans 3:23 NIV*). Jesus Christ came to repair the breach in the relationship between God and humans. He reconciled God and man through his death on the cross (see Section 10.9), hence, giving humans another chance to relate with God. The Bible is mainly a book that documented various aspects of the relationship between God and man. Illustrating how man had breached the expectations of God, the warnings from God about these breaches, the consequences of missing the mark, and the efforts God has made to reconcile man to himself. The stories are all geared towards stimulating man to do better in this relationship so that they can reap the benefits God has prepared for man as a result of this relationship:

> ¹² For the eyes of the Lord are on the righteous
> and his ears are attentive to their prayer,
> but the face of the Lord is against those who do evil."
> 13 Who is going to harm you if you are eager to do good? 14 But even if you should suffer for what is right, you are blessed. "Do not fear their threats[b]; do not be frightened." (1 Peter 3: 12–14 NIV).

Unfortunately, many followers of Christ tend to disregard the work required to be on the path of righteousness. Such people believe that Christ has done all the work and there is nothing else for his followers to do other than to have faith in Christ. By having faith in Christ, grace will take care of the rest of it. As a result, many followers of Christ tend to frequently fail in bearing good fruit. You are often to come in contact with many individuals professing immeasurable love for God on one hand but fail to extend such love to their fellow human beings. Christ reiterated the importance of loving one another shortly before his crucifixion:

> ³⁴ A new commandment I give to you, that you love one another: just as I have loved you, you also are to love one another. ³⁵ By this all people will know that you are my disciples if you have love for one another." (John 13: 34–35 ESV).

Faith alone cannot accomplish this requirement. To love God and one another requires certain level of work and sacrifice from the individual. Righteousness cannot be accomplished if one neglects to do the work he is expected to do:

> ¹⁴ What good is it, my brothers, if someone says he has faith but does not have works? Can that faith save him? ¹⁵ If a brother or sister is poorly clothed and lacking in daily food, ¹⁶ and one of you says to them, "Go in peace, be warmed and filled," without giving them the things needed for the body, what good is that? ¹⁷ So also faith by itself, if it does not have works, is dead. (James 2:14–26 ESV).

Christ warned about this complacency and clearly stated that it is only those who do the will of God that will enter the Kingdom of heaven. The keyword here is "do", which is an action on the part of the individual. People who neglect to keep the laws of God are not doing his will and are referred to as lawless ones, who will be judged harshly despite their professing to have faith in him:

THE WAY–BECOMING A FOLLOWER OF CHRIST

> [21] "Not everyone who says to me, 'Lord, Lord,' will enter the kingdom of heaven, but the one who does the will of my Father who is in heaven. [22] On that day many will say to me, 'Lord, Lord, did we not prophesy in your name, and cast out demons in your name, and do many mighty works in your name?' [23] And then will I declare to them, 'I never knew you; depart from me, you workers of lawlessness.' (Matthew 7: 21–23 ESV).

In Galatians, Paul asserted that followers of Christ have already crucified their fleshly desires, hence, the reason they bear the fruits of the spirit, which cannot be regulated by any law (not under the law):

> [24] Those who belong to Christ Jesus have crucified the flesh with its passions and desires. (Galatians 5:24 NIV).

The act to crucify oneself is a type of work, that requires the effort of the individual to accomplish. Notice that Paul did not ask them to relax and let the grace crucify them, but each individual will have to make the necessary effort to discipline himself and exercise self-restraint over those natural desires that could inflame the body to sin ([25] *Since we live by the Spirit, let us keep in step with the Spirit–Galatians 5:24 NIV*).

In summary, walking along the righteous path implies following the footsteps of Christ, and abandoning previous lifestyles not conforming with the new life, which one has been called into. The target is basically striving to be holy:

> [14] As obedient children, do not be conformed to the passions of your former ignorance, [15] but as he who called you is holy, you also be holy in all your conduct, [16] since it is written, "You shall be holy, for I am holy." [17] And if you call on him as Father who judges impartially according to each one's deeds, conduct yourselves with fear throughout the time of your exile, [18] knowing that you were ransomed from the futile ways inherited from your forefathers, not with perishable things such as silver or gold, [19] but with the precious blood of Christ, like that of a lamb without blemish or spot. [20] He was foreknown before the foundation of the world but was made manifest in the last times for the sake of you [21] who through him are believers in God, who raised him from the dead and gave him glory, so that your faith and hope are in God.
>
> [22] Having purified your souls by your obedience to the truth for a sincere brotherly love, love one another earnestly from a pure heart, [23] since you have been born again, not of perishable

seed but of imperishable, through the living and abiding word of God; (1 Peter 1: 14–24 ESV).

While on earth, Christ accomplished two primary things: showing mankind how to walk or navigate the righteous path in this world and opening the door of salvation for man. So, to be a follower of Christ is to emulate the standards he has already established. He hinted at this in Mathew 16:

> [24] Then Jesus told his disciples, "If anyone would come after me, let him deny himself and take up his cross and follow me. (Mathew 16: 24).

Christianity is not a joyride that once one opens his mouth to profess that he is born-again and say few lines of prayers, that is the end of the matter, and he can live as he/she so desires, and grace takes care of the rest. To follow Christ requires some level of work to be done, in preparation for the final judgement that will happen at the end of age. Hence, believing, and confessing Christ, is one step towards the goal of passing the final test, so as to be promoted to the status of a son of God. Walking the righteous path is akin to modelling ones live to match those of Christ:

> [6] He that saith he abideth in him ought himself also so to walk, even as he walked. (1 John 2:6 KJV).

The way Christ lived on earth provides the plumbline to measure ours. One could consider the life of Christ as a straight regression line that shows the ideal line of progression, whereas ours is like a sinusoidal line we are trying to fit into the regression line. The confidence interval of this regression line (margin of error around this line) is very slim, as the requirements to follow Christ are quite strict, unlike the way of the world, where all sorts of perverted behaviours are acceptable. Satan's way is to allow man to do all they will (*"Do what thou wilt shall be the whole of the Law,"*). This is the reason the antichrist is referred to as the man of lawlessness. To demonstrate that to follow him is not an easy road, Christ described it as a narrow gate that very few find, contrasting it with the way of the world, which he termed the broad gate that many follow:

> [13] "Enter by the narrow gate. For the gate is wide and the way is easy that leads to destruction, and those who enter by it are many. [14] For the gate is narrow and the way is hard that leads to life, and those who find it are few. (Matthew 7: 13–14 ESV).

THE WAY—BECOMING A FOLLOWER OF CHRIST

Even though salvation is free, the followers of Christ are expected to do certain things to merit the final reward. No doubt some level of sacrifice is required (*deny himself and take up his cross*) for one to be able to follow Christ (walk the path of righteousness). For instance, after Christ declared that *"unless you eat the flesh of the Son of Man and drink his blood, you have no life in you"* (John 6:53 ESV), most of his disciples who had been following him stopped following him and returned to their former ways of life, it was too difficult for them to take in:

> [66] After this many of his disciples turned back and no longer walked with him. (John 6:66 ESV).

Some of the things followers of Christ are expected to do were articulated by Christ in the Sermon on the Mount (Mathew 5: 13–48). All through his mission Christ gave specific instructions in addition to those presented in Mathew 5, to his followers with respect to what they should or should not do and how they should conduct themselves in the world. And he practically demonstrated all these:

> [15] For I have given you an example, that you also should do just as I have done to you. [16] Truly, truly, I say to you, a servant is not greater than his master, nor is a messenger greater than the one who sent him. [17] If you know these things, blessed are you if you do them. (John 13:15–17 ESV).

These examples are the works that anyone that wishes to follow Christ must do. Christ expects his followers to do these, which means they are critical. The works that Christ did daily while on earth were like the template of righteousness that each follower of Christ must adhere to (*he will repay each person according to what he has done*). The works produce fruits. The Holy Spirit assists the followers of Christ to accomplish the tasks that will yield good fruits. Any follower of Christ found not to be producing good fruits will be cut off from Christ:

> "I am the true vine, and my Father is the vinedresser. [2] Every branch in me that does not bear fruit he takes away, and every branch that does bear fruit he prunes, that it may bear more fruit. [3] Already you are clean because of the word that I have spoken to you. [4] Abide in me, and I in you. As the branch cannot bear fruit by itself, unless it abides in the vine, neither can you, unless you abide in me. [5] I am the vine; you are the branches. Whoever abides in me and I in him, he it is that bears much fruit, for apart from me you can do nothing. [6] If anyone does not

abide in me he is thrown away like a branch and withers; and the branches are gathered, thrown into the fire, and burned. (John 15: 1–6 ESV).

Note that the branch that will be cut off is the branch that is already part of the vine. This means that one can lose his status as a branch of the vine, even after becoming a follower of Christ. Believing in Christ, getting baptised are just steps towards being grafted into the true vine. This means that at any point along the life of the individual (after being grafted in), he/she could lose what he has initially received (promise of salvation). For instance, Judas believed, was baptised and casted out demons like other apostles. However, he was cut off from the vine by hist of betrayal. Simon the magician also believed, got baptised and followed Philip for a while before he was exposed by Peter as one in the bond of iniquity:

> [13] Even Simon himself believed, and after being baptized he continued with Philip. And seeing signs and great miracles performed, he was amazed (Acts 8: 13 ESV).

The final judgement will be based on this: what everyone has accomplished with regards to this template of righteousness set by Christ. Anyone found to be slacking in these and not doing what is expected will be cast out:

> [11] "But when the king came in to look at the guests, he saw there a man who had no wedding garment. [12] And he said to him, 'Friend, how did you get in here without a wedding garment?' And he was speechless. [13] Then the king said to the attendants, 'Bind him hand and foot and cast him into the outer darkness. In that place there will be weeping and gnashing of teeth.' (Mathew 22: 11–13 ESV).

Christ used the parable of the wedding feast (narrated in Mathew 22) to describe this. Many were called to the banquet, but they are expected to come to the banquet in an appropriate costume. The banquet is free, so is the invitation, none of the people invited merited to be invited in such a royal banquet, but there is a caveat that all invited must do their part, by attending in an appropriate clothing. Similarly, salvation is free, but people are expected to come to receive it in appropriate clothing, which is akin to the robe of righteousness (Revelation 22:14). Anyone not wearing this garb of righteousness will be cast out from the fold of

Christ in the end. At the marriage supper of the Lamb the bride of Christ will wear fine linen, that depicts their righteous deeds:

> for the marriage of the Lamb has come,
>   and his Bride has made herself ready;
> ⁸ it was granted her to clothe herself
>   with fine linen, bright and pure"— for the fine linen is the righteous deeds of the saints. (Revelation 19: 7–8 ESV).

A simple way to view this is that when one becomes a follower of Christ, he is given a white garment. The actions of the follower of Christ after this point, will either soil the white garment or keep it white. The goal is that at the final judgement, this garment should be kept unsoiled and spotless.

To understand this more, it might be worth considering that the ultimate target of every follower of Christ is to find his way back to the Garden of Eden, where Adam once lived in bliss before being ejected from it after transgressing the commands of God. To re-enter this garden, one must be elevated to the status of a son of God. Christ did the heavy lifting, by removing the barrier that precludes humans from assessing the garden. Hence, anyone can re-enter the garden if he so desires, but such individuals should be prepared to do the necessary work required. The first step to this walk is acknowledging Christ and the redemptive work he has done and abiding in him. The second step is to do the necessary work that enables us to follow the path he walked. Acknowledging the lordship of Christ is a fundamental aspect of the journey, because without Christ nothing can be accomplished:

> ⁴ Abide in me, and I in you. As the branch cannot bear fruit by itself, unless it abides in the vine, neither can you, unless you abide in me. (John 15:4 ESV).

But how does one abide in Christ? To abide in him is essentially to be in sync with him. The target of every follower of Christ is to be in union with him. To be in union with him is to be in alignment with him by following the footstep he walked while on earth. Hence, matching one's life to that of Christ and maintaining regular communication with him–in good and in bad seasons. Through this, one can develop a healthy relationship with Christ, where he knows every aspect of one's life. Christ wants to know us and only those he knows will he accept into his kingdom:

> [21] "Not everyone who says to me, 'Lord, Lord,' will enter the kingdom of heaven, but the one who does the will of my Father who is in heaven. [22] On that day many will say to me, 'Lord, Lord, did we not prophesy in your name, and cast out demons in your name, and do many mighty works in your name?' [23] And then will I declare to them, 'I never knew you; depart from me, you workers of lawlessness.' (Matthew 7:21–23 ESV).

A rule of thumb for any follower of Christ when faced with any situation is to ask, "what would Christ do under this circumstance", the honest answer to this question, will guide the individual in taking the right course of action. John made this clear in his letter where he urged anyone who wishes to abide in him to walk as Christ walked:

> 4 Whoever says "I know him" but does not keep his commandments is a liar, and the truth is not in him, 5 but whoever keeps his word, in him truly the love of God is perfected. By this we may know that we are in him: *6 whoever says he abides in him ought to walk in the same way in which he walked.* (1 John 2:4–6 ESV).

James also hammered this in, in his letter where he urged followers of Christ to be doers of the word:

> [21] Therefore put away all filthiness and rampant wickedness and receive with meekness the implanted word, which is able to save your souls.
> [22] But be doers of the word, and not hearers only, deceiving yourselves
> [27] Religion that is pure and undefiled before God the Father is this: to visit orphans and widows in their affliction, and to keep oneself unstained from the world. (James 1: 21–22; 27 ESV).

Paul also hinted at this walk of righteousness in Ephesians:

> I therefore, a prisoner for the Lord, urge you to walk in a manner worthy of the calling to which you have been called, [2] with all humility and gentleness, with patience, bearing with one another in love, [3] eager to maintain the unity of the Spirit in the bond of peace. (Ephesians 4: 1–3 ESV).

The aspiration to enter the Kingdom of God can be likened to the process of entering and graduating from a university to obtain a degree. To graduate from a university, one must first get admitted into the university. Repentance and baptism is the basic requirement for admission into this figurative university. Once admitted, the individual is granted the privilege to undergo the necessary training that will enable him/her to graduate from the university. Obviously, no one outside this university can graduate from it unless they get enrolled. For a long time, no man was able to undertake the tasks required to graduate from this university until Christ arrived on the scene. He successfully enrolled in the university and graduated from it with flying colors. His death on the cross could be likened to his taking the final degree examination, and his resurrection paying the tuition for all others who wishes to enrol in the university. Thus, anyone who believes in him can enrol in this university, free of charge. All that is required is for one to present himself to be enrolled into the university, attend lectures, and keep doing his coursework and exams, and passing them. In this analogy, the lecturers who teach and train the student represent the work of the Holy Spirit, who teaches, trains and build up the individual in the work of righteousness, so that he can be passing his tests and be able to graduate in the final exams.

To enrol into the Kingdom of God, one must accept Christ as his Lord and Saviour. The individual must be ready for the death of his old self, and his rebirth through Christ. Christ is the only way that leads men back to God.:

> [7] So Jesus again said to them, "Truly, truly, I say to you, I am the door of the sheep. [8] All who came before me are thieves and robbers, but the sheep did not listen to them. [9] I am the door. If anyone enters by me, he will be saved and will go in and out and find pasture. (John 10: 7–9 ESV).

Only Christ's credentials can open the doors and no other. No other path can lead one to the gate of the sought after Kingdom of God:

> "I am the way, and the truth, and the life. No one comes to the Father except through me. (John 14: 6 ESV).

11.3.1 The Narrow Path

The journey of a follower of Christ through the world (the path of righteousness) could be construed as walking through a very narrow path running through a city amidst other thoroughfares and distractions that could lead one astray from the path that leads to their final destination. Imagine the world as this city, filled with many paths that run in different directions leading to different destinations. Only one path out of these leads to the Kingdom of God. That path is the path of righteousness that leads man back to God. There are other paths (religions, ideologies, values, philosophies, cultures, traditions) running in many directions in the world with many allures and benefits that can enchant people. However, these paths ultimately lead to destruction, whereas the narrow path is the only path that leads to the sought after Kingdom of God. These paths at times intersect with the path of righteousness and present critical decision points for the person to either take them and veer off the path of righteous or continue his walk on the right path.

There are lots of dynamics and complexities associated with this walk. Before commencing the journey to follow Christ, an individual can be at any of these worldly paths. The resolve to follow Christ commences at the point the individual turns away from the alluring worldly paths, to walk along the narrow path. This is commonly known as repentance. It starts when one realises that he has been on the wrong path and decides to turn into the right one. For repentance to happen, one must have heard of the right path and believe that it leads to a better destination. This is when he hears the gospel and believed in it. After repentance, comes the confession: confessing that Christ is the son of God who came to save man. At this point, one is ready to be baptised to become a new individual–be born again. To be born again is just one of the early stages in this walk, because after this point one must start to walk through this narrow path to the destination. Walking through this path yields fruit. Consider there are milestones along this path, and when one reaches a milestone, he gains some points (fruits). This stage is akin to one attending lectures and taking the semester courses and exams, to move up the rungs of the academic ladder. At certain points along this walk, there would be many challenges and distractions that would confront the individual, which could force him out of this narrow path. Every stage has a huddle (trials and temptations). To progress, one is expected to overcome the huddles to be promoted to the next level. The agents of Satan stand by the side of this narrow path presenting many allures of life to distract people from this path. Hence, the reason God provides the Holy Spirit to help those on this path to reach the destination.

11.3.2 Receiving the Holy spirit

Consider the Holy Spirit as the interface through which God interacts with things (animate or inanimate). God is holy and cannot directly interact with unholy things, else he will destroy such things, if they come in direct contact with him. Hence, God uses the Holy Spirit to work on things to mould them into what he wants (to perfect them). Remember that God used the Holy Spirit to interact with the formless and dark earth, to recreate it:

> ² Now the earth was formless and empty, darkness was over the surface of the deep, and the Spirit of God was hovering over the waters. (Genesis 1:2 ESV).

At some point after baptism, one will receive the Holy Spirit. At times the Holy Spirit may be received at the point of baptism like what happened to Christ after he was baptised by John:

> ²¹ When all the people were baptized, it came to pass that Jesus also was baptized; and while He prayed, the heaven was opened. ²² And the Holy Spirit descended in bodily form like a dove upon Him, and a voice came from heaven which said, "You are My beloved Son; in You I am well pleased." (Luke 3:21–24 NKJV).

But in most cases, it is received after baptism. It took the apostles over three years of following Christ in his mission to receive the Holy Spirit after his resurrection (John 20: 22) and fully at the Pentecost. In the same vein, the new converts in Samaria did not immediately receive the Holy Spirit after being baptised by Phillip, until Peter and John arrived from Jerusalem:

> ¹⁴ When the apostles in Jerusalem heard that Samaria had accepted the word of God, they sent Peter and John to Samaria. ¹⁵ When they arrived, they prayed for the new believers there that they might receive the Holy Spirit, ¹⁶ because the Holy Spirit had not yet come on any of them; they had simply been baptized in the name of the Lord Jesus. ¹⁷ Then Peter and John placed their hands on them, and they received the Holy Spirit. (Acts 8: 14–17 NIV).

In rare occasions, the Holy Spirit could be received before baptism. In the case of Cornelius, while Peter was still preaching the gospel to him and others in his household, the Holy Spirit fell on them, thereby forcing

Peter's hands to immediately baptise them. It seems that if this hadn't happened, Peter may have found it difficult to baptise Cornelius:

> [44] While Peter was still speaking these words, the Holy Spirit came on all who heard the message. [45] The circumcised believers who had come with Peter were astonished that the gift of the Holy Spirit had been poured out even on Gentiles. [46] For they heard them speaking in tongues and praising God.
> Then Peter said, [47] "Surely no one can stand in the way of their being baptized with water. They have received the Holy Spirit just as we have." [48] So he ordered that they be baptized in the name of Jesus Christ. (Acts 10: 44–48 NIV).

The Holy Spirit performs many functions in the life of followers of Christ to support them in the existential journey. Among other things, he is a helper, advocate, and teacher of truth:

> [26] But the Advocate, the Holy Spirit, whom the Father will send in my name, will teach you all things and will remind you of everything I have said to you. (John 14: 26 NIV).

> 12 "I have much more to say to you, more than you can now bear. 13 But when he, the Spirit of truth, comes, he will **guide you into all the truth**. He will not speak on his own; he will speak only what he hears, and he will tell you what is yet to come. (John 16: 12–13 NIV).

> [26] "But when the **Helper** comes, whom I will send to you from the Father, the Spirit of truth, who proceeds from the Father, he will bear witness about me. [27] And you also will bear witness, because you have been with me from the beginning. (John 15: 26 ESV).

He also empowers the followers of Christ to do good work:

> [38] how God anointed Jesus of Nazareth with the Holy Spirit and power, and how he went around doing good and healing all who were under the power of the devil, because God was with him. (Acts 10: 38 NIV).

> 26 In the same way, the Spirit *helps us in our weakness*. We do not know what we ought to pray for, but the Spirit himself *intercedes for us* through wordless groans. 27 And he who searches our hearts knows the mind of the Spirit, because the Spirit intercedes for God's people in accordance with the will of God. (Romans 8:26–27 NIV).

> 7 Now to each one the manifestation of the Spirit is given for the common good. 8 To one there is given through the Spirit a message of wisdom, to another a message of knowledge by means of the same Spirit, 9 to another faith by the same Spirit, to another gifts of healing by that one Spirit, 10 to another miraculous powers, to another prophecy, to another distinguishing between spirits, to another speaking in different kinds of tongues,[a] and to still another the interpretation of tongues.[b] 11 All these are the work of one and the same Spirit, and he distributes them to each one, just as he determines. (1 Corinthians 12: 7–11 NIV).
>
> 8 But you will **receive power** when the Holy Spirit comes on you; and you will be my witnesses in Jerusalem, and in all Judea and Samaria, and to the ends of the earth." (Acts 1:8 NIV).

After one receives the Holy Spirit, he comes to be taught and guided in preparation for test and trials that will be encountered as one progresses through the narrow path. Christ was guided into the wilderness by the Holy Spirit after his baptism to be fortified and prepared for the coming temptation of Satan:

> Then Jesus was led by the Spirit into the wilderness to be tempted by the devil. ² After fasting forty days and forty nights, he was hungry. ³ The tempter came to him and said, "If you are the Son of God, tell these stones to become bread." (Matthew 4: 1–3 NIV).

When one yields to workings of the Holy Spirit, it produces fruits:

> ²² But the fruit of the Spirit is love, joy, peace, forbearance, kindness, goodness, faithfulness, ²³ gentleness and self-control. (Galatians 5:22–23 NIV).

By walking with the Holy Spirit on this journey, one is empowered to overcome all the huddles and temptations on the path:

> ³³ God is my strength and power: and he maketh my way perfect (2 Samuel 22:33 KJV).
>
> ¹⁶ So I say, walk by the Spirit, and you will not gratify the desires of the flesh. ¹⁷ For the flesh desires what is contrary to the Spirit, and the Spirit what is contrary to the flesh. They are in conflict with each other, so that you are not to do whatever you want. ¹⁸ But if you are led by the Spirit, you are not under the law.

> [19] The acts of the flesh are obvious: sexual immorality, impurity and debauchery; [20] idolatry and witchcraft; hatred, discord, jealousy, fits of rage, selfish ambition, dissensions, factions [21] and envy; drunkenness, orgies, and the like. I warn you, as I did before, that those who live like this will not inherit the kingdom of God. (Galatians 5:22-26 NIV).

Many followers of Christ tend to be delayed at various stages on this path, hence, prevented from reaching the ultimate destination. When one steps away from this narrow path and goes into the other paths, he gets exposed to things that would make him to sin against God and man. His journey on the righteous path gets interrupted at this point, until he finds his way back. Hence, progression of an individual through this path could be stunted by sin or permanently stopped, depending on how he responds after the transgression. However, the ability to retrace one's steps and find his way back to the narrow path is a key aspect of this journey. There is a danger associated with one getting off this path. If one continues to be on the wrong path and unfortunately dies at this point, he would be condemned, because he failed short of the mark before his death. Conversely, if one who has been sinning and have been on the wrong path, suddenly realises himself and gets back unto the right path before his death, he shall not be condemned:

> [11] Say to them, 'As surely as I live, declares the Sovereign Lord, I take no pleasure in the death of the wicked, but rather that they turn from their ways and live. Turn! Turn from your evil ways! Why will you die, people of Israel?'
> [12] "Therefore, son of man, say to your people, 'If someone who is righteous disobeys, that person's former righteousness will count for nothing. And if someone who is wicked repents, that person's former wickedness will not bring condemnation. The righteous person who sins will not be allowed to live even though they were formerly righteous.' [13] If I tell a righteous person that they will surely live, but then they trust in their righteousness and do evil, none of the righteous things that person has done will be remembered; they will die for the evil they have done. [14] And if I say to a wicked person, 'You will surely die,' but they then turn away from their sin and do what is just and right— [15] if they give back what they took in pledge for a loan, return what they have stolen, follow the decrees that give life, and do no evil—that person will surely live; they will not die. (Ezekiel 33:11-15 NIV).

This is where grace, mercy and continual repentance come into play. These are three key elements that work in favor of those who wish to follow the footsteps of Jesus Christ:

> 4 But when the kindness and love of God our Savior appeared, 5 he saved us, not because of righteous things we had done, but because of his mercy. He saved us through the washing of rebirth and renewal by the Holy Spirit, 6 whom he poured out on us generously through Jesus Christ our Savior, 7 so that, having been justified by his grace, we might become heirs having the hope of eternal life. (Titus 3:4–7 NIV).

The Holy Spirit, mercy and grace come from God (prerogatives of God), while repentance is the responsibility of man. When one repents and through God's mercy re-enters the narrow path, he starts from where he stopped on this journey. Depending on how far he went astray it may take a while for the individual to get to this point. The person may even be taken back some steps, so he can be retested with previous huddles.

11.3.3 Mercy of God

Mercy functions by blocking or tempering the application of God's law, when an individual contravenes them. This was demonstrated in the story of the adulterous woman and Jesus, where Jesus applied mercy on the woman caught in the act, instead of enforcing the prescribed punishment for contravening that law against adultery:

> 3 The teachers of the law and the Pharisees brought in a woman caught in adultery. They made her stand before the group 4 and said to Jesus, "Teacher, this woman was caught in the act of adultery. 5 In the Law Moses commanded us to stone such women. Now what do you say?" 6 They were using this question as a trap, in order to have a basis for accusing him.
>
> But Jesus bent down and started to write on the ground with his finger. 7 When they kept on questioning him, he straightened up and said to them, "Let any one of you who is without sin be the first to throw a stone at her." 8 Again he stooped down and wrote on the ground.
>
> 9 At this, those who heard began to go away one at a time, the older ones first, until only Jesus was left, with the woman still standing there. 10 Jesus straightened up and asked her, "Woman, where are they? Has no one condemned you?"

[11] "No one, sir," she said.

"Then neither do I condemn you," Jesus declared. "Go now and leave your life of sin." (John 8:3–11 NIV).

God is a merciful and loving father and is willing to forgive humans as much as they repent and ask to be forgiven. The Psalmist latched on the knowledge of the mercy of God when he declared:

> Let your ears be attentive
>   to the voice of my pleas for mercy!
>
> [3] If you, O LORD, should mark iniquities,
>   O Lord, who could stand?
> [4] But with you there is forgiveness,
>   that you may be feared. (Psalm 130: 2–4 ESV).

The prayer of Manasseh also comes to mind at this point. The Prayer of Manasseh is an extra biblical text that contains the prayer of repentance of Manasseh, the 14th king of Judah, who was considered in the Bible as one of the most idolatrous kings of Judah (II Kings 21:1–18; II Chronicles 33:1–9). The Bible did not record the contents of the prayer but hinted that it is recorded in the "the records of the seers" (II Chronicles 33:19).

Manasseh committed a lot of atrocities in Judah. However, after being taken captive by the Assyrians (II Chronicles 33:13), he asked for mercy in the prayer and was forgiven by God, despite his atrocious past:

> [19] His prayer and how God was moved by his entreaty, as well as all his sins and unfaithfulness, and the sites where he built high places and set up Asherah poles and idols before he humbled himself—all these are written in the records of the seers. (2 Chronicles 33:19 NIV).

Many followers of Christ are caught up at this stage, where they continuously loop through the sin-repentance cycle. Sinning against God could be compared to breaking a code in programming. Every programmer will tell you how frustrating it is for someone to continuously be introducing errors in a code that breaks them and requires the programmer to fix this error. God created man to function in a certain way. Sin altered the original design of man, and each time one sins, he alters his nature, and God will have to refix him.

Whereas Christ admonishes all he has forgiven, not to sin again, most of us end up going back to the same sin we have been forgiven, hence, making no real progress on this journey.

11.3.4 Grace at work

Now enters grace, which could be construed as a favor from God. Grace is bestowed on humans as a gift from God, to enable them to overcome earthly challenges:

> [7] But grace was given to each one of us according to the measure of Christ's gift. (Ephesians 4: 7 ESV).

Although many Christians tend to associate grace with the New Testament dispensation, grace has been in operation across human history with a few examples captured in the Old Testament. God was portrayed as gracious in many Old Testament passages[1]:

> The Lord is compassionate and gracious,
> slow to anger, abounding in love. (Psalm 103:8 NIV).

Grace is given to humans in different measures, to enable them to overcome specific challenges along the path of righteousness, so they can grow into maturity in this journey and become like Christ:

> [16] Let us therefore come boldly unto the throne of grace, that we may obtain mercy, *and find grace to help in time of need* (Hebrews 4:16 KJV).

As grace is given for specific purposes and to individuals, the type and measure of grace given to one differs from that given to another. Only God decides what measure of grace is appropriate for a particular individual, but we can assume that whatever type and measure of grace allotted to one is sufficient for the purpose it was given (*"My grace is sufficient for you, for my power is made perfect in weakness." - 2 Corinthians 12:9 NIV*).

It is purely a prerogative of God and is unmerited. It can manifest in different ways. For instance, it can serve as an aid that God gives to humans to help them to navigate through the narrow path. Grace can help one to overcome a particular weakness and shortcomings that may have stunted one's progress along the narrow path. For example, a person might be caught up in the loop of sin-repentance-forgiveness that has

1. Waite, "What is Grace", 1

kept the individual at a particular point along this journey, but when God pours out his grace, such individual could be energised to overcome the weakness/challenge, to escape the loop and move on to the next huddle. Paul hinted at this in 2 Corinthians 12, when he wrote about his weakness, which God assured him, there was sufficient grace to cater for this.

Grace can also prevent someone from being in certain situations that could make him to stumble. For instance, it can manifest as protection from harm. Noah was able to escape the flood because he found grace with God:

> 7 And the Lord said, I will destroy man whom I have created from the face of the earth; both man, and beast, and the creeping thing, and the fowls of the air; for it repenteth me that I have made them.
> 8 But Noah found grace in the eyes of the Lord.
> (Genesis 6:8 KJV).

Grace can also enable one to achieve great things that ordinarily, the individual may not have been able to. Hence, grace is an enabler that helps the followers of Christ to successfully walk through the righteous path. This contrasts with the views of modern-day Christians who project grace as a licence to do all sorts of things, while pushing the required work of righteousness to the background. As a result of this view about grace, many have abused the grace of God, considering it as a licence to sin. Such individuals believe they are under the protection of grace and hence, can indulge in sinful lifestyle as much as they wish, and it would not impact on their relationship with God (because grace will take care of it). Such Christians believe they can do these, because they are not under the law but under grace, which is a distorted view of what Paul taught. Even Paul cautioned about this inordinate way of thinking:

> 11 In the same way, count yourselves dead to sin but alive to God in Christ Jesus. 12 Therefore do not let sin reign in your mortal body so that you obey its evil desires. 13 Do not offer any part of yourself to sin as an instrument of wickedness, but rather offer yourselves to God as those who have been brought from death to life; and offer every part of yourself to him as an instrument of righteousness. 14 For sin shall no longer be your master, because you are not under the law, but under grace.
> 15 What then? Shall we sin because we are not under the law but under grace? By no means! (Romans 6: 11–15 NIV).

A careful reading of the above passage will show exactly what Paul was advocating. For a follower of Christ, who is under grace, such a person is considered dead to sin, because his members will not be allowed to sin by the grace made available to him. The desire to sin will be minimised by grace. This contrasts with the view that one under grace can wilfully sin and counting on grace to wipe it off. This also tallies with John's opinion about this:

> [9] No one who is born of God will continue to sin, because God's seed remains in them; they cannot go on sinning, because they have been born of God. (1 John 3:9 NIV).

Under this context, grace provides a preventive aid against sin, rather than acting as a post-sin remediation. Post-sin remediation is where the mercy of God comes into play. Understandably, humans are weak, and Christians can still occasionally fall into sin (not wilfully, I must add), but due to human imperfections, which is why God made provisions for mercy and forgiveness.

Again, forgiveness is a prerogative of God that emanates from his merciful nature. Mercy steps in to prevent the application of punishment due to sin. Mercy in most cases goes with certain preconditions such as repentance from the heart (the turning away from sin and turning toward God) and asking for forgiveness. When, one sins and repents, what follows is for the individual to ask for forgiveness from God. Then God will apply his mercy and forgiveness. This can happen at any time even at the dying moment. The thief on the cross with Jesus, asked for forgiveness and was forgiven instantly, shortly before his death. Again, there were two thieves on that cross, one was forgiven, the other was not, because one repented and asked for forgiveness, the other did not. On rare occasions God can also decide to apply mercy on someone without them expressly asking for it. The adulterous woman that was brought to Christ by the scribes and Pharisees for condemnation, received this sort of mercy (without her expressly asking for it, even though Christ having looked at her heart had seen she must have repented and probably asking for forgiveness and mercy in her spirit), which spared her from being stoned, as her accusers had wished:

> [10] When Jesus had lifted up himself, and saw none but the woman, he said unto her, Woman, where are those thine accusers? hath no man condemned thee?

> ¹¹ She said, No man, Lord. And Jesus said unto her, Neither do I condemn thee: go, and sin no more. (John 8:10–12 KJV).

To buttress the point that Paul was focusing on preventing sin from happening, when talking of grace, he urged in the passage for Christians not to provide a leeway for sin to enter and reign over them (*Therefore do not let sin reign in your mortal body so that you obey its evil desires–Romans 6: 8 NIV*). To rise above the powers of sin, Paul recommended that believers should not make themselves available to sin (Romans 6:13), but to rather subject themselves to God (*but rather offer yourselves to God - Romans 6:13 NIV*). It is only by doing so that sin shall not prevail over the individual (*For sin shall no longer be your master, because you are not under the law, but under grace - Romans 6:14*). This idea was also pushed forward by Paul in his letter to Galatians 5, where he urged them to ensure they are led by the Spirit, so they cannot gratify the desires of the flesh and live above the law:

> ¹⁶ So I say, walk by the Spirit, and you will not gratify the desires of the flesh. ¹⁷ For the flesh desires what is contrary to the Spirit, and the Spirit what is contrary to the flesh. They are in conflict with each other, so that you are not to do whatever you want. ¹⁸ But if you are led by the Spirit, you are not under the law. (Galatians 5:16–18 ESV).

He went ahead to differentiate between the acts of flesh and the fruits of the spirit (Galatians 5:19–25 ESV). By doing so, he was making it clear for followers of Christ to know when they are being led by the Spirit, or when they are being led by flesh. Invariably, what he was saying was that a person exhibiting the acts of the flesh as stipulated is not led by the Spirit, hence, such a person is still under the law. However, for those exhibiting the fruits of the Spirit they are being led by the Spirit and hence, not under the law. This makes perfect sense, considering that the law was made for humans to keep. A human who wishes to ascend from his current fleshly status must stop indulging in the acts of the flesh, and rather clothe himself with the light of the Spirit (led by the Spirit). When one begins to walk and be led by the Spirit, the law for humans ceases to exist, and he would be subjected under the law of the Spirit.

Hence, what Paul was essentially saying was that through grace, one can be aided not to subject themselves to sin (not make themselves *an instrument of wickedness*), but rather be subjected to God, and in so doing prevail over sin. To make this clearer for those who might still

THE WAY—BECOMING A FOLLOWER OF CHRIST

misunderstand what he was saying, he had added that by no means should people assume that being under grace is a licence to sin:

> ¹⁵ What then? Shall we sin because we are not under the law but under grace? By no means! Romans 6: 15 NIV.

Believers of the "*once saved always saved*" doctrine are even pushing this weird view about grace to the limits by asserting that once someone has been saved (become born again), no matter what the individual does subsequently, it will not impact on the person's salvation, because salvation was sealed at the point the person was initially saved. This is a fallacy to say the least. God clearly stated that a righteous person can end up in a bad place if he sins after being righteous in the past:

> ²⁴ But when the righteous turneth away from his righteousness, and committeth iniquity, and doeth according to all the abominations that the wicked man doeth, shall he live? All his righteousness that he hath done shall not be mentioned: in his trespass that he hath trespassed, and in his sin that he hath sinned, in them shall he die. (Ezekiel 18: 24 KJV).

This error is arising from the misunderstanding of what salvation is all about. Being born-again is merely a step to being saved and does not equate to salvation. As a matter of fact, it is only at the end of ages that anyone will know whether they are saved or not. Being born again, even though, is an important step toward salvation, is not a guarantee for salvation. Being born again legally makes one a descendant of Christ, however, not adhering to the commands of Christ and abiding in him can make him to disown the individual:

> ²³ And then will I declare to them, 'I never knew you; depart from me, you workers of lawlessness.' (Matthew 7:23 ESV).

Hence, the mantra of "*once saved always saved*" is a misleading fallacy as no human has at yet been saved. There are several instances of people who started well in the Bible and ended badly. A classic case is Judas who followed Christ for three years, and ended up in hell:

> ²⁴ The Son of man goeth as it is written of him: but woe unto that man by whom the Son of man is betrayed! it had been good for that man if he had not been born. (Matthew 26: 24 KJV).

Christ stated that people who have been in him can also be cut off:

[2] Every branch in me that beareth not fruit he taketh away: and every branch that beareth fruit, he purgeth it, that it may bring forth more fruit. (John 15:2 KJV).

Peter also weighed in on this:

[20] If they have escaped the corruption of the world by knowing our Lord and Savior Jesus Christ and are again entangled in it and are overcome, they are worse off at the end than they were at the beginning. [21] It would have been better for them not to have known the way of righteousness, than to have known it and then to turn their backs on the sacred command that was passed on to them. [22] Of them the proverbs are true: "A dog returns to its vomit," and, "A sow that is washed returns to her wallowing in the mud." (2 Peter 2:20–22 NIV).

Also, John referred to certain followers of Christ who he referred to as antichrists:

[19] They went out from us, but they were not of us; for if they had been of us, they would no doubt have continued with us: but they went out, that they might be made manifest that they were not all of us (1 John 2:19 KJV).

Thus, despite the benefits from grace, one is still expected to play his part in the work of righteousness. The patriarchs such as Enoch, Methusaleh, Noah, Seth, Abraham, Jacob, and Joseph all paid their dues, while walking this path of righteousness, even before Moses codified the laws in the 10 commandments. So, it is baffling when many professing followers of Christ try to avoid walking this path by using grace as a substitute for walking the path of righteousness, despite Christ expressly stating that he wants his followers to do these:

"If anyone would come after me, let him deny himself and take up his cross and follow me. (Matthew 16:24 ESV).

The importance of work is replete across the Bible. The scripture cannot be set apart. Anyone relying on grace in this way, tend to forget that Christ stated the following:

[13] But the one who endures to the end will be saved. (Mathew 24:13 ESV).

Endurance is a form of work that followers of Christ are expected to undertake/imbibe.

> Therefore, since we have been justified by faith, we have peace with God through our Lord Jesus Christ. ² Through him we have also obtained access by faith into this grace in which we stand, and we rejoice in hope of the glory of God. ³ Not only that, but we rejoice in our sufferings, knowing that suffering produces endurance, ⁴ and endurance produces character, and character produces hope, ⁵ and hope does not put us to shame, because God's love has been poured into our hearts through the Holy Spirit who has been given to us. (Romans 5: 1–5 ESV).

Ezekiel stressed on this while encouraging people to continue to do the necessary things required to be on the path of righteousness, otherwise, they could lose their righteousness:

> ¹² "And you, son of man, say to your people, The righteousness of the righteous shall not deliver him when he transgresses (Ezekiel 33:12 KJV).

A lot of people misconstrue Paul's construct of grace even though he warned against this–people abusing the gift of grace. Paul rather advocated for people to strive to live righteously. Paul was a strong advocate of working to reach the finish line. He described the walk of righteousness as a race:

> ²⁴ Do you not know that in a race all the runners run, but only one receives the prize? So run that you may obtain it. ²⁵ Every athlete exercises self-control in all things. They do it to receive a perishable wreath, but we an imperishable. ²⁶ So I do not run aimlessly; I do not box as one beating the air. ²⁷ But I discipline my body and keep it under control, lest after preaching to others I myself should be disqualified. (1 Corinthians 9 ESV).

> ¹² Not that I have already obtained this or am already perfect, but I press on to make it my own, because Christ Jesus has made me his own. ¹³ Brothers, I do not consider that I have made it my own. But one thing I do: forgetting what lies behind and straining forward to what lies ahead, ¹⁴ I press on toward the goal for the prize of the upward call of God in Christ Jesus. (Philippians 3: 12–14 ESV).

He hinted at this also in 2 Timothy, where he believes he has done the necessary work and awaiting the promised reward:

> 7 I have fought the good fight, I have finished the race, I have kept the faith. 8 Henceforth there is laid up for me the crown of

righteousness, which the Lord, the righteous judge, will award to me on that day, and not only to me but also to all who have loved his appearing. (2 Timothy 4: 7–8 ESV).

11.3.5 The Dynamics of Navigating the Narrow Path

The preceding sections have explored the role of the core elements (repentance, mercy, forgiveness, grace, and the Holy Spirit) at play in one's walk along the narrow path. Each of these plays prominent role in shaping the outcome of the walk. Through these elements, one can continue to make progress on this journey, trudging on and striving to be on the righteous path till the time he dies. All that he has accomplished while walking on this path will be recorded and used to judge him in the end:

> [12] And I saw the dead, small and great, standing before God, and books were opened. And another book was opened, which is the Book of Life. And the dead were judged according to their works, by the things which were written in the books. [13] The sea gave up the dead who were in it, and Death and Hades delivered up the dead who were in them. And they were judged, each one according to his works. (Revelation 20: 12–13 NIV).

Anyone deemed worthy based on what has been written down in their books would be transformed into the next generation of humans (the sons of God) who would enter the Kingdom of God and inherit the new earth. Many will declare themselves born-again, but will eventually not make it in the end, because their works were found wanting. Many are called but few are chosen. Paul enumerated some of the things expected from a true follower of Christ:

> [9] Let love be genuine. Abhor what is evil; hold fast to what is good. [10] Love one another with brotherly affection. Outdo one another in showing honor. [11] Do not be slothful in zeal, be fervent in spirit, serve the Lord. [12] Rejoice in hope, be patient in tribulation, be constant in prayer. [13] Contribute to the needs of the saints and seek to show hospitality.
> [14] Bless those who persecute you; bless and do not curse them. [15] Rejoice with those who rejoice, weep with those who weep. [16] Live in harmony with one another. Do not be haughty but associate with the lowly. Never be wise in your own sight. [17] Repay no one evil for evil but give thought to do what is honorable in the sight of all. [18] If possible, so far as it depends on

you, live peaceably with all. [19] Beloved, never avenge yourselves, but leave it to the wrath of God, for it is written, "Vengeance is mine, I will repay, says the Lord." [20] To the contrary, "if your enemy is hungry, feed him; if he is thirsty, give him something to drink; for by so doing you will heap burning coals on his head." [21] Do not be overcome by evil, but overcome evil with good. (Romans 12: 9–14 ESV).

11.4 BECOMING A FOLLOWER OF CHRIST

A Christian is an individual who has chosen to follow the footsteps of Jesus Christ, to become like him. The process of becoming a Christian takes several stages, with each stage bringing the individual closer to the nature of Christ. There are key things that a follower of Christ is expected to do to accomplish the goal of becoming like Christ. These are the things that distinguish a Christian from a non-Christian. The first step in this process is the realization and conviction that one has been on the wrong path. This realization often comes with the hearing and understanding of the gospel and believing the truth of the gospel. In most cases, this is triggered when an individual encounters the knowledge of the true light (learnt about the truth of Christ), after he has been brought the good news. It may be difficult for someone born in a Christian family to recognise this experience, as the individual may take several things for granted. In most cases, this conviction may come later in the life of the individual when he experiences the power of the true light. Most people are triggered to experience this after they fall into hardship or difficult situations in life.

At this point, the individual has the choice of either continuing on the path he has been or change course. The point where the individual starts to turn away from his former ways, and choose the way that leads to God, is the start of his repentance process. When the individual turns towards God, he has essentially turned his back on darkness and facing the true light. Subsequently, the individual will get baptised, signifying the death of his former life and the start of a new life in Christ. This new life will consist of doing things Christ had commanded his followers to do–striving to enter through the narrow gate.

To summarise, the process of becoming a follower of Christ starts with hearing the good news about him, believing that good news, turning to God (repenting) as a result of the enlightenment the good news has brought, getting baptised, and walking through the narrow way of righteousness to earn the reward of being allowed into the Kingdom of God:

> [15] And he said to them, "Go into all the world and proclaim the gospel to the whole creation. [16] Whoever believes and is baptized will be saved, but whoever does not believe will be condemned (Mark 16: 15–16 KJV).

11.4.1 The Repentance Process

Despite common belief that suggests that repentance is an instantaneous event, that swiftly transforms an unbeliever from a sinner to a saint, in reality, it is more of a process for many than an event. To repent means to change direction, to turn away from something to face another thing, reverse direction, reverse a line of action, change of mind/course of action (*And the Lord repented of the evil which he thought to do unto his people–Exodus 32:14 NIV*). Repenting towards God simply mean turning away from where one was headed and turning towards God. It normally takes time to walk from the point where the individual started turning away, to where God is (the expected standard of God), depending on how far away someone has walked away from God, before repenting. Broadly speaking, there are three key stages that mark the repentance process of many individuals: the trigger point, the long wait, and continual renewal of mind.

11.4.1.1 The trigger point

Arguably, the most significant part of the repentance process is the trigger point–the instant when an individual decides to repent. Without this, the process cannot even proceed. This trigger point is what many usually consider as repentance. However, after this initial point, a lot of effort would be required for the individual to be fully transformed as he walks closer and closer to God. A lot of things could trigger this desire to repent, such as hardship (e.g. the prodigal son), encountering God's power (Philippian Jailer–Acts 16:25 - 40), confronted by the truth (e.g. Paul's conversion), God's kindness and favor (e.g. Zacchaeus), encountering new information (e.g. Dionysius and Damaris and other Atheneans–Acts

THE WAY—BECOMING A FOLLOWER OF CHRIST

17:34), receiving the gospel e.g. at the Pentecost when over three thousand Jews and others present in Jerusalem repented:

> [37] When the people heard this, they were cut to the heart and said to Peter and the other apostles, "Brothers, what shall we do?"
>
> [38] Peter replied, "Repent and be baptized, every one of you, in the name of Jesus Christ for the forgiveness of your sins. And you will receive the gift of the Holy Spirit. [39] The promise is for you and your children and for all who are far off—for all whom the Lord our God will call."
>
> [40] With many other words he warned them; and he pleaded with them, "Save yourselves from this corrupt generation." [41] Those who accepted his message were baptized, and about three thousand were added to their number that day. (Acts 2: 37-41 NIV).

Even now while reading this book, the reader can be triggered to repent towards God. As a matter of fact, any non-Christian who has made it this far in this book, might be good candidate, as something is drawing you to God. Take a pause and ask yourself why you have been drawn to this book? Is there some inner force pulling you closer to the gospel? God is always eager to welcome his children when they get convinced that they have been on the wrong path and decide to turn to God:

> [12] "Even now," declares the Lord,
> "return to me with all your heart,
> with fasting and weeping and mourning."
>
> [13] Rend your heart
> and not your garments.
> Return to the LORD your God,
> for he is gracious and compassionate,
> slow to anger and abounding in love,
> and he relents from sending calamity. (Joel 2:12-13 NIV).

For someone who has not come under the light of Christ they will be wallowing in the darkness, until they realise that they have been on the wrong path. At this point they will turn towards the light of God:

> [21] testifying both to Jews and to Greeks of repentance toward God and of faith in our Lord Jesus Christ. (Acts 20: 21 ESV).

Turning towards God is the first aspect, then continuing on this right path as one draws closer to God is another aspect, as it demonstrates one's willingness to yield to God. The yielding of the individual in this way will allow God to commence the work of cleaning up the individual. The parable of the prodigal son clearly illustrates this process. At some point in his life, the prodigal son came to himself, having fallen on hard times. That was his trigger moment, when it hit him that he has been on the wrong path and needs to return to his father. Notice that after this point, he turned and started making his way towards his father. It probably took him a while before he eventually got close to his father's house. Interestingly, his father seems to have been eagerly waiting for his return, despite all he has done. Seeing him from way off, his father ran towards him to welcome him back into the fold:

> But while he was still a long way off, his father saw him and felt compassion, and ran and embraced him and kissed him. (Luke 15: 20 NIV).

He was still wearing his rags (symbolising the artefacts of his sins) as he was incapable of getting a fine linen in his present condition (symbolising that one cannot forgive himself, God will have to do it for the individual). At his approach, his father reclothed him with a fine robe, dressed him up to look like a prince and prepared a banquet for him. This symbolises how God washes away the sins of a repentant son and reclothes him with the garb of righteousness.

Most people usually stop sinning long after they have repented. They stop sinning because they have come under the influence of the light. Fortunately, God being so kind is happy to accept humans once they turn towards him, despite the stains of sin on them. Again, the parable of the Prodigal son aptly illustrates this. The father went and embraced his son, despite the rags he probably had on as clothes and the stench of his dirt, considering he has been working in a pig farm.

11.4.1.2 *The long wait*

Repentance is normally a long-term process for many. There are rare occasions where an individual completely stops sinning at an instant. In most cases, even after someone has decided to repent and remain fully committed to God, he may gradually find himself returning to sin. A lot of things could lead to this, in most cases due to human weakness.

However, despite what seems to be weakness and failure of the individual to consistently stay without sin, this is a critical stage when God slowly purifies the individual from within. For some, this process could take a very long time to be completed, as every aspect of the individual where sin has tainted will be cleaned and repaired. During this stage every fabric of sinful nature will be uprooted from the individual, till it gets to a point where most things the person formerly used to enjoy, will stop enticing him/her. The individual will no longer be deriving pleasure from those things. A physical manifestation of this is that the individual will start losing desire to engage in certain things he used to do. Even when he tries to do these, he will hardly derive the joy and excitement he used to experience while indulging in the acts before. In place of the excitement will be the remorse. Gradually, all the negative desires will flee from him/her, and he will start developing interests in other things that are benign and holy. The Holy Spirit diligently works on the individual in different ways to bring him in conformity to the life of Christ. At times, this may be subtle promptings for one to desist from doing certain things, to leave a place or occasion that could lead him back to sin. At times the Holy Spirit can apply stronger force (applying the hard break) when an individual has been weakened and was fully heading towards actions that lead him to sin. Spiritually sensitive people normally recognise this as the hand of God coming to the rescue, by preventing them from sinning:

> And God is faithful; he will not let you be tempted beyond what you can bear. But when you are tempted, he will also provide a way out so that you can endure it. (1 Corinthians 10:13 NIV).

It must be considered that it took over three years for the disciples of Christ who were following him to be completely transformed to receive the Holy Spirit. Even after spending years with Christ, Peter lied and denied him, and the other disciples abandoned Christ when he needed them most, as their faith was terribly shaken by the arrest and death of Christ on the cross.

11.4.1.3 Continual renewal of the mind

A crucial part of the repentance process is the continual renewal of the mind and relying on God's mercy, to ask for forgiveness, whenever one steps out of line. As has been explored in Section 9.2.3, the mind is a battle ground, hence every individual will have to make continual efforts to sanitise his mind so that only righteous and holy thoughts are entertained within his mind. When the mind is cleaned, half of the battle is won. This is one of the key ways to push negative thoughts away from an individual in pursuit of holiness. Paul advocated for this in many of his epistles:

> "Finally, brethren, whatsoever things are true, whatsoever things are honest, whatsoever things are just, whatsoever things are pure, whatsoever things are lovely, whatsoever things are of good report; if there be any virtue, and if there be any praise, think on these things." (Philippians 4:8 KJV).

> [2] Do not conform to the pattern of this world, but be transformed by the renewing of your mind. Then you will be able to test and approve what God's will is—his good, pleasing and perfect will. (Romans 12:2 NIV).

> 5 We demolish arguments and every pretension that sets itself up against the knowledge of God, and we take captive every thought to make it obedient to Christ. (2 Corinthians 10:5 NIV).

The renewal of the mind is very important, considering that it is a constant struggle for man to completely stay clean from sin, due to his nature. Paul had the following to say about his own struggles:

> [22] For I delight in the law of God according to the inward man. [23] But I see another law in my members, warring against the law of my mind, and bringing me into captivity to the law of sin which is in my members. (Romans 7:22–23 NKJV).

11.4.2 Baptism and Being Born Again–The Rewiring of Man's DNA

After believing and repenting towards God, the next step is to be baptised. Baptism is a very important stage in the life of a Christian. It is the doorway that leads humans into a new life in Christ. Baptism signifies death of the old life and being born into a new life. When one is submerged under water, it signifies the death of the old self, and when the person remerges from the water, he has come into a new life (see Section 10.9.1). Hence, after being baptised, one has become born again and all his past sins washed away by the water. In a nutshell, the individual has become a descendant of Christ (reborn by Christ) and no longer a descendant of Adam. Thus, the individual is no longer a carrier of the corrupted gene of Adam, rather, his gene has been rewired to that of Christ:

> ³ Do you not know that all of us who have been baptized into Christ Jesus were baptized into his death? ⁴ We were buried therefore with him by baptism into death, in order that, just as Christ was raised from the dead by the glory of the Father, we too might walk in newness of life. (Romans 6: 3-4 ESV).

The importance of baptism cannot be understated, considering that even Christ went through it, to the amazement of John the Baptist:

> ¹³ Then Jesus came from Galilee to John at the Jordan to be baptized by him. ¹⁴ And John tried to prevent Him, saying, "I need to be baptized by You, and are You coming to me?"
> ¹⁵ But Jesus answered and said to him, "Permit it to be so now, for thus it is fitting for us to fulfil all righteousness." (Matthew 3:13-15 NKJV).

To make clear what happens during baptism, the Holy Spirit descended on Christ as soon as he rose from the water and God's voice reconfirms that Christ is his son:

> ¹⁶ And Jesus, when he was baptized, went up straightway out of the water: and, lo, the heavens were opened unto him, and he saw the Spirit of God descending like a dove, and lighting upon him:
> ¹⁷ And lo a voice from heaven, saying, This is my beloved Son, in whom I am well pleased. (Matthew 3: 16-17 KJV).

So technically speaking Christ was reborn by God at this point, the same manner the descendants of Adam will be reborn in Christ, at baptism.

The necessity for baptism could be traced back to the event at the Garden of Eden, when Adam's original nature (DNA) was changed after he fell to the trick of Satan. With corruption of Adam's DNA, all his seeds were also corrupted. Hence, to restore man to his original nature, the old man would have to die so that a new man can be birthed. This was what Christ tried to explain to Nicodemus, that the fallen nature of man (the corrupted DNA of man) cannot enter the Kingdom of God. This makes sense, considering that as soon as Adam's DNA was corrupted by Satan, he was cast out from the Garden, hence, it would not make sense to readmit man into the garden in his fallen state. Man has to be born again to enter the Kingdom of God:

> ³ Jesus answered him, "Truly, truly, I say to you, unless one is born again he cannot see the kingdom of God." ⁴ Nicodemus said to him, "How can a man be born when he is old? Can he

> enter a second time into his mother's womb and be born?" ⁵ Jesus answered, "Truly, truly, I say to you, unless one is born of water and the Spirit, he cannot enter the kingdom of God. ⁶ That which is born of the flesh is flesh, and that which is born of the Spirit is spirit. (John 3: 3–6 ESV).

Some Bible translations have this as born from above as against born again:

> Jesus replied, "I tell you for certain that you must be born from above before you can see God's kingdom!" (CEV).

> Jesus replied, 'I tell you this: Unless a person is born from above, they cannot understand the kingdom of God.' (EASY).

> Jesus replied, "Amen, Amen, I tell you: Unless someone is born from above, he cannot see the kingdom of God." (EHV).

This stems from the fact that the original Greek word ἄνωθεν (*anothen*) has multiple meanings: from above, again, from the beginning, for a long time.

In John 3: 5, Christ re-emphasised that man must be born of water and Spirit. Recall, that when Adam was created God breathed into him, to give him life. This the same Spirit Christ is referring to here that must be in place for man to be born again. In John 20, Christ breathed the Spirit into his disciples:

> ²² And with that he breathed on them and said, "Receive the Holy Spirit. (John 20: 22 NIV).

Hence, what Christ was telling Nicodemus was that man has been corrupted and must be recreated/re-born, not from earthly perspective (going back into his mother's womb), but from above (from the Spirit), almost in the same way that Adam was created:

> "Yes, indeed," Christ answered him, "I tell you that unless a person is born again from above, he cannot see the Kingdom of God." (CJB).

When Adam was moulded from the mud, he was inanimate (dead), until God breathed the Spirit into him. Hence, baptism is a replication of this process: when a person is completely immersed in the water, he is dead, when he re-emerges, the Spirit activates him into a new life (*"Truly, truly, I say to you, unless one is born of water and the Spirit, he cannot enter the kingdom of God*). No man can enter the kingdom of God without

THE WAY—BECOMING A FOLLOWER OF CHRIST

being born again from above, because the DNA of man was corrupted by Satan. This corrupted DNA must be changed to its original makeup before man can be accepted into the Kingdom of God.

Obviously, this notion that man can only be redeemed if only they are reborn of Christ, sounds like an outlandish story that many will not want to believe. Hence, it requires a considerable degree of faith on the part of humans; to believe they have become the true descendants of Christ through baptism. This is the faith Paul preached. The faith required for the salvation of man that has been under sin:

> [22] But the scripture hath concluded all under sin, that the promise by faith of Jesus Christ might be given to them that believe. (Galatians 3:22 KJV).

> [16] He that believeth and is baptized shall be saved; but he that believeth not shall be damned. (Mark 16:16 KJV).

The essence of being born-again is to bring man to a new life that will lead him to a redeemable state, so he can ascend to the sonship class of beings, which God has prepared for him. A man that has been baptised is no longer expected to walk in his old ways, but to model his life after Christ:

> [17] Now this I say and testify in the Lord, that you must no longer walk as the Gentiles do, in the futility of their minds. [18] They are darkened in their understanding, alienated from the life of God because of the ignorance that is in them, due to their hardness of heart. [19] They have become callous and have given themselves up to sensuality, greedy to practice every kind of impurity. [20] But that is not the way you learned Christ!— [21] assuming that you have heard about him and were taught in him, as the truth is in Jesus, [22] to put off your old self, which belongs to your former manner of life and is corrupt through deceitful desires, [23] and to be renewed in the spirit of your minds, [24] and to put on the new self, created after the likeness of God in true righteousness and holiness... (Ephesians 4: 17–24).

Hence, being born-again is a step towards the "evolution" of humans to the next level (becoming the sons of God–see Section 14.7, for detailed discussion on this topic). To become a son of God is to directly be created by God. Hence, every Christian will have to be recreated/re-born by the Spirit of God, in order to access the Kingdom of God. This is a pre-requisite otherwise no access can be granted to flesh from the earth:

> [63] The Spirit gives life; the flesh counts for nothing. The words I have spoken to you—they are full of the Spirit and life. (John 6:63 NIV).

> [15] The Spirit you received does not make you slaves, so that you live in fear again; rather, the Spirit you received brought about your adoption to sonship. And by him we cry, "Abba, Father." (Romans 8:15 NIV).

Peter also alluded to this in his epistle:

> [23] Being born again, not of corruptible seed, but of incorruptible, by the word of God, which liveth and abideth for ever. (1 Peter 1: 23 KJV).

11.4.3 Bearing of good fruit

A true follower of Christ is expected to bear good fruit. The fruit is the totality of the output from an individual, which distinguishes one person from another:

> [16] Ye shall know them by their fruits. Do men gather grapes of thorns, or figs of thistles?
> [17] Even so every good tree bringeth forth good fruit; but a corrupt tree bringeth forth evil fruit.
> [18] A good tree cannot bring forth evil fruit, neither can a corrupt tree bring forth good fruit.
> [19] Every tree that bringeth not forth good fruit is hewn down, and cast into the fire.
> [20] Wherefore by their fruits ye shall know them. (Matthew 7:14–20KJV).

This expectation to produce good fruit is so serious that any follower of Christ found not to be producing good fruit would be cut off from the flock.

> "I am the true vine, and my Father is the vinedresser. [2] *Every branch in me that does not bear fruit he takes away, and every branch that does bear fruit he prunes, that it may bear more fruit.* (John 15:1–2 ESV).

This passage directly from Christ clearly stated that any Christian who is not producing the expected fruit will be cut off from Christ. Hence, one is expected to continue to produce good fruit until the end:

THE WAY—BECOMING A FOLLOWER OF CHRIST

> ⁴³ Therefore I tell you, the kingdom of God will be taken away from you and given to a people producing its fruits. (Matthew 21:43 ESV).

What matters is the state of one's heart at the end (Ezekiel 18:21–28 KJV). To produce good fruit, one must continuously abide in Christ. To abide in Christ, one must obey the commandments of Christ (John 15:3–11 ESV):

> ²⁸ And now, little children, abide in him, so that when he appears we may have confidence and not shrink from him in shame at his coming. ²⁹ If you know that he is righteous, you may be sure that everyone who practices righteousness has been born of him. (1 John 2:28–29 ESV).

The commandments are hinged on love of God and love for one another. This is where everything hinges:

> ³⁷ Jesus replied, "'You must love the Lord your God with all your heart, all your soul, and all your mind.' ³⁸ This is the first and greatest commandment. ³⁹ A second is equally important: 'Love your neighbor as yourself.' ⁴⁰ The entire law and all the demands of the prophets are based on these two commandments." (Matthew 22:36–40 NLT).

> ¹² "This is my commandment, that you love one another as I have loved you. ¹³ Greater love has no one than this, that someone lay down his life for his friends. ¹⁴ You are my friends if you do what I command you. ¹⁵ No longer do I call you servants, for the servant does not know what his master is doing; but I have called you friends, for all that I have heard from my Father I have made known to you. ¹⁶ You did not choose me, but I chose you and appointed you that you should go and bear fruit and that your fruit should abide, so that whatever you ask the Father in my name, he may give it to you. ¹⁷ These things I command you, so that you will love one another. (John 15:12–17 ESV).

> ⁷ Beloved, I am writing you no new commandment, but an old commandment that you had from the beginning. The old commandment is the word that you have heard. ⁸ At the same time, it is a new commandment that I am writing to you, which is true in him and in you, because the darkness is passing away and the true light is already shining. ⁹ Whoever says he is in the light and hates his brother is still in darkness. ¹⁰ Whoever loves his brother abides in the light, and in him there is no cause for

stumbling. [11] But whoever hates his brother is in the darkness and walks in the darkness, and does not know where he is going, because the darkness has blinded his eyes. (1 John 2:7–11 ESV).

[14] For the entire law is fulfilled in keeping this one command: "Love your neighbor as yourself."[(Galatians 5: 14 NIV).

Christians are expected to demonstrate the love for one another in deeds, and not in words alone. Their profession of faith must be backed up by commensurate acts of love towards others:

[15] If a brother or sister is naked and destitute of daily food, [16] and one of you says to them, "Depart in peace, be warmed and filled," but you do not give them the things which are needed for the body, what does it profit? (James 2:15–16 NKJV).

The gospel and epistle contain various instructions on practical things Christians are expected to do:

[11] For this is the message that ye heard from the beginning, that we should love one another.

[12] Not as Cain, who was of that wicked one, and slew his brother. And wherefore slew he him? Because his own works were evil, and his brother's righteous.

[13] Marvel not, my brethren, if the world hate you.

[14] We know that we have passed from death unto life, because we love the brethren. He that loveth not his brother abideth in death.

[15] Whosoever hateth his brother is a murderer: and ye know that no murderer hath eternal life abiding in him.

[16] Hereby perceive we the love of God, because he laid down his life for us: and we ought to lay down our lives for the brethren.

[17] But whoso hath this world's good, and seeth his brother have need, and shutteth up his bowels of compassion from him, how dwelleth the love of God in him?

[18] My little children, let us not love in word, neither in tongue; but in deed and in truth.

[19] And hereby we know that we are of the truth, and shall assure our hearts before him.

[20] For if our heart condemn us, God is greater than our heart, and knoweth all things.

> ²¹ Beloved, if our heart condemn us not, then have we confidence toward God.
>
> ²² And whatsoever we ask, we receive of him, because we keep his commandments, and do those things that are pleasing in his sight.
>
> ²³ And this is his commandment, That we should believe on the name of his Son Jesus Christ, and love one another, as he gave us commandment.
>
> ²⁴ And he that keepeth his commandments dwelleth in him, and he in him. And hereby we know that he abideth in us, by the Spirit which he hath given us. (1 John 3: 11–24 KJV).

Paul also re-emphasised this in Ephesians:

> ²³ and to be renewed in the spirit of your minds, ²⁴ and to put on the new self, created after the likeness of God in true righteousness and holiness.
>
> ²⁵ Therefore, having put away falsehood, let each one of you speak the truth with his neighbor, for we are members one of another. ²⁶ Be angry and do not sin; do not let the sun go down on your anger, ²⁷ and give no opportunity to the devil. ²⁸ Let the thief no longer steal, but rather let him labor, doing honest work with his own hands, so that he may have something to share with anyone in need. ²⁹ Let no corrupting talk come out of your mouths, but only such as is good for building up, as fits the occasion, that it may give grace to those who hear. ³⁰ And do not grieve the Holy Spirit of God, by whom you were sealed for the day of redemption. ³¹ Let all bitterness and wrath and anger and clamor and slander be put away from you, along with all malice. ³² Be kind to one another, tenderhearted, forgiving one another, as God in Christ forgave you. (Ephesians 4: 23–32 ESV).

In the same vein Christians are expected not to be overly attached to the things of the world, as that would distract them from loving God as much as they should:

> ¹⁵ Do not love the world or the things in the world. If anyone loves the world, the love of the Father is not in him. ¹⁶ For all that is in the world—the desires of the flesh and the desires of the eyes and pride of life—is not from the Father but is from the world. ¹⁷ And the world is passing away along with its desires, but whoever does the will of God abides forever. (1 John 2:7–11 ESV).

The call is for everyone to become a true follower of Christ. The door is open for all, but not all who are called to walk through this path will eventually make it to the kingdom. A sifting will be conducted at the end and every individual's fruit and work assessed. The outcome of this final calibration is what will determine if one can be allowed into the Kingdom of God or not:

> [14] For many are called, but few are chosen. (Matthew 22:14 KJV).

11.4.4 Be discerning

In addition to loving God and one another, Christians are expected not to be gullible, but to be discerning in their physical and spiritual dealings. They should be able to detect falsehood from both man and spirits. This way, they will not be led astray by evil spirits, false prophets and deceivers. Many Christians have failed in this regard and have fallen prey to false teachers and prophets, and evil spirits masquerading as angels of light. This was why John urged Christians to test every spirit. He may have encountered many false spirits in his time, necessitating his admonition:

> Beloved, do not believe every spirit, but test the spirits to see whether they are from God, for many false prophets have gone out into the world. [2] By this you know the Spirit of God: every spirit that confesses that Jesus Christ has come in the flesh is from God, [3] and every spirit that does not confess Jesus is not from God. This is the spirit of the antichrist, which you heard was coming and now is in the world already. (1 John 4: 1–3 ESV).

Christians are supposed to emulate the practice of the Berean believers who received Paul and Silas after they were smuggled out of Thessalonica. These Jews were quick to crosscheck every message they received with the truth of the Scriptures:

> [11] Now these Jews were more noble than those in Thessalonica; they received the word with all eagerness, examining the Scriptures daily to see if these things were so. [12] Many of them therefore believed, with not a few Greek women of high standing as well as men. (Acts 17:11–12 ESV).

11.4.5 Unequal Yoking

Christians must avoid being yoked with the devils. As hinted in Section 9.2, many cultural and religious practices, norms, and practices in various places were inspired by the dark forces, who once ruled various parts of the world. Many non-discerning Christians fell into this trap by thinking they can reconcile/unite culture with ways of Christ. These cultural practices, act as doorways through which evil forces can enter and engage with the mind of the individual, before subsequently taking full control of their actions.

> ¹⁴ Be ye not unequally yoked together with unbelievers: for what fellowship hath righteousness with unrighteousness? and what communion hath light with darkness?
> ¹⁵ And what concord hath Christ with Belial? or what part hath he that believeth with an infidel?
> ¹⁶ And what agreement hath the temple of God with idols? for ye are the temple of the living God; as God hath said, I will dwell in them, and walk in them; and I will be their God, and they shall be my people.
> ¹⁷ Wherefore come out from among them, and be ye separate, saith the Lord, and touch not the unclean thing; and I will receive you.
> ¹⁸ And will be a Father unto you, and ye shall be my sons and daughters, saith the Lord Almighty. (2 Corinthians 6:14–18 KJV).

Christians are urged to separate themselves from abhorrent practices and worldly lifestyles that can yoke them with the dark forces. Through avoidance of such unequal yoking, Christians can be sanctified from the rest of the world.

Despite what other religions might say, Christ was unequivocal when he stated that he was the only way to God. No other way was made available to man for redemption. Mixing the values of Christ with those of other religious figures is an unequal yoking that should be avoided. Christians are rather urged to bring the good news to everyone, so that interested individuals can come into the fold. Evangelism is what is expected of followers of Christ and not mingling and yoking with the world, because even though they are in the world, they are not of the world (John 17:16) and expected not to participate in the obnoxious practices of the world:

> ¹⁹ If you were of the world, the world would love you as its own; but because you are not of the world, but I chose you out of the world, therefore the world hates you. (John 15: 19 ESV).

> ² Do not conform to the pattern of this world, but be transformed by the renewing of your mind (Romans 12:2 NIV).

> ¹⁵ Do not love the world or anything in the world. If anyone loves the world, love for the Father is not in them. ¹⁶ For everything in the world—the lust of the flesh, the lust of the eyes, and the pride of life—comes not from the Father but from the world. ¹⁷ The world and its desires pass away, but whoever does the will of God lives forever. (1 John 2:15–17 NIV).

11.4.6 The Great Commission

Finally, Christians are called to take the good news to all nations. The gospel, which Jesus handed over to his Jewish disciples are meant to be spread to other nations, so that all descendants of Adam, despite their nationalities and former allegiance to the renegade gods, should receive the good news–that God is ready to bring them into his kingdom.

> ¹⁸ Then Jesus came to them and said, "All authority in heaven and on earth has been given to me. ¹⁹ Therefore go and make disciples of all nations, baptizing them in the name of the Father and of the Son and of the Holy Spirit, ²⁰ and teaching them to obey everything I have commanded you. And surely I am with you always, to the very end of the age." (Matthew 28:18–20 ESV).

The duty of Christians is to bring this information to the knowledge of all so that no one can use ignorance as an excuse in the final judgement. Everyone is meant to hear about this, the choice to believe or not is left for the individual who the message came to. God's goal is to reclaim the nations, which he previously gave to the renegade gods. During the Pentecost when the apostles officially commenced their apostolic mission on a large scale, the message was brought to many of the nations named in the Table of Nations (Genesis 10). The Pentecost event was more or less a reversal of the Tower of Babel event, when the people were separated by God by giving them multiple tongues (Genesis 11: 6–9). At the Pentecost, the apostles seemed to have spoken in the original tongues of men before the confusion of the tongues, hence, people from the various nations were able to hear and understand what they were saying:

> [5] And there were dwelling at Jerusalem Jews, devout men, out of every nation under heaven.
> [6] Now when this was noised abroad, the multitude came together, and were confounded, because that every man heard them speak in his own language.
> [7] And they were all amazed and marvelled, saying one to another, Behold, are not all these which speak Galilaeans?
> [8] And how hear we every man in our own tongue, wherein we were born?
> [9] Parthians, and Medes, and Elamites, and the dwellers in Mesopotamia, and in Judaea, and Cappadocia, in Pontus, and Asia,
> [10] Phrygia, and Pamphylia, in Egypt, and in the parts of Libya about Cyrene, and strangers of Rome, Jews and proselytes,
> [11] Cretes and Arabians, we do hear them speak in our tongues the wonderful works of God.
> [12] And they were all amazed, and were in doubt, saying one to another, What meaneth this? (Acts 2: 5-12 KJV).

The apostles' message on that day was a unifying one, calling on the people from all the nations that God had handed over to the renegades to return to him:

> [38] Then Peter said unto them, Repent, and be baptized every one of you in the name of Jesus Christ for the remission of sins, and ye shall receive the gift of the Holy Ghost. (Acts 2: 38 KJV).

God empowered the apostles so that their message was backed up by practical demonstration of the power of God over the gods of the nations:

> [19] Behold, I give unto you power to tread on serpents and scorpions, and over all the power of the enemy: and nothing shall by any means hurt you. (Luke 10:19 KJV).

The apostles were bringing down principalities in the various territories they took the gospels to. By changing the minds of the people towards God, the powers of the principalities dwindled. As the gospel continued to spread, the powers of the principalities over nations essentially collapsed and the gods relegated to the background.

11.5 CONFRONTATIONAL GOSPEL

Despite the apparent innocuousness of the gospel, the dark world which perceives its potency view it as dangerous. This is because the gospel confronts the lies of the dark world with the truth of the light. It is a disruptor of existing practices instituted by Satan, the renegade gods, principalities, and demons. Hence, they resist it and do all they can to thwart it or distract people from receiving it. The gospel came to dispel their lies and evils. The gospel is the light shining over darkness. Christ alluded to this when he told his disciples he had not come to bring peace but to bring division. The division among those who believe in the light and those who prefer to cling to the darkness. The division can run even through families, separating children from parents and siblings from among each:

> 34 "Do not think that I have come to bring peace to the earth. I have not come to bring peace, but a sword. 35 For I have come to set a man against his father, and a daughter against her mother, and a daughter-in-law against her mother-in-law. 36 And a person's enemies will be those of his own household. 37 Whoever loves father or mother more than me is not worthy of me, and whoever loves son or daughter more than me is not worthy of me. 38 And whoever does not take his cross and follow me is not worthy of me. 39 Whoever finds his life will lose it, and whoever loses his life for my sake will find it. (Matthew 10: 34–39 ESV).

Hence, it is usually viewed by the dark world as confrontational, and they fight it with all their might. The world under the influence of Satan fights the gospel because it brings a direct attack to the gates of hell. It undermines the authority of the fallen ones over the nations. This was the reason why the earlier Christians were highly persecuted, and many killed. As they brought the gospel to different nations and people, and with many accepting the gospels, the apostles were whittling down the powers of the fallen ones over the nations. They were inadvertently causing upheaval in the dark world and the dark forces had to move against them. They were perceived as dangerous and troublemakers:

> 5 "We have found this man to be a troublemaker, stirring up riots among the Jews all over the world. He is a ringleader of the Nazarene sect (Acts 24:5 NIV).

Modern Christians have acquiesced, thus, letting the dark forces to breathe. They have conformed their teaches to the worldly values, to avoid the persecution of the world. Hence, the gospel they present to the world is a diluted gospel that has reduced potency against the dark world. However, this will come to head during the end time when the dark forces will be allowed to briefly reign. An end time revival will come with the rise of the beast system (Section 12.2), and Christians will once again be persecuted, hunted down, and killed as they will be viewed as standing in the way of the establishment of the kingdom of Satan on earth.

One of the simplest ways to know the true gospel, is to see how the world reacts to it. Any gospel that is generally accepted and well received by the world is likely to be a false gospel. Conversely, any gospel that is opposed, rejected, or attacked by the world as not conforming to worldly values is a true gospel. The true gospel hits at the core of the dark world; hence, they attack it. Jesus warned his disciples of this, so that his followers will be fully prepared for the inevitable confrontation from the world to the gospel:

> [18] "If the world hates you, know that it has hated me before it hated you. [19] If you were of the world, the world would love you as its own; but because you are not of the world, but I chose you out of the world, therefore the world hates you. [20] Remember the word that I said to you: 'A servant is not greater than his master.' If they persecuted me, they will also persecute you. (John 15:18–20 ESV).

> [16] "Behold, I am sending you out as sheep in the midst of wolves, so be wise as serpents and innocent as doves. [17] Beware of men, for they will deliver you over to courts and flog you in their synagogues, [18] and you will be dragged before governors and kings for my sake, to bear witness before them and the Gentiles. (Matthew 10: 16–33 ESV).

CHAPTER 12

New World Order: The Foundations of the Last Empire of Satan

"We have before us the opportunity to forge for ourselves and for future generations a new world order, a world where the rule of law, not the law of the jungle, governs the conduct of nations. When we are successful, and we will be, we have a real chance at this new world order, an order in which a credible United Nations can use its peacekeeping role to fulfil the promise and vision of the U.N.'s founders"–*Comments by George H. W. Bush's on the Air Strikes Against the Iraqis, New York Times January 17, 1991.*

"By the end of this decade we will live under the first one world government that has ever existed in the society of nations…a government with absolute authority to decide the basic issues of human survival. One world government is inevitable"–*Pope John Paul II*[1].

"Now is a time when things are shifting. We're going to–there's going to be a new world order out there, and we've got to lead it. And we've got to unite the rest of the free world in doing it."–Joe Biden, 2022[2].

1. Martin, "The Keys of This Blood", 45
2. Sommerlad, "What is the 'New World Order'", 1

12.1 THE RECREATION OF THE ATLANTEAN CIVILIZATION

A popular buzzword in the mouth of many world leaders these days is the "New World Order". This phrase is awkwardly invoked by political and religious leaders in critical speeches of global importance. The manner the phrase is interjected into speeches suggests there is some kind of hidden mandate for leaders to introduce the phrase to the world–as a way to let the world know of what is coming. This is in line with cosmic legalism, which holds that nothing can be done on earth, without the inhabitants of earth accepting it. The increasing frequency of the usage of the phrase around the world since the last few decades, indicates the imminency of its emergence.

This phrase portends different things to different people and is subject to multiple interpretations. However, despite the benign façade around the phrase, it connotes one thing–the building of a new world system that would entail the unification of the entire world under one government. In other words, the establishment of a global empire that will surpass other previous empires in strength and might. This would be a totalitarian global government that would have real power, strong enough to control the entire world. Advocates of the global government believes that such a government with enormous powers would efficiently solve all the problems and challenges of the current world system, and institute mechanisms that will guarantee global "Peace and Safety".

Despite the controversy trailing it, with some branding it a conspiracy theory,[3] there is no doubt that there have been concerted efforts towards the establishment of a new world system that would be remarkably different from the current system of governance and nationhood. Snippets of this concept have been around for a long time, mainly hidden in cryptic symbols and texts such as those crafted into the Unted States' one-dollar bill (*Novus Ordo Seclorum*). Burja[4] notes that:

> The prospect of a world government has been seen as the inevitable future of humanity for centuries if not millennia. Many luminaries—from Immanuel Kant to H.G. Wells—spoke and wrote passionately in its favor, arguing it would produce a utopian world free of war, strife, perhaps even want, where humanity

---

3. Sommerlad, "What is the 'New World Order'", 1; Flores, "The New World Order", 1

4. Burja, "The First World", 1

finally applied its talents to taming and remaking nature. Others issued dire prophecies and warnings of an inescapable dystopia, wrought by a great and terrible political Leviathan.

In contemporary times, this idea for a new word system was floated to the world around 1973, when the Trilateral Commission was established with one of its key objectives being the creation of a new international economic order[5]. The purveyors of this ideology project to the people that this is the best panacea to the many challenges of the world. In 1975, the Club of Rome opined through its publication *Mankind at the Turning Point* that *the world has cancer and the cancer is man*. The report concluded that the solution of various crises of the world that it explored can be developed only in a global context, with full and explicit recognition of the emerging world system ... a new world economic order and a global resources allocation system[6].

On the surface, the move for a *'New World Order'* is packaged as a geopolitical, socioeconomic reform and reorganisation of the current world system. However, esoterically, the move is part of a hidden agenda to usher in the rule of the antichrist–an individual that will arise during the end times, empowered by Satan to rule the entire earth and draw the worship of the world away from the God to himself. The central idea is to establish a world government that would be under the absolute control of a man, who will redistribute the world's resources whichever way he deems fit. This government will emerge at a time of great crisis that would befall the world. Henry A. Kissinger captured this in his famous quote about the emergence of a new world order:

> "The one thing man fears is the unknown. When presented with this scenario, individual rights will be willingly relinquished for the guarantee of their well-being granted to them by a World Government, a New World Order." [\EXT]

Advocates of the *New World Order,* believe they have been chosen to bring this about, with the hope of a reward from their master, when his reign comes. This idea is symbolically captured in the design of the one-dollar bill. The bill contains an image of an unfinished pyramid. Below this pyramid is a Latin inscription (*Novus Ordo Seclorum*), which translates into New Order of the Ages. Above the pyramid is a capstone with an all-seeing eye (the Eye of Providence), with another Latin inscription

---

5. Oracle Films, "The Agenda", 1
6. Oracle Films, "The Agenda", 1

above it stating *Annuit cœptis*, which translates to "He has favored our undertakings." Putting all these symbolisms together, the creators of this design are cryptically indicating that they have been commissioned to create a New World Order, that will complete the unfinished pyramid, with Satan at its head (the all-seeing eye capstone)–"*He has favored our undertakings [in creating a] New Order of the Ages* ". The completion of this pyramid is the core of the new world order ideology. The unfinished pyramid in this case represents the unfinished empire of Satan, which was abruptly terminated by God in ages long past.

This idea for the establishment of a *New World Order*, is being stimulated by a hidden agenda of a select few to recreate an Atlantean-like civilization on earth. There was a time Satan held sway on this earth. This was Satan's golden era, before the present-day humans were created, when the beings on earth worshipped Satan and he in turn brings the worship to God. Hence, the entire earth was under his rule, until it got into his mind to ascend to heaven above the host of heavens, to make himself equal to God, leading to the war in heaven. A glimpse of this was provided in Isaiah's prophesy against Babylon, when God alluded to the downfall of Satan as part of the prophesy:

> [12] "How you are fallen from heaven,
>   O Day Star, son of Dawn!
> How you are cut down to the ground,
>   you who laid the nations low!
> [13] You said in your heart,
>   'I will ascend to heaven;
> above the stars of God
>   I will set my throne on high;
> I will sit on the mount of assembly
>   in the far reaches of the north;
> [14] I will ascend above the heights of the clouds;
>   I will make myself like the Most-High.' (Isaiah 14: 12–14 ESV).

Here, it is mentioned that the entity being referred here laid the nations low, alluding to the fact that he subdued the nations of the world. This idea was expounded in subsequent verses, which hinted that he shook kingdoms:

> 'Is this the man who made the earth tremble,
>   who shook kingdoms,
> [17] who made the world like a desert

and overthrew its cities,
who did not let his prisoners go home?' (Isaiah 14: 16–14 ESV).

Satan's influence and attachment to the earth was also alluded to in Job, when twice, he appeared among other sons of God, to present themselves to God (Job 1: 6–7 and Job 2: 1–2). He told God he came from the earth. A claim that suggests he was in the gathering as the representative of the earth.

The Atlantean civilization or other similar pre-adamic civilizations are all attempts to recreate the golden age of Satan's rule on earth. Satan still looks at this era, when the civilization he built was at its peak, with admiration, and aims to rebuild this civilization. He held sway around the earth during this era and essentially assumed a godlike status during this time, hence his desire to recreate this civilization on earth. God has granted Satan this opportunity which would last for a brief period:

> [EPI] ⁵ The beast was given a mouth to utter proud words and blasphemies and to exercise its authority for forty-two months. ⁶ It opened its mouth to blaspheme God, and to slander his name and his dwelling place and those who live in heaven. ⁷ It was given power to wage war against God's holy people and to conquer them. And it was given authority over every tribe, people, language and nation. ⁸ All inhabitants of the earth will worship the beast—all whose names have not been written in the Lamb's book of life, the Lamb who was slain from the creation of the world. [/EPI]

However, Satan will try to utilise this opportunity to make another attempt at overthrowing God. It is believed that Satan will attempt to recreate this civilization using a synergy of artificial intelligence, quantum computing, robotics, genetics, nanotechnology, blockchain, and other advanced technologies. As a matter of fact, the various tools to accomplish this are already in place on earth and going through final phases of optimisation, before they are fully integrated.

During this time (the new Atlantis era), the world as we currently know it will drastically change. The rebellious angels, the fallen Watchers, and the renegade gods, will be present on earth, as they prepare to take full control of the entire earth. These principalities who have been behind the scenes while controlling affairs of various governments of the world (*Ephesians 6:12*), will be forced into the open, when they are forced down from the Second Heaven (where they have been sojourning since their expulsion from the presence of God) to the earth:

> Michael and his angels fought with the dragon; and the dragon and his angels fought, [8] but did not prevail, nor was a place found for them in heaven any longer. [9] So the great dragon was cast out, that serpent of old, called the Devil and Satan, who deceives the whole world; he was cast to the earth, and his angels were cast out with him. (Revelation 12:7-9 NKJV).

Even those chained in the abyss, will be released from their dungeons into the earth when the dimensions are ripped open through technologically advances currently being conducted around the world. The Nephilim and other humanoid beings that have been imprisoned or those forced into hiding, will creep out from all the crevices they have been hiding in, to exact their full revenge on mankind. Their ultimate goal would be to take over the earth and make it their habitation, as they have been evicted from other realms where they have been hiding in. The Book of Jubilees 10: 8-9, noted that about 90% of the Nephilim spirits were restrained from interfering on the earth until the end of age when they will be released from their restrain. Humans will literally be living among these strange beings (*For as were the days of Noah, so will be the coming of the Son of Man–Mathew 24: 37 ESV*). This verse clearly suggests that the world at the end of age will resemble those in Noah's time. And a key feature of Noah's era was the presence of the Nephilim, tormenting humans and extreme level of immorality. Hence, the world will resemble the time of Noah, infested with the Nephilim and false gods. The Nephilim will be the foot soldiers of these entities that will re-emerge on earth at this time.

The nations will be ruled by these entities, who together with Satan, will try to mobilise an army to launch another attack against God. Part of Satan's plans for the end time is the recreation of the ancient civilization, and the transformation of humans (change the DNA of humans) into those of the beings that were on earth before man. First step to achieve this plot is the hybridisation of humans with angelic DNA, to produce Nephilim. Posthumanism/Transhumanism is part of this plot, as it aims to transform humans by mingling humans with Artificial Intelligence and machines (see Section 12.5). Any human that succumbs to this plot will cease to be human as his nature will drastically change. This goes contrary to the plans of God for man, as God wishes to transform humans to sons of God (a class of celestial beings far above the current state of humans).

With all the relevant technologies in place, Satan will proceed to inspire the establishment of a new world government made up of ten kings with the antichrist at its head. These ten kingdoms the Beast System is a replication of the ten kingdoms of Atlantis. Plato noted that Atlantis had ten rulers[7], who were the sons of Poseidon: *Atlas, Gadeirus, Ampheres, Evaemon, Mneseus, Autochthon, Elasippus, Mestor, Azaes and Diaprepes.* This government will introduce a new world order on earth, dissimilar from previously existing world orders. The role of this empire of Satan is to take full control of the earth, eradicate God-fearing people in the first phase, and finally eradicate all humans, such that the earth will be repopulated by different beings loyal to Satan. The core plan is to turn the earth into the domain of Satan and his angels:

> [10] The thief cometh not, but for to steal, and to kill, and to destroy (John 10:10 KJV).

12.2 THE BEAST SYSTEM–THE FINAL EMPIRE OF SATAN

"Collective security today must encompass not only the security of nations. But also mankind's security in a global environment that has proven vulnerable to debilitating changes wrought by man's own endeavors. Thus, in setting an American agenda for a new world order, we must begin with a profound alteration in traditional thought,"–*culled from "On the Threshold of the New World Order: A Rebirth for the United Nations", a speech delivered at Clayton Hall in 1992, by Joe Biden.*

Satan has made several attempts to recreate the pre-human civilization that once existed on earth. These are the empires of Satan, through which Satan had tried to regain full control and foist his rule over the earth, once again. Since God had prohibited the dark forces or any other celestial being to have direct charge over the earth after the rebellion and war in heaven, Satan had to work through human proxies, willing to do his biddings. This has been his modus operandi. Throughout history, Satan has tried to galvanise the world into one formidable force to challenge the heavenly authority of God. He nearly succeeded in the

---

7. Study Country, "What are the 10 kingdoms", 1

NEW WORLD ORDER: THE FOUNDATIONS OF THE LAST EMPIRE OF SATAN

corruption of the entire world before God struck with the great flood. Yet, he was unrelenting in the post-diluvian era. Soon after the flood, Satan inspired the re-emergence of giants/nephilim and establishment of empires to rule the entire world, starting from Nimrod to several other empires that had ruled over the earth. During the time of Nimrod, the world was galvanised into a formidable force to the extent that they were motivated to build a tower that could allow them to reach the heavens (Section 6.7). Subsequent empires that emerged also had this same motivation to unify the world and to have total control over all humans.

During the end time, God will briefly allow Satan to establish an empire that will have control over the entire world. Satan will exercise his authority over all on earth for a brief period during this time:

> "It will be for a time, times and half a time. When the power of the holy people has been finally broken, all these things will be completed." (Daniel 12:7 NIV).

> ² But exclude the outer court; do not measure it, because it has been given to the Gentiles. They will trample on the holy city for 42 months (Revelation 11:2 NIV).

This empire of Satan is the so-called Beast System/Government and will last for three and half years before it is destroyed. This is the final empire of Satan, as its destruction will lead to the imprisonment of Satan and his subsequent destruction in the lake of fire. This empire is usually given the moniker, *Beast System*, because of its figurative representation in both Daniel and Revelation. It was represented as a beast in Revelation 13:1–8 and Revelation 17:3, with seven heads and ten horns:

> 13 The dragon stood on the shore of the sea. And I saw a beast coming out of the sea. It had ten horns and seven heads, with ten crowns on its horns, and on each head a blasphemous name. ² The beast I saw resembled a leopard but had feet like those of a bear and a mouth like that of a lion. The dragon gave the beast his power and his throne and great authority. ³ One of the heads of the beast seemed to have had a fatal wound, but the fatal wound had been healed. The whole world was filled with wonder and followed the beast. ⁴ People worshiped the dragon because he had given authority to the beast, and they also worshiped the beast and asked, "Who is like the beast? Who can wage war against it?" (Revelation 13: 1–5 NIV).

This is the same beast that was shown to Daniel as the fourth beast, with 10 horns:

> [7] "After that, in my vision at night I looked, and there before me was a fourth beast—terrifying and frightening and very powerful. It had large iron teeth; it crushed and devoured its victims and trampled underfoot whatever was left. It was different from all the former beasts, and it had ten horns.
>
> [8] "While I was thinking about the horns, there before me was another horn, a little one, which came up among them; and three of the first horns were uprooted before it. This horn had eyes like the eyes of a human being and a mouth that spoke boastfully. (Daniel 7: 7 -8 NIV).
>
> 'The fourth beast is a fourth kingdom that will appear on earth. It will be different from all the other kingdoms and will devour the whole earth, trampling it down and crushing it. (Daniel 7:23 NIV).

This beast is the one-world government that would soon emerge. The system will have control over the seven continents of the world (*the seven heads are seven mountains on which the woman is seated–Revelation 17:9 ESV*), which would be subdivided into 10 regions that would be under the control of ten kings:

> [12] And the ten horns that you saw are ten kings who have not yet received royal power, but they are to receive authority as kings for one hour, together with the beast (Revelation 17:10 ESV).

At the head of this beast government is the little horn, who the other horns will subject their powers to. This little horn is the figurative representation of the antichrist. God will allow Satan to do as he wishes during this time. The Apocalypse of Baruch also touched on this empire:

> 5. And after these things a fourth kingdom shall arise, whose power shall be harsh and evil far beyond those which were before it, and it shall rule many times as the forests on the plain, and it shall hold fast the times, and shall exalt itself more than the cedars of Lebanon. 6. And by it the truth shall be hidden, and all those who are polluted with iniquity shall flee to it, as evil beasts flee and creep into the forest. (Apocalypse of Baruch XXXIX: 5–6).

Satan has long been preparing for this time, which he would try to seize to relaunch attack on God, once again. Satan's ultimate desire is to overthrow or kill God, so he would become the supreme being:

> [9] Out of one of them came another horn, which started small but grew in power to the south and to the east and toward the Beautiful Land. [10] It grew until it reached the host of the heavens, and it threw some of the starry host down to the earth and trampled on them. [11] It set itself up to be as great as the commander of the army of the Lord; it took away the daily sacrifice from the Lord, and his sanctuary was thrown down (Daniel 8:9–11 NIV).

He would use the earth as his launching pad for this campaign against God, with artificially engineered humans (post humans) used as part of the array of weapons in the warfare. Humans are connected to God through the spirit of God in them. Satan reckons he can utilise this connection to get to God. Through advanced technologies that would be facilitated by the mark of the beast, humans loyal or trapped in this regime will be turned into a weaponised hive mind against God.

The Beast System will have power over the world's political, social, financial, economic, and religious systems. It will have a heavy-handed control on virtually all facets of life. This empire will directly be under the authority of the antichrist and indirectly under Satan. This empire will be characterised by authoritarianism, highly reduced human population and infiltration of the earth by extra-terrestrial beings. To have absolute control over humanity, Satan will attempt to drastically reduce the population of mankind. Judging by current world population, about two billion people would die from the events of this period. These will mostly come through starvation, wars that will involve the use of nuclear and other dangerous weapons, pandemics, that will arise through bio-weapons, and persecution of those opposed to the government:

> They were given power over a fourth of the earth to kill by sword, famine and plague, and by the wild beasts of the earth." (Revelation 6: 8).

This time would be ten times (if not more) worse than a combination of Pol Pot's and Hitler's Nazi regime, as the antichrist runs a tightly controlled government. Everyone would constantly be monitored by various technological means that would even be linked to human mind. The Nephilim and other extra-terrestrials will make a comeback to the earth to support Satan in taking full control of the earth.

Literarily, the earth will be filled with darkness and wickedness during this time. God will allow this to happen, as it will facilitate the pulling down of the dark forces from the heavens to the earth. Spiritually, like attracts like. Hence, when the earth has become dark and wicked, all dark and wicked forces will naturally gravitate towards the earth.

12.3 SATAN'S MASTER PLAN TO RECAPTURE THE WORLD

Satan has always plotted to surreptitiously recapture the world using human proxies, who are unaware of his goal. This plan has been active across all generations, with Satan having made several attempts to take back the world. However, God has continuously restrained Satan's attempt to achieve this. However, towards the end time, God will allow Satan to achieve this. The restrainer will be removed to allow Satan to temporarily rule over the earth.

To establish his rule on earth, Satan through the antichrist will establish a highly repressive government that will go after and crush all opposing voices in the world, to gain full control. This would be worse than what Hitler or any other repressive government did in the past. Passages from the Revelation and Daniel suggest that the world will initially be reorganized with ten rulers (kings) in charge, who will eventually hand over their powers to the antichrist:

> [12] And the ten horns that you saw are ten kings who have not yet received royal power, but they are to receive authority as kings for one hour, together with the beast. [13] These are of one mind, and they hand over their power and authority to the beast. [14] They will make war on the Lamb, and the Lamb will conquer them, for he is Lord of lords and King of kings, and those with him are called and chosen and faithful." Revelation 17:12–14 ESV).

> [24] The ten horns are ten kings who will come from this kingdom. After them another king will arise, different from the earlier ones; he will subdue three kings. [25] [He] will speak against the Most-High and oppress his holy people and try to change the set times and the laws. The holy people will be delivered into his hands for a time, times and half a time.[a] [26] "'But the court will sit, and his power will be taken away and completely destroyed forever'". (Daniel 7:24–26 NIV).

Through advanced technologies such as artificial intelligence, nanotechnology, satellite technology, quantum computing, digital ID, blockchain, digital currencies (crypto currency, Central Bank Digital Currency (CBDC)), big data analytics, high-powered mobile communication network (5G and above), and internet of things, the antichrist will attempt to create a world, where he can closely monitor what every person is doing or thinking, at all times. The technologies will enable the antichrist to maintain total surveillance and control. This stems from his desire is to create a world where he would have a semblance of being omniscient and omnipresent. People will be controlled through devices that dictate what they can or cannot do. There are several digital identification projects that are at various levels of development. One of the ambitious ones is the ID2020 (now incorporated in the Digital Impact Alliance project), which aims to provide IDs for 2 billion undocumented people around the world (Jordan, 2016). The idea behind this project is to ensure that everyone living in the world is documented and linked to a unique identifier. With biometric-linked digital ID technology, people can be identified and tracked with high level of accuracy, and with digital currencies, their financial activities can be monitored and controlled[8]. The integration of digital ID and digital currencies is a dangerous cocktail that will ensure that the financial activities of people across the globe can accurately be monitored and controlled. People's access to the financial and other activities can be restricted based on these two protocols alone. In 2023, OpenAI (the developers of ChatGPT) launched an ambitious cryptocurrency and digital ID project named WorldCoin. The project's key feature is the "orb" which gives it the ability to verify users' identity by scanning their eyes[9]. Among other things, Artificial Intelligence (AI) will be utilised to grant entry to aliens into the world. The infamous quote of Elon Musk comes to mind (*"with Artificial Intelligence, we are summoning the demons"*)[10]. Currently, AI is bridging the physical and the spiritual realms. It is uncanny that the current Administration of the United States, named their biggest AI project as a Stargate Project. The Stargate Project is aiming to build up to 20 large AI data centers in the United States, to support AI innovations, with an initial investment of $100 billion and plans for up to $500 billion by 2029[11]. As discussed in

8. Levi, "The Elite's", 1
9. Hart, "What is Worldcoin", 1
10. Mack, "Elon Musk", 1
11. Forbes, "The Stargate Project", 1

Section 6.7.1, a start in ancient times is an instrument that creates an interdimensional portal between the physical and spiritual realms. Despite every other name this project could have been tagged, I can hardly find any reason why "stargate" was chosen as an appropriate name for a data center project, if not a declaration of its intent and purpose. Hence, literally speaking, this project is probably aiming to achieve the same thing that the ancients have tried to do–create an AI-enabled interdimensional portal through which the fallen ones can freely access the earth. One of the most dangerous aspects of AI, the so called artificial general intelligence (AGI), expected to morph into the artificial superintelligence (ASI), with an intellectual scope beyond human intelligence, would be developed around 2027[12]. According to an IBM report, "*at the most fundamental level, this superintelligent AI has cutting-edge cognitive functions and highly developed thinking skills more advanced than any human*"[13]. The ramifications of such a development are too dangerous to humanity, in order words, humans would have created an entity that could totally control them.

Efforts have been intensified around the world in the development and optimisation of these technologies. For instance, 5G technology is being upgraded to 6G. The 6G cellular technology (still in development) is expected to provide diverse connectivity at microsecond speeds[14]. The technology will deploy ultra-high radio frequencies with greater bandwidth capacity (carry more data) and latency (one thousand times faster latency) than preceding generations. Equipped with AI capabilities, the 6G and subsequent higher generations will "*serve as a distributed neural network that provides communication links to fuse the physical, cyber, and biological worlds, truly ushering in an era in which everything will be sensed, connected, and intelligent*"[15]. On the quantum computing space, giant leaps are daily being made. D-Wave's Advantage quantum computer has 5000 qubits (quantum bit) that can enable it to crunch massive amount of data in microseconds[16]. This quantum computer towers well above IBM's Condor with 1121 qubit capacity[17]. Yet other companies

12. Futurism, "Artificial Superintelligence", 1
13. Mucci and Stryker, "What is artificial", 1
14. Becher and Urwin, "What Is It?", 1
15. Huawei, "6G: The Next", 1
16. D-Wave, "The Most Connected", 1
17. Gambetta, "The hardware and software", 1

such as Microsoft, Xanadu, and Quantum Computing Inc. (QCI) are pouring a lot of effort in developing more quantum computing systems.

Needless to say; all these technologies, currently in the hands of various governments and private companies will fully come under the control of the antichrist, who would deploy them to his advantage. The ramification of the synergy of these technologies is profound. For the first time in recorded human history, the possibility of being able to identify, track and control everyone on earth in real time is within the grasp of humanity. The prophecy in Revelation 13:16–17 that people cannot buy and sell unless they have a particular identifier (mark of the beast–see Section 12.3.4), given over two thousand years ago is becoming a reality. The integration of these technologies will power the beast system and enable the antichrist to have a tight grip on the world. Anyone who opposes the rule and government of the antichrist would be crushed. Those who survive will be endangered species during this time, that would relentlessly be pursued and persecuted via several technological means. Countries are currently building network of spy satellites that can track people across the globe[18]. Reuters recently reported that the *"The National Reconnaissance Office is developing the most capable, diverse, and resilient space-based intelligence, surveillance, and reconnaissance system the world has ever seen,"*[19]. According to the report, the NRO, which is a United States intelligence agency is building these classified constellation of spy satellites to offer the most persistent, pervasive and rapid coverage of activities on Earth, that "No one can hide," from. Through the deployment of spy satellites, it would become difficult for anyone to hide from this extremely tyrannical regime. Global data from these satellites can be analysed by quantum-enabled AIs in microseconds. Larry Ellison, the founder of Oracle Founder, is advocating for an AI Surveillance state whereby AI will be used to analyse data from network of cameras, hence providing constant monitoring and surveillance of people and make them be on their best behaviour:

> "The police will be on their best behavior because we're constantly watching and recording everything that's going on. Citizens will be on their best behavior because we're constantly recording and reporting everything that's going on. It's unimpeachable"[20].

18. Roulette and Taylor, "Exclusive: Musk's SpaceX", 1
19. Exclusive: "Musk's SpaceX"
20. Khanum, "Oracle Founder Larry", 1

Mass surveillance of the people will lead to crackdown on perceived dissidents of the regime. Obviously, many followers of Christ who will recognise this period as the time of the antichrist, will be highly persecuted for not kowtowing to the regime. They will be treated as provocateurs and rebels, and many will be killed, and some imprisoned. There will also be other non-Christians in the secular world who will oppose the establishment of the empire of Satan. They will essentially oppose it because it would be a highly restrictive and repressive government, that will not recognise even the basic rights of people. Many people will lose their rights and freedoms they have been used to. However, they will be severely dealt with. This is the period Jesus Christ described as the Great Tribulation (Section 12.3.3). This will be a very horrible time:

> [21] As I watched, this horn was waging war against the holy people and defeating them, [22] until the Ancient of Days came and pronounced judgment in favor of the holy people of the Most-High, and the time came when they possessed the kingdom. (*Daniel 7: 21–22 NIV*).

The establishment of this empire will commence with worldwide deception (the emergence of the rider of the white horse with a bow–rainbow). This will happen when the First Seal is broken (Revelation 6:1–2). The aim of this global deception is the corruption of the world and humans and increased levels of sin and immorality, to enable evil spirits to breakthrough the restraining barriers to enter and operate better on earth (evil attracts evil, while light attracts lights). The second stage (the Second Seal–Revelation 6:3–4) will be marked by increased wars around the earth (nation against nation, and kingdom against kingdom). The purpose of these wars will be to disrupt the existing global geopolitical dynamics, to create a new political system. These will culminate in geopolitical realignments that will eventually lead to the emergence of the last 10 kings briefly instituted to govern the earth. The antichrist will eventually subdue the ten kings and force them to hand over all their powers to him. Part of the plan to establish the beast system is the drastic reduction of the world's population to a level that the system can easily control and manage. These wars and other events will be the causative agents of global population reduction.

12.3.1 THE EMERGENCE OF THE ANTICHRIST AND ESTABLISHMENT OF THE BEAST SYSTEM

There are indications in the Bible that the emergence of the antichrist will initially be unnoticed by many around the world, especially those who are not well versed in the Bible and not keenly watching out for key events that will usher in the antichrist. Daniel was given a series of visions that spanned a couple of years, which cryptically detailed the rise of the antichrist and the inauguration of his global rule. The unlocking of the cryptic hints in the vision will enable one to identify the emergence of this system and the identity of this individual at the appropriate time.

The antichrist will be a human, that would progressively acquire power until he emerges on the global stage as a world leader. At this point, Satan would empower him with immense power that will enable him to exercise massive authority and influence across the world. His initial appearance on the global political stage will be very innocuous that he will largely not be recognises as a heinous individual with evil intents. Daniel described the individual as *"the little horn"*, suggesting that he will initially be of relatively low political significance in the early stages, but will gradually become extremely powerful.

Daniel was shown this vision of four prominent kingdoms or empires that will emerge on the earth. These kingdoms were represented with beast of different characteristics and demeanour. Of particular interest to Daniel was the fourth beast, described to have ten horns (which represent 10 kings of this kingdom). When he sought the explanation about this terrifying fourth beast, he was told that this kingdom will devour the entire earth.

This fourth beast is essentially describing the last empire of Satan, which the antichrist will eventually lead. This empire/kingdom will be a confederation of different powerful nations of the world, that would be made up of 10 major blocks. This confederation would be multipolar in nature with the 10 kings exercising authority over their specific jurisdiction. Each of this block will have a leader/king in charge, overseeing its affairs, and together they will run affairs of the entire world. The forging of this empire would come through political and economic domination of other countries, so that the phase of influence of this empire would spread globally. This confederation will make war on other countries of the world, until it subdues them (*The fourth beast is a fourth kingdom that will appear on earth. It will be different from all the other kingdoms and will devour the whole earth, trampling it down and crushing it–Daniel 7:23 NIV)*. At the inception of this kingdom, the antichrist will be in the shadows, while this empire is being forged. Then he would appear on the stage at some point when this empire has appeared on the global stage.

The emergence of the antichrist on the global stage will happen when the world is reeling from the impact of global upheaval caused by extreme natural disasters, wars, pandemic, and global financial meltdown. This will be a time of global crisis that the world has not witnessed before. The end time upheavals are symbolically captured in Revelation as the four horsemen (white horse–deception, red horse–wars, black horse–economic collapse and famine, and pale horse–synergy of wars, economic collapse, hunger, diseases/pandemic, and attacks by beasts (animals or hybrids e.g. werewolves), culminating in largescale death across the world):

> ² And I looked, and behold, a white horse! And its rider had a bow, and a crown was given to him, and he came out conquering, and to conquer.
>
> ³ When he opened the second seal, I heard the second living creature say, "Come!" ⁴ And out came another horse, bright red. Its rider was permitted to take peace from the earth, so that people should slay one another, and he was given a great sword.
>
> ⁵ When he opened the third seal, I heard the third living creature say, "Come!" And I looked, and behold, a black horse! And its rider had a pair of scales in his hand. ⁶ And I heard what seemed to be a voice in the midst of the four living creatures, saying, "A quart of wheat for a denarius, and three quarts of barley for a denarius, and do not harm the oil and wine!"
>
> ⁷ When he opened the fourth seal, I heard the voice of the fourth living creature say, "Come!" ⁸ And I looked, and behold, a pale horse! And its rider's name was Death, and Hades followed him. And they were given authority over a fourth of the earth, to kill with sword and with famine and with pestilence and by wild beasts of the earth. (Revelation 6: 2–8 ESV).

He will emerge as a global problem solver, who would help the world manage the myriads of disasters it would be facing at that time. The rise of the antichrist will come about, amidst wars. His emergence will be forged in war. Through intrigues and political shenanigans, he will become so powerful. This is a key marker people should watch out for to be able to identify the emergence of the antichrist. There would be wars across many parts of the world, and there would be tremendous shift in the political landscape in the Near East. He will have great political and military prowess, that will enable him to exercise his authority across the world. A detailed analysis of these geopolitical wars in the Near East is presented in a previous work *The Final Battle for Earth*.[21]

The trigger for this war was shown to Daniel in Chapter 8, which follows the vision he had earlier seen in Chapter 7. In this Chapter he was shown how Iran represented as a ram would be charging at other countries around it, until it gets subdued by the goat (possibly representing a confederation of other Islamic countries (most likely the Sunnis) headed by Turkey) forged to counter the influence of the Iran in the region. The Turkish President Tayyip Erdogan had called for the formation of such an Islamic Alliance, targeted against Israel (to counter "the growing threat of expansionism" from Israel)[22]. This may be a forerunner of the confederation that will be forged against Iran in the last days. The defeat of Iran will pave the way for Turkey to emerge as a leading country in this region. Out of this new Islamic confederation initially headed by Turkey will emerge four blocks, when the first leader of confederation is killed:

> [8] The goat became very great, but at the height of its power the large horn was broken off, and in its place four prominent horns grew up toward the four winds of heaven. (Daniel 8: 8 NIV).

From one of these new four blocks, the antichrist will emerge:

> [9] Out of one of them came another horn, which started small but grew in power to the south and to the east and toward the Beautiful Land. [10] It grew until it reached the host of the heavens, and it threw some of the starry host down to the earth and trampled on them. [11] It set itself up to be as great as the commander of the army of the Lord; it took away the daily sacrifice from the Lord, and his sanctuary was thrown down. [12] Because of rebellion, the Lord's people and the daily sacrifice were given over to it. It prospered in everything it did, and truth was thrown to the ground. (Daniel 8: 9–12 NIV).

At his emergence, he will subdue three out of the ten kings of the empire to take their place:

> [8] "While I was thinking about the horns, there before me was another horn, a little one, which came up among them; and three of the first horns were uprooted before it. This horn had

---

21. Anejionu, "The Final Battle", 47.
22. Reuters, "Turkey's Erdogan", 1

eyes like the eyes of a human being and a mouth that spoke boastfully. (Daniel 7: 8 NIV).

This will change the balance of power in the multipolar confederation, with the antichrist acquiring more power. And shortly afterwards, he will convince/persuade the rest to handover their powers to him:

> [12] "The ten horns you saw are ten kings who have not yet received a kingdom, but who for one hour will receive authority as kings along with the beast. [13] They have one purpose and will give their power and authority to the beast. (Revelation 17: 12–13 NIV).

He will change the laws and global world order and will be given authority to rule the world and crush his enemies for three and half years. The highlight of the antichrist regime would be the point he invades Israel with his army as they march straight into Jerusalem, where he would declare himself to be God and command everyone to worship him as such. This is the point Jesus Christ warned his followers to watch out for–when the abomination of desolation would happen, marking the beginning of the Great Tribulation (see Section 12.3.3). He would demand to be worshipped as God and anyone who refuses would be killed. This is the period that many Christians would be martyred and coincides with the opening of the Fifth Seal of Revelation:

> [9] When he opened the fifth seal, I saw under the altar the souls of those who had been slain because of the word of God and the testimony they had maintained. [10] They called out in a loud voice, "How long, Sovereign Lord, holy and true, until you judge the inhabitants of the earth and avenge our blood?" [11] Then each of them was given a white robe, and they were told to wait a little longer, until the full number of their fellow servants, their brothers and sisters, were killed just as they had been. (Revelation 6: 9–11 ESV).

This three and half year duration is a key that links the little horn of Daniel 7 to the antichrist. In Revelation, the antichrist was also given three and half years (42 months/1260 days to exercise his authority over the earth). Another fact that ties this little horn of the fourth beast to the antichrist is the fact that he will make war against the saints and blaspheme God until the authority is taken from him (Daniel 7: 21–22 NIV).

The emergence of the antichrist and his rule may take around 6 years and a couple of months to come to conclusion. This period will cover the period he would be in the background and when he will fully emerge as the world leader commanding worship from all, before he is defeated. In the vision, Daniel was told that the fulfilment will take 2300 days (about 6 years 3 months):

> [13] Then I heard a holy one speaking, and another holy one said to him, "How long will it take for the vision to be fulfilled—the vision concerning the daily sacrifice, the rebellion that causes desolation, the surrender of the sanctuary and the trampling underfoot of the Lord's people?"
> [14] He said to me, "It will take 2,300 evenings and mornings; then the sanctuary will be reconsecrated." (Daniel 8: 13–14 NIV).

Daniel was instructed to conceal details of the aspects of the vision he was given concerning the 2300 evenings and mornings, hence, no one can say with certainty how long this period will last, or what it will encompass:

> [26] "The vision of the evenings and mornings that has been given you is true, but seal up the vision, for it concerns the distant future." (Daniel 8: 26 NIV).

Although many have associated this vision of ram and goat with an earlier generation closer to the time of Daniel, especially the encounter between the Alexander the Great and the defeat of the Medo-Persian empire, Gabriel who interpreted this vision for Daniel reiterated that the vision was meant for the end times:

> "Son of man," he said to me, "understand that the vision concerns the time of the end." (Daniel 8: 17 NIV).

> "I am going to tell you what will happen later in the time of wrath, because the vision concerns the appointed time of the end." (Daniel 8: 19 NIV).

Jesus Christ also referred to the vision of Daniel concerning the abomination of desolation as a marker for the commencement of the Great Tribulation. Jesus Christ made this remark during the Roman Empire, long after the demise of the Greek Empire. Hence, confirming that this vision will only be fully accomplished at the end times.

12.3.2 The False Prophet–The Beast System Executor

Besides the antichrist and Satan, there is another prominent figure that will rank high in the Beast System. This individual was symbolised in the Revelation as the False Prophet (second beast). Based on the description provided in the passage, this individual will be the chief propagandist of the Beast System and executor general of the instructions of the antichrist:

> [11] Then I saw another beast rising out of the earth. It had two horns like a lamb and it spoke like a dragon. [12] It exercises all the authority of the first beast in its presence, and makes the earth and its inhabitants worship the first beast, whose mortal wound was healed. [13] It performs great signs, even making fire come down from heaven to earth in front of people, [14] and by the signs that it is allowed to work in the presence of the beast it deceives those who dwell on earth, telling them to make an image for the beast that was wounded by the sword and yet lived. [15] And it was allowed to give breath to the image of the beast, so that the image of the beast might even speak and might cause those who would not worship the image of the beast to be slain. [16] Also it causes all, both small and great, both rich and poor, both free and slave, to be marked on the right hand or the forehead, [17] so that no one can buy or sell unless he has the mark, that is, the name of the beast or the number of its name. [18] This calls for wisdom: let the one who has understanding calculate the number of the beast, for it is the number of a man, and his number is 666. (Revelation 13: 11–18 ESV).

Unmasking of the identities of the individuals that will assume the role of the antichrist (the first beast) and the false prophet (second beast) has for a long time been at the top of eschatological quests. Many prominent individuals, especially high-ranking religious leaders have at one time, or the other been fingered as prime candidates for the false prophet role. This is largely based on the religious connotation associated with the description of this fellow as a false prophet, who would make the people to worship the antichrist. Hence, many are convinced that this individual would be an influential religious figure who would be able to convince the whole world to worship the beast.

However, eschatology enthusiasts who engage in this line of thought might be looking in the wrong direction, and this view may not necessarily be true. A re-examination of the description of this individual provided by John in the above passage (*Revelation 13: 11–18 ESV*), indicates that the false prophet does not necessarily have to be a religious figure to function in this role or influence the entire world. The authority of this individual will not emanate from a prominent religious position he already has but rather is derived from the authority of the antichrist (It exercises all the authority of the first beast in its presence). As a matter of fact, this individual would be as powerful as the antichrist, and would be the one the people will interface more with, during this period.

His key role is to direct worship and loyalty of the people to the antichrist. This individual who is clearly very dangerous and wicked would appear to people as someone with benign intentions (two horns like a lamb and it spoke like a dragon). Key attributes of this individual would be his charisma and oratorical prowess to convince the people. He will also have supernatural powers that will enable him to perform various outstanding things on earth to help support his work for the antichrist. The false prophet will be someone they world would respect and adore such that he is able to convince and deceive them, especially when he starts to perform many apparent wonders on earth ([14] and by the signs that it is allowed to work in the presence of the beast it deceives those who dwell on earth).

A prominent accomplishment of the false prophet would be the animation of the image of the beast and the implementation of the mark of the beast across the world. This is the point where he will showcase his wicked nature to the entire world:

> [15] And it was allowed to give breath to the image of the beast, so that the image of the beast might even speak and might cause those who would not worship the image of the beast to be slain. [16] Also it causes all, both small and great, both rich and poor, both free and slave, to be marked on the right hand or the forehead (Revelation 13:16 ESV).

The animated (so that the image of the beast might even speak) image of the beast mentioned in this passage could be an AI-powered robot, holographic image or perhaps live television broadcast of the antichrist. Obviously, these technologies were not in the world when John saw this vision, and he described the vision as close as he could. The description could fit any of these modern tech-generated features.

In my earlier work *The Final Battle for Earth*,[23] I argued that the false prophet could be a technology giant, political leader, religious leader, diplomat, etc. This conclusion that the false prophet would most likely be a tech giant was based on the fact that advanced technology would play a key role in the establishment and operations of the Beast System, especially in the animation of the image of the beast and implementation of the mark of the beast. While I believe that this argument is still valid, I am currently more inclined towards the idea that the false prophet role will be taken up by a great world leader or politician. That individual could be a well-recognised and respected political leader that is giving a position of authority, which he could use to command-and-control technological giants, religious leaders, the world financial and economic system, and diplomats, to achieve the stated goals. I strongly believe that the antichrist will place the individual who already commands the respect of the people across the world in a high-ranking global position, that will enable him to exercise his functions in the Beast System. This individual would have demonstrated his experience and abilities to globally implement obnoxious policies that are highly abhorrent to God, yet acceptable to the people. This is because in his role as the false prophet, all policies and tasks he would be implementing will be repulsive to God, hence, it makes sense that he must have shown his capabilities and prowess to conduct such an operation without incurring the wrath of the people. Just few current and past political leaders, currently fit this bill (having global appeal and far-reaching influence). The true identity of this individual will be revealed just shortly after the rise of the antichrist, and anyone keenly watching at this time will surely recognise the fellow.

12.3.3 The Great Tribulation–The Violent Takeover of the World and Establishment of the rule of Satan

The Great Tribulation is a key event of the end time. It is also referred to as the time of Jacob's trouble (Jeremiah 30: 4–10). It is a period when the world will be subjected to excruciating suffering and hardship, as the antichrist intensifies effort to take full control of the entire world, by crushing any opposing voices. The beginning of this event will be marked by a certain critical action by an individual who will eventually be revealed as the antichrist. This action by the individual is figuratively referred to

---

23. Anejionu, "The Final Battle", 89.

in the Bible as the "*abomination of desolation*". This event would amount to the desecration of the temple of God in Jerusalem. Christ was clear on this as he warned his followers to watch out for this critical event, which would be a clear indicator that the Great Tribulation has commenced:

> [15] "So when you see the abomination of desolation spoken of by the prophet Daniel, standing in *the holy place* (let the reader understand), [16] then let those who are in Judea flee to the mountains. [17] Let the one who is on the housetop not go down to take what is in his house, [18] and let the one who is in the field not turn back to take his cloak. [19] And alas for women who are pregnant and for those who are nursing infants in those days! [20] Pray that your flight may not be in winter or on a Sabbath. [21] For then there will be Great Tribulation, such as has not been from the beginning of the world until now, no, and never will be. [22] And if those days had not been cut short, no human being would be saved. (Mathew 24: 15-22 ESV).

This passage is a direct reference to another passage in Daniel regarding the emergence of the antichrist (little horn):

> [27] He will confirm a covenant with many for one 'seven.' In the middle of the 'seven' he will put an end to sacrifice and offering. And at *the temple* he will set up an abomination that causes desolation, until the end that is decreed is poured out on him. (Daniel 9: 27 NIV).

This abomination of desolation was revealed to Daniel by Gabriel, who came to deliver a message from God, concerning the fate of Israel, from the time they were in exile to the last days. The abomination of desolation is linked to the invasion of Israel by the antichrist army, who will match into Jerusalem to desecrate it. There, he would declare himself as God. Paul also alluded to this event as a key marker to be watched out for:

> [3] Let no man deceive you by any means: for that day shall not come, except there come a falling away first, and that man of sin be revealed, the son of perdition;
> [4] Who opposeth and exalteth himself above all that is called God, or that is worshipped; so that he as God sitteth in the temple of God, shewing himself that he is God. (2 Thessalonians 2: 3-4 KJV).

Before the abomination of desolation happens, Israel, which prior to this event, would have been enjoying relative peace with her Islamic neighbours, due to a seven-year peace treaty previously brokered by the antichrist, will be surrounded by the armies of the antichrist, after he calls of the peace deal:

> [20] "But when you see Jerusalem surrounded by armies, then know that its desolation has come near. [21] Then let those who are in Judea flee to the mountains, and let those who are inside the city depart, and let not those who are out in the country enter it, [22] for these are days of vengeance, to fulfill all that is written. [23] Alas for women who are pregnant and for those who are nursing infants in those days! For there will be great distress upon the earth and wrath against this people. [24] They will fall by the edge of the sword and be led captive among all nations, and Jerusalem will be trampled underfoot by the Gentiles, until the times of the Gentiles are fulfilled. (Luke 21: 20–24 ESV).

The invading armies would most likely be predominated by armies of surrounding Muslim countries, who would use that as an opportunity to avenge all that Israel had done to them in the past (*for these are days of vengeance, to fulfil all that is written–Luke 21:22 ESV*).

Although Israel and the Middle East will be the epicenter of the war, the Great Tribulation will affect everyone around the world. Access to necessities will be restricted to only those that have pledged allegiance to the antichrist. This is one of the core roles of the mark of the beast, which would serve among other things as an identifier of those loyal to the beast system (see Section 12.3.4 for further discussion about this). The Apocalypse of Baruch divided the events of this period into 12 cadences that intensify as the events are rolled out:

> XXVII. And He answered and said unto me : " Into twelve parts is that time divided, and each one of them is reserved for that which is appointed for it. 2. In the first part there shall be the beginning of commotions. 3. And in the second part (there shall be) slayings of the great ones. 4. And in the third part the fall of many by death. 5. And in the fourth part the sending of the sword. 6. And in the fifth part famine and the withholding of rain. 7. And in the sixth part earthquakes and terrors. 8. [Wanting.] 9. And in the eighth part a multitude of spectres and attacks of the Shedim. 10. And in the ninth part the fall of fire. 11. And in the tenth part rapine and much oppression. 12. And in the eleventh part wickedness and unchastity. 13. And

in the twelfth part confusion from the mingling together of all those things aforesaid. 14. For these parts of that time are reserved and shall be mingled one with another and minister one to another. 15. For some shall leave out some of their own, and receive (in its stead) from others; and some shall complete their own and that of others, so that those may not understand who are upon the earth in those days that this is the consummation of the times. (Apocalypse of Baruch XXVII: 1-15).

XXVIII. " Nevertheless, whosoever understandeth shall then be wise. 2. For the measure and reckoning of that time are two parts a week of seven weeks." (Apocalypse of Baruch XXVIII: 1-2).

The unprecedented hardship and suffering associated with this period will be occasioned by the unrelenting attempt by the antichrist to establish the rule of Satan over the entire world. This is akin to a violent takeover of the world; hence, it will be bloody and excruciating for the enemies of the regime. Virtually all opposing voices will be crushed. The antichrist will elevate himself to the level of God and will demand worship from all. Anyone who refuses to subject himself under the authority of the antichrist, will be punished severely and many will be killed and others imprisoned:

> [5] The beast was given a mouth to utter proud words and blasphemies and to exercise its authority for forty-two months. [6] It opened its mouth to blaspheme God, and to slander his name and his dwelling place and those who live in heaven. [7] It was given power to wage war against God's holy people and to conquer them. And it was given authority over every tribe, people, language and nation. [8] All inhabitants of the earth will worship the beast—all whose names have not been written in the Lamb's book of life, the Lamb who was slain from the creation of the world. (Revelation 13: 5-8 NIV).

Interspaced with the persecution of the antichrist are super intense geophysical events (widespread earthquakes, volcanic eruptions, wildfires, heat waves, tsunamis, floods, hailstorms, hurricanes, tornadoes, storms) that would be occurring around the world, causing unprecedented record-breaking natural disasters, that would increase the sufferings of the people. There would be frequent occurrence of extreme weather events across the globe. The Apocalypse of Baruch described this period

(Great Tribulation) as the last black water, where humans will face unprecedented hardship:

> Hear therefore the interpretation of the last black waters which are to come [after the black] : this is the word: 2. Behold! the days come, and it shall be when the time of the age has ripened, And the harvest of its evil and good seeds hath come, That the Mighty One will bring upon the earth and its inhabitants and upon its rulers Perturbation of spirit and stupor of heart. 3. And they will hate one another, And provoke one another to fight, And the mean shall rule over the honourable, And those of low degree shall be extolled above the famous, 4. And the many shall be delivered into the hands of the few, And those who are nothing shall rule over the strong, And the poor shall have abundance beyond the rich, And the impious shall exalt themselves above the heroic, 5. And the wise shall be silent, And the foolish shall speak, Neither shall the thought of men be then confirmed, Nor the counsel of the mighty, Nor shall the hope of those who hope be confirmed; 6. Moreover, it shall be when those things which were predicted have come to pass, That confusion shall fall upon all men, And some of them shall fall in battle, And some of them shall perish in anguish, And some of them shall be destroyed by their own. 7. Then the Most-High will reveal those peoples whom He hath prepared before, And they shall come and make war with the leaders that shall then be left. 8. And it shall come to pass that whosoever getteth safe out of the war shall die in the earthquake, and whosoever getteth safe out of the earthquake shall be burned by the fire, and whosoever getteth safe out of the fire shall be destroyed by famine. [9. And it shall come to pass that whosoever of the victors and the vanquished getteth safe out of and escapeth all these things aforesaid shall be delivered into the hands of My servant Messiah. 10. For all the earth will devour its inhabitants. (The Apocalypse of Baruch LXX:1–9).

Christians and Jews will be the most affected during this period as many Christians will recognise the antichrist and oppose his dictates, and hence, draw his wrath. Jews will be persecuted as part of Satan's agenda to rid the world of Jews, who God chose as his people. This is similar to the same ambition Hitler had during World War II. Revelation notes that many Christians would be imprisoned and beheaded for refusing to worship the antichrist and do his biddings:

> ¹⁰ "If anyone is to go into captivity,
>   into captivity they will go.
> If anyone is to be killed with the sword,
>   with the sword they will be killed." *(Revelation 13: 10 NIV).*

However, there are others who will succumb under the persecution that would be unleashed against them and acquiesced to the Beast System. Christ warned that this period will be very harsh for Christians. They entire world under the Beast System would be turned against them, as they would be regarded as troublemakers and rebels against the new world order. Treachery, deception and lies will rule the day, and love will tremendously diminish, as the hardship being experienced at this time will intensify the selfishness of humans:

> ⁹ "Then they will deliver you up to tribulation and put you to death, and you will be hated by all nations for my name's sake. ¹⁰ And then many will fall away and betray one another and hate one another. ¹¹ And many false prophets will arise and lead many astray. ¹² And because lawlessness will be increased, the love of many will grow cold. ¹³ But the one who endures to the end will be saved. ¹⁴ And this gospel of the kingdom will be proclaimed throughout the whole world as a testimony to all nations, and then the end will come. (Mathew 24: 9–14 NIV).

The false prophets mentioned in the above passage will be those who will convince Christians that events they are experiencing at that time are not part of the end time, but a normal global geopolitical transition. They will encourage many to take the mark of the beast as good citizens of the world. They will explain away the technologies used to implement the mark as just advancement of humanity and not part of the long-awaited end time events. These prophets will align with the beast system and will encourage followers to pledge allegiance to the beast.

Even though, Israel and Christians will be made to bear the initial brunt of the antichrist, his heavy handedness will spread to the rest of the world as he crushes opposition to establish his authority over the entire world. People will be given the choice to either worship the antichrist and pay allegiance to the beast system or be killed *(Revelation 13: 5–10 NIV)*. Millions will be killed during this period. The great multitude from all nations seen around the throne of God at the opening of the 6th seal, were the direct product of the Great Tribulation. These were people massacred during this period:

> ⁹ After this I looked, and behold, a great multitude that no one could number, from every nation, from all tribes and peoples and languages, standing before the throne and before the Lamb, clothed in white robes, with palm branches in their hands, ¹⁰ and crying out with a loud voice, "Salvation belongs to our God who sits on the throne, and to the Lamb!" ¹¹ And all the angels were standing around the throne and around the elders and the four living creatures, and they fell on their faces before the throne and worshiped God, ¹² saying, "Amen! Blessing and glory and wisdom and thanksgiving and honor and power and might be to our God forever and ever! Amen."
>
> ¹³ Then one of the elders addressed me, saying, "Who are these, clothed in white robes, and from where have they come?" ¹⁴ I said to him, "Sir, you know." And he said to me, "These are the ones coming out of the Great Tribulation. They have washed their robes and made them white in the blood of the Lamb. (Revelation 7: 9–14 ESV).

Many non-believers will embrace the new world order to save their skin or having been enticed by the allures and promises of the antichrist to establish a better world through the new world order and advanced technologies:

> The whole world was filled with wonder and followed the beast. ⁴ People worshiped the dragon because he had given authority to the beast, and they also worshiped the beast and asked, "Who is like the beast? Who can wage war against it?" (Revelation 13: 3–4 NIV).

Every tool will be deployed by the antichrist and his agents to coerce the people into submission to the Beast System. Many people will be marvelled by his military might and power, and the wonders he would perform through technology. Some people will initially be excited to be part of the system and its apparent promising prospects for human evolution. However, his rule will increasingly become authoritarian, and the rights of the people gradually taken away as the antichrist demands absolute loyalty from all people. People will gradually be turned into slaves of the Beast System, as AI increasingly begins to take charge of critical infrastructures and decisions required to run the world. At this point many people will realise the danger the antichrist and his system pose and would try to rebel against the system. However, it would be difficult for them to extricate themselves from the system, as anyone who pledged allegiance to the antichrist would have been sealed with the mark of the beast. By this time many Christians would have been killed or forced underground, and the antichrist will turn his aggression on the rest of humanity.

In terms of Biblical timing, the Great Tribulation will happen as part of the events of the 5th Seal of the Revelation, after the precursor events (birth pains of the tribulation) associated with the previous four seals. There are markers in Mathew 24 and Revelation 6, that were placed to help people understand this. Revelation noted that at the opening of the 5th Seal, souls of martyrs were crying to God to avenge their death, and they were asked to wait patiently for more of their brethren to be killed:

> ^{9} When he opened the fifth seal, I saw under the altar the souls of those who had been slain because of the word of God and the testimony they had maintained. ^{10} They called out in a loud voice, "How long, Sovereign Lord, holy and true, until you judge the inhabitants of the earth and avenge our blood?" ^{11} Then each of them was given a white robe, and they were told to wait a little longer, until the full number of their fellow servants, their brothers and sisters were killed just as they had been. (Revelation 6: 9–11 NIV).

This event will precede the opening of the 6th Seal, when the rebellious angels will be cast down from the heavens. Although, it has previously been opined that the Great Tribulation is part of the 6th Seal event,[24] this view tends to pale in the light of the fact that Jesus Christ clearly stated that the events associated with the 6th Seal, will occur immediately after the Great Tribulation. In Mathew 24, Christ said that immediately after the tribulation, the stars will fall from heaven. He stated that this event will be used by the elect to know when he is coming, so they would not be deceived by the emergence of false christs and false prophets:

> ^{29} "Immediately after the tribulation of those days the sun will be darkened, and the moon will not give its light, and the stars will fall from heaven, and the powers of the heavens will be shaken. ^{30} Then will appear in heaven the sign of the Son of Man, and then all the tribes of the earth will mourn, and they will see the Son of Man coming on the clouds of heaven with power and great glory. ^{31} And he will send out his angels with a loud trumpet call, and they will gather his elect from the four

---

24. Anejionu, "The Final Battle", 68.

winds, from one end of heaven to the other. (Mathew 24: 29–31 NIV).

This same event that will happen immediately after the Great Tribulation is presented in the Revelation as the beginning of the event of the opening of the 6th Seal, when rebellious angels will be forced down to the earth as a result of their defeat from war in heavens, and they will fall like fruits from the fig tree:

> [12] When he opened the sixth seal, I looked, and behold, there was a great earthquake, and the sun became black as sackcloth, the full moon became like blood, [13] and the stars of the sky fell to the earth as the fig tree sheds its winter fruit when shaken by a gale. [14] The sky vanished like a scroll that is being rolled up, and every mountain and island was removed from its place. [15] Then the kings of the earth and the great ones and the generals and the rich and the powerful, and everyone, slave and free, hid themselves in the caves and among the rocks of the mountains, [16] calling to the mountains and rocks, "Fall on us and hide us from the face of him who is seated on the throne, and from the wrath of the Lamb, [17] for the great day of their wrath has come, and who can stand?" (Revelation 6:12–17).

There is no doubt that these two passages (Mathew 24: 29–31 and Revelation 6:12–17) are describing the same events (earthquake, solar and lunar eclipse, falling of the stars from the sky, appearance of Christ from the sky), although certain details were missing. For instance, Revelation did not mention that the angels will gather the elect at this point, and Mathew did not demarcate the event according to the seals. If this event is marking the coming of Christ as can be seen from the two passages, it indicates that the Great Tribulation had already happened as part of the events of the 5th Seal. Although, the Revelation did not explicitly identify the 5th Seal event as the Great Tribulation, it hinted at it (Revelation 6:9–11). This passage indicated that the followers of Christ were being killed at this time in great numbers, yet more were expected to be killed before the deaths can be avenged. This places the Great Tribulation to be part of the 5th Seal event, as by the opening of the next seal, Christ was at the verge of coming with his angels to render justice on the world. Even the kings of earth recognised that wrath of God was at hand:

> "Fall on us and hide us from the face of him who is seated on the throne, and from the wrath of the Lamb, [17] for the great day of

their wrath has come, and who can stand?" (Revelation 6:16–17 ESV).

It is not clear how long the Great Tribulation will last, but there are indications that it would be for three and half years (approximately 42 months). Some hints were given in the Revelation about the duration. The first hint is in Chapter 11, where John was told that the Gentiles will trample Jerusalem for 42 months and that the two witnesses will prophesy from the city during this time for 1260 days (approximately 42 months):

> "Go and measure the temple of God and the altar, with its worshipers. ² But exclude the outer court; do not measure it, because it has been given to the Gentiles. They will trample on the holy city for 42 months. ³ And I will appoint my two witnesses, and they will prophesy for 1,260 days, clothed in sackcloth."

The second hint was provided in Revelation 13, which described the inception of the antichrist rule over the world, he was allowed 42 months to rule:

> ⁵ The beast was given a mouth to utter proud words and blasphemies and to exercise its authority for forty-two months. (Revelation 13: 5 NIV).

The third hint was provided in Revelation 12, where the woman was hidden from the dragon/Satan and nourished in the wilderness for 1260 days (beyond the reach of the dragon):

> ⁶ The woman fled into the wilderness to a place prepared for her by God, where she might be taken care of for 1,260 days. (Revelation 12: 6 NIV).

This confirms that the power of the dragon and the antichrist to cause harm to her would have dwindled or vanished after 1260 days.

Although it is anticipated that the Great Tribulation will last for 42 months, there are indications that it may not last that long, because the time will deliberately be shortened by Christ, to avoid the elimination of all followers of Christ on the earth:

> ²² And if those days had not been cut short, no human being would be saved. But for the sake of the elect those days will be cut short. (Mathew 24: 22 NIV).

How this shortening of days will happen was not made clear. However, considering that specific number of days or months were given, it seems that each day within this period may not be a full 24 hours as we currently have. Some geophysical shift at the time, could facilitate the shortening of times. Scientists have found evidence that indicates that earth's shifting system could cause day length variations[25]. Tremendous geophysical shifts are expected as part of the end time havocs that will befall inhabitants of the earth, hence, the day length at this time could drastically be shortened. Revelation may have hinted that this will happen and by what degree. It noted that during the events of the 4th Trumpet a third of sun, moon, and stars will be affected, resulting in shorter day light and nighttime by a third. This suggests that a normal day will be shortened by one third:

> The fourth angel blew his trumpet, and a third of the sun was struck, and a third of the moon, and a third of the stars, so that a third of their light might be darkened, and a third of the day might be kept from shining, and likewise a third of the night– (Revelation 8: 12 ESV).

Daniel noted that God can change times and seasons:

> [21] He changes times and seasons;
>   he deposes kings and raises up others.
> He gives wisdom to the wise
>   and knowledge to the discerning. (Daniel 2:21 NIV).

12.3.4 The Mark of the Beast: Satan Gene Top-up Super Max

During the last days, every human being will be presented with the opportunity to reject Satan and accept Christ as their king and saviour, and vice versa. The Bible calls this period the final test. Satan's strategy is to put stumbling blocks that would prohibit humans from accepting Christ. Part of this strategy would be deceit, coercion, and ultimately the mark of the beast (MOTB) that will be used to seal off any opportunity for anyone who takes it to be saved.

The MOTB is a form of an identifier for all those who have pledged allegiance to the antichrist and Satan. It is a conclusive seal that separates humans who have chosen to accept the antichrist as their god and those who did not. This mark will determine those who can participate in the

---

25. Hill, "A Day is Not", 1

Beast System and those who will not. This is similar to the practice in the ancient times where slave masters brand their slaves, to show ownership. The concept of the mark of the beast was introduced in Revelation 13, where John was describing the attributes of the second beast of the end time aka the false prophet:

> [16] It also forced all people, great and small, rich and poor, free and slave, to receive a mark on their right hands or on their foreheads, [17] so that they could not buy or sell unless they had the mark, which is the name of the beast or the number of its name.
> [18] This calls for wisdom. Let the person who has insight calculate the number of the beast, for it is the number of a man. That number is 666. (Revelation 13: 16–18 NIV).

The mark of the beast is a popularly discussed topic among Christians, even though no one yet knows exactly what the final form of this mark would be. Many speculations are rife on what the mark of the beast would look like, but none can say with certainty what this will eventually look like or how it would be implemented. However, one thing that is clear is that this mark would play important role in the final empire of Satan (the Beast System), which would be headed by the antichrist. People may initially not recognise this for what is it is as it would slowly be introduced to the world. At this point, people will be encouraged to accept it to enable them function in the technologically charged world. However, as time progresses, encouragement will turn to coercion and restrictions of access to certain critical necessities. At this point, the MOTB will be sold to the public as an essential part of the system, which everybody must accept. This will be the point it would become a mandatory requirement for all, and non-adherence to the law would lead to harsh consequences. Many will recognise it for what it is, and everyone will be given the opportunity to reject or accept it.

The MOTB will have both physical and spiritual relevance. Its practical relevance would be to serve as a pass that will enable people to function or freely participate in the economic activities in the system (buying and selling). There are several technologies currently in place or at various stages of development and integration, that could be used to restrict people's access to money as well as buying and selling. Its spiritual implication is to serve as a seal that would prohibit any human who received it from being redeemed by Christ, because they have committed themselves wholly to Satan via the antichrist:

> ⁹ And the third angel followed them, saying with a loud voice, If any man worship the beast and his image, and receive his mark in his forehead, or in his hand,
>
> ¹⁰ The same shall drink of the wine of the wrath of God, which is poured out without mixture into the cup of his indignation; and he shall be tormented with fire and brimstone in the presence of the holy angels, and in the presence of the Lamb:
>
> ¹¹ And the smoke of their torment ascendeth up for ever and ever: and they have no rest day nor night, who worship the beast and his image, and whosoever receiveth the mark of his name. (Revelation 14: 9–11 KJV).

This suggests that the mark has the potency to make humans irredeemable. Considering the fact that usually any human who repents and calls on God for forgiveness will be forgiven, this passage suggests that the mark does something to the individual that makes the person irredeemable. As can be seen in various passages in the Revelation, those who received the mark were adamant about repenting. Even at the height of the wrath of God being poured out on the earth, those with the mark instead cursed God for punishing them rather than repenting:

> ⁸ The fourth angel poured out his bowl on the sun, and the sun was allowed to scorch people with fire. ⁹ They were seared by the intense heat and they cursed the name of God, who had control over these plagues, but they refused to repent and glorify him. (Revelation 16: 8–9 NIV).
>
> 20 The rest of mankind who were not killed by these plagues still did not repent of the work of their hands; they did not stop worshiping demons, and idols of gold, silver, bronze, stone and wood—idols that cannot see or hear or walk. 21 Nor did they repent of their murders, their magic arts, their sexual immorality or their thefts. (Revelation 9: 20 -21 NIV).

The mark of the beast will change the individual who received it, such that they are incapable of repenting. It will most likely come as a digital identification technology with neuro-nanotechnology capabilities that could corrupt the gene and hijack the minds of the individual who receives it. These will be implemented as part of the posthuman evolution scheme that will be championed during the end times, which is promising humans, transformation to the next generation of humanoid. However, this will render humans to irredeemable species (see Section

12.5). This is linked to Satan's ultimate plan for mankind, which is to degrade the gene of humans so that they will become irredeemable and cannot achieve the original purpose God created them for.

The engineering/tampering of the gene is essentially a topping up of the satanic gene in humans, which had waned over the years. Satan has made several attempts to corrupt the original gene of humans. The first attempt was with Adam, which debased humans from beings of light to beings of mud. Then through the fallen watchers, who Satan might have inspired to lust after earthly women, which resulted in the birthing of the Nephilim. At the time of Noah, humanity was nearly corrupted with genes of the watchers, that God had to intervene with the flood to disrupt this (see Section 5.5). The MOTB will be Satan's final attempt to accomplish this agenda. He reckons that if humans are somehow genetically modified, they will no longer be technically considered humans. Christ's second coming is to complete the redemptive work he started in his first coming by restoring man to his full nature, which God originally intended. But if there are no humans in the real sense because their genes have been tampered with, such humans will become irredeemable, and there would not be need for Christ to come back a second time. Salvation through Christ's blood is only meant for the redemption of humans and not for other beings. This is why Satan attacks human DNA.

Furthermore, the MOTB will hijack the minds of the people such that they are incapable of making independent decisions or go against the beast. The beast will have all who had taken its mark under its full control, even the thoughts of man can be read by the system, through its many technologies. Soon after the end of COVID 19 pandemic, Yuval Noah Harari, an Israeli historian, opined in several interviews that humans are hackable[26]. He also insinuated that human brains will be hacked, and artificial intelligence will use data obtained from an individual to manipulate users into doing its bidding[27]. As a matter of fact, he suggested that humans have already been hacked, and people will look back in time and recognise the period when this happened. He insinuated that humans were hacked during the Corona Virus pandemic:

> "... people could look back in a hundred years and identify the corona virus epidemic as the moment when a new regime of surveillance took over, especially surveillance under the skin,

---

26. Harari, "AI and the future", 1; Moon, "Humans are hackable", 1; Political Incorrectness, "We Can Hack", 1; 60 Minutes, "Yuval Noah Harari", 1.
27. Delbert, "AI Will Hack", 1

which I think is maybe the most important development of the 21st century, is this ability to hack human beings, to go under the skin, collect biometric data, analyse it and understand people better than they understand themselves. This I believe is maybe the most important development of the 21st century. "(Political Incorrectness, 2022)

"In this time of crisis, you have to follow science. It is often said that you never allow a good crisis to go to waste, because a crisis is an opportunity to also do good reforms that in normal time, people will never agree to. But in a crisis, you see we have no chance, so, let's do it." (Political Incorrectness, 2022).

The possibility of the changing of humans via DNA was also suggested by Klaus Schwab, the founder of the World Economic Forum (WEF). In a 2022 interview available on YouTube, he stated the following:

> "One of the features of the 4th industrial revolution, we are doing is that it doesn't change what you are doing, it changes you. If you take genetic editing just as an example, it's you who are changed, and of course it has big impact on your identity." (Everyday on Blast, 2022).

There is every indication that the mark of the beast will play a big role in the expected transformation of humans.

12.3.5 Satan's war on human DNA

Satan has a key interest to disrupt or damage human DNA. He sees man as a threat, as he believes that God used humans to replace him. His goal is to ensure that humans never ascend to become sons of God. He launched his main salvo at Adam at the garden of Eden. This caused humanity to fall from the original height God had created him in. Since then, he has assiduously worked to bring man into a lower state of being, by tampering with his DNA, to completely render him irredeemable from his fallen state. Furthermore, by degrading humans, Satan can weaponize them against God. The human being is a powerful supercomputer, and if Satan can re-engineer humans, they will outperform any existing computer system. Having a network of connected human beings linked to AI, could be turned into powerful weapon that could be used in the war against God, as humans have direct connection to God through the spirit.

Hence, Satan has continued to wage war against man and his DNA, through genetic innovations, technology, chemicals, and mind control. Satan is attempting to modify human DNA through direct and indirect approaches. Direct approaches include sexual intercourse such as what occurred at the Garden of Eden, as well as during the incursion of the watchers, leading to the birth of Nephilim. Direct approach could also be achieved through medical procedures that aim to re-engineer human DNA, using advanced nanotechnology and genetics. Indirect approaches are achieved through environmental conditioning, demonic possession, and consummation of toxic foods. Researchers have proven that human gene can be changed/influenced by thoughts/mind and environment.

The mingling of humans with AI and machines will be the climax of the genetic tampering. Satan would promise humans that the modification of their genes will lead to their transformation to better humans with increased powers and abilities. But these will turn out to be deceptive promise that would rather destroy every fabric of humanity in them, and turn them to accursed beings, that would be irredeemable.

12.3.6 Deception to draw out the righteous

During the Great Tribulation, the antichrist and his agents will fake many false appearances of Christ to draw out the elect from their hiding places. Christ's warned Christians to run as soon as they observe the abomination of desolation (Mathew 24: 15–18 NIV). He also urged them to run from one place to the other to avoid being captured:

> [23] When you are persecuted in one place, flee to another. Truly I tell you, you will not finish going through the towns of Israel before the Son of Man comes. (Mathew 10: 23 NIV).

He admonished them to only raise up their heads from their hiding places when they observe certain things that suggests he was around:

> [26] People will faint from terror, apprehensive of what is coming on the world, for the heavenly bodies will be shaken. [27] At that time they will see the Son of Man coming in a cloud with power and great glory. [28] When these things begin to take place, stand up and lift up your heads, because your redemption is drawing near." (Luke 21: NIV).

However, before the approach of Christ and his angels, Satan will try to draw out Christians before this time. As the hardship of the tribulation intensifies, believers will be longing for rapture and deliverance from the persecutions of the antichrist, hence, many will believe any sign/wonder that may seem to be from God. Many false christs who will be at various places around the world will attempt to deceive people including some Christians not grounded in the scripture:

> [23] Then if anyone says to you, 'Look, here is the Christ!' or 'There he is!' do not believe it. [24] For false christs and false prophets will arise and perform great signs and wonders, so as to lead astray, if possible, even the elect. [25] See, I have told you beforehand. [26] So, if they say to you, 'Look, he is in the wilderness,' do not go out. If they say, 'Look, he is in the inner rooms,' do not believe it. [27] For as the lightning comes from the east and shines as far as the west, so will be the coming of the Son of Man. [28] Wherever the corpse is, there the vultures will gather. (Mathew 24: 23–28 NIV).

Many who are ungrounded in eschatology may even be led to believe that Jesus has made changes to his plans on how he will appear on the day of the lord. Hence, the warning from Jesus Christ to believers not to fall into such traps. They are to remain in hiding until they see the son of man coming down from heaven. Only then are they expected to raise their heads from their hiding places, to welcome the lord.

12.4 THE RESURGENCE OF THE WORSHIP OF RENEGADE GODS

Ancient gods are making their way back into many nations and cultures, and this move will be intensified during the last days. Their strategy was to weaken the Christian church (the custodians of the truth of God in the society), to enable them to erode the truth from the world. A key strategy adopted to weaken the churches was through the infiltration of the church by dark elements who slowly made their way to the top echelon. Soon after the Second Vatican Council, Pope Paul VI on June 29, 1972, wrote a letter that was hidden for many years and later published in 2018, by Fr. Leonardo Sapienza (regent of the Pontifical Household), in the book The Barque of Paul ("La barca di Paolo") stating the following:

"... We would say that, through some mysterious crack—no, it's not mysterious; through some crack, the smoke of Satan has entered the Church of God. There is doubt, uncertainty, problems, unrest, dissatisfaction, confrontation.

"The Church is no longer trusted. We trust the first pagan prophet we see who speaks to us in some newspaper, and we run behind him and ask him if he has the formula for true life. I repeat, doubt has entered our conscience. And it entered through the windows that should have been open to the light: science." [28].

"... It was thought that, after the Council, sunny days would come for the history of the Church. Nevertheless, what came were days of clouds, of storms, of darkness, of searching, of uncertainty ... We tried to dig abysses instead of covering them ..."[29]

Indeed, the smoke of Satan has infiltrated the Christian church as many occult practitioners, and members of secret societies have made their way to the top hierarchy of various Christian churches. In *Windswept House: A Vatican Novel*, a non-fiction novel written by Malachi Martin (a former Jesuit priest, who served as secretary to Cardinal Augustin Bea during preparations for the Second Vatican Council), the author describes a satanic ritual conducted at Saint Paul's Chapel inside the Vatican City, on June 29, 1963, to enthrone Lucifer in the church. The book alleged that high-ranking churchmen who were plotting to destroy the Church from within, took oaths signed with their own blood. The book tells the story of an organized international attempt by these powerful Vatican forces and secular compatriots to force a pope to abdicate, giving way to successor that will fundamentally change orthodox faith and help in establishing a New World Order[30]. The effects of the infiltration of the churches are reflected in many scandals that have been rocking the Christian churches in the past couple of years, leading to many falling away from the faith.

Both the secular and religious spaces are being taking over by influences of these gods. The spirit of deception which has been unleashed on the earth is aiding the spread of false doctrines permeating the space. Many practices previously considered obnoxious in the society are now largely acceptable. People are constitutionally being allowed to do as they

28. Aletia, "What did Paul VI mean", 1
29. Zuhlsdorf, "29 June 1972. Paul VI", 1
30. Martin, *Windswept House*, 7, 297 -300

wish, when it comes to morals and societal norms–the world has literally been turned upside down. With the failure of the church to nip this in the bud, citizens of many former traditional Christian countries especially in the western world have largely abandoned the church, to follow these ancient gods–masked in various forms, in the modern era.

Witchcraft and occult practices are now widespread among the high and low across the world. Coupled with this is the proliferation of false prophets and counterfeit churches, which have made many to be disillusioned about Christianity. In western world many have abandoned God and their Christian values and have embraced witchcraft and occultic practices. In Africa, many are abandoning Christianity and "going back to their roots" (the traditional worship of many deities). In their mind Jesus Christ and Christianity are a western construct used by colonialists to conquer nations in the continent. These young generation of Africans cannot reconcile the fact that the same people who introduced Jesus Christ to them were also the same that participated in the slave trade, colonised them, and stole their natural resources. Moreover, they argue that even the West who brought Jesus Christ to them has abandoned him. These are manifestations of deceptive spirits operating on earth currently. Many practitioners of traditional religion who before now were pushed into the background by Christianity are back in full glare. These disenchanted individuals are boldly poking fun at Jesus Christ and ridiculing various passages in the Bible, which seemingly sound ridiculous or contradictory.

Contributing to these issues is the proliferation of charlatans parading as pastors and prophets in the Christian churches. These charlatans have polluted the gospel with false teachings, demonic doctrines and false miracles. However, charlatanism succeeded in the church, because for long, many Christian preachers and scholars ignored some of the "hard meat" in the Bible and continuously fed the flock with "baby milk". The outcome of this is that many followers of Christ are half-baked in the truths of God and cannot withstand any rigorous scrutiny of their faith in God. These also gave leeway for many Christians to accept false doctrines, especially prosperity gospel that has produced inordinate quest of wealth by many Christians.

Needless to say that what is currently being witnessed on earth are still preparatory steps to the overrunning of this world by these false deities and spirits. The worship of the false gods will be intensified during the end times when the gods will literally be walking the earth. People will gravitate towards them, as they would claim to be the real creators of humans, who have come back to help humanity evolve to a higher level of consciousness. They will enthral the people with many apparent benefits such as satisfying human desires, increased wealth and prosperity, increased sexual immorality and so on, which many will be yearning for. This will lead to the great fallen away (rebellion/apostasy) hinted at Paul in 2 Thessalonians 2:3. All these will culminate to the people not being able to repent even while facing immediate danger:

> 20 The rest of mankind who were not killed by these plagues still did not repent of the work of their hands; they did not stop worshiping demons, and idols of gold, silver, bronze, stone and wood—idols that cannot see or hear or walk. 21 Nor did they repent of their murders, their magic arts, their sexual immorality or their thefts. (Revelation 9: 20–21).

12.5 TRANSHUMANISM TO POSTHUMANISM: SATAN'S FALSE 'EVOLUTION' PROMISE TO HUMANS

Transhumanism is "the belief or theory that the human race can evolve beyond its current physical and mental limitations, especially by means of science and technology" (Oxford Dictionary). Transhumanists believe that humans (*homo sapiens*) are due for another stage of evolution. This evolution will be a mix of organic and inorganic materials to enhance the current state and abilities of humans. The belief is fundamentally based on the assumption that the human condition can be enhanced through technological innovations. *It is rooted in the belief that humans can and will be enhanced through genetic engineering and information technology in addition to anticipated advances in bioengineering, artificial intelligence, and molecular nanotechnology. This will result in the iteration of Homo sapiens enhanced or augmented, but still fundamentally human*[31].

Transhumanism is essentially a belief that humans can inorganically be transformed to become superior beings, without the help of God. This transformation clearly differs from what God intends for humans (see Section 14.7). This belief which has long remained in the theoretical domain is no longer farfetched and has progressed from theoretical research to practical attempts to augment humans. Giant strides are being

---

31. World Economic Forum, "What is transhumanism", 1

made by several companies in human augmentation[32]. A defence strategic document jointly published by the UK Ministry of Defence (MOD) and their German counterpart (Bundeswehr Office of Defence Planning - BODP) in 2021, opines that human augmentation has the potential to transform the society, security and defence over the next three decades[33]. The document notes that *"future wars will be won, not by those with the most advanced technology, but by those who can most effectively integrate the unique capabilities of both people and machines"*. Neuralink has successfully implanted wireless brain chip into a human, in an attempt to connect human brains to computers to help tackle complex neurological conditions[34]. Many rival tech companies such as the Swiss-based École Polytechnique Fédérale in Lausanne (EPFL), have also done this.

On the face of it, transhumanism exudes a benign ambience (helping man to overcome certain physical limitations and challenges that inhibits his potentials), however, it has a very sinister motive lurking behind the façade. There are spiritual and ethical ramifications of the goal of transhumanists to transform humans into an enhanced state, outside the route God had planned. Although, transhumanism covers a broad spectrum of human enhancement, ranging from mechanical augmentation of parts of the human body, to genetic modifications and implants; its ultimate goal is the promise to change humans by completely eradicating ageing and death, so that humans can attain eternity and be like God. The Guardian in its 2018 editorial noted that *"the idea of technologically enhancing our bodies is not new. But the extent to which transhumanists take the concept is. In the past, we made devices such as wooden legs, hearing aids, spectacles and false teeth. In future, we might use implants to augment our senses so we can detect infrared or ultraviolet radiation directly or boost our cognitive processes by connecting ourselves to memory chips. Ultimately, by merging man and machine, science will produce humans who have vastly increased intelligence, strength, and lifespans; a near embodiment of gods"*[35].

This sums up the agenda of transhumanist–making humans to be like God. This was the same promise Satan made to Eve, that by eating the fruit, she will be like God:

32. InnoVirtuoso, "10 Remarkable", 1
33. UK Ministry of Defence, "Human Augmentation", 1
34. BBC, "Elon Musk says"
35. The Guardian, "No death and an", 1

> [4] "You will not certainly die," the serpent said to the woman. [5] "For God knows that when you eat from it your eyes will be opened, and you will be like God, knowing good and evil." (Genesis 3: 4–5 NIV).

Whereas God had promised the transformation or glorification of humans into sons of God (see Section 14.7), Satan is promising the transformation of humans into sons of Satan–human and machine hybrid. These merger of humans and machines is one of the indicators of the end-time as captured by Daniel:

> [43] And whereas thou sawest iron mixed with miry clay, they shall mingle themselves with the seed of men: but they shall not cleave one to another, even as iron is not mixed with clay. (Daniel 2:43 KJV).

The above passage from Daniel was referring to the ten *toes of the feet of the statue that Nebuchadnezzar saw in a dream–Daniel 2: 42)*. The ten toes were representative of the ten kingdoms that will emerge during the end time–the Beast System. The dream suggests that the mixing of iron and clay is the hallmark of the last kingdom of Satan on earth, which implies that during this time, most people on earth will be hybrids– a mixture of humans (clay) and machines (iron). This is the kingdom that the stone hewn in heaven will crush.

In line with its agenda to radically change humanity, transhumanism has progressively evolved into posthumanism. Posthumanism is a philosophical concept that challenges the traditional understanding of human nature and existence. It is a direct outcome of transhumanism and pushes the theory to the extreme. Whereas transhumanists advocate for mainly augmentation of humans (more of human than machines), Posthumanists are calling for the drastic change of the nature of humans from what it currently is to a new form of being[36]. With posthumanism, humans as we currently know it will cease to exist and be replaced by another being emanating from the former. As humans are progressively transformed with modern electronics, self-replicating nanobots, genetic modification, and artificial intelligence, they will start losing their human nature. This would get to a point when humans will become more of machine than human. At this point, they can no longer be considered humans anymore. Potentially, a posthuman could become a digital copy of a human being that can be integrated with other things, and functions

36. Sus, "Posthumanism vs Transhumanism", 1

as any other computer. Advocates are pushing for a time when human consciousness could be uploaded like any other data to the cloud[37]. This is one of the angles being pursued for eternity of human via science.

A human who had significantly been altered will no longer represent the human species; hence, it would become a posthuman[38]. This worldview is based on the belief that the human species in its current form does not represent the end of its development, but rather its beginning[39]. In a nutshell, Satan's desire is to destroy humans and replace them with something else that is remarkably different from what God created. And he would do this with fake promises of enlightenment and longevity.

This calls for extreme caution and humans should be wary of taking anything, device or medication that has the potential of changing their genes, especially towards the end time. Proponents of posthumanism are promising humanity gene enhancements (such as engineering double helix to triple helix genes) that could give people additional super capabilities (see Section 12.5). Potential application of nano robotics, bioengineering and Artificial Intelligence in the medical field is mind-blowing. Only recently, Larry Ellison (the Chairman of Oracle), disclosed, during a meeting at the White House that *AI could revolutionise cancer detection, treatment, and vaccine development, offering groundbreaking capabilities* in healthcare such as aiding production of personalised mRNA vaccines robotically created for each patient in 48 hours[40]. Despite its apparent benefit and innocuous façade, the ramification of such an agenda is frightening, to say the least. Ability of letting nano robots to run wild in the human body, interact with gene, could lead to the hijacking of the individual. The genetic code of such an individual could be changed to anything the AI determines. Humans will literally be at the mercy of AI, and their existence will be in their hands. These are the sort of promises and many more that will be used in the end times to lure humans in accepting to be genetically modified into new sets of beings.

The prospects of having posthumans on earth are real. As a matter of fact, the presence of posthumans on earth is not far fetch and is a key part of the Beast System. It is where the present generation is headed, according to the Bible and based on current pace of technological

---

37. Neuroba, "Can Consciousness Be", 1; Wagner, "AI and Consciousness", 1; Weber, "Could you move", 1

38. Encyclopedia.com, "Transhumanism", 1

39. Bostrom, "The Transhumanist", 6

40. Economic Times, "Oracle's Larry Ellison", 1

innovations in genetics, nanotechnology and artificial intelligence. There are strong speculations that singularity could be reached by 2027[41]. This is a hypothetical point in the future where AI becomes so advanced that it fundamentally changes society and human existence. There is an ongoing rush across the world for the development of artificial superintelligence (a hypothetical software-based artificial intelligence (AI) system with an intellectual scope beyond human intelligence–an intelligence that surpasses human intelligence in almost every field, including scientific creativity, general wisdom, and social skills)[42]. The emergence of ASI comes with a lot of ramifications for the human race. ASI integrated with advanced nanotechnology can be implanted in humans. This will automatically change the genetic makeup of humans. During a recent interview, Ray Kurzweil, a renowned computer scientist and transhumanist predicts that immortality will be reached by 2032[43]. He opines that ASI will emerge by 2029, but humans can only be truly integrated with them by 2030's when advanced nanotechnology are in place. At this point, ASI can effortlessly be embedded inside humans, with thousands or even millions of nanobots swimming through every part of the human body. As a result, humans will technically become hybrids:

> ... with the exponential growth of computation, we'll soon have the ability to rapidly test billions of possible molecular sequences to find cures ultimately for all diseases. By around 2032, people who are diligent with their health are going to reach what we call Longevity Escape Velocity. This is when scientific breakthroughs will add more time to our remaining life expectancy than is going by right now. As you live through a year you get back about four months of life from scientific progress so you're only losing about eight months of your life expectancy for each year that you live. But as I've said, medicine is advancing exponentially so by around 2032, we'll be getting back a whole year of life as we live through a year and after that we'll get back more than a year back for each year that we live. So, we'll be going backwards in time as far as our health is concerned. As we emerge with AI in this way we will become a hybrid species. We'll still be human, but we'll be enhanced by AI. Do you consider people who have cochlear implants or pacemakers or prosthetic limbs to be less alive? Of course not! These are early examples of merging with

41. Goertzel, "Artificial Superintelligence", 1
42. Mucci and Stryker, "What is artificial", 1
43. This Is World. "All My Predictions", 1

machines. Our machines are going to continue to shrink in size and gain power to the point where they are invisible and inside our bodies, as we emerge with technology. We will no longer be limited by our biology. We'll be free to live life without limits.

People will have own cerebral cortex and an artificial cerebral cortex thanks to this artificial cortex will they be able to search for information just like we do today using Google?

Well, let me start by explaining how we're going to connect our brains to the cloud. Nanotechnology is an emerging field that's manipulating materials measured in nanometers. One nanometer is one billionth of a meter. For perspective the head of a pin is about a million nanometers wide. Scientists are in the early days of figuring out how to build Nanorobots, the size of cells that will function like today's robots: sensing data, processing information, taking action, communicating with each other, all on a molecular level. This idea might sound futuristic, but my research shows a steady trend leading to a nanotechnology revolution in the next 15 years. The amount of computation that once took up an entire floor of a building now fits on a smartphone in your pocket and soon what now fits in your pocket will fit inside a blood cell and will be far more powerful in the 2030s and 2040s. Nanobots will swim in our bloodstream, uh they'll perform medical tasks with precision: deliver drugs straight to the source, drill through clogged arteries, ultimately they will go into our brains non-invasively through our capillaries, provide wireless communication between our neocortex which is the top layer of our brains and additional digital neurons hosted in the cloud. Think of it like having your phone but in your brain. If you ask a question your brain will be able to go out to the cloud similar to the way you do on your phone now only will be instant there won't be any input or output issues, and you won't realize it has been done. The answer just will appear in your brain like it is part of you. Some people say they don't want Nanobots in their body but lots of people didn't want to use early cell phones either. Yet today they take them everywhere and never leave home without them.

Once we connect our brains to the cloud, our intelligence won't be limited by the small size of our skulls and ultimately it will expand a millionfold.

AI's enthusiasts see the technology as a mechanism for transhumanism–for transcendence of the mortal flesh. They view AI as a stepping stone to a "successor species or some kind of merger of mind and machine"[44]. The existential question currently being asked is whether humans will be allowed to survive once ASI is in place, or if everyone would be forced to change by integrating with AI and other technologies. Stephen Hawking in 2014, told the BBC that "the development of full artificial intelligence could spell the end of the human race".[45] In a recent interview with Ross Douthat, Peter Thiel, the co-owner of Palantir, a leading US software company devoted to generation of AI-powered insights for surveillance and military intelligence, hesitated when asked if he thinks the human race should survive[46]. This is a very dangerous curve that humans are dangerously and blindly about to make.

Theologically speaking, if humans in their current form are wiped out or replaced by hybrids, there is no reason for Christ to come again. This was possibly why Christ posed the question:

> Nevertheless, when the Son of Man comes, will he find faith on earth?" (Luke 18:8 ESV).

The key issue here is that at the current pace of innovation, humans will be incapable of rescuing themselves from the mess posthumanism once that line is crossed. This is why Christ said he would cut the period short:

> [22] "If those days had not been cut short, no one would survive, but for the sake of the elect those days will be shortened. (Mathew 24:22 NIV).

This is the future that awaits man, if Christ does not return to put a stop to it. This period is the point when Christ will appear on the scene, to disrupt these activities and shatter the Empire of Satan:

> [34] Thou sawest till that a stone was cut out without hands, which smote the image upon his feet that were of iron and clay, and brake them to pieces. (Daniel 2: 34 KJV).

> 45 Forasmuch as thou sawest that the stone was cut out of the mountain without hands, and that it brake in pieces the iron, the brass, the clay, the silver, and the gold; the great God hath made known to the king what shall come to pass hereafter: and the dream is certain, and the interpretation thereof sure. (Daniel 2: 45 KJV).

44. Interesting Times with Ross Douthat, "A.I., Mars and Immortality", 1
45. Rincon, "Stephen Hawking's warnings",1
46. Interesting Times with Ross Douthat, "A.I., Mars and Immortality", 1

CHAPTER 13

The Second Coming of Christ

13.1 WHY IS CHRIST COMING BACK TO EARTH?

Christians are looking forward to the second coming of Christ. He promised his disciples that he would come back. So, why is he coming back?

During his first coming, Christ core task was to rectify the wrongs of man, to repair the broken relationship between God and man. Hence, reopening the door of salvation for the sons of Adam, so that they can reclaim their lost glory. The mission of his second coming is mainly to complete the following tasks: reclaiming the nations that have been under dark rulers for God, defeating Satan and the antichrist, establishing an empire on earth, which he will rule for a time (before handing it over to God), eradicating sin on earth, judging the world, and establishing God's kingdom on earth.

The second coming of Christ will occur after the 10 kings of the Beast System have been instituted to govern the world. Hence, the emergence of the 10 kings is a strong indicator that the coming of Jesus Christ is around the corner.

13.2 RECLAIMING THE NATIONS

One of the key tasks that Christ would do during his second coming is the reclamation of all the nations for God and re-establishing God's authority over the world. These nations that were once under the authority of renegade sons of God (see Section 7.1 and Section 7.2), will be reclaimed for God. The process of reclaiming these nations began from the Great Commission (see Section 11.4.6), when Christ charged his disciples to take the good news of their redemption (gospel) to all the nations.

On his return to earth, he will complete the process, by bringing war and judgment against the enemies of God. The end game of the second coming is the establishment of the kingdom of God on earth. The prelude to the establishment of the Kingdom of God on earth is the Millenium reign of Christ. This is the period Christ will reign on earth for one thousand years. This Millennial reign in literal terms is the Empire of Christ (*Imperium Christus*). To establish this empire, Christ will have to crush all authority (human and spiritual) exercising power or influence over the earth that is opposed to God:

> The Lord said unto my Lord, Sit thou at my right hand, until I make thine enemies thy footstool.
> ² The LORD shall send the rod of thy strength out of Zion: rule thou in the midst of thine enemies. (Psalm 110: 12 KJV).

The establishment of this empire will be executed systematically and will touch every fundamental element of nature. This process will be activated at the opening of the 7th Seal as hinted in Revelation 8. This 7th Seal essentially contains the blueprint of God's war plan against Satan and his armies. These will culminate in the so-called Battle of Armageddon, when Christ and his angelic army will face those of the antichrist around the *Hill of Megiddo* in Israel (see Revelation 16:12–16 and Section 13.8). Even though the battle will be swift, the process of eradicating all dark forces from the earth will be completed at the end of the Millennial reign, when Satan will finally be defeated in the final war and final judgement rendered on all humans that have once lived on earth. At this point, the earth and heavens will be cleansed and renewed (a new earth and a new heaven) devoid of all evils. Only then will the Kingdom of God be truly established on earth and across all the heavens.

13.3 DELIVERING THE EARTH TO GOD

Another important thing Christ will do during the end time is to deliver the world from the clutches of Satan and handing it back to God. Prior to the second coming of Christ, Satan will be allowed a brief period to exercise control over all the world, as has been explored in the preceding chapter. This will be the only period Satan will be allowed unrestrained access to the world, so he can exercise total control over the earth. Hence, virtually all nations of the world will be under the authority of the antichrist.

However, at his second coming, Christ will reverse the process by crushing the antichrist and the Beast System he established and take back the nations of the world by establishing his authority over them. So basically, Christ is coming to overthrow the government and rule of Satan established over the world. After this, Christ will rout out every enemy of God, wherever they are. This will be a thorough operation that will span through the Millennial reign of Christ when all enemy forces are conquered and subjected under the authority of Christ. Then Christ will deliver the earth to God, at the end of the Millennial reign. At this point the kingdom of God will commence. Paul captured this in his first letter to the Corinthians by stating that:

> [24] Then comes the end, when he delivers the kingdom to God the Father after destroying every rule and every authority and power. [25] For he must reign until he has put all his enemies under his feet. [26] The last enemy to be destroyed is death. [27] For "God has put all things in subjection under his feet (1 Corinthians 12: 24–27 ESV).

13.4 ENFORCEMENT OF GOD'S JUDGEMENT ON EARTH

Another thing Christ will be doing at his second coming is to execute God's judgement against all the enemies of God. This will commence with a very fierce war in the heavens between the angels of Christ and the rebellious angels of Satan. At their defeat in the cosmic realms, they will be forced down to the physical realm (the earth), where the war will continue. This will continue with the execution of the wrath of God upon various parts of the earth: astronomical bodies (sun, star, moon), the ecosystem, and humanity. Then, the defeat of Satan and his cohorts. As a matter of fact, the enforcement of the judgment of God on these entities is a prominent goal of the second coming of Christ. Whilst Christ came as the saviour in his first coming, during the second coming, he will come as a judge and king. At the end, he will sit on the judgement seat, where he will judge all (the white throne judgement), separating the good and the bad. Only those who met the expectation would be allowed into the kingdom of God, and the bad are destroyed in eternal fire (Revelation 20: 11–15).

13.5 THE END TIMES–A SELECTION PERIOD

The end times is a popular phrase used to describe a period when the world will be in upheaval as it goes through series of tumultuous events, before going into a new era/age. Many mainly focuses on the troubling aspects of this period and losing sight of its main goal–to extract the best crop of humans to become sons of God.

Across the ages, the earth has continuously gone through a filtration process, where the best is selected out of it. In this regard, the world serves as a testing ground for the selection of those deemed qualified to become the sons of God. In every age, God picks out the *best of the best* of the beings on the earth from the rest. These *best of the bests* are those who have merited the grades to be promoted to the next level of humans–the sons of God. Those who did not make this grade are destroyed.

The final test for this age will happen at the end times of this age. This period is not only meant for testing, but for cleansing and purification of the next generation of humans. It could be considered as the last crucible of purification. Christ alluded to it in Revelation as buying *gold refined by fire*":

> [18] I counsel you to buy from me gold refined by fire, so that you may be rich, and white garments so that you may clothe yourself and the shame of your nakedness may not be seen, and salve to anoint your eyes, so that you may see. [19] Those whom I love, I reprove and discipline, so be zealous and repent. (Revelation 3: 18-19 ESV).

Daniel was also told about this period of great distress that will result to the production of the two groups of humans–those with everlasting life and those that will be destroyed in everlasting shame and contempt:

> "There will be a time of distress such as has not happened from the beginning of nations until then. But at that time your people—everyone whose name is found written in the book—will be delivered. [2] Multitudes who sleep in the dust of the earth will awake: some to everlasting life, others to shame and everlasting contempt. [3] Those who are wise will shine like the brightness of

the heavens, and those who lead many to righteousness, like the stars for ever and ever. (Daniel 12: 1–3 NIV).

The hardship and sufferings of end-times are essentially, the heat of the crucible through which the best of the best of humans are produced. During the end time every human on earth will be given the opportunity to prove his worth, through the series of events that will be unleashed upon the earth during this time. At the end of this period, sin would be eradicated. Daniel hints at this in the following passage:

[24] "Seventy weeks are decreed about your people and your holy city, to finish the transgression, to put an end to sin, and to atone for iniquity, to bring in everlasting righteousness, to seal both vision and prophet, and to anoint a most holy place." (Daniel 9:24 ESV).

Jesus Christ described the initial stages of the end time tribulation as birth pains that would be increasing in frequency and intensity as the child is about to be born. This is a symbolic representation that the earth will go through birth pains and delivery period, to give birth to a new specie of humans–the sons of God. Micah also hinted at this, while prophesying about the first and second coming of Christ:

> Therefore he shall give them up until the time
>   when she who is in labor has given birth;
> then the rest of his brothers shall return
>   to the people of Israel.
> [4] And he shall stand and shepherd his flock in the strength of the Lord,
>   in the majesty of the name of the Lord his God.
> And they shall dwell secure, for now he shall be great
>   to the ends of the earth.
> [5] And he shall be their peace. (Micah 5: 3–5).

Revelation using the mystery of the woman and the dragon also alluded to this birthing process and the accompanying pains:

> And a great sign appeared in heaven: a woman clothed with the sun, with the moon under her feet, and on her head a crown of twelve stars. [2] She was pregnant and was crying out in birth pains and the agony of giving birth. [3] And another sign appeared in heaven: behold, a great red dragon, with seven heads and ten horns, and on his heads seven diadems. [4] His tail swept down a third of the stars of heaven and cast them to the earth. And the dragon stood before the woman who was about to give birth, so that when she bore her child he might devour it. [5] She gave birth to a male child, one who is to rule all the nations

with a rod of iron, but her child was caught up to God and to his throne, ⁶ and the woman fled into the wilderness, where she has a place prepared by God, in which she is to be nourished for 1,260 days. (Revelation 12:1–6 ESV).

These narratives were also consistent with depiction of these events in various extrabiblical apocalyptic books. The Apocalypse of Baruch alluded to it in the following way:

> 31. For that time shall arise which bringeth affliction; for it shall come and pass by with quick vehemence, and it shall be turbulent, coming in the heat of indignation. 32. And it shall come to pass in those days that all the inhabitants of the earth will be moved one against another, because they know not that My judgement hath drawn nigh., 33. For there shall not be found many wise at that time, And the intelligent shall be but a few: Moreover, even those who know shall most of all be silent. 34. And there shall be many rumours and tidings not a few, And the doings of phantasmata shall be manifest, And promises not a few be recounted Some of them (shall prove) idle, And some of them shall be confirmed. 35. And honour shall be turned into shame, And strength humiliated into contempt, And probity destroyed, And beauty shall become ugliness. * 36. And many shall say to many at that time : Where hath the multitude of intelligence hidden itself, And whither hath the multitude of wisdom removed itself? ' 37. And whilst they are meditating these things, Then envy shall arise in those who had not thought aught of themselves (?), And passion shall seize him who is peaceful, And many shall be roused in anger to injure many, And they shall raise up armies in order to shed blood, And in the end they shall perish together with them. 38. And it shall come to pass at the self-same time, That a change of times shall manifestly appear to every man, Because in all those times they polluted themselves, And practised oppression, And walked every man in his own works, And remembered not the Law of the Mighty One. 39. Therefore a fire shall consume their thoughts, And in flame shall the meditations of their reins be tried For the Judge shall come and will not tarry. 40. Because each of the inhabitants of the earth knew when he was committing iniquity, And they have not known My Law by reason of their pride. 41. But many shall then assuredly weep, Yea, over the living more than over the dead." (Apocalypse of Baruch XLVIII:29–41).

All things considered, the end time is a period designed to produce something desirable to God, which has undergone intense purification and scrutiny. The chaffs are removed while the substance is retained:

> [40] As therefore the tares are gathered and burned in the fire; so shall it be in the end of this world. [41] The Son of man shall send forth his angels, and they shall gather out of his kingdom all things that offend, and them which do iniquity; [42] And shall cast them into a furnace of fire: there shall be wailing and gnashing of teeth. [43] Then shall the righteous shine forth as the sun in the kingdom of their Father. Who hath ears to hear, let him hear. (Matthew 13:40-43 KJV).

13.6 THE GREAT TRIBULATION-A TEST OF LOYALTY, REFINEMENT AND INOCULATION PROCESS

As has been hinted in preceding sections, the overarching aim of the Great Tribulation (a key aspect of the end times), is to serve as a mechanism to test and prove the loyalty of humans to God, before they are transformed into a higher level of beings–sons of God. This new level of beings will be like angels, as hinted by Jesus Christ in Luke 20:

> [34] And Jesus said to them, "The sons of this age marry and are given in marriage, [35] but those who are considered worthy to attain to that age and to the resurrection from the dead neither marry nor are given in marriage, [36] for they cannot die anymore, because they are equal to angels and are sons of God, being sons of the resurrection. (Luke 20:34-36).

The Great Tribulation will provide the opportunity for the final selection of the last generation of humans that will be transformed into the sons of God. Christ alluded to it in Revelation as the "hour of trial" *(Revelation 3: 10 ESV)*.

The generation of humans that will go through the Great Tribulation will intentionally be exposed to the allures of Satan through the antichrist, as a way to test their loyalty to God:

> [24] For there shall arise false Christs, and false prophets, and shall shew great signs and wonders; insomuch that, if it were possible, they shall deceive the very elect. (Mathew 24:24 KJV).

Those who fail to succumb to these tricks will be subjected to the wrath of Satan that would be unleashed against those who refuse to bow and worship him as God. God will allow Satan to unleash all his arsenal on humanity. The antichrist would push believers to their limits during the Great Tribulation, that only those who truly love God and Jesus Christ can withstand. The faith of many shall be shaken thoroughly, as lawlessness thrives, and the strong delusion is cast on the earth by the fallen ones:

> [10] and with all unrighteous deception among those who perish, because they did not receive the love of the truth, that they might be saved. [11] And for this reason God will send them strong delusion, that they should believe the lie, [12] that they all may be condemned who did not believe the truth but had pleasure in unrighteousness. (2 Thessalonians 2:10-12 NKJV).

God intends to use Satan as an instrument to thoroughly test humans. By persecuting Christians, Satan would at this time, presume that he was establishing his empire on earth (by eliminating all opposed to his rule). However, God will inadvertently be using him to refine and test the faith of humans. This test is necessary to prevent any future disobedience or rebellion from the new breed of sons of God that would emerge from the human race. God is not going to allow unpurified and untested humans into His kingdom, because they will closely interact with Him. Hence, God is taking his time to sift humans so that only the *créme de la créme* can inherit this status. He does not want to promote humans who would rebel or go against his words after they have been promoted. Considering what happened with Adam, Satan and other fallen angels, God is taking his time to refine and test humans, before elevating them. Having experienced the rebellion of angels in the past, God is not intending to take any more chances, hence, he will thoroughly test the loyalty of man in keeping his commands and serving him eternally. Humans are going to be promoted to a very high level with great responsibilities, hence, only those found worthy can be allowed to ascend to this level:

> [10] Many will be purified, made spotless and refined, but the wicked will continue to be wicked. None of the wicked will understand, but those who are wise will understand. (Daniel 12:10 NIV).

Viewed from this standpoint, the Great Tribulation experience will serve as an inoculation of the sons of God. Satan tricked angels to rebel against God, Satan also tricked Adam and Eve to disobey God, hence, to forestall future occurrence of this, God will immunise the sons of God from falling for such temptations after their elevation, by exposing them to the pressure cooker of the Great Tribulation. Hence, before this promotion to the sons of God level, Satan would be allowed to test/tempt every human being on earth, with all he can, just the same way (if not more) that he tricked and tempted the rebellious angels.

Peter in his first epistle, alluded to this trial of faith that would lead to the salvation of souls at the end of age when Jesus appears:

> [7] That the trial of your faith, being much more precious than of gold that perisheth, though it be tried with fire, might be found unto praise and honour and glory at the appearing of Jesus Christ (1 Peter 1: 7 KJV).

The above passage also buttresses the fact that the Great Tribulation is also a period of refinement. Just as heat brings out the best in metals, the period will serve as a furnace for the purification of humans, especially lukewarm Christians. The heat from the Great Tribulation suffering will burnout all impurities that limit them from becoming the sons of God:

> [18] I counsel you to buy from me gold refined by fire, so that you may be rich, and white garments so that you may clothe yourself and the shame of your nakedness may not be seen, and salve to anoint your eyes, so that you may see. (Revelation 3: 18 KJV).

This refinement has been going on in all generations. For instance, the early Christians were highly persecuted. Many of them martyred. Other generations of Christians down the line also went through their own persecutions and trials. But the Great Tribulation provides the opportunity for the last batch of Christians and humanity in general to be tested before the best are selected. This last batch of Christians are those that will be highly compromised by the world (the Laodicean Church):

> [15] "'I know your works: you are neither cold nor hot. Would that you were either cold or hot! [16] So, because you are lukewarm, and neither hot nor cold, I will spit you out of my mouth. [17] For you say, I am rich, I have prospered, and I need nothing, not realizing that you are wretched, pitiable, poor, blind, and naked. [18] I counsel you to buy from me gold refined by fire, so that you may be rich, and white garments so that you may clothe yourself and the shame of your nakedness may not be seen, and

salve to anoint your eyes, so that you may see. [19] Those whom I love, I reprove and discipline, so be zealous and repent. [20] Behold, I stand at the door and knock. If anyone hears my voice and opens the door, I will come in to him and eat with him, and he with me. [21] The one who conquers, I will grant him to sit with me on my throne, as I also conquered and sat down with my Father on his throne. [22] He who has an ear, let him hear what the Spirit says to the churches.'" (Revelation 3 ESV).

Hence, the need for them to go through the Great Tribulation. This Laodicean Church will go through the Great Tribulation with the rest of the world because although they profess to be followers of Christ, their lifestyle closely matches with the rest of the world, hence, the need to test their heart and allegiance before they are deemed worthy to be admitted into the rank of the sons of God.

13.6.1 The Two Parallel Worlds of the Great Tribulation

During the Great Tribulation there will be two parallel worlds: one world will be completely under the control of the antichrist (the Beast System) with those participating in it all having the mark of the beast. This world will be a highly advanced society, powered by technologically advanced solutions and predominant AI activities. In this society extra-dimensional beings will freely mingle with humans. This will look almost like the normal world with some semblance of governance, but highly controlled, regimented, and repressive. In this tyrannical regime, humans will be subservient to aliens from other realms and dimensions, as well to demons and principalities.

In addition to this world that is controlled by the Beast System, there will be an outlier world, that will largely stay underground. This world will be filled with those who managed to escape the Beast System. They will mainly be in hiding, away from the major cities and not participating in any sociopolitical, financial, or economic activities associated with the Beast System. People living in this parallel world will constantly be hunted by agents of the antichrist who will be cracking down on them, to bring them into the world of the antichrist. This is the world where many believers still alive (the remnant Christians) will be living in before Christ returns. The suffering will be unimaginable and only those with absolute faith in Christ can endure it till the end. At the inception of the Beast System, which will slowly creep in on the inhabitants of the earth, many people (Christians and non-Christians) will lose their life, many imprisoned, as people will openly challenge the Beast System. The rest will be subjected to increasing persecution and hardship. As times goes on with the intensification of the crackdown, many believers will be forced underground. This is the period that calls for endurance of the saints:

> Here is a call for the endurance of the saints, those who keep the commandments of God and their faith in Jesus.[a] (Revelation 14: 12 ESV).

> [10] Do not fear what you are about to suffer. Behold, the devil is about to throw some of you into prison, that you may be tested, and for ten days you will have tribulation. Be faithful unto death, and I will give you the crown of life. (Revelation 2:12: 12 ESV).

This period of great distress is expected to last for roughly three and half years, although it will somehow be shortened to preserve the lives of Christians from the antichrist (Mathew 24:21–22). Despite the hardships, Christ expects his followers to overcome the antichrist by not letting him to break them to the point they will bow down in worship of Satan. He outlined many rewards for all those who will not succumb to the pressures from the antichrist:

> [25] Only hold fast what you have until I come. [26] The one who conquers and who keeps my works until the end, to him I will give authority over the nations, [27] and he will rule them with a rod of iron, as when earthen pots are broken in pieces, even as I myself have received authority from my Father. [28] And I will give him the morning star. (Revelation 2:25–28 ESV).

> [21] The one who conquers, I will grant him to sit with me on my throne, as I also conquered and sat down with my Father on his throne. (Revelation 3:21 ESV).

> [12] The one who conquers, I will make him a pillar in the temple of my God. (Revelation 3:12 ESV).

> [5] The one who conquers will be clothed thus in white garments, and I will never blot his name out of the book of life. (Revelation 3:5 ESV).

> To the one who conquers I will grant to eat of the tree of life, which is in the paradise of God.' (Revelation 2:7 ESV).

To the one who conquers I will give some of the hidden manna, and I will give him a white stone, with a new name written on the stone that no one knows except the one who receives it.' (Revelation 2:17 ESV).

By resisting the antichrist and refusing to bow or worship him, such believers are also proving their loyalty to God and their worthiness to merit the coming promotion as the sons of God.

> ⁵ He that overcometh, the same shall be clothed in white raiment; and I will not blot out his name out of the book of life, but I will confess his name before my Father, and before his angels. (Revelation 3: 4–5 KJV).

> These are they which came out of Great Tribulation, and have washed their robes, and made them white in the blood of the Lamb. (Revelation 7: 14 KJV).

> ¹⁹ Those whom I love, I reprove and discipline, so be zealous and repent. (Revelation 3: 19 ESV).

> ⁴ Thou hast a few names even in Sardis which have not defiled their garments; and they shall walk with me in white: for they are worthy. (Revelation 3: 4 KJV).

> ¹² Beloved, do not be surprised at the fiery trial when it comes upon you to test you, as though something strange were happening to you. ¹³ But rejoice insofar as you share Christ's sufferings, that you may also rejoice and be glad when his glory is revealed. ¹⁴ If you are insulted for the name of Christ, you are blessed, because the Spirit of glory and of God rests upon you. (1 Peter 4:12–14 ESV)

Those who endured will eventually reign with Christ and allowed into the Kingdom of God:

> ¹¹ Here is a trustworthy saying:
>   If we died with him,
>   we will also live with him;
> ¹² if we endure,
>   we will also reign with him. (2 Timothy 2:8–11–12 NIV).

However, those who failed to conquer and found unworthy will not be permitted into the Kingdom of God, but rather end up in the lake of fire:

> ⁷ The one who conquers will have this heritage, and I will be his God and he will be my son. ⁸ But as for the cowardly, the faithless, the detestable, as for murderers, the sexually immoral, sorcerers, idolaters, and all liars, their portion will be in the lake that burns with fire and sulfur, which is the second death." (Revelation 21: 7–8 ESV).

The Apocalypse of Ezra alluded to this as the unavoidable narrow path that must be taken by humans to access the Kingdom of God:

> 3. And he answered and said to me: If a sea be set? in a wide place, so that it is broad and unlimited, 4. but its entrance is set in a narrow place, so that it is like a river; 5. And if a man desire to enter upon the sea, and to behold it and master it, if then he do not pass through the narrow, how shall he be able to come into the broad? 6. [Hear] again another thing: There is a city that is built and set? in a large place of the valley,' and that city is full of many good things; 7. And its entrance is narrow and set on a height,* so that there is fire on the right hand, and on the left deep waters; 8. and a single path is set between these two, between the fire and the waters, so that that path only sufficeth for a man's footstep alone. If now that city be given 9. for an inheritance, unless that heir pass through the danger that is set, how shall he be able to receive his inheritance?
>
> 10. And I said to him: It is indeed so, my Lord! And he answered and said to me: So also is Israel's portion; 11. for, for their sakes I made the world: and when Adam transgressed my commandments, that which had been made was condemned. 12. And on this account the entrances of this [present] world became narrow and full of sighing and travail and many dangers, and much weariness [together with sicknesses and pains]; 13. but the entrances of that future world are broad and carefree, and produce fruits that do not die. 14. Unless, then, the living pass through the tribulation and these evils, they shall not be able (to receive) what has been kept for them. (Apocalypse of Ezra VII: 3–14).

13.7 THE SLOW DEMISE OF THE BEAST SYSTEM

Immediately after the Great Tribulation and just before Christ appears on earth, there are certain events that would occur on the earth that is designed to shake the Beast System and the people all over the world. These are events planned as part of the actions that will be taken against the world to enable the overthrowing of Satan and antichrist from their rule over the world. The taking over of the world from Satan and establishment of the empire of Christ will be actualised through carefully orchestrated series of events that would involve the forces of nature marshalled out against the world. These events would serve as tell-tale signs of the imminency of second coming of Christ.

There would be many extreme geophysical events and the forces of nature such as earthquakes, tsunamis, floods, landslides, volcanic eruptions, drought, etc; will be unleashed against the earth to destabilise the Beast System. This will lead to tremendous natural disasters, widespread destructions, pandemics, wars, and loss of lives, across the world. Normal activities in the Beast System will be severely disrupted, and the sufferings of the people living in this system will intensify. Astronomic bodies such as asteroids will be weaponised and launched against the earth. As the Beast System struggles to mitigate the impact of one disaster, another would hit the world in another place. There would be utter chaos with intensifying rhythm of disasters, as the final crunch time approaches. The powers of heaven shall utterly be shaken:

> [24] But in those days, after that tribulation, the sun shall be darkened, and the moon shall not give her light,
> [25] And the stars of heaven shall fall, and the powers that are in heaven shall be shaken.
> [26] And then shall they see the Son of man coming in the clouds with great power and glory. (Mark 13: 24–26 KJV).

These will suddenly creep upon the world when the antichrist and his followers would have assumed that they have eradicated all Christians from the world or pushed them to the fringes of insignificance. The initial chaotic period (wars and persecutions) that would trail the emergence of the antichrist and establishment of the Beast System, would have been brought under control with many opposing voices (considered as troublemakers) having been eliminated or forced into hiding. At this time, the antichrist would have relaxed that he has finally established his empire on the earth and gotten everything under control. Then suddenly these events would be unleashed on the earth:

> ³ For when they shall say, Peace and safety; then sudden destruction cometh upon them, as travail upon a woman with child; and they shall not escape. (1 Thessalonians 5:3 ESV).

This period will commence with the opening of the 6th Seal and span through the 7th Seal events, which contains details of the wrath of God that would be unleashed on the earth. At the opening of the 6th Seal, the powers that be on earth at this time will realise that their time was up, and Christ was literally at the doorsteps of the earth to wrench the world from them:

> ¹² I watched as he opened the sixth seal. There was a great earthquake. The sun turned black like sackcloth made of goat hair, the whole moon turned blood red, ¹³ and the stars in the sky fell to earth, as figs drop from a fig tree when shaken by a strong wind. ¹⁴ The heavens receded like a scroll being rolled up, and every mountain and island was removed from its place.
> ¹⁵ Then the kings of the earth, the princes, the generals, the rich, the mighty, and everyone else, both slave and free, hid in caves and among the rocks of the mountains. ¹⁶ They called to the mountains and the rocks, "Fall on us and hide us from the face of him who sits on the throne and from the wrath of the Lamb! ¹⁷ For the great day of their wrath has come, and who can withstand it?" (Revelation 6: 12–17 NIV).

The events that will unfold at the opening of the 7th Seal are contained in carefully planned stages, that are orchestrated with the blowing of each of the seven trumpets. The events will be calibrated in such a cadence that will overwhelm the Beast System. The first trumpet will unleash strange fires and flares that would burn one third of the terrestrial environment, affecting vegetation and possibly other aspects of the terrestrial ecosystem:

> ⁶ Now the seven angels who had the seven trumpets prepared to blow them. ⁷ The first angel blew his trumpet, and there followed hail and fire, mixed with blood, and these were thrown upon the earth. And a third of the earth was burned up, and a third of the trees were burned up, and all green grass was burned up–Revelation 8: 6–7 ESV).

As the Beast System tries to literally put out these mysterious fires, which they would blame on climate change, the events of the second trumpet will be unleashed on the marine environment, with an asteroid striking the sea, devastating one third of this ecosystem:

> The second angel blew his trumpet, and something like a great mountain, burning with fire, was thrown into the sea, and a third of the sea became blood. ⁹ A third of the living creatures in the sea died, and a third of the ships were destroyed. (Revelation 8: 8–9 ESV).

This event would also likely be attributed to climatic change. At this point, the encumbered Beast System will start to take stringent steps to address this latest disaster.

Following this would be the devastation of the fresh water with the blowing of the Third trumpet. The poisoning of the fresh water sources across the world will lead to the death of many:

> ¹⁰ The third angel blew his trumpet, and a great star fell from heaven, blazing like a torch, and it fell on a third of the rivers and on the springs of water. ¹¹ The name of the star is Wormwood. A third of the waters became wormwood, and many people died from the water, because it had been made bitter (Revelation 8: 10–11 ESV).

Then the celestial bodies (sun, moon, and stars) that illuminate the world would be hit next, hence, plunging the world into partial darkness both during the day and the night):

> The fourth angel blew his trumpet, and a third of the sun was struck, and a third of the moon, and a third of the stars, so that a third of their light might be darkened, and a third of the day might be kept from shining, and likewise a third of the night– (Revelation 8: 12 ESV).

Having taking care of the various environments that sustains the existence of humans on earth, the actions will shift to direct attacks on human population. At this point the gun is turned towards the people in the Beast System, who participated in the persecution of believers during the Great Tribulation. The 5th Trumpet unleashed events that greatly tormented humans. The bottomless pit will be opened, and dark forces would be allowed into the earth in vast numbers:

> And the fifth angel blew his trumpet, and I saw a star fallen from heaven to earth, and he was given the key to the shaft of the bottomless pit.[2] He opened the shaft of the bottomless pit, and from the shaft rose smoke like the smoke of a great furnace, and the sun and the air were darkened with the smoke from the shaft. [3] Then from the smoke came locusts on the earth, and they were given power like the power of scorpions of the earth. [4] They were told not to harm the grass of the earth or any green plant or any tree, but only those people who do not have the seal of God on their foreheads. [5] They were allowed to torment them for five months, but not to kill them, and their torment was like the torment of a scorpion when it stings someone. [6] And in those days people will seek death and will not find it. They will long to die, but death will flee from them. (Revelation 9:1 -6 ESV).

The opening of the bottomless pit is likely the opening of a portal into the dark dimension by certain activities that would be conducted on the earth at this time. The dark forces that would be unleashed on the earth are the so-called dark matter from another dimension. Recall that the angels restrained most of the demonic forces that were roaming the earth after the flood; and only allowed a few (10%), to be operating on the earth after their leader petitioned God not to restrain all of them. The Book of Jubilees 10: 4–13, provided the account of what happened during this time where only one tenth of the evil forces were allowed to operate on the earth (see Section 6.5). The blowing of the 5th Trumpet will lead to the opening of a portal into the dimension where the remaining 90% of demonic forces have been restrained for generations. These would be the locusts that will greatly torment the people.

The passage in Revelation indicates that a fallen angel would provide the knowledge (key) that would be used to reap open this portal (a star fallen from heaven to earth, and he was given the key to the shaft of the bottomless pit). The opening of this portal is most likely going to be through such scientific activities such as those being conducted at CERN, that are fixated on understanding other dimensions and origin of the universe. The motive behind this move (most likely instigated by Satan), would be to enlist energies or beings from the other dimension, to counter the wrath of God, when the earth will be reeling from the effects of the wrath of God. Perhaps they would be trying to harness the energies of dark matter or antimatter in this war with God. However, this move would backfire and turn sour, when the entities that would come through the bottomless pit will turn against the inhabitants of the earth to torment them.

As the world grapples with the tormenting plague that has besieged the world for five months, the next devastating event will happen, with the world plunged into war, that would be inspired by four fallen angels who had been imprisoned at the Euphrates:

> [13] Then the sixth angel blew his trumpet, and I heard a voice from the four horns of the golden altar before God, [14] saying to the sixth angel who had the trumpet, "Release the four angels who are bound at the great river Euphrates." [15] So the four angels, who had been prepared for the hour, the day, the month, and the year, were released to kill a third of mankind. 16 The number of mounted troops was twice ten thousand times ten thousand; I heard their number. (Revelation 9: 13–15 ESV).

Judging from the passage, about two hundred million (*twice ten thousand times ten thousand*) soldiers will be participating in this war. This war may be between nations who may at this point be trying to pull away from the Beast System. Daniel's prophecy revealed that this kingdom will be a mixture of iron and clay, hence not united:

> [42] As the toes were partly iron and partly clay, so this kingdom will be partly strong and partly brittle. [43] And just as you saw the iron mixed with baked clay, so the people will be a mixture and will not remain united, any more than iron mixes with clay. (Daniel 2: 42–43 NIV).

The Beast System would likely prevail against these nations, as it survived after this period, trudging on to hold the world in its clutches. At the end of this war, one third of the world population would have died from this war.

The world still reeling from the pains of the events, will be plunged into more devastating events unleashed in the second wave of judgement, planned to further destabilise the Beast System. By this time, the antichrist would have realised that the world was slipping away from its hands, due to the events orchestrated by a more powerful external force. He will make frantic efforts to hold on to power. Then, the events of the 7th Trumpet will be unfolded. The 7th Trumpet is the climax of the wrath of God, and the event that will be leading the final defeat of the Beast System (the kingdom of Satan). This can be gleaned from the declarations coming from the heaven when the 7th Trumpet was blown:

¹⁵ The seventh angel sounded his trumpet, and there were loud voices in heaven, which said:

> "The kingdom of the world has become
> the kingdom of our Lord and of his Messiah,
> and he will reign for ever and ever." (Revelation 11: 15 NIV).

The events of the 7th Trumpet are also phased into 7 key events termed plagues. The plagues were almost a repetition of the events of the 7 trumpets but with more devastating impacts. The first plague caused great havoc on the terrestrial environment (land) by causing a festering boil pandemic across the world. The second plague also followed similar pattern of impacting the marine environment, but this time killing every living thing in the sea (contrasting that of the Second Trumpet that killed one third of the things in the sea). The third polluted the fresh water, and turned them into blood:

> ² The first angel went and poured out his bowl on the land, and ugly, festering sores broke out on the people who had the mark of the beast and worshiped its image.
> ³ The second angel poured out his bowl on the sea, and it turned into blood like that of a dead person, and every living thing in the sea died.
> 4 The third angel poured out his bowl on the rivers and springs of water, and they became blood. (Revelation 16: 2–3 NIV).

Following these would be the fourth and fifth plagues, which unleashed more terror against the inhabitants of the world. The fourth trumpet unleashed intense heat wave on the earth, that terribly scotched the people:

> ⁸ The fourth angel poured out his bowl on the sun, and the sun was allowed to scorch people with fire. ⁹ They were seared by the intense heat and they cursed the name of God, who had control over these plagues, but they refused to repent and glorify him (Revelation 16: 8–9 NIV).

This plague will terribly disfigure the people in the Beast System. The flesh of humans will be scotched with festering burns that will leave the skins of the people hanging out in ugly mix of dry and fresh skin flakes. The impact of this heat wave will probably be intensified by the complications from the mark of the beast device, which would have altered the genetic makeup of the individuals. However, the people will be conditioned to accept this as normal, as their minds at this point has been hijacked and their thoughts continuously being manipulated by AI linked to the Beast System.

The fifth trumpet targeted the seat of power of the Beast System, destroying it and plunging it into darkness:

> 10 The fifth angel poured out his bowl on the throne of the beast, and its kingdom was plunged into darkness. People gnawed their tongues in agony 11 and cursed the God of heaven because of their pains and their sores, but they refused to repent of what they had done. (Revelation 16: 10–11 NIV).

This plague is literally, the official declaration of war against the Beast System by Christ. It is Christ's way of poking Satan in the eyes, to let him know his time was up. Not taking this lying down, the antichrist and the false prophet will at this point begin to mobilise the world to form a formidable force against the coming of Christ. The mobilization will culminate in the antichrist gathering a global army to await the arrival of Christ and his angelic army in Israel:

> The sixth angel poured out his bowl on the great river Euphrates, and its water was dried up to prepare the way for the kings from the East. 13 Then I saw three impure spirits that looked like frogs; they came out of the mouth of the dragon, out of the mouth of the beast and out of the mouth of the false prophet. 14 They are demonic spirits that perform signs, and they go out to the kings of the whole world, to gather them for the battle on the great day of God Almighty.
> 15 "Look, I come like a thief! Blessed is the one who stays awake and remains clothed, so as not to go naked and be shamefully exposed."
> 16 Then they gathered the kings together to the place that in Hebrew is called Armageddon. (Revelation 16: 13–16 NIV).

While the antichrist is still preparing for the coming war, the events of the 7th plague will be unleashed. The plague is packed full of terribly events that would shock the world into stupor, shortly before Christ and his army arrive at the scene. These events include lightning strikes, thunders, rain of hundred-pound weight hailstones plunging down on earth, and the greatest earthquake the world had ever seen. This earthquake will split Jerusalem into three parts, possibly destabilising the armies of the antichrist already gathered there and plunging them into disarray and destroying important military equipment and logistics for the war.

The earthquake will also shake and level the mountains and cause great tsunamis that will flood and possibly submerge various islands across the world. Major cities in different countries would be levelled. Other key events lined up for this period include the gathering of the elect, the first resurrection, and the fall of Babylon the Great and the Battle of Armageddon:

> [17] The seventh angel poured out his bowl into the air, and out of the temple came a loud voice from the throne, saying, "It is done!" [18] Then there came flashes of lightning, rumblings, peals of thunder and a severe earthquake. No earthquake like it has ever occurred since mankind has been on earth, so tremendous was the quake. [19] The great city split into three parts, and the cities of the nations collapsed. God remembered Babylon the Great and gave her the cup filled with the wine of the fury of his wrath. [20] Every island fled away and the mountains could not be found. [21] From the sky huge hailstones, each weighing about a hundred pounds, fell on people. And they cursed God on account of the plague of hail, because the plague was so terrible. (Revelation 16: 17–21 NIV).

These last sets of events would immediately precede the coming of Christ and his army. The events are planned to shock and destabilise the armies of Satan, that they would not know what hits them next:

> [43] But know this, that if the master of the house had known in what part of the night the thief was coming, he would have stayed awake and would not have let his house be broken into. [44] Therefore you also must be ready, for the Son of Man is coming at an hour you do not expect. (Matthew 24:43–44 ESV).

The destruction of *Babylon the Great* (see Section 13.8), a powerhouse in the Beast System would happen at this time. The destruction of this city/country cryptically tagged *Babylon the Great* is targeted to bring further destabilization to the Beast System and unleashing further confusion among the remaining armies of the antichrist. There would be chaos in their camps as various critical infrastructure and logistics prepared for the war would have been rendered useless. This would be the state of the world when Christ and his angelic armies would hit the ground, to finish off the war.

13.8 THE FALL OF BABYLON THE GREAT

One of the highlights of the events contained in the 7th plague is the destruction of a location (country/city) identified as Babylon the Great (mystery Babylon). Babylon the Great is considerably a very important part of the Beast System that three chapters of Revelation (Revelation 17, 18 and 19) are dedicated almost entirely to the description of its nature and abrupt destruction. Despite having almost three chapters dedicated to it, the identity of which country or city would become Babylon the Great in the end times has remained a mystery. Over generations, these has generated great ruckus among eschatological scholars. Like many other mysteries in the Revelation, many scholars and preachers have progressively associated the mystery Babylon with the Roman Empire, the Vatican-cum-Catholic Church, the European Union, Jerusalem or the United States. The confusion surrounding the mystery Babylon emanates from the way it is described in the Revelation. In addition to its being described as a city, the mystery Babylon is also presented as the great harlot, that rides the beast. This implies it controls the Beast System. This adds to the confusion. One thing that is clear is that the mystery Babylon is not the ancient Babylon, but another country or city that will have similar characteristics as the ancient Babylon. John described it as mystery, because even though it had the nature and significance of the ancient Babylon, it was unlike it in various respects, and still unrevealed as at the time of his writings.

The ancient Babylon was the capital city of a very great kingdom. Due to its prominence, it was used to represent the kingdom. The mystery Babylon referred to in the Revelation would be expected to be as great as its ancient counterpart and could symbolically represent a country associated with it. John described it as a mystery because it was not existing on earth as at the time the revelation was being giving to him. It was a mystery because even though the country looked as great as the ancient Babylon, which has ceased to exist, it was remarkably different. Hence, it should be assumed that the greatest nation on earth in the last days, would be the prime candidate to represent this mystery Babylon. This country would have to be taken out of the scene, for the reordering of the world's geopolitics to be accomplished.

The first mention of Babylon in Revelation was after the blowing of the 7th Trumpet, when the three angels were announcing the contents of the final wrath of God on the earth and its inhabitants:

> [8] A second angel followed and said, "'Fallen! Fallen is Babylon the Great,' which made all the nations drink the maddening wine of her adulteries." (Revelation 14: 8 NIV).

This declaration by the second angel, suggests that Babylon the Great had tremendous influence over all the nations of the world. This influence was negative, suggesting the nations were corrupted and turned away from God to follow Satan and other gods, hence the use of adultery in its description. The passage also suggests that as at this time (7th Trumpet), Babylon the Great is yet to be destroyed, but has come under the line of fire of God.

The second time Babylon the Great was mentioned was after the seventh angel poured out his bowl into the air (the 7th Plague event), when it was said that God remembered Babylon:

> God remembered Babylon the Great and gave her the cup filled with the wine of the fury of his wrath. (Revelation 16: 19 NIV).

The phraseology used here suggests that this was the time of reckoning for Babylon the Great when God decides to exert punishment upon it. The chapter following this passage alluded to this, as one of the seven angels who executed the last phase of the wrath of God, took the liberty to show John what Babylon the Great was and what happened at its destruction:

> One of the seven angels who had the seven bowls came and said to me, "Come, I will show you the punishment of the great prostitute, who sits by many waters. [2] With her the kings of the earth committed adultery, and the inhabitants of the earth were intoxicated with the wine of her adulteries." (Revelation 17: 1–2 NIV).

Based on the description presented in Revelation 17, Babylon the Great, would be the seat of power of the False Prophet (the enforcer of the Beast Systems orders), rather the seat of power of antichrist, as widely speculated.

The first clue to this conclusion is presented with the symbology of the woman riding the beast with seven heads and ten horns:

> [3] And he carried me away in the Spirit into a wilderness, and I saw a woman sitting on a scarlet beast that was full of blasphemous names, and it had seven heads and ten horns. (Revelation 17: 3 ESV).

The identity of this beast is unambiguous, considering the description proffered by the angel. This beast that the woman was riding is the Beast System. This imagery suggests that the woman had a controlling power over the nations of the world, because it was empowered (carried) by the Beast System to execute its commands against the people and nations of the world:

> [18] And the woman that you saw is the great city that has dominion over the kings of the earth." (Revelation 17: 18 ESV).

Recall that the false prophet will exercise all the authorities of the antichrist, to get the whole world to worship the beast:

> [12] It exercises all the authority of the first beast in its presence, and makes the earth and its inhabitants worship the first beast, whose mortal wound was healed (Revelation 13: 12 ESV).

The second clue is found in the fact that Babylon the Great deceived and corrupted the nations of the world (turned them away from God). It made the nations participate in her adulterous nature and killed the servants of God:

> "Hallelujah!
> Salvation and glory and power belong to our God,
> [2] for his judgments are true and just;
> for he has judged the great prostitute
>   who corrupted the earth with her immorality,
> and has avenged on her the blood of his servants." (Revelation 19: 1–2 ESV).

> [4] The woman was arrayed in purple and scarlet, and adorned with gold and jewels and pearls, holding in her hand a golden cup full of abominations and the impurities of her sexual immorality. [5] And on her forehead was written a name of mystery: "Babylon the great, mother of prostitutes and of earth's abominations." (Revelation 17: 4–5 ESV).

The symbology of adultery, harlotry or prostitution is usually used to represent the state of a nation turning away from worshipping the true God, to worship false gods. Hence, in this regard, Babylon the Great will allow fallen entities to inhabit its territory, and make the nations to turn away from God, to worship the antichrist by corrupting them:

> "Fallen, fallen is Babylon the great!
> She has become a dwelling place for demons,

> a haunt for every unclean spirit,
> a haunt for every unclean bird,
> a haunt for every unclean and detestable beast.
> ³ For all nations have drunk
> the wine of the passion of her sexual immorality,
> and the kings of the earth have committed immorality with her,
> and the merchants of the earth have grown rich from the power
> of her luxurious living." *(Revelation 17: 2-3 ESV)*.

The third clue is based on the fact that the woman was drunk with the blood of the saints:

> ⁶ And I saw the woman, drunk with the blood of the saints, the blood of the martyrs of Jesus. (Revelation 17: 6 ESV).

This suggests that the woman (Babylon the Great) killed those saints, who refused to bow down to the image of the beast. Recall that it is the false prophet that would be killing the followers of Christ for their refusal to compromise and pledge allegiance to the antichrist (see Section 12.3.2).

These descriptions of Babylon the Great essentially tally with that used to describe the attributes of the False Prophet who will deceive the entire world and make them to worship the antichrist:

> and makes the earth and its inhabitants worship the first beast, whose mortal wound was healed. ¹⁴ and by the signs that it is allowed to work in the presence of the beast it deceives those who dwell on earth (Revelation 13: 13-14 ESV).

In my earlier work,[1] I had concluded that Jerusalem would be Babylon the Great, considering that it was referred to as the great city and would be the religious seat of power of the antichrist. However, emerging facts are suggesting that although Jerusalem would be one the seats of power of the antichrist, it will not be Babylon the Great. The mystery Babylon is most likely going to be the United States or a city in it (most likely New York), from where the false prophet would be operating from. One of the clues to support this is based on the angel's declaration that Babylon the Great has done many evil things to other countries, hence her punishment would be doubled. No country in contemporary world has influenced other countries more than the United States. Through the United Nations, NATO and direct interference, the United States has

---

1. Anejionu, "The Final Battle", 129-36

influenced governments and people across the globe. As a matter of fact, the world is currently under the masked United States Empire. Babylon the Great also lived in luxury and glorified herself:

> ⁵ for her sins are heaped high as heaven,
>   and God has remembered her iniquities.
> ⁶ Pay her back as she herself has paid back others,
>   and repay her double for her deeds;
>   mix a double portion for her in the cup she mixed.
> ⁷ As she glorified herself and lived in luxury,
>   so give her a like measure of torment and mourning,
> since in her heart she says,
>   'I sit as a queen,
> I am no widow,
>   and mourning I shall never see.'
> ⁸ For this reason her plagues will come in a single day,
>   death and mourning and famine,
> and she will be burned up with fire;
>   for mighty is the Lord God who has judged her."
> (Revelation 18: 5–8 ESV).

Based on this, it seems the antichrist would largely be operating mainly from Jerusalem (pretending to be God), while the false prophet will be operating from the United States. Hence, it will be destroyed before the Battle of Armageddon that will take place in Israel, to dislodge the Beast System.

The fall of Babylon the Great will set off series of events during the end times that will reorganize the global geopolitics. Other countries will try to step into the vacuum left by the demise of the great nation, and in the process of this, there would be wars and global tension.

Needless to say that despite the compelling argument presented in the preceding paragraphs, the identity of the mystery Babylon is not conclusive. The confusion here on the correct identity of the mystery Babylon stems from the fact that Satan like other entities does not really know when the end time seals would be opened. Hence, in every generation, he prepares some individuals to take up the role of the antichrist, false prophet and the country that would serve as mystery Babylon. For instance, during the days of the early church, Rome would have been the perfect candidate for the mystery Babylon, Emperor Nero Claudius Caesar Augustus Germanicus (Lucius Domitius Ahenobarbus) the antichrist. Similarly, during World War II, Satan must have thought the end time seals may have been opened and positioned Hitler as the antichrist and Joseph Goebbels, the false prophet. During this period, Nazism was the budding beast system and Germany, Babylon the great.

Hence, there is a possibility that another country more powerful than the United States that would emerge in the future may be position as the mystery, if Christ tarries in his second coming.

13.9 THE DAY OF THE LORD - THE BATTLE OF ARMAGEDDON AND THE DEFEAT OF THE BEAST SYSTEM

The day of the Lord marks the day that Christ will come down to earth in power and glory to defeat Satan and reclaim the earthly kingdom from him:

> [12] For the Lord of hosts has a day
>   against all that is proud and lofty,
>   against all that is lifted up—and it shall be brought low
> (Isaiah 2:12 ESV).

Even though it is themed "the day of the Lord", there are indications that events surrounding this day might linger for more than a day. This day is so important that it has been prophesied from the Old Testament to the New Testament. The prophecies of many ancient prophets including those contained in Enoch 1, Isaiah 34, Jeremiah 46, Amos 5, Joel 2, and Zechariah 14, touched on this topic with varying degrees of detail. The Book of Enoch captured it in great detail:

> The Holy Great One will come forth from His dwelling,
> 4. And the eternal God will tread upon the earth, (even) on Mount Sinai,
> [And appear from His camp]
> And appear in the strength of His might from the heaven of heavens.
>
> 5. And all shall be smitten with fear
> And the Watchers shall quake,
> And great fear and trembling shall seize them unto the ends of the earth.

6. And the high mountains shall be shaken,
And the high hills shall be made low,
And shall melt like wax before the flame

7. And the earth shall be [wholly] rent in sunder,
And all that is upon the earth shall perish,
And there shall be a judgement upon all (men).

8. But with the righteous He will make peace.

And will protect the elect,
And mercy shall be upon them.

And they shall all belong to God,
And they shall be prospered,
And they shall [all] be blessed.

[And He will help them all],
And light shall appear unto them,
[And He will make peace with them].

9. And behold! He cometh with ten thousands of [His] holy ones
To execute judgement upon all,
And to destroy [all] the ungodly:

And to convict all flesh
Of all the works [of their ungodliness] which they have ungodly committed,
And of all the hard things which ungodly sinners [have spoken] against Him. (Book of Enoch 1: 3 -9).

The day of the Lord is the highlight of the end time events. A day planned for the overthrow of the kingdom of Satan and his rule over the earth, to initiate the process of installing the kingdom of God on earth. Shortly before this day, there would be key events that would happen on the earth to announce this day including blood moon, eclipse, and earthquake (Revelation 16: 18 NIV):

> [30] "And I will show wonders in the heavens and on the earth, blood and fire and columns of smoke. [31] The sun shall be turned to darkness, and the moon to blood, before the great and awesome day of the Lord comes. [32] And it shall come to pass that everyone who calls on the name of the Lord shall be saved. For in Mount Zion and in Jerusalem there shall be those who escape,

as the Lord has said, and among the survivors shall be those whom the Lord calls. (Joel 2: 1–32 ESV).

These catastrophic events will be triggered by the passage of the Destroyer across the earth, shortly before the appearance of Christ. The Destroyer (Exodus 12:23) is the nickname for Planet Niburu/Planet X (a weaponised planet supposedly 4 times bigger than the earth[2]), whose close shave with the earth will cause tremendous havoc on earth.[3] On this day, God will begin to exact in full measure his judgement against his enemies:

> [10] That day is the day of the Lord God of hosts,
>   a day of vengeance,
>   to avenge himself on his foes.
> The sword shall devour and be sated
>   and drink its fill of their blood.
> For the Lord God of hosts holds a sacrifice
>   in the north country by the river Euphrates. (Jeremiah 46:10 ESV).

The climax of this day is the Battle of Armageddon. This is the battle that will be fought between the armies of Christ and those of the antichrist and will take place at a place known as Armageddon, in the outskirts of Jerusalem, hence, the Battle of Armageddon. At the point the battle, the antichrist and his army would encamp around Jerusalem:

> [2] For I will gather all nations against Jerusalem to battle; and the city shall be taken, and the houses rifled, and the women ravished; and half of the city shall go forth into captivity, and the residue of the people shall not be cut off from the city.
> [3] Then shall the LORD go forth, and fight against those nations, as when he fought in the day of battle. (Joel 3: 2–3 ESV).

Hence, for the battle at that place, to first wrench Jerusalem out of his hands. The control of Jerusalem is pivotal to the spiritual scheme of things. That is also where God has designated to be his seat of power. Hence, Satan's attempt to occupy it, to disrupt God's plan. The Battle of Armageddon would be a decisive battle that would conclusively decide the fate of the world. Each side in the battle will throw all they could into the battle.

---

2. Broussard, "Is Planet X", 1.
3. The Kolbrin Bible also detailed the havoc caused by the Destroyer in Egypt.

Satan had long prepared for this day, as it would determine his continued hold on the earth or his ultimate defeat and beginning of his demise. Prior this day, Satan, the antichrist, and the false prophet will mobilise the nations under the 10 kings to wage war against the incoming army of Christ. They might probably sell a lie to the world that an external (alien) force is about to invade the earth, and the entire world needs to come together to fight this malevolent external force. They may explain that all the unprecedented natural disasters that had been hitting the earth prior this time was orchestrated by the external enemy forces, as part of their plot to take over the earth. While this excuse would be partly true, the motive behind it is false. Satan will paint the armies of Christ as the bad guys, coming to destroy the world, while Satan and his army are the good guys trying to protect it. The unwise will buy this story and join forces with the antichrist army to await the arrival of the heavenly army. Hence, the nations will gather around Jerusalem to await the day of the Lord:

> Behold, the day of the Lord cometh, and thy spoil shall be divided in the midst of thee.
> ² For I will gather all nations against Jerusalem to battle; and the city shall be taken, and the houses rifled, and the women ravished; and half of the city shall go forth into captivity, and the residue of the people shall not be cut off from the city.
> ³ Then shall the LORD go forth, and fight against those nations, as when he fought in the day of battle.
> ⁴ And his feet shall stand in that day upon the mount of Olives, which is before Jerusalem on the east, and the mount of Olives shall cleave in the midst thereof toward the east and toward the west, and there shall be a very great valley; and half of the mountain shall remove toward the north, and half of it toward the south.
> ⁵ And ye shall flee to the valley of the mountains; for the valley of the mountains shall reach unto Azal: yea, ye shall flee, like as ye fled from before the earthquake in the days of Uzziah king of Judah: and the LORD my God shall come, and all the saints with thee. (Zechariah 14: 1–5 KJV).

The above prophesy from Zechariah matches that in Joel 3. Joel's prophesy also presented this as a summoning of the nations of the world to gather against Isreal in Jerusalem, where Christ will decimate them:

> Proclaim this among the nations:
> Consecrate for war;
> > stir up the mighty men.
> Let all the men of war draw near;
> > let them come up.
> ¹⁰ Beat your plowshares into swords,
> > and your pruning hooks into spears;
> > let the weak say, "I am a warrior."
>
> ¹¹ Hasten and come,
> > all you surrounding nations,
> > and gather yourselves there.
> Bring down your warriors, O Lord.
> ¹² Let the nations stir themselves up
> > and come up to the Valley of Jehoshaphat;
> for there I will sit to judge
> > all the surrounding nations.
>
> ¹³ Put in the sickle,
> > for the harvest is ripe.
> Go in, tread,
> > for the winepress is full.
> The vats overflow,
> > for their evil is great.
>
> ¹⁴ Multitudes, multitudes,
> > in the valley of decision!
> For the day of the Lord is near
> > in the valley of decision.
> ¹⁵ The sun and the moon are darkened,
> > and the stars withdraw their shining.
>
> ¹⁶ The Lord roars from Zion,
> > and utters his voice from Jerusalem,
> > and the heavens and the earthquake.
> But the Lord is a refuge to his people,
> > a stronghold to the people of Israel. (Joel 3, 13–17 ESV).

Joel's prophecy about the winepress was re-echoed by one of the angels in Revelation 14, indicating that that event was the same event that Joel captured in his prophesy:

> ¹⁷ Another angel came out of the temple in heaven, and he too had a sharp sickle. ¹⁸ Still another angel, who had charge of the fire, came from the altar and called in a loud voice to

him who had the sharp sickle, "Take your sharp sickle and gather the clusters of grapes from the earth's vine, because its grapes are ripe." [19] The angel swung his sickle on the earth, gathered its grapes and threw them into the great winepress of God's wrath. [20] They were trampled in the winepress outside the city, and blood flowed out of the press, rising as high as the horses' bridles for a distance of 1,600 stadia. (Revelation 14:17–20 ESV).

Christ will show his mettle against Satan by handing him a heavy blow at this battle. It appears the battle will be swift, that the armies of the antichrist wouldn't know what hits them.

A cryptic description of the armies of Christ was presented in Joel 2. The armies were described as fierce and menacing, consuming their surroundings with fire. It seems from Joel's description that the armies were using armoured vehicles that were going across obstacles, in the battle:

Blow a horn in Zion! Give the sound of danger on My holy mountain! Let all the people of the land shake in fear, for the day of the Lord is coming. The day is near. [2] It will be a day of darkness, a day of clouds and much darkness. A large and powerful army will come like darkness spreading over the mountains. There has never been anything like it, and there will never be anything like it again for all time to come. [3] Fire destroys in front of them and behind them. The land is like the garden of Eden in front of them, but a desert waste is left behind them. Nothing gets away from them. [4] They look like horses. They run like war horses. [5] As they jump on the tops of the mountains they sound like war-wagons. They sound like a fire burning up the dry grass, like a powerful army ready for battle. [6] Nations suffer in front of them. All faces turn white. [7] They run like strong men. They go over the wall like soldiers. They each walk straight on, and do not turn from their paths. [8] They do not push each other. Each one walks in his path. When they break through those who fight against them, their path is not changed. [9] They rush upon the city. They run on the wall. They go into the houses through the windows like a robber. [10] The earth shakes in front of them. The heavens shake. The sun and the moon become dark, and the stars stop shining. [11] The Lord thunders in front of His army. His army has too many to number. Those who obey His Word are powerful. The day of the Lord is very great and fills people with fear and wonder. Who can live through it? (Joel 2: 1–11 NLV).

There would be many casualties of this war that blood will literally flow for miles (1,600 stadia, about 180 miles):

> [20] And the winepress was trodden outside the city, and blood flowed from the winepress, as high as a horse's bridle, for 1,600 stadia. (Revelation 14; 20 ESV).

On this day, the nations that have come up against the Lord will utterly be destroyed:

> 11 Then I saw heaven opened, and behold, a white horse! The one sitting on it is called Faithful and True, and in righteousness he judges and makes war. 12 His eyes are like a flame of fire, and on his head are many diadems, and he has a name written that no one knows but himself. 13 He is clothed in a robe dipped in[b] blood, and the name by which he is called is The Word of God. 14 And the armies of heaven, arrayed in fine linen, white and pure, were following him on white horses. 15 From his mouth comes a sharp sword with which to strike down the nations, and he will rule[c] them with a rod of iron. He will tread the winepress of the fury of the wrath of God the Almighty. 16 On his robe and on his thigh he has a name written, King of kings and Lord of lords.
>
> 17 Then I saw an angel standing in the sun, and with a loud voice he called to all the birds that fly directly overhead, "Come, gather for the great supper of God, 18 to eat the flesh of kings, the flesh of captains, the flesh of mighty men, the flesh of horses and their riders, and the flesh of all men, both free and slave,[d] both small and great." 19 And I saw the beast and the kings of the earth with their armies gathered to make war against him who was sitting on the horse and against his army. (Revelation 19: 11–19 ESV).

Powerful weapons probably more devastating than nuclear bomb will be used in this battle. Zechariah gave a snippet of the effects of this weapon on the people, where humans will literally be turned into skeletons in an instant (while still standing):

> [12] And this shall be the plague wherewith the Lord will smite all the people that have fought against Jerusalem; Their flesh shall consume away while they stand upon their feet, and their eyes shall consume away in their holes, and their tongue shall consume away in their mouth. (Zechariah 14: 12 KJV).

The appearance of the Lord in the battle ground would also cause great panic and confusion among the antichrists forces that they will turn against each other:

> [13] And it shall come to pass in that day, that a great tumult from the Lord shall be among them; and they shall lay hold everyone on the hand of his neighbour, and his hand shall rise up against the hand of his neighbour.
> [14] And Judah also shall fight at Jerusalem; and the wealth of all the heathen round about shall be gathered together, gold, and silver, and apparel, in great abundance. (Zechariah 14: 13–14 KJV).

The key casualties of this war would be Satan, the antichrist, and the false prophets, who would be captured alive by the angelic army of Christ. In addition to these key figures of the Beast System, other casualties of this war would be the leaders of the nations that went with the antichrist to fight Christ's army, the soldiers (including the generals, and commanders) that participated in this war, and every other person who had anything to do with this war (to eat the flesh of kings, the flesh of captains, the flesh of mighty men, the flesh of horses and their riders, and the flesh of all men, both free and slave, both small and great - Revelation 19:17).

The antichrist and the false prophet would be thrown into the lake of fire, while their human collaborators would be killed. These will be the ones that would emerge at the Second Resurrection, when they will receive their judgement and eventually get thrown into the lake of fire:

> 20 And the beast was captured, and with it the false prophet who in its presence[e] had done the signs by which he deceived those who had received the mark of the beast and those who worshiped its image. These two were thrown alive into the lake of fire that burns with sulfur. 21 And the rest were slain by the sword that came from the mouth of him who was sitting on the horse, and all the birds were gorged with their flesh. (Revelation 19: 20–21 ESV).

> XL. The last leader of that time shall be left alive, when the multitude of his hosts shall be put to the sword, and he shall be bound, and they shall take him up to Mount Zion, and My Messiah shall convict him of all his impieties, and shall gather and set before him all the works of his hosts. 2. And afterwards he shall put him to death, and protect the rest of My people

> which shall be found in the place which I have chosen. 3. And his principate shall stand for ever, until the world of corruption is at an end, and until the times afore said are fulfilled. 4. This is thy vision, and this is its interpretation." (Apocalypse of Baruch Xl: 1–3).

Satan would be arrested and imprisoned for a thousand years, before he is ultimately thrown into the lake of fire. One may ask why Satan had to be imprisoned first rather than being thrown into the lake of fire like the other leaders of his camp? To hazard a guess on this, it could be that he has a prison sentence he has not yet served. So, he needs to serve this sentence from a previous crime, before his final sentencing to the lake of fire.

13.10 TAKEOVER OF THE KINGDOM OF THE WORLD

After the Battle of Armageddon and the resounding defeat of Satan and his armies, the kingdoms of the world will finally come under the control of Christ:

> [9] And the Lord shall be king over all the earth: in that day shall there be one Lord, and his name one. (Zechariah 14: 9 KJV).

This was also made clear in the pronouncement that followed the sounding of the 7th Trumpet, declaring that the kingdom of the earth has finally become the kingdom of God:

> [15] The seventh angel sounded his trumpet, and there were loud voices in heaven, which said:
>
> "The kingdom of the world has become
>   the kingdom of our Lord and of his Messiah,
>   and he will reign for ever and ever." (Revelation 11:15 NIV).

This declaration provides another confirmation that before this time, the kingdoms of the world were under Satan. Thus, the demise of the Beast System leaves a vacuum that would be occupied by the Empire of Christ.

13.11 SANITISATION OF THE HEAVENS

It's instructive to understand that the end times events will not only take place on the earth, but certain specific events will also happen across the heavenly realms. As a matter of fact, the battles will commence in the heavenlies, where Satan and other fallen angels will be defeated and chased down to the earth, before the coming of Christ:

> [29] "Immediately after the tribulation of those days the sun will be darkened, and the moon will not give its light, and the stars will fall from heaven, and the powers of the heavens will be shaken. (Mathew 24: 29 ESV).

The rebellious host of heaven (starting from those who joined Satan in his rebellion, and the sons of the Most-High judged in Psalm 82) will be chased down from the Second Heaven where they have settled; to the earth, where they would be killed like men. They shall fall like figs from the skies (see Isaiah 34 and 6th Seal of Revelation 6: 12–17). Hence, the earth will be their graveyard. Isaiah 34, hinted at this about the judgement of the nations and their hosts. The hosts being referred to in the passage, are the principalities (the renegade gods) ruling over these nations:

> Draw near, O nations, to hear,
>   and give attention, O peoples!
> Let the earth hear, and all that fills it;
>   the world, and all that comes from it.
> [2] For the Lord is enraged against all the nations,
>   and furious against all their host;
>   he has devoted them to destruction, has given them over for slaughter.
> [3] Their slain shall be cast out,
>   and the stench of their corpses shall rise;
>   the mountains shall flow with their blood.
> [4] All the host of heaven shall rot away,
>   and the skies roll up like a scroll.
> All their host shall fall,
>   as leaves fall from the vine,
>   like leaves falling from the fig tree. (Isaiah 34: 1- 8 ESV).

The essence of their removal from these heavenly places is part of the sanitisation of the heaven that will need to happen for a new heaven to emerge, devoid of these bad eggs. These wicked rulers have desecrated the heavens and the earth, and after their defeat, the heavens and earth will be sanitised, and a new heaven and earth will have to be created. The concept of a new heaven and earth is more like a refresh of the heaven and earth, where evil forces have been removed. This sanitisation of the heavens, when the rebellious angels are thrown down to the earth happened at the opening of the 6th Seal, just right before the wrath of God commences:

> [12] And I beheld when he had opened the sixth seal, and, lo, there was a great earthquake; and the sun became black as sackcloth of hair, and the moon became as blood;
> [13] And the stars of heaven fell unto the earth, even as a fig tree casteth her untimely figs, when she is shaken of a mighty wind.
> [14] And the heaven departed as a scroll when it is rolled together; and every mountain and island were moved out of their places. (Revelation 6: 12–14 KJV).

CHAPTER 14

The Empire of Christ

> ⁶ For unto us a child is born, unto us a son is given: and the government shall be upon his shoulder: and his name shall be called Wonderful, Counsellor, The mighty God, The everlasting Father, The Prince of Peace.
> ⁷ Of the increase of his government and peace there shall be no end, upon the throne of David, and upon his kingdom, to order it, and to establish it with judgment and with justice from henceforth even for ever. The zeal of the Lord of hosts will perform this. (Isaiah 9:6–7 KJV)

14.1 THE EMPIRE OF CHRIST—THE MILLENNIAL REIGN OF CHRIST

> ²⁷ And the kingdom and the dominion
> and the greatness of the kingdoms under the whole heaven
> shall be given to the people of the saints of the Most High;
> his kingdom shall be an everlasting kingdom,
> and all dominions shall serve and obey him.' (Daniel 7: 27 ESV).

The Empire of Christ is a rulership that Christ will setup on earth upon his return. The establishment of this empire will follow the defeat of the kingdom of Satan (Beast System). Christ will set up his rule on the earth and subdue every other earthly kingdom (*For he must reign, till he hath put all enemies under his feet* - 1 Corinthians 15:25). The establishment of this empire by Christ is in preparation of the establishment of the Kingdom of God on earth (when God will rule the universe from the earth). God has planned to have his seat of power headquartered on earth. This makes the earth a strategically important piece of estate in cosmic affairs. Hence, the reason, Satan and his cohorts want to have the earth and fight for it to finish.

The construct "Empire of Christ" was chosen to depict that this rule of Christ will function almost like other empires that had existed on earth, except for having Christ at its helm. This construct brings out the practicalities of this kingdom as a physicalised kingdom, and not just only a spiritual kingdom. Nations of the world will be paying homage and tribute to Christ, in recognition of his authority as the ruler of the world.

The Empire of Christ should best be perceived as an intermediary period sandwiched between the demise of the kingdom of Satan (the Beast System) and the inception of the Kingdom of God. This empire will last for one thousand years; hence, it is commonly referred to as the Millennial Reign of Christ. Christ will use the opportunity to cleanse the earth of all forms of impurities, before God descends to setup his throne on the earth. David alluded to this reign in Psalm 110, where he captured the moment God was reassuring Christ of this reign and promising to make his enemies his footstool:

> The Lord says to my Lord:
>   "Sit at my right hand,
> until I make your enemies your footstool."
> ² The LORD sends forth from Zion
>   your mighty scepter.
>   Rule in the midst of your enemies!
> ³ Your people will offer themselves freely
>   on the day of your power,
>   in holy garments; from the womb of the morning,
>   the dew of your youth will be yours.
> ⁴ The LORD has sworn
>   and will not change his mind,
> "You are a priest forever
>   after the order of Melchizedek."
> ⁵ The Lord is at your right hand;
>   he will shatter kings on the day of his wrath.
> ⁶ He will execute judgment among the nations,
>   filling them with corpses;
> he will shatter chiefs

over the wide earth (Psalm 110: 1-6 ESV).

In terms of eschatological chronology, this will commence after the events of the 7th Trumpet. The announcement for the commencement of this Empire of Christ was made immediately after the 7th Trumpet was blown. This suggests that the events that follows that declaration, will facilitate the establishment of the reign of Christ over the entire world:

> [15] The seventh angel sounded his trumpet, and there were loud voices in heaven, which said:
>
> > *"The kingdom of the world has become*
> > *the kingdom of our Lord and of his Messiah,*
> > *and he will reign for ever and ever."*
>
> [16] And the twenty-four elders, who were seated on their thrones before God, fell on their faces and worshiped God, [17] saying:
>
> > "We give thanks to you, Lord God Almighty,
> > the One who is and who was,
> > *because you have taken your great power*
> > *and have begun to reign.* (Revelation 11:15-17 NIV).

This is yet another confirmation that up until this moment, the kingdom of the world was under the control of Satan, hence, Christ will be coming with his army to wrench it from Satan's hand and establish his rule over the world.

Although, many do not see this, Nebuchadnezzar's dream (Daniel 2), which Daniel interpreted, presented one of the clearest indications of this empire. Nebuchadnezzar was given a vision of an image of consisting of metals of varying nature, representing all the empires of the world (starting from his reign to the end times). The core characteristics of each empire were depicted with the quality of metal they were made of. But one interesting fact was that a mysterious stone, which Daniel later identified as Christ would crush the last empire in this vision, to establish his kingdom that will fill the entire earth:

> [31] "You saw, O king, and behold, a great image. This image, mighty and of exceeding brightness, stood before you, and its appearance was frightening. [32] The head of this image was of fine gold, its chest and arms of silver, its middle and thighs of bronze, [33] its legs of iron, its feet partly of iron and partly of clay. [34] As you looked, a stone was cut out by no human hand, and it struck the image on its feet of iron and clay, and broke

them in pieces. ³⁵ Then the iron, the clay, the bronze, the silver, and the gold, all together were broken in pieces, and became like the chaff of the summer threshing floors; and the wind carried them away, so that not a trace of them could be found. But the stone that struck the image became a great mountain and filled the whole earth. (Daniel 2:31–35 ESV).

Daniel identified the Babylonian Empire headed by Nebuchadnezzar as the *head of gold* (Daniel 2: 38) of this image. After this empire there would be others, which would be inferior to the Babylonian Empire: the Medo-Persian Empire (silver), the Greek Empire (bronze), the Roman Empire (iron), the Ottoman Empire (clay and iron). This clay and iron empire will re-emerge during the end times (the revived Ottoman Empire–details of this were discussed in "The Final Battle"[1]), from where the antichrist empire (10 kings/10 toes of the image) would be established:

> ¹⁰ they are also seven kings, five of whom have fallen, one is, the other has not yet come, and when he does come he must remain only a little while. ¹¹ As for the beast that was and is not, it is an eighth but it belongs to the seven, and it goes to destruction. (Revelation 17: 10–11 ESV).

It is this eight empire (the Beast System) that Jesus Christ (*the stone honed by no human hand*) will strike, and eventually crush every artifact of it (*For he must reign, till he hath put all enemies under his feet*–1 Corinthians 15:25 AKJV), in order to establish his empire on earth (But the stone that struck the image became a great mountain and filled the whole earth). Christ will start to crush the worldly empires and kingdoms, starting with that established by the antichrist:

> ⁶ Your right hand, O Lord, glorious in power,
>   your right hand, O Lord, shatters the enemy.
> ⁷ In the greatness of your majesty you overthrow your adversaries;
>   you send out your fury; it consumes them like stubble.
> (Exodus 15:6–7 ESV).

The vision also showed that Christ's dominion over the earth will gradually spread from Jerusalem to fill the entire earth. This tallies with the Millennial Reign, the period set out for Christ to spread his imperial influence around the world. The gradual spread of this empire was alluded to in several parables by Christ:

---

1. Anejionu, "The Final Battle", 48–55.

THE EMPIRE OF CHRIST

> [18] Then Jesus asked, "What is the kingdom of God like? What shall I compare it to? [19] It is like a mustard seed, which a man took and planted in his garden. It grew and became a tree, and the birds perched in its branches."
>
> [20] Again he asked, "What shall I compare the kingdom of God to? [21] It is like yeast that a woman took and mixed into about sixty pounds of flour until it worked all through the dough." (Luke 13: 18-20 NIV).

This spreading indicates that influence of the reign of Christ on earth will gradually spread till it has covered the entire world. He will gradually subdue every other empire/or kingdom opposed to his authority, so that only his, can tower above all. That's a key objective of his reign, to bring all to subjugation to God, then he will hand the earth back to God:

> [24] Then comes the end, when he delivers the kingdom to God the Father after destroying every rule and every authority and power. [25] For he must reign until he has put all his enemies under his feet. [26] The last enemy to be destroyed is death. [27] For "God has put all things in subjection under his feet." But when it says, "all things are put in subjection," it is plain that he is excepted who put all things in subjection under him. [28] When all things are subjected to him, then the Son himself will also be subjected to him who put all things in subjection under him, that God may be all in all. (1 Corinthians 15: 24-28 ESV).

This spreading of the dominion of Christ over the earth will mostly be accomplished by the servants of Christ (the 144000, and the *sons of God*), who will help to establish and spread the influence of Christ's empire across the nations of the earth. Some of the *sons of God*, will be assigned several territories of the world to control, while taking orders and directive from Christ sitting on his throne in Jerusalem. A key allusion to the participation of the sons of God in the reign of Christ is contained in 2 Timothy:

> For if we died with Him,
> We shall also live with Him.
> [12] If we endure,
> We shall also reign with Him. (2 Timothy 2:11-12 NKJV).

The Empire of Christ will commence immediately after the crushing defeat of the antichrist and his army at the Battle of Armageddon. With the key participants of this battle, Satan, antichrist, and the false prophet captured, and the rest of their armies demolished, Christ will begin the process of establishing his reign over the earth. His angelic army will go across the world conducting a mop up operation, rounding up the remnants of the Beast System armies and leaders, until all enemy forces are subdued (Psalm 110: 1–6).

It must be factored in that because Satan's influence was deeply infused in the world, it will take a considerably time to rid the earth of all the negative artifacts of Satan. Hence, the necessity for the one thousand years, required to deconstruct all the dark paraphernalia of Satan and the Beast System.

Many tend to assume that as soon as Christ shows up and defeats the antichrist, a whole new world (remarkably different from previous one), ensues; with all the bad elements eliminated. However, this is not the case, based on various snippets from the Bible. The true situation is that the world's population will be drastically reduced due to the events of the end times (cutting across the Great Tribulation and the Wrath of God era). However, there would be different categories of people still on earth that could broadly be classified as those loyal to Christ's rule and those who are not. Psalm 110 stated that Christ will rule among his enemies:

> [2] The Lord sends forth from Zion
> your mighty scepter.
> Rule in the midst of your enemies! (Psalm 110: 2 ESV).

14.2 THE WORLD AFTER THE DEFEAT OF THE ANTICHRIST

Shortly after the defeat of the antichrist and his army in Jerusalem by Christ and his angelic army, which would mark the end of the Beast System, the world will be in a state of chaos, due to the devastating impacts of the Great Tribulation and the wrath of God. The world would be remarkably different, with many national boundaries redrawn, as an aftermath of the Beast System's reorganisation of the world order. The ruins around various parts of the world that had been under the brief rule of the antichrist will start to emerge. The devastation of the earth following the various geophysical events that had trailed the antichrist reign would be enormous. Simply put, the world would be in wrecked state.

In terms of demographics, there would be survivors of the Beast System and those who resurrected. The survivors will be a mixture of different kinds of people living on the earth at this time–believers in Christ and non-believers. In the first category are the remnants–the followers of Christ who survived the previous tumultuous periods of the Great Tribulation and Wrath of God (the 7 trumpets period). Also, during this time, the dead in Christ (1 Thessalonians 4:16–17) would have resurrected and transformed (into the new generation of humans) alongside other followers of Christ who made it alive through this period (the remnants who had remained faithful and steadfast all through the tumultuous period of the last days). These transformed humans have become the *sons of God (see Section 14.7)*, with incredible abilities and immortal bodies. The transformed humans will almost be like humans, with additional abilities. Their nature will be like that of Christ after he resurrected, and was mingling with his disciples at will. These *sons of God* will reign with Christ in the empire that will at that time be operating from Jerusalem:

> [6] Blessed and holy is the one who shares in the first resurrection! Over such the second death has no power, but they will be priests of God and of Christ, and they will reign with him for a thousand years. (Revelation 20: 6 ESV).

Also, in that world would be those humans who are not followers of Christ but survived the onslaught of the end times. Among these would be two groups, those who took the mark of the Beast and suffering the consequences there off and those who did not, but somewhat managed to go through the period undetected by agents of the Beast System. At the Battle of Armageddon, the victims will mostly be those around the battleground, mainly the armies of the antichrist who encamped around the frontlines:

> "Come, gather for the great supper of God, 18 to eat the flesh of kings, the flesh of captains, the flesh of mighty men, the flesh of horses and their riders, and the flesh of all men, both free and slave,[d] both small and great." 19 And I saw the beast and the kings of the earth with their armies gathered to make war against him who was sitting on the horse and against his army. (Revelation 19: 17- 21 ESV).

There may also be those who escaped from the battle, judging from Joel's prophesy:

> ³² And it shall come to pass that everyone who calls on the name of the Lord shall be saved. *For in Mount Zion and in Jerusalem there shall be those who escape,* as the Lord has said, and among the survivors shall be those whom the Lord calls. (Joel 2:32 ESV).

This leaves room for the existence of other people (non-followers of Christ) still on earth after the demise of the Beast System. Hence, at the commencement of the Millennial Reign of Christ, there will still be enemies of God still on earth, hence Christ will be ruling in the midst of his enemies (The *Lord* shall send the rod of thy strength out of Zion: rule thou in the midst of thine enemies–Psalm 110:2). These enemies will eventually be subdued before the end of the Millennial Reign and judged accordingly for their actions against God:

> ¹⁵ From his mouth comes a sharp sword with which to strike down the nations, and he will rule them with a rod of iron. He will tread the winepress of the fury of the wrath of God the Almighty. ¹⁶ On his robe and on his thigh he has a name written, King of kings and Lord of lords. (Revelation 19: 15–16 ESV).

Due to the chaos and wide-range destruction around the earth in the period preceding the reign of Christ, some efforts would be required to put things back in place and restore the world order. The situation in the world at this time implies there would be a lot of work to be done by the angels and the sons of God, to restore the world into a stable and peaceful place. This is part of God's plan to regain control of the Earth. As a matter of fact, this phase will lead to the establishment of a new world order (that would be culminating into a new heaven and a new earth), remarkably different from the old order established by the antichrist:

> There will be no more death'or mourning or crying or pain, for the old order of things has passed away." (Revelation 21: 4 NIV).

Part of the work to be done at this time would be clearing up operation mainly conducted by the warring angels of Christ and possibly assisted by the 144000 chosen for the occasion. This task will take years to accomplish. The angels will be rounding up all those who have taken the mark of the beast from every corner of the world, as well as eliminating the fallen angels and demonic forces that aligned with Satan and the antichrist during their reign. It is highly likely that mini battles will be happening at various parts of the world as these entities put in their last fight for survival. Eventually, they will be defeated and thrown into the same lake of fire where the antichrist and the false prophet have been thrown, after their defeat at the Battle of Armageddon:

> [9] And the third angel followed them, saying with a loud voice, If any man worship the beast and his image, and receive his mark in his forehead, or in his hand,
> [10] The same shall drink of the wine of the wrath of God, which is poured out without mixture into the cup of his indignation; and he shall be tormented with fire and brimstone in the presence of the holy angels, and in the presence of the Lamb:
> [11] And the smoke of their torment ascendeth up for ever and ever: and they have no rest day nor night, who worship the beast and his image, and whosoever receiveth the mark of his name. (Revelation 14: 9–11 KJV).
>
> "For behold, the day is coming,
> Burning like an oven,
> And all the proud, yes, all who do wickedly will be stubble.
> And the day which is coming shall burn them up,"
> Says the Lord of hosts. (Malachi 4: 3 NIV).

14.3 RATIONALE FOR THE EMPIRE OF CHRIST

There are several reasons behind Christ establishing his empire on earth. These include: the gathering of Israelites, the restoration of Israel's place in the divine plan, teaching the world about the mysteries and ways of God, revealing the righteousness of God, maintaining law and order on the earth, and preparing the world to receive the throne of God.

This period when Christ is reigning on earth will be the final opportunity giving to humanity to understand how the kingdom of God operates, before God comes to set up his throne on earth. God is perfect and holy, and since he plans to setup his throne on earth, everything on earth will have to be made perfect and holy, before God arrives. Hence, the nations will be coming to Jerusalem yearly, to pay homage to Christ and learn from him:

> In the last days the mountain of the Lord's temple will be established as the highest of the mountains;

> it will be exalted above the hills,
>   and peoples will stream to it.
>
> ² Many nations will come and say,
>
> "Come, let us go up to the mountain of the LORD,
>   to the temple of the God of Jacob.
> He will teach us his ways,
>   so that we may walk in his paths." (Micah 4:1–3 NIV).

> ² And it shall come to pass in the last days, that the mountain of the LORD's house shall be established in the top of the mountains, and shall be exalted above the hills; and all nations shall flow unto it.
>   ³ And many people shall go and say, Come ye, and let us go up to the mountain of the Lord, to the house of the God of Jacob; and he will teach us of his ways, and we will walk in his paths: for out of Zion shall go forth the law, and the word of the *Lord* from Jerusalem. (Isaiah 2:1–3 KJV).

Another key event that would be happening at the second coming of Christ is the gathering of the people into various nations. These nations will be based on the racial characteristics of the original nations of the earth and will differ from the artificial constructs of countries that have been in place in the world. The nations will be under the authority of Christ who will be reigning from Jerusalem. The agents of Christ will be made rulers of these nations and through them, their inhabitants are taught the ways and commands of God, in preparation for the final judgement.

During his reign on earth, Christ will reveal the righteousness of God, through the way he executes judgement on the adversaries of God and rewards those who have been faithful and loyal to his commandments:

> "Great and amazing are your deeds,
>   O Lord God the Almighty!
> Just and true are your ways,
>   O King of the nations!
> ⁴ Who will not fear, O Lord, and glorify your name?
> For you alone are holy.
>   All nations will come and worship you, for your righteous acts have been revealed." (Revelation 15:3–4 ESV).

Although, the above proclamation was made right before the unleashing of the final seven plagues of God on earth, the purging of the enemies of God continued throughout the Millennial Reign of Christ.

He will also maintain law and order on the earth during his reign, so that the world will be at peace. Like an emperor, his commands will be going forth from Jerusalem, and his agents will carry them out to the letter across the nations. Under the authority of Christ, the world will be peaceful. All belligerent nations and bellicose individuals, will be forced to maintain peace:

> The law will go out from Zion,
>   the word of the Lord from Jerusalem.
> ³ He will judge between many peoples
>   and will settle disputes for strong nations far and wide.
> They will beat their swords into plowshares
>   and their spears into pruning hooks.
> Nation will not take up sword against nation,
>   nor will they train for war anymore. (Micah 4:1–3 NIV).

> For out of Zion shall go forth the law,
>   and the word of the LORD from Jerusalem.
> ⁴ He shall judge between the nations,
>   and shall decide disputes for many peoples;
> and they shall beat their swords into plowshares,
>   and their spears into pruning hooks;
> nation shall not lift up sword against nation,
>   neither shall they learn war anymore.
>
> ⁵ O house of Jacob,
>   come, let us walk
>   in the light of the LORD. (Isaiah 2:3–5 ESV).

It is uncanny how these prophesies from Isaiah and Micah mirrors each other. This confirms that these prophecies are true and must come to past. Another thing to point out here is that Israel is important in the plans of God. God's seat of power will be in Jerusalem and the people of Israel will be the prime servants of God in Jerusalem. Hence, Israel has to be restored, and the Israelites who had previously been scattered around the world will be gathered at the second coming of Christ.

14.4 THE GATHERING OF THE ELECT (SECOND EXODUS)

The scripture holds that at the second coming of Christ, he will send out his angels to gather the elect from every corner of the earth, where they have been:

> [30] "Then will appear the sign of the Son of Man in heaven. And then all the peoples of the earth will mourn when they see the Son of Man coming on the clouds of heaven, with power and great glory. [31] And he will send his angels with a loud trumpet call, and they will gather his elect from the four winds, from one end of the heavens to the other. (Mark 13:26–27 NIV).

The key question here is: who are those people referred to as 'his elect'? This generates a lot of controversy as there seems to be a lot of confusion on who these elects are. A prominent assumption is that elects are the followers of Christ littered across the world, who survived the Great Tribulation.

However, this belief is inaccurate. The elects being referred here are a select group of people. The term elect means chosen. Biblically, this term "chosen" is usually associated with the nation of Israel, who were chosen among all the other nations by God, as his portion (see Section 7.1). However, the relationship between Israel and God turned soar, when Israel turned against God, and he scattered them across the world.

The scattering of the sons of Jacob happened in various stages. The prominent ones are when the 10 tribes (from northern kingdom of Israel) were taken into exile and never returned to their land. Hence, they are referred to as the lost tribes. Presumably these exiles found their way into various parts of the world. The second major scattering was when the Jews in the Kingdom of Judah (made up of the two remaining tribes of Israel (Judah and Benjamin –the southern kingdom of Israel), were taken into captivity in Babylon. Although some of them returned to the land, a proportion of them did not. The last wave of scattering occurred during the Siege of Jerusalem in AD 70, when the Roman empire army sacked Jerusalem, soon after the crucifixion of Christ. This scattering mainly affected the descendants of the Jews who returned from the Babylonian captivity. In addition, to these events, there are also indications that some Hebrews that are currently settled in other parts of the world, such as those in Western, Central, and Southern Africa, may have escaped from Egypt, even before the Exodus and meshed up with the indigenous people at these places of settlement[2]. For instance, there is a belief that Eri, the first king/priest of the Ibos [Igbos] in Nigeria fled Egypt with some of his comrades, before the Egyptians started cracking down on them. Leigh[3] stated that:

> "Though this is the most widely accepted version of how Eri came to Earth, others believe that Eri was one of the seven sons of Gad, who was one of the 12 sons of Jacob in the Bible. These references can be found in Genesis 46:15–18 and Numbers 26:16–18. It is believed that Eri was a high priest during the reign of Joseph. Just before the impending exodus of Israelites from Egypt, he fled with a group of his closest comrades to the Ezu and Omambala Rivers, which are both found in Anambra. Once arriving at this place, Eri made it a home for his comrades and descendants to thrive."

One of God's key promises recorded in various prophetic books in the Bible, was the promise to return the scattered Israelites from every part of world where they had been scattered to their home country during the end times. Ezekiel had several oracles about this:

> [13] I will bring them out from the nations and gather them from the countries, and I will bring them into their own land. (Ezekiel 34:13 NIV).

> [42] Then you will know that I am the LORD, when I bring you into the land of Israel, the land I had sworn with uplifted hand to give to your ancestors. [43] There you will remember your conduct and all the actions by which you have defiled yourselves, and you will loathe yourselves for all the evil you have done. [44] You will know that I am the LORD, when I deal with you for my name's sake and not according to your evil ways and your corrupt practices, you people of Israel, declares the Sovereign LORD." (Ezekiel 20:42–44 NIV).

> [25] "Therefore this is what the Sovereign Lord says: I will now restore the fortunes of Jacob and will have compassion on all the people of Israel, and I will be zealous for my holy name. [26] They will forget their shame and all the unfaithfulness they showed toward me when they lived in safety in their land with no one to make them afraid. [27] When I have brought them back from the nations and have gathered them from the countries of their

---

2. Leigh, Eri: Mythical King, 1; Oduah, "Nigeria's Igbo Jews", 1
3. Leigh, Eri: "Mythical King", 1

enemies, I will be proved holy through them in the sight of many nations. ²⁸ Then they will know that I am the Lord their God, for though I sent them into exile among the nations, I will gather them to their own land, not leaving any behind. ²⁹ I will no longer hide my face from them, for I will pour out my Spirit on the people of Israel, declares the Sovereign Lord." (Ezekiel 39:25–29 NIV).

'This is what the Sovereign Lord says: I will take the Israelites out of the nations where they have gone. I will gather them from all around and bring them back into their own land. ²² I will make them one nation in the land, on the mountains of Israel. There will be one king over all of them and they will never again be two nations or be divided into two kingdoms. ²³ They will no longer defile themselves with their idols and vile images or with any of their offenses, for I will save them from all their sinful backsliding and I will cleanse them. They will be my people, and I will be their God.

²⁴ "'My servant David will be king over them, and they will all have one shepherd. They will follow my laws and be careful to keep my decrees. ²⁵ They will live in the land I gave to my servant Jacob, the land where your ancestors lived. They and their children and their children's children will live there forever, and David my servant will be their prince forever. ²⁶ I will make a covenant of peace with them; it will be an everlasting covenant. I will establish them and increase their numbers, and I will put my sanctuary among them forever. ²⁷ My dwelling place will be with them; I will be their God, and they will be my people. ²⁸ Then the nations will know that I the Lord make Israel holy, when my sanctuary is among them forever.'" (Ezekiel 37:21–28 NIV).

Isaiah also, prophesied about this gathering:

¹⁰ In that day the Root of Jesse will stand as a banner for the peoples; the nations will rally to him, and his resting place will be glorious. ¹¹ In that day the Lord will reach out his hand a second time to reclaim the surviving remnant of his people from Assyria, from Lower Egypt, from Upper Egypt, from Cush, from Elam, from Babylonia, from Hamath and from the islands of the Mediterranean.

¹² He will raise a banner for the nations
    and gather the exiles of Israel;
he will assemble the scattered people of Judah

from the four quarters of the earth.
(Isaiah 11: 10–12 NIV).

⁵ Fear not, for I am with you;
 I will bring your offspring from the east,
 and from the west I will gather you.
⁶ I will say to the north, Give up,
 and to the south, Do not withhold;
bring my sons from afar
 and my daughters from the end of the earth,
⁷ everyone who is called by my name,
 whom I created for my glory,
 whom I formed and made."(Isaiah 43:5–7 ESV).

As a matter of fact, Joel's prophesy insinuates that part of the reason Christ will decimate most of the nations during the Battle of Armageddon is to punish them for the atrocities the nations committed against Israel in the past:

> "For behold, in those days and at that time, when I restore the fortunes of Judah and Jerusalem, ² I will gather all the nations and bring them down to the Valley of Jehoshaphat. And I will enter into judgment with them there, on behalf of my people and my heritage Israel, because they have scattered them among the nations and have divided up my land, ³ and have cast lots for my people, and have traded a boy for a prostitute, and have sold a girl for wine and have drunk it. (Joel 3:1–3 ESV).

Judging from the above prophesy, the gathering of the elect might be a trap for the antichrist and the Beast System. When Israelites are gathered in Israel, the antichrist will be tempted to mobilise his army against them, so as to bring them under his rule. This will make it easier for Christ and his army to get many of them, with their pants down.

Ezekiel's prophesy against Gog (Ezekiel 38) was targeting this moment, when Gog (the antichrist), will gather nations against Israel. The prophesy suggests that God will draw Gog with his entire army to encamp against the restored Israel. This hook in the jaw appears to be the gathering of Isreal, who the antichrist cannot resist to attack:

> The word of the Lord came to me: ² "Son of man, set your face against Gog, of the land of Magog, the chief prince of Meshek and Tubal; prophesy against him ³ and say: 'This is what the

Sovereign Lord says: I am against you, Gog, chief prince of Meshek and Tubal. [4] I will turn you around, put hooks in your jaws and bring you out with your whole army—your horses, your horsemen fully armed, and a great horde with large and small shields, all of them brandishing their swords. [5] Persia, Cush and Put will be with them, all with shields and helmets, [6] also Gomer with all its troops, and Beth Togarmah from the far north with all its troops—the many nations with you.

[7] "'Get ready; be prepared, you and all the hordes gathered about you, and take command of them. [8] After many days you will be called to arms. In future years you will invade a land that has recovered from war, whose people were gathered from many nations to the mountains of Israel, which had long been desolate. They had been brought out from the nations, and now all of them live in safety. [9] You and all your troops and the many nations with you will go up, advancing like a storm; you will be like a cloud covering the land.

[10] "'This is what the Sovereign Lord says: On that day thoughts will come into your mind, and you will devise an evil scheme. [11] You will say, "I will invade a land of unwalled villages; I will attack a peaceful and unsuspecting people—all of them living without walls and without gates and bars. [12] I will plunder and loot and turn my hand against the resettled ruins and the people gathered from the nations, rich in livestock and goods, living at the center of the land. [13] Sheba and Dedan and the merchants of Tarshish and all her villages will say to you, "Have you come to plunder? Have you gathered your hordes to loot, to carry off silver and gold, to take away livestock and goods and to seize much plunder?"'

[14] "Therefore, son of man, prophesy and say to Gog: 'This is what the Sovereign Lord says: In that day, when my people Israel are living in safety, will you not take notice of it? [15] You will come from your place in the far north, you and many nations with you, all of them riding on horses, a great horde, a mighty army. [16] You will advance against my people Israel like a cloud that covers the land. In days to come, Gog, I will bring you against my land, so that the nations may know me when I am proved holy through you before their eyes.

[17] "'This is what the Sovereign Lord says: You are the one I spoke of in former days by my servants the prophets of Israel. At that time they prophesied for years that I would bring you against them. [18] This is what will happen in that day: When Gog attacks the land of Israel, my hot anger will be aroused, declares the Sovereign Lord. [19] In my zeal and fiery wrath I declare that

THE EMPIRE OF CHRIST

at that time there shall be a great earthquake in the land of Israel. [20] The fish in the sea, the birds in the sky, the beasts of the field, every creature that moves along the ground, and all the people on the face of the earth will tremble at my presence. The mountains will be overturned, the cliffs will crumble and every wall will fall to the ground. [21] I will summon a sword against Gog on all my mountains, declares the Sovereign Lord. Every man's sword will be against his brother. [22] I will execute judgment on him with plague and bloodshed; I will pour down torrents of rain, hailstones and burning sulfur on him and on his troops and on the many nations with him. [23] And so I will show my greatness and my holiness, and I will make myself known in the sight of many nations. Then they will know that I am the Lord.'" (Ezekiel 38: 1-23 NIV).

Furthermore, the description of what will happen on that day when God goes against Gog and his army, matches the description of what will happen on the day of the Lord (Battle of Armageddon–see Section 13.9) prophesied in other books such Zechariah and Joel, such as a great earthquake that will shake the entire world (Ezekiel 38:19/Revelation 16:18), Gog's soldiers killing each other (Ezekiel 38:22/Zechariah 14:13) and hailstorm and fire (Ezekiel 38: 18-22/Revelation 16:21).

These events were also captured as part of the events of the 7th plague (the Battle of Armageddon) in Revelation 16:

[17] The seventh angel poured out his bowl into the air, and out of the temple came a loud voice from the throne, saying, "It is done!" [18] Then there came flashes of lightning, rumblings, peals of thunder and a severe earthquake. No earthquake like it has ever occurred since mankind has been on earth, so tremendous was the quake. [19] The great city split into three parts, and the cities of the nations collapsed. God remembered Babylon the Great and gave her the cup filled with the wine of the fury of his wrath. [20] Every island fled away and the mountains could not be found. [21] From the sky huge hailstones, each weighing about a hundred pounds, fell on people. And they cursed God on account of the plague of hail, because the plague was so terrible. (Revelation 16: 17-21 NIV).

There are key pointers in the passage (Ezekiel 38) that confirms that this prophesy is referring to the end time gathering of Israel, not a prior gathering of Isreal. This gathering referred to in the prophesy would happen after the current state of Israel had been made desolate by the Beast

System. A key pointer is that the land had just been restored with the gathering. This suggests the land is recovering from something:

> In future years you will invade a land that has recovered from war, whose people were gathered from many nations to the mountains of Israel, which had long been desolate. They had been brought out from the nations, and now all of them live in safety. (Ezekiel 38: 8 NIV).
>
> [12] I will plunder and loot and turn my hand against the resettled ruins and the people gathered from the nations, rich in livestock and goods, living at the center of the land. (Ezekiel 38: 12 NIV).

Stretching this further, Isaiah 11 hints at the route the Israelites will take to reach their land, stating that the Red Sea (Egyptian sea) as well as the Euphrates will be dried to allow some of them passage. Others will also come from Assyria. This is a strong suggestion that the exiles will come from different directions into Israel:

> [13] Ephraim's jealousy will vanish,
>   and Judah's enemies will be destroyed;
> Ephraim will not be jealous of Judah,
>   nor Judah hostile toward Ephraim.
> [14] They will swoop down on the slopes of Philistia to the west;
>   together they will plunder the people to the east.
> They will subdue Edom and Moab,
>   and the Ammonites will be subject to them.
> [15] The Lord will dry up
>   the gulf of the Egyptian sea;
> with a scorching wind he will sweep his hand
>   over the Euphrates River.
> He will break it up into seven streams
>   so that anyone can cross over in sandals.
> [16] There will be a highway for the remnant of his people
>   that is left from Assyria,
> as there was for Israel
>   when they came up from Egypt. (Isaiah 11: 10–16 NIV).

The drying up of Euphrates is a key to understanding the time in question, which links this gathering to the end time and the Battle of Armageddon. Revelation noted that the Euphrates will dry up at the pouring out of the 6th bowl by the angel, which is an event that happened prior to the preparation for the Battle of Armageddon:

¹² The sixth angel poured out his bowl on the great river Euphrates, and its water was dried up to prepare the way for the kings from the East. ¹³ Then I saw three impure spirits that looked like frogs; they came out of the mouth of the dragon, out of the mouth of the beast and out of the mouth of the false prophet. ¹⁴ They are demonic spirits that perform signs, and they go out to the kings of the whole world, to gather them for the battle on the great day of God Almighty.

¹⁵ "Look, I come like a thief! Blessed is the one who stays awake and remains clothed, so as not to go naked and be shamefully exposed."

¹⁶ Then they gathered the kings together to the place that in Hebrew is called Armageddon. (Revelation 16: 12–16 NIV).

Based on the foregoing, there is enough evidence to support the conclusion that elects who will be gathered when Christ returns the second time are the descendants of the Israelites who were scattered when Israel and Judah went on exile (the so-called lost tribes of Israel). Again, this is a bloodline thing. Everyone from the bloodline of Jacob (the house of Israel) belongs to this group. This people will be gathered by the angels of God (based on their DNA), from wherever they have been residing back into their land Jerusalem. Many of these people have lost their identity and do not even know they are Israelites as the prophesies foretold about the curses of Israel (Deuteronomy 28), but their DNA would be used to trace their roots.

14.4.1 End-time Gathering versus 1948 Reconstitution of State of Israel

Although many believe that the gathering and restoration of Israel as prophesied had already happened, a close examination of the prophesies will reveal that is a future event that is yet to happen. The end-time gathering is markedly different from the reconstitution of the State of Israel that occurred in 1948, in several ways.

Firstly, the true gathering referred to in the prophesies will happen during the second coming of Christ, and not decades before. The gathering is part and parcel of the second coming of Christ. Secondly, after the gathering, Christ will reign as the sovereign king of the house of Israel and the rest of the world. This is not currently the case with the state of Israel, and several other follow-up events in the prophesies concerning the gathering are yet to occur. Thirdly, the children of Israel will be gathered by the angels of Christ from every part of the world, whereas the gathering of 1948 happened through human mechanism, and it was mainly people who were in or formerly living in Europe. The creation of the State of Israel was midwifed by the Zionism Movement[4] and not angels. As a matter of fact, Uganda was considered a possible country where the people from Europe would have been resettled. The Ugandan Proposal presented by Theodor Herzl (the founder of the modern Zionist movement) to Joseph Chamberlain (the British colonial secretary) and other high-ranking officials in 1903, would have seen the Ashkenazi and Krymchaks in Russia resettled in a part of Uganda[5].

It is important to note at this point that being an Israelite by DNA does not guarantee that one will eventually enter the land of Israel at the gathering or the Kingdom of God for that matter. But the land is only reserved for those who are obedient to the commandments of God and Jesus. The gathering and journey back to Israel will happen in phases just like in the first Exodus. Firstly, the exiled Israelites will be led out of the various nations where they had been, into some place of safety (wilderness). This initial phase may be catalysed by the hardship and persecution of the Beast System. In the wilderness, they will be refined to prepare them for their eventual return to the land. Rebellious ones will be judged and prevented from entering. Those found worthy will be led back into the land of Israel:

> [33] As surely as I live, declares the Sovereign Lord, I will reign over you with a mighty hand and an outstretched arm and with outpoured wrath. [34] I will bring you from the nations and gather you from the countries where you have been scattered—with a mighty hand and an outstretched arm and with outpoured wrath. [35] I will bring you into the wilderness of the nations and there, face to face, I will execute judgment upon you. [36] As I judged your ancestors in the wilderness of the land of Egypt, so I will judge you, declares the Sovereign Lord. [37] I will take note of you as you pass under my rod, and I will bring you into the bond of the covenant. [38] I will purge you of those who revolt and rebel against me. Although I will bring them out of the land where they are living, yet they will not enter the land of Israel. Then you will know that I am the *Lord*. (Ezekiel 20: 33–38 NIV).

---

4. History.com Editors, "Israel", 1
5. Jewish Virtual Library, "Zionist Congress", 1

This is like what happened during the first exodus, where after Moses led the Israelites out of Egypt into the wilderness, all the rebellious ones died in the wilderness and did not make it into the promised land.

Ezekiel 34 which focused on the gathering of Israel, alluded to this mixture of good and bad among the gathered people using the metaphor of rams and goats among the flock of messiah that have been gathered to the land:

> [17] "'As for you, my flock, this is what the Sovereign Lord says: I will judge between one sheep and another, and between rams and goats. [18] Is it not enough for you to feed on the good pasture? Must you also trample the rest of your pasture with your feet? Is it not enough for you to drink clear water? Must you also muddy the rest with your feet? [19] Must my flock feed on what you have trampled and drink what you have muddied with your feet?
>
> [20] "'Therefore this is what the Sovereign LORD says to them: See, I myself will judge between the fat sheep and the lean sheep. [21] Because you shove with flank and shoulder, butting all the weak sheep with your horns until you have driven them away, [22] I will save my flock, and they will no longer be plundered. I will judge between one sheep and another'". (Ezekiel 34: 17-22 NIV).

There are also indications that people from other nations may join Israelites during this time. Isaiah hinted that some foreigners would join the descendants of Jacob during this time to enter the land. However, these foreigners who will join the camp of Israel will not have equal status with the citizens of the land:

> The Lord will have compassion on Jacob;
>   once again he will choose Israel
>   and will settle them in their own land.
> Foreigners will join them
>   and unite with the descendants of Jacob.
> [2] Nations will take them
>   and bring them to their own place.
> And Israel will take possession of the nations
>   and make them male and female servants in the Lord's land.
> They will make captives of their captors
>   and rule over their oppressors (Isaiah 14: 1-2 NIV).

14.4.2 Regrouping of the Nations

In addition to the gathering of the elects, I also believe there will be other minor future gatherings during the Millennial Reign, where people will be grouped according to their respective bloodlines, to recreate the original 70 nations of the world that emerged from the sons of Noah (Section 7.1). This will result in a new world order, where every individual living on the earth will be taken to their original nation. This could be gleaned from Revelation 20, which mentioned the existence of *"nations at the four corners of the earth"*, which were apparently not considered part of the house of Israel. There are many snippets in the Bible that suggest this:

> [16] Then the survivors from all the nations that have attacked Jerusalem will go up year after year to worship the King, the Lord Almighty, and to celebrate the Festival of Tabernacles (Zechariah 14:16 NIV).

> [16] "'After this I will return,
> and I will rebuild the tent of David that has fallen;
> I will rebuild its ruins,
>   and I will restore it,
> [17] that the remnant of mankind may seek the Lord,
>   and all the Gentiles who are called by my name,
>   says the Lord, who makes these things [18] known from of old.'" (Acts 15:16–17).

There are indications that the gathered people will be joined by those who had resurrected. It seems that each nation would have their resurrected ones joining those who survived the onslaught of the final days, under the antichrist rule. These would be the people that will enter the Millennial Reign. The idea of having those that has been transformed or the resurrected ones living among those that have not, is not inconceivable. After his resurrection, Christ mingled with his disciples. As a matter of fact, the disciples that were going to Emmaus, did not recognise Christ or perceive him as a non-human. Mathew noted that some people resurrected at the crucifixion of Christ and appeared to many:

> [52] And the graves were opened; and many bodies of the saints which slept arose,
>   [53] And came out of the graves after his resurrection, and went into the holy city, and appeared unto many (Matthew 27: 52–53 KJV).

THE EMPIRE OF CHRIST

The biblical passage in Matthew 24:31 states that these elects will be gathered from the four winds [of the earth], and from one end of the heaven to the other (*and they will gather his elect from the four winds, from one end of the heavens to the other*), suggesting that among those that will be gathered will be the living (*from the four winds [of the earth]* and those who resurrected (*from one end of the heavens to the other*). This notion is supported by other passages in the Bible that suggests that the dead who resurrected will be part of people that would be seen during this time, who will enter the Kingdom of God:

> [11] And I say unto you, That many shall come from the east and west, and shall sit down with *Abraham, and Isaac, and Jacob,* in the kingdom of heaven. (Matthew 8:11 KJV).

> 'This is what the Sovereign Lord says: My people, I am going to open your graves and bring you up from them; I will bring you back to the land of Israel. [13] Then you, my people, will know that I am the Lord, when I open your graves and bring you up from them. [14] I will put my Spirit in you and you will live, and I will settle you in your own land. Then you will know that I the Lord have spoken, and I have done it, declares the Lord.'" (Ezekiel 37: 12–14 NIV).

Also, among those who will be gathered at this time, will be those who have already been transformed as the sons of God, and those who unfortunately have not. To buttress this point, during this period in Israel, there would be sin offerings and sacrifices happening. This begs the question that if everyone in the Millennial reign has been transformed, there would no longer be sin and necessity for sin offering. Presumably, this is not so, because both guilt and sin offerings were still being offered at this time, suggesting that there are some people in the land who may still be committing sin:

> "'This is the place where the priests shall boil the guilt offering and the sin offering, and where they shall bake the grain offering, in order not to bring them out into the outer court and so transmit holiness to the people." (Ezekiel 46: 20 NIV).

As stated earlier, during this time in the world, there would be people who did not take the mark of the beast and somehow managed to survive the purge of that time. These people who have not yet accepted Christ as their saviour will be giving opportunity during the Millennial Reign to come under the authority of Christ and God. These are those who will be taught the ways of God. Anyone who after this period of grace, still refuses to accept Christ will not be permitted to enter the Kingdom of God, which would fully materialise at the end of the Millennial Reign, after the final defeat of Satan. This was also reiterated while Christ was admonishing his followers on the sacrifice required to enter the Kingdom of God:

> [24] Strive to enter in at the strait gate: for many, I say unto you, will seek to enter in, and shall not be able.
>
> [25] When once the master of the house is risen up, and hath shut to the door, and ye begin to stand without, and to knock at the door, saying, Lord, Lord, open unto us; and he shall answer and say unto you, I know you not whence ye are:
>
> [26] Then shall ye begin to say, We have eaten and drunk in thy presence, and thou hast taught in our streets.
>
> [27] But he shall say, I tell you, I know you not whence ye are; depart from me, all ye workers of iniquity.
>
> [28] There shall be weeping and gnashing of teeth, when ye shall see Abraham, and Isaac, and Jacob, and all the prophets, in the kingdom of God, and you yourselves thrust out.
>
> [29] And they shall come from the east, and from the west, and from the north, and from the south, and shall sit down in the kingdom of God. (Luke 13:24–29 KJV).

[12] But the children of the kingdom shall be cast out into outer darkness: there shall be weeping and gnashing of teeth. (Matthew 8:1 KJV).

This reference about "Then shall ye begin to say, We have eaten and drunk in thy presence, and thou hast taught in our streets," points to the time of Millennial Reign, and not the first coming of Christ, as many have been led to believe. The first supporting evidence about this is based on the fact that the entire passage was referring to the time shortly preceding the emergence of the Kingdom of God. Secondly, there are biblical passages that suggest that Christ will be close to the people during his one thousand-year reign:

> [3] and many peoples shall come, and say:
> "Come, let us go up to the mountain of the Lord,
>   to the house of the God of Jacob,
>   that he may teach us his ways
>   and that we may walk in his paths." (Isaiah 2:3 ESV).

Hence, these people who will be shut out of the kingdom, having lived in proximity with Christ (eating and drinking in his presence) during the Millennial Reign would have assumed that they have gained access to the Kingdom of God. This is the error Christ wanted to correct so that they can disabuse their minds and get their acts together.

Supposedly, not all the transformed humans will be permanent residents of Jerusalem at this time, but they will have the pass to enter Jerusalem at will or when necessary such as during the feasts (*People will come from east and west and north and south, and will take their places at the feast in the kingdom of God*). Christ will be in Jerusalem, the seat of power of this new empire with a select few of the transformed humans (the elects) alongside the patriarchs, prophets, and apostles. While the rest of the *sons of God* from other nations (bloodlines) would be assigned different duties across the world towards the spreading of the influence of the Kingdom of God across every nation of the world. These people from the other nations will be coming to Jerusalem yearly to pay homage to Christ. Any nation that refuses to make this annual pilgrimage will be severely punished (Zechariah 14:16).

This suggests that some people from some of these nations will not willingly be making this pilgrimage, because they will feel subjugated by the nation of Israel who will be the ruling class at this time. This may be the source of grudge that will give Satan the leeway after his one thousand-year imprisonment to be able to deceive people from these nations again, to make a final attempt to launch attack against Christ and the people with him in Israel (see Section 14.13).

This is expected, considering that in every empire, there would be those who do not fully subject themselves to the authorities. Hence, in these nations, there would be a mix of both the good and bad, but they will all be forced to adhere to the commands of Christ. This period was captured by Isaiah in the prophesy about the shoot from Jesse that will emerge at the end time, where the lamb and wolf will live side-by-side:

> He will strike the earth with the rod of his mouth;
> with the breath of his lips he will slay the wicked.
> ⁵ Righteousness will be his belt
> and faithfulness the sash around his waist.
>
> ⁶ The wolf will live with the lamb,
> the leopard will lie down with the goat,
> the calf and the lion and the yearling together;
> and a little child will lead them.
> ⁷ The cow will feed with the bear,
> their young will lie down together,

> and the lion will eat straw like the ox.
> ⁸ The infant will play near the cobra's den,
> and the young child will put its hand into the viper's nest.
> ⁹ They will neither harm nor destroy
> on all my holy mountain,
> for the earth will be filled with the knowledge of the LORD
> as the waters cover the sea. (Isaiah 11: 1–9 NIV).

There is a likelihood that few humans who were non-believers but somehow managed to survive the antichrist's regime without taking the mark, could still be saved if they truly repent and accept Christ. This might be those who would be performing sin and guilt offering, which would assist their transformation.

However, salvation is foreclosed for only those who took the mark, as they will not be considered humans needing salvation.

14.4.3 Are the Elects the 144000 people?

There have also been suggestions that the elects are the 144000. But evidence presented in Biblical passages about the gathering does not seem to align with the notion that the elects are the same as the 144000 people that were sealed.

The 144000 are rather a subgroup of the elects, because they are also drawn from the tribes of Israel:

> ⁴ Then I heard the number of those who were sealed: 144,000 from all the tribes of Israel. (Revelation 7: 4 NIV).

The elects will be gathered from all over the world to a place (a particular location), whereas the 144000 were sealed wherever they were. The 144000 were called the servants of God.

> "Do not harm the earth or the sea or the trees, until we have sealed the servants of our God on their foreheads." ⁴ And I heard the number of the sealed, 144,000, sealed from every tribe of the sons of Israel. (Revelation 7: 3–4 ESV).

They will play critical roles during the Great Tribulation, in protecting and guiding the remnants, as well as special roles during the Millennial Reign. They may also play important role in the gathering of the Israelites.

14.5 THE GREAT BANQUET: THE MARRIAGE SUPPER OF THE LAMB

The Marriage Supper of the lamb is one of the most overlooked portions of the end times events in Revelation. However, this event is so critical that it can help to unravel most of the mysteries in Revelation. The event is the pinnacle, the end goal of the end times events that every follower of Christ should be working to take part in. The Marriage Supper of the lamb is the ceremony marking the meeting/union of Christ and his prime servants on earth (most likely the 144000 people). This view of the 144000 being the bride of Christ is based on the fact that they did not defile themselves, they are blameless, and are the first fruit of mankind offered to God:

> No one could learn the song except the 144,000 who had been redeemed from the earth. 4 These are those who did not defile themselves with women, for they remained virgins. They follow the Lamb wherever he goes. They were purchased from among mankind and offered as firstfruits to God and the Lamb. 5 No lie was found in their mouths; they are blameless. (Revelation 14:3–5 ESV).

They were also presented to have God's special attention (being sealed to protect them from the wrath of God–Revelation 7:3–4). In addition, they will occupy very special position beside Christ when he comes to earth (they followed him wherever he goes–Revelation 14: 1–5). This places them as the *crème* de la *crème* of followers of Christ, and suggesting they were being prepared for a special purpose–to become the bride of Christ. In addition, they were presented as virgins who have not defiled themselves with women. This is almost a pointer to the five wise virgins in Mathew 25:1–13. In that parable, the ten virgins were the potential bride waiting to meet the groom (Christ), however, only half of them made it into the wedding banquet. The 144000 are a subgroup of followers of Christ who made it through.

Prior to this time, the most popular view was that marriage was between Christ and his followers who made it to Heaven. Supposedly, these followers are a combination of those that have been raptured and those that have been martyred during the Great Tribulation. In *The Final Battle for Earth*,[6] I also took this position that this marriage of Christ and end

---

6. Anejionu, "The Final Battle", 140.

time martyrs will happen in Heaven. However, upon re-examination, I am leaning towards a view contrary to this general view, that this event (marriage supper of the Lamb) will take place on the earth rather than in Heaven. After the marriage, Christ will take his bride to his chambers–his kingdom (the Millennial reign). The common view that this event happened in heaven was because the announcement was made while Christ was still in Heaven, and many assumed that the marriage will happen in Heaven before Christ comes back to the earth, which justifies the reason why the announcement was made while he was still there. However, following the pattern of the symbolic announcements in Revelation, most of the announcements/declarations where for events that were about to happen on earth afterwards, and not immediately and not in Heaven. For instance, the declaration of the three angels (in Revelation 14: 6–13) were for things that happened afterwards on earth.

The clues to the earthly marriage supper of the lamb can be found in the declaration about the marriage supper of the Lamb:

> [6] Then I heard what seemed to be the voice of a great multitude, like the roar of many waters and like the sound of mighty peals of thunder, crying out,
>
> > "Hallelujah!
> > For the Lord our God
> >   the Almighty reigns.
> > [7] Let us rejoice and exult
> >   and give him the glory,
> > for the marriage of the Lamb has come,
> >   and his Bride has made herself ready;
> > [8] it was granted her to clothe herself
> >   with fine linen, bright and pure"—
> >
> > for the fine linen is the righteous deeds of the saints.
>
> [9] And the angel said to me, "Write this: Blessed are those who are invited to the marriage supper of the Lamb." (Revelation 19: 6–9 ESV).

A careful read of the passage will indicate that the purpose of the announcement was not that the marriage was happening there in heaven, but to declare that the moment for the marriage supper has arrived, as the bride has made herself ready, for her bridegroom to come and take her to his chamber. There was no mention of the event happening in

Heaven. Rather, the next thing that followed the announcement was the appearance of Christ and his army on earth:

> [11] Then I saw heaven opened, and behold, a white horse! The one sitting on it is called Faithful and True, and in righteousness he judges and makes war. (Revelation 19: 11 ESV).

This is in line with the ancient Jewish marriage custom, where the bridegroom will come to take her bride to his chamber[7] and not the other way round. The Lord (the bridegroom) will come from heaven to where the bride is (the earth) to take her into his chamber (the Millennial reign). Christ alluded to this when he said he would come like a thief in the night:

> [42] Therefore, stay awake, for you do not know on what day your Lord is coming. [43] But know this, that if the master of the house had known in what part of the night the thief was coming, he would have stayed awake and would not have let his house be broken into. [44] Therefore you also must be ready, for the Son of Man is coming at an hour you do not expect.

This marriage supper event will happen as part of the "thief in the night" event. Two key things will be happening during this event: Christ coming to fight Satan and take over the world, and Christ coming to take his bide into his kingdom. The "thief in the night" phrase is the surprise element that Christ would utilise to storm Satan ("master of the house") and his forces. It is pertinent to note that the announcement of the marriage supper was made right after the destruction of Babylon the Great, which suggests that the destruction of Babylon the Great is the key marker that will signal the imminent arrival of Christ and his army.

This will also tally with the first resurrection as the groom takes the rest of his faithful followers (the wedding guests) into his empire/kingdom. John also alluded to this in Revelation 16, after the 6th Bowl, which was to serve as a final call for people to get ready for the imminent arrival of Christ:

> [15] ("Behold, I am coming like a thief! Blessed is the one who stays awake, keeping his garments on, that he may not go about naked and be seen exposed!"). (Revelation 16:15 ESV).

The brides are the five wise virgins who patiently waited for the bridegroom, even though he may have tarried. In the parable of the 10

---

7. Got Questions Ministries, "What is the marriage", 1; Mooney, "What is the", 1

virgins waiting for the groom (*Mathew 25: 1–13 NIV*), the virgins were on earth waiting for the groom.

Instructively, this parable followed Mathew 24, where Christ enumerated to his disciples what to expect during the Great Tribulation. It was as if he was asking them to prepare to endure the sufferings of the Great Tribulation and wait for his arrival. Only those who made themselves ready for the occasion will be allowed into the banquet (marriage supper of the Lamb).

Furthermore, in Revelation 14, there was a snippet about the meeting of Christ and the 144000 at Mount Zion:

> Then I looked, and there before me was the Lamb, standing on Mount Zion, and with him 144,000 who had his name and his Father's name written on their foreheads. ² And I heard a sound from heaven like the roar of rushing waters and like a loud peal of thunder. The sound I heard was like that of harpists playing their harps. ³ And they sang a new song before the throne and before the four living creatures and the elders. No one could learn the song except the 144,000 who had been redeemed from the earth. (Revelation 14:1–3 ESV).

This event from the passage above is happening when Christ returned on earth, possibly after the Battle of Armageddon, when Christ and the 144000 met. The Mount Zion referred here is on earth and not in Heaven. It is near to Mount of Olives. Christ will set his feet on Mount of Olives during the Battle of Armageddon:

> And in that day His feet will stand on the Mount of Olives,
> Which faces Jerusalem on the east. (Zechariah 14:4 NKJV).

To make this clear, John said he heard a new song from heaven that sounded like harpists playing their harps, suggesting that there were two distinct places involved in the vision, Mount Zion and Heaven–the event was happening on Mount Zion, and the song was coming from Heaven.

It is illogical to presume that the meeting between Christ and the 144000 will happen prior the commencement of the battle or during the battle. Christ initial preoccupation as he enters the earth with his army is to defeat the antichrist and his army to secure the earth. If he embarks on the marriage before the battle, the element of surprise would dissipate. Furthermore, the joyful and serene nature of the description of their meeting rather suggests the battle was over and won, and the songs from the harpist from heaven were to celebrate this win.

Furthermore, in the parable of the Wedding Banquet, the army of the king dealt with those enemies who killed the servant of the king, before the wedding banquet occurred:

> ⁵ "But they paid no attention and went off—one to his field, another to his business. ⁶ The rest seized his servants, mistreated them and killed them. ⁷ The king was enraged. He sent his army and destroyed those murderers and burned their city.
>
> ⁸ "Then he said to his servants, 'The wedding banquet is ready, but those I invited did not deserve to come. ⁹ So go to the street corners and invite to the banquet anyone you find.' (Mathew 22: 5-8 NIV).

In addition, the 144000 were following Christ wherever he went. This must be a reference to them following Christ as he establishes his rule across the world.

14.5.1 End time Lessons from the Parable of the Ten Virgins

The Parable of the ten virgins is a very scary parable when one considers it deeply. They were all virgins (so supposedly living a good life). They all had lamps, meaning that they had the light:

> "At that time the kingdom of heaven will be like ten virgins who took their lamps and went out to meet the bridegroom. ² Five of them were foolish and five were wise. ³ The foolish ones took their lamps but did not take any oil with them. ⁴ The wise ones, however, took oil in jars along with their lamps. (Matthew 25: 1-4 NIV).

They ten virgins became drowsy and fell asleep. Hence, at some point while they waited for the coming of the groom, they lost some of their spiritual strength or got drowsy by the cares of this world and were no longer watching for the coming of the groom.

> ⁵ The bridegroom was a long time in coming, and they all became drowsy and fell asleep.
>
> ⁶ "At midnight the cry rang out: 'Here's the bridegroom! Come out to meet him!'
>
> ⁷ "Then all the virgins woke up and trimmed their lamps. ⁸ The foolish ones said to the wise, 'Give us some of your oil; our lamps are going out.'

⁹ "'No,' they replied, 'there may not be enough for both us and you. Instead, go to those who sell oil and buy some for yourselves.'

¹⁰ "But while they were on their way to buy the oil, the bridegroom arrived. The virgins who were ready went in with him to the wedding banquet. And the door was shut.

¹¹ "Later the others also came. 'Lord, Lord,' they said, 'open the door for us!'

¹² "But he replied, 'Truly I tell you, I don't know you.'

¹³ "Therefore keep watch, because you do not know the day or the hour". (Matthew 25: 1–13 NIV).

But the differentiating thing is that five had extra oil in their reserve tanks, the other five did not. That is to say, whereas five of them had what it takes to sustain the light they have, the other five did not. Had the groom come early, the ten virgins would have made it with the oil that was in their lamps. However, the groom tarried, thus, the oil in the lamps was no longer sustaining the lamp and had to be replenished. This boils down to the fact that the five wise ones prepared for any contingency that may arise, whereas the other five described as being foolish did not prepare for this. Hence, they missed out. This parable is clear for all followers of Christ to be fully prepared for all end time contingencies that might arise.

14.6 THE FIRST RESURRECTION AND THE TRANSFORMATION OF HUMANS

The First Resurrection is a prominent event of the end time, when the dead in Christ will come to live to be with him in his kingdom. This is one of the key promises of Christ to his followers, that in the end he will raise all who believed in him from the dead:

> ³⁹ And this is the Father's will which hath sent me, that of all which he hath given me I should lose nothing, but should raise it up again at the last day.
>
> ⁴⁰ And this is the will of him that sent me, that every one which seeth the Son, and believeth on him, may have everlasting life: and I will raise him up at the last day. (John 6: 39–40 KJV).

It is important to note that this raising up will occur on the *last day* and not before. In Revelation 20, John saw the souls of those who died during the Great Tribulation coming to live again to reign with Christ on earth:

> Also I saw the souls of those who had been beheaded for the testimony of Jesus and for the word of God, and those who had not worshiped the beast or its image and had not received its mark on their foreheads or their hands. They came to life and reigned with Christ for a thousand years. ⁵ The rest of the dead did not come to life until the thousand years were ended. This is the first resurrection. (Revelation 20: 4–5 ESV).

The angel told Daniel about this event:

> ² And many of those who sleep in the dust of the earth shall awake, some to everlasting life, and some to shame and everlasting contempt. ³ And those who are wise shall shine like the brightness of the firmament; and those who turn many to righteousness, like the stars for ever and ever (Daniel 12: 2–3 RSV).

This event is so important that many extra biblical books such as the Apocalypse of Esdras, Apocalypse of Baruch, and Antiquities of Philo have many passages that covered it with varying levels of detail. The angel speaking to Baruch told him the following:

> 2. Then shall all who have fallen asleep in hope of Him rise again. And it shall come to pass at that time that the treasuries shall be opened in which is preserved the number of the souls of the righteous, and they shall come forth, and a multitude of souls shall be seen together in one assemblage of one thought, and the first shall rejoice and the last shall not be grieved. 3. For they know that the time hath come of which it is said, that it is the consummation of the times. 4. But the souls of the wicked, when they behold all these things, shall then waste away the more. 5. For they shall know that their torment hath come and their perdition hath arrived.' (Apocalypse of Baruch XXX: 2–5).

Although there was no clear indication of exactly when this event happened in the Revelation timeline, it is logical to conclude that this event is part of the events that followed the pouring out of the 7th Bowl. This is based on the description of things that happened on earth after the 7th Bowl, especially the great earthquake that literally shook and levelled the earth (*every island fled away, and no mountains were to be found*):

> ¹⁸ And there were flashes of lightning, rumblings, peals of thunder, and a great earthquake such as there had never been since

man was on the earth, so great was that earthquake. ¹⁹ The great city was split into three parts, and the cities of the nations fell, and God remembered Babylon the great, to make her drain the cup of the wine of the fury of his wrath. ²⁰ And every island fled away, and no mountains were to be found. ²¹ And great hailstones, about one hundred pounds each, fell from heaven on people; and they cursed God for the plague of the hail, because the plague was so severe. (Revelation 19: 18–21 ESV).

This great earthquake may have been one of the tools used to activate the first resurrection, as it will shake the entire earth and open up the graves. Hence, the dead will resurrect shortly before Christ appears with his army to confront the forces of the antichrist. Paul provided additional insight to this in 1 Thessalonians 4, while reminding the followers of Christ of the promise of resurrection made by Christ:

> 15 For this we declare to you by a word from the Lord,[a] that we who are alive, who are left until the coming of the Lord, will not precede those who have fallen asleep. 16 For the Lord himself will descend from heaven with a cry of command, with the voice of an archangel, and with the sound of the trumpet of God. And the dead in Christ will rise first. 17 Then we who are alive, who are left, will be caught up together with them in the clouds to meet the Lord in the air, and so we will always be with the Lord (1 Thessalonians 4:15–17 ESV).

Here, Paul indicated that four events will be occurring almost at the same time. The first is the descent of Christ and his angels from Heaven to earth. The second is the resurrection of the dead. The third is the transformation of the bodies of those alive at this time into new bodies (to match those of the resurrected ones). The fourth is the meeting of Christ and his entourage in the clouds by the transformed humans. Hence, both the dead and the living will have the same body, like that of Christ after his resurrection. This new generation of humans (the transformed humans) will meet Christ and his angelic army in the air (space) and join them on their way to the earth.

This meeting of Christ in the air by the transformed and resurrected humans is more like a welcome party to receive Christ as the legitimate king of the earth. These are the vanguards from the earth welcoming Christ as the rightful king of the earth. This is to fulfil cosmic legalism. The earth belongs to humans, and before any external force can ruler over it, humans must allow that to happen. In other words, only humans can legally hand over authority over the earth to the external entity. Recall that God handed over the earth to Adam, hence, transformed humans are the legitimate owners of the earth. With Christ first coming having redeemed man from the sins of Adam, it reopened the door for humans to regain their lost status (the way they had originally been designed). Hence, the transformed humans have the same status that Adam had before his fall and can legitimately hand over the rule of the earth to Christ.

According to Paul, this event will happen at the last trump, which might be an allusion to the 7th Trumpet, which is the last trumpet that contains the 7th Plagues. The foregoing presentation about the first resurrection contrasts with the general notion about the rapture, which generally mixes the events of the first resurrection with the notion that Christ will extract his followers out of the earth before the commencement of the Great Tribulation. The perspective adopted here matches with what the Bible teaches, that the followers of Christ will go through the Great Tribulation to be purified to inherit their imperishable gift. In 2 Thessalonians, Paul confirmed that the coming of Christ and the resurrection of the dead will happen after the apostasy (rebellion) has occurred and the antichrist (the man of lawlessness) has been revealed to the world (has appeared on earth and assumed the role of the antichrist):

> Concerning the coming of our Lord Jesus Christ and our being gathered to him, we ask you, brothers and sisters, ² not to become easily unsettled or alarmed by the teaching allegedly from us—whether by a prophecy or by word of mouth or by letter—asserting that the day of the Lord has already come. ³ Don't let anyone deceive you in any way, for that day will not come until the rebellion occurs and the man of lawlessness is revealed, the man doomed to destruction. ⁴ He will oppose and will exalt himself over everything that is called God or is worshiped, so that he sets himself up in God's temple, proclaiming himself to be God (2 Thessalonians 2:1–4 NIV).

14.7 *FILII DEI* (SONS OF GOD)–THE ULTIMATE PRIZE FOR HUMANS

The "*sons of God*" are a new generation of beings that will emerge from the crucibles of the earth. The entire purpose of every man on earth is to attain this next level of evolution. The books in the Bible contain the guiding principles that will enable any human to reach this enviable goal.

The entire creation is awaiting this moment when this new generation of beings emerges from the cocoon of the earth to take their rightful place in the Kingdom of God:

> [19] For the creation waits in eager expectation for the children of God to be revealed. [20] For the creation was subjected to frustration, not by its own choice, but by the will of the one who subjected it, in hope [21] that the creation itself will be liberated from its bondage to decay and brought into the freedom and glory of the children of God.
>
> [22] We know that the whole creation has been groaning as in the pains of childbirth right up to the present time. [23] Not only so, but we ourselves, who have the firstfruits of the Spirit, groan inwardly as we wait eagerly for our adoption to sonship, the redemption of our bodies. [24] For in this hope we were saved. But hope that is seen is no hope at all. Who hopes for what they already have? (Romans 8:22–24 NIV).

God created Adam to occupy a special place in his kingdom, but his fall from grace brought a disconnection that disrupted this plan of God. Hence, a new plan was put in motion to select from the human race, only the best. The selection process is very rigorous as God does not want further disruptions to his plan by having these new *sons of God* doing things that will disrupt his plans.

The emergence of the *sons of God* will occur during the last phases of the end times events. The term "*sons of God*" is used in the Bible to describe beings directly created by God. This contrasts the term "*sons of men*", which is associated with humans–for instance the descendants of Adam. Sons of men are earthly offsprings of men (beings procreated by men). Hence, "*sons of God*" is usually ascribed to angelic beings. Adam is an exception, he was also described as a son of God (the son of Enos, the son of Seth, the son of *Adam, the son of God–Luke 3:38*), because God formed him with his hands (in this sense God was Adam's direct parent), just like God directly created angels. Adam was a specially created son of God, however, when he fell, he lost this status and became a mortal, that can die. However, God made a way for man to regain this status of *sons of God*, through the salvation brought by Christ:

> [3] Blessed be the God and Father of our Lord Jesus Christ, which according to his abundant mercy hath begotten us again unto a lively hope by the resurrection of Jesus Christ from the dead,

> ⁴ To an inheritance incorruptible, and undefiled, and that fadeth not away, reserved in heaven for you,
> ⁵ Who are kept by the power of God through faith unto salvation ready to be revealed in the last time. (1 Peter 1: 3–5 KJV).

Thus, anyone who believes and follows the commandments of Christ, will be transformed from a mortal man to a *son of God* in the end. The *sons of God* will be restored to their original state before death was brought in through the fall of Adam:

> ²⁰ But in fact Christ has been raised from the dead, the firstfruits of those who have fallen asleep. ²¹ For as by a man came death, by a man has come also the resurrection of the dead. ²² For as in Adam all die, so also in Christ shall all be made alive. (1 Corinthians 15: 20–22 KJV).

This is the goal of mankind, to attain this status of *sons of God*. Hence, the task set before every man is to strive to be found worthy to merit the last day elevation from the level of a *son of man* to the level of *son of God* (to become what Adam was originally created as).

It must be understood that the *sons of God* are a select group of people that will cut across all generations. Hence, not every human will attain this status. The followers of Christ are expected to emulate him, who came as a *son of man* (14 And the Word was made flesh, and dwelt among us–John 1: 14 KJV), but successfully finished his work, to become a *son of God*, and obtain the transformed body (immortal body) after his resurrection. He was described as the first fruit of this new generation of mankind:

> ²⁰ But in fact Christ has been raised from the dead, the firstfruits of those who have fallen asleep. ²¹ For as by a man came death, by a man has come also the resurrection of the dead. ²² For as in Adam all die, so also in Christ shall all be made alive. ²³ But each in his own order: Christ the firstfruits, then at his coming those who belong to Christ. (1 Corinthians 15: 20–23 ESV).

In terms of their nature, the sons of God will be like angels with immortal bodies (see Section 12.3). Christ alluded to this when answering questions about the resurrection:

> ³⁰ At the resurrection people will neither marry nor be given in marriage; they will be like the angels in heaven. (Matthew 22:30 NIV).

This was also alluded to in Daniel that the transformed humans will shine like stars:

> ² Multitudes who sleep in the dust of the earth will awake: some to everlasting life, others to shame and everlasting contempt. ³ Those who are wise will shine like the brightness of the heavens, and those who lead many to righteousness, like the stars for ever and ever. (Daniel 12: 1–3 NIV).

Paul expounded on the transformation of humans and the nature of the transformed body in 1 Corinthians 15, while providing a commentary on the resurrection of Christ and the dead:

> ⁵⁰ I tell you this, brothers: flesh and blood cannot inherit the kingdom of God, nor does the perishable inherit the imperishable. ⁵¹ Behold! I tell you a mystery. We shall not all sleep, but we shall all be changed, ⁵² in a moment, in the twinkling of an eye, at the last trumpet. For the trumpet will sound, and the dead will be raised imperishable, and we shall be changed. ⁵³ For this perishable body must put on the imperishable, and this mortal body must put on immortality. ⁵⁴ When the perishable puts on the imperishable, and the mortal puts on immortality, then shall come to pass the saying that is written:
> "Death is swallowed up in victory."
> ⁵⁵ "O death, where is your victory?
> O death, where is your sting?" (1 Corinthians 15: 50–55 KJV).

Here, Paul alluded to the fact that these new bodies will be different from the natural ones and would be imperishable–immortal bodies. Only those who have merited this new body can be allowed into the Kingdom of God.

This makes sense, considering that when the throne of God descends to the earth (Revelation 21: 1–3), it will arrive in all its ramifications and glory. Just like the way it is currently in the heaven. It would not be diluted for humans. Rather, humans would have to be transformed to conform to the nature of beings found in heaven. No mortal body can get into heaven, where God's throne is. Hence, when the Kingdom of God is set up on earth, only those with immortal bodies can enter it. The transformed body is a body that can access both the earth and heavenly environments. Adam was able to interact with God in this body. Christ after his resurrection was interacting with his disciples, as well as presenting himself in the heavenly temple. He also ascended to God's throne with this body.

Also, Baruch was told almost the same thing about the resurrected bodies:

> XLIX. In what shape will those live who live in Thy day? Or how will the splendour of those who (are) after that time continue? 3. Will they then resume this form of the present, And put on these entrammeling members, Which are now involved in evils, And in which evils are consummated Or wilt Thou perchance change these things which have been in the world, As also the world?' "
>
> L. And He answered and said unto me: "Hear, Baruch, this word, And write in the remembrance of thy heart all that thou shalt learn. 2. For the earth shall then assuredly restore the dead, Which it now receiveth, in order to preserve them. It shall make no change in their form, But as it hath received, so shall it restore them And as I delivered them unto it, so also shall it raise them. 3. For then it will be necessary to show to the living that the dead have come to life again, and that those who had departed have returned (again). 4. And it shall come to pass, when they have severally recognized those whom they now know, then judgement shall grow strong, and those things which before were spoken of shall come.
>
> LI. "And it shall come to pass, when that appointed day hath gone by, that then shall the aspect of those who are condemned be afterwards changed, and the glory of those who are justified. 2. For the aspect of those who now act wickedly shall become worse than it is, as they shall suffer torment. 3. Also (as for) the glory of those who have now been justified in My Law, who have had understanding in their life, and who have planted in their heart the root of wisdom, then their splendour shall be glorified in changes, and the form of their face shall be turned into the light of their beauty, that they may be able to acquire and receive the world which doth not die, which is then promised to them. 4. For over this above all shall those who come then lament, that they rejected My Law, and stopped their ears that they might not hear wisdom or receive understanding. 5. When therefore they see those, over whom they are now exalted, (but) who shall then be exalted and glorified more than they, they shall respectively be transformed, the latter into the splendour of angels, and the former shall yet more waste away in wonder at the visions and in the beholding of the forms. 6. For they will first behold, and afterwards depart to be tormented. 7. But those

who have been saved by their works, And to whom the Law hath been now a hope, And understanding an expectation, And wisdom a confidence, To them wonders will appear in their time. 8. For they shall behold the world which is now invisible to them, And they shall behold the time which is now hidden from them. 9. And time shall no longer age them. 10. For in the heights of that world shall they dwell, And they shall be made like unto the angels, And be made equal to the stars, And they shall be changed into every form they desire, From beauty into loveliness, And from light into the splendour of glory. 11. For there shall be spread before them the extents of Paradise, and there shall be shown to them the beauty of the majesty of the living creatures which are beneath the throne, and all the armies of the angels, who [are now held fast by My word, lest they should appear, and] are held fast by a command, that they may stand in their places till their advent cometh. 12. Moreover, there shall then be excellency in the righteous surpassing that in the angels. 13. For the first shall receive the last, those whom they were expecting, and the last those of whom they used to hear that they had passed away. 14. For they have been delivered from this world of tribulation, And laid down the burthen of anguish. 15. For what then have men lost their life, And for what have those who were on the earth exchanged their soul? 16. For then they chose (not) for themselves this time, Which, beyond the reach of anguish, could not pass away But they chose for themselves that time, Whose issues are full of lamentations and evils, And they denied the world which ageth not those who come to it, And they have rejected the time of glory, So that they shall not come to the honour of which I told thee before (The Apocalypse of Baruch, XLIX, L, LI).

The opportunity is giving to every man to aspire to become a *son of God*, because as many as received him he gave them power to become sons of God:

> [12] But as many as received him, to them gave he power to become the sons of God, even to them that believe on his name: [13] Which were born, not of blood, nor of the will of the flesh, nor of the will of man, but of God. (John 1: 12–13 KJV).

Once again John in this passage reiterated that *sons of God* are born of God (John 1: 13 KJV). It is pertinent to note that this verse does not necessarily say that anyone that receives has become a *son of God* but such person has been *empowered to become* a *son of God* (if the person does the right thing and follows in the footstep of Christ who was the first fruit of this transformed humans). Following the footsteps of Christ is not a tea party. There are lots of sacrifices and self-denials to be made while striving to walk in the righteous path (see Section 11.3). Paul alluded to these as the sufferings that must be endured, which does not compare with the future glory that awaits those who conquered:

> [18] For I consider that the sufferings of this present time are not worth comparing with the glory that is to be revealed to us. [19] For the creation waits with eager longing for the revealing of the sons of God. (Romans 8:18-19 NIV).

Despite this opportunity made open to all humans to evolve into a higher status, only a few can attain this. Only the best of the best from this world will be allowed into the next world. Esdras was told that the next world coming (the Kingdom of God) is made for a few, unlike the present world that is made for many:

> VIII. And he answered and said to me: This world hath the Most-High made for the sake of many, but that which is to come for the sake of few. 2. But I will expound a parable, O Ezra: as when thou shalt ask the earth and it shall say to thee what dust it yieldeth more abundantly, that from which cometh the potsherd, or that from which cometh gold? so is the work of this world. 3. Many have been created, but few live. (Apocalypse of Ezra VIII: 1 - 3).
>
> [5z.] Thou, however, because thou hast said there not many righteous but few... ? hear (the answer) to this: [52.] ? If thou have precious stones and few, against the number of these do thou set lead and clay !3 [53-] And I said: How, O Lord, is that possible ? (54.| And he answered and said to me: Not only so, but ask the earth, and she shall tell thee ; speak to her, and she shall recount to thee. [55.] Say to her: Gold hast thou brought forth, and silver, and copper, and iron, and lead, and clay; -[56.] But the silver is more (abundant) than gold, and copper than silver, and iron than copper, and lead [57.] Do thou, then, than iron, and clay than lead reckon up? and see, what things are precious and to be desired,' 9 the many or the few? [58.] And I answered and said : O Lord my Lord: Things abundant are what are worthless, and things few are precious. [59.] And he answered and said to me: Do thou, then, reckon up in thine own mind what thou hast thought! Because everyone who hath

> a little that (is) rare rejoiceth over it more than that one who hath what is abundant.
>
> [60.] So also is the promise of my judgement; for I rejoice [and delight] over the few who live? because they it is who now strengthen my glory, and for whose sake my name is now extolled. [61.] And I am not pained over the multitude of those who are perishing; for these are they who now are made like a breath, and as the smoke are they counted, and are comparable unto the flame; who are burnt and extinguished. (Apocalyse of Ezra VII: 51 - 61).
>
> 37. And he answered and said to me: Some things thou hast spoken aright and according to thy words, 38. Because in truth I take no thought about the fashioning of the evil doers, or about their death, or about their judgement, or about their perdition; 39. but I delight (rather) over [the coming of] the fashioning of the righteous, and over their life, and over the recompence of their reward. For as thou hast said so shall it be. 40. Mankind is like Seed sown 41. For as the husbandman [who] soweth many seeds and planteth many plants, but not all the seeds live in due season, nor indeed do all the plants strike root ; so also they who have come into the world do not all live. (Apocalypse of Ezra VIII: 37 - 41).

The call to become a son of God has gone out to many people, but not all can make it, because as Christ said "For many are called, but few are chosen" (Matthew 22:14 KJV).

In the parable where the above quote came from, a king had prepared a wedding banquet for his son and initially sent out invitations to a select group of people (most likely his friends), but they refused to come to the banquet, preoccupied with earthly affairs. Infuriated, he opened the invitation to everyone available. However, one of those invited to the wedding banquet came in an inappropriate clothing and was removed from the event:

> [10] So those servants went out into the highways, and gathered together all as many as they found, both bad and good: and the wedding was furnished with guests. [11] And when the king came in to see the guests, he saw there a man which had not on a wedding garment: [12] And he saith unto him, Friend, how camest thou in hither not having a wedding garment? And he was speechless. [13] Then said the king to the servants, Bind him hand and foot, and take him away, and cast him into outer darkness,

there shall be weeping and gnashing of teeth. (Matthew 22:10–13 KJV).

This is a clear indication that even though the call to become *sons of God* is opened to virtually any human, only those who have done the right thing will be accepted into this select group of humans. In Revelation, we learn that the deeds of each individual will determine the type of garment the person would wear: *for the fine linen is the righteous deeds of the saints (Revelation 19:8 ESV)*.

It is instructive to note here that Christ compared the wedding banquet to the Kingdom of God (Kingdom of heaven). This parable is related to the parable of the 10 virgins, but with each parable focusing on the various aspects of the event. Whereas the parable of the virgins focused on the bride (the virgins), the parable here focused on the invited guests. The clue to recognise that these two parables are related is the fact that the guest who did not make it into the wedding feast was thrown out into the darkness where there is wailing and weeping, which is similar to the treatment that was meted out to the five foolish virgins. Each of these two parables were pointing at the end time separation of the good and the bad.

From the foregoing, it could be inferred that there are two broad categories of humans that will become the Sons of God. First is the 144000, the bride of Christ (described as the first of redeemed humans). The second will be the humans who were transformed during the First Resurrection (the guests invited to the wedding). Each of this group will be allowed into the wedding feast, the kingdom/empire of Christ symbolised as the Marriage Supper of the lamb (see Section 14.5).

The sons of God will be put in charge of certain aspects of the Kingdom of God. There are indications from many passages in the Bible that certain responsibilities will be given to the sons of God in the Kingdom of God. In the Parable of the Talents, which immediately followed the Parable of the Ten Virgins, a man going on a journey entrusted certain responsibilities to his servants. On his return, he assessed how each of them carried out their allocated responsibility. Those adjudged to have performed well were given more responsibilities:

> [21] His master said to him, 'Well done, good and faithful servant. You have been faithful over a little; I will set you over much. Enter into the joy of your master.' (Matthew 25: 21 ESV).

This is a clear indication, that on his return the deeds of all humans will be assessed, and this will determine the reward that each will receive. Part of this reward might be a position in the empire of Christ. Christ will require administrators that will be in charge of the affairs of the empire, and who else would occupy these positions than the sons of God? In Revelation 20 thrones were set up and those who had been given authority to judge sat on them. In the same vein the transformed humans (the *sons of God*) reigned with Christ for a thousand years:

> [4] Then I saw thrones, and seated on them were those to whom the authority to judge was committed. Also, I saw the souls of those who had been beheaded for the testimony of Jesus and for the word of God, and those who had not worshiped the beast or its image and had not received its mark on their foreheads or their hands. They came to life and reigned with Christ for a thousand years. (Revelation 20: 4 ESV).

"Reigning with Christ" implies some administrative position in the Millennial Reign. This is another indication that the sons of God will be utilised to perform certain roles in the Empire of Christ.

The responsibilities of the sons of Gods might even go beyond earthy responsibilities to something much more esteemed in the wider sphere of things in the universe. For instance, as part of the end time wars in Heavens, Satan and his angels who had occupied the Second Heaven, from where they have been operating from will be chased down to the earth and crushed (Revelation 12:7–9). The position previously occupied by Satan and his angels will have to be taken over by other beings. I strongly believe that the *sons of God* will assume some of these vacant positions. Christ hinted that *they will be like the angels in heaven. (Matthew 22:30 NIV)*. Hence, they can undertake some of duties that angels normally do. This might be the reason Satan has always planned to stop humans to rise from their current position, because God intends to replace him and his angels with humans who have been elevated to the rank of *sons of God*. This was captured in Hebrews 2, where Paul confirmed that next world will be subjected under mankind, albeit those who have been promoted to the sons of God status:

> [5] It is not to angels that he has subjected the world to come, about which we are speaking. [6] But there is a place where someone has testified:

> "What is mankind that you are mindful of them,
>   a son of man that you care for him?
> ⁷ You made them a little lower than the angels;
>   you crowned them with glory and honor
> ⁸   and put everything under their feet.
>
> In putting everything under them, God left nothing that is not subject to them. Yet at present we do not see everything subject to them⁹ But we do see Jesus, who was made lower than the angels for a little while, now crowned with glory and honor because he suffered death, so that by the grace of God he might taste death for everyone. (Hebrews 2:5–8 NIV).

Whatever God had planned for man must be so enviable that Satan could not fathom humans taking up those responsibilities:

> "Eye has not seen, nor ear heard,
> Nor have entered into the heart of man
> The things which God has prepared for those who love Him."
> (1 Corinthians 2:9 NKJV).

Paul hinted in 1 Corinthians that sons of God will judge angels:

> ³ Know ye not that we shall judge angels? how much more things that pertain to this life? 1 Corinthians 6:3 KJV).

Therefore, there is an enormous glory and reward awaiting the *sons of God* in the plans of God.

14.7.1 PRIEST FROM EVERY NATION

Despite the fact that Israelites will have a special place in the Empire of Christ and the subsequent Kingdom of God that would be established on earth, they will not be the only racial group that will be transformed. People from other nations will also be transformed into sons of God. These people will be in their respective nations from where they can visit Jerusalem to tabernacle with Christ, until the end of the Millennial Reign of Christ. Revelation 5 clearly stated that Christ redeemed people from every tribe and nation (and not just from Israel), whom he had made priests:

> and by your blood you ransomed people for God
>   from every tribe and language and people and nation,

> [10] and you have made them a kingdom and priests to our God, and they shall reign on the earth." (Revelation 5:9–10 ESV).

There are also other references in the Bible that mentioned that people from various nations and tongues were found around the throne of God:

> [9] After this I looked, and there before me was a great multitude that no one could count, from every nation, tribe, people and language, standing before the throne and before the Lamb. They were wearing white robes and were holding palm branches in their hands. (Revelation 7: 9 NIV).

This also tallies with the argument earlier presented that Christ will redeem the people from various nations who had previously been under the rulership of the renegade gods.

14.8 THE EARTH AND NOT HEAVEN IS THE FINAL RESIDENCE OF HUMANS

There is a general notion that seems to indicate that the final abode of humans is in the Heaven. However, various Biblical passages point the other way–that man's final home is rather the earth–well, the new earth. For all beings made by God, he allocated a place for them. For man, God gave the earth to him as his residence, and at the end of the age, man will take full charge of the earth and occupy it. Various snippets in the Bible suggest that man will inherit this earth:

> [11] But the meek shall inherit the earth; and shall delight themselves in the abundance of peace. (Psalm 37:11 KJV).

> [5] Blessed are the meek: for they shall inherit the earth. (Mathew 5:5 KJV).

The idea that man's final destination is the Heaven stems from the misunderstanding of what happens to the souls of humans when they die. The doctrine that portends that when the righteous die, they head off to Heaven to live permanently with God and the angels, is not necessarily accurate, judging from Biblical facts. The main task before humans as far as God is concerned is not for them to go to Heaven per se, but to regain their status as the *sons of God* he has created them to be from the beginning, so they can re-enter the Garden of Eden. As has been seen from the preceding sections, this elevation to become *sons of God*, will take place at the end of age. Hence, God has prepared a temporary place, where the dead can await the final judgement. This temporary place is not Heaven, where God's throne is located, and the angels reside.

In reality, when humans die its three components are split: body, spirit and soul. While the flesh (body) decays and returns to dust, the spirit of the individual goes back to God:

> and the dust returns to the ground it came from,
>   and the spirit returns to God who gave it. (Ecclesiastes 12:7 NIV).

The soul goes before God to be assessed/judged:

> [27] And as it is appointed unto men once to die, but after this the judgment. (Hebrews 9: 27 KJV).

As the soul journeys to God, all that he has done will be shown to him: the good deeds and the bad deeds. This is more like a recap of his entire life from birth to death. By the time the soul reaches to where God is, he would have self-assessed himself, that whatever the verdict of the judgement is, would be just and fair that he cannot dispute it. At this point, depending on where the individual's deeds stand on the scale of judgement, he may head off to a good place known as Abraham's bosom if he did well while alive, or to a horrible place known as Hades/Sheol (the so-called hell):

> [4] Behold, all souls are mine; as the soul of the father, so also the soul of the son is mine: the soul that sinneth, it shall die. (Ezekiel 18:4 KJV).

These places are holding places where the souls of humans temporarily await the final judgement, when the souls that sinneth will be incinerated in the lake of fire. Some light was shown on what happens to the soul after death in the discourse in the Apocalypse of Ezra. For the unrighteous, after their death, they are cast into Shoel and made aware of what they have missed and what destiny awaits them in the end. These are what causes their torment while they await the final judgement:

> [78.] But concerning death the teaching is: When the decisive decree of judgement goeth forth from the Most-High concerning a man that he shall die, as the spirit separateth from the body, that it may be sent to him who gave it, it first of all

> worshippeth the glory of God. [79.] But if it be of the deniers, or of those who have not kept the ways of the Most-High, or of those who have hated the God-fearers— [80.] these souls enter not into the chambers, but henceforth are in torment, sighing and anguished, in seven ways. [81.] The first way: that they have resisted the Law of the Most-High. [82.] The second way: that - they are unable to repent and do good works whereby to live. [83.] The third way: that they see the reward laid up for those who have believed. [84.] The fourth way: when they know and understand the torment that is prepared for them at the last. [Wherein the souls of the ungodly shall be reproached; because while they had the time for service they did not subject themselves to the commandments of the Most-High.] [85.] The fifth way: that they see the chambers of the other souls, that are guarded by angels in great quietness. [86.] The sixth way: that they see the torment which is made ready for them henceforth.
>
> [87.] The seventh way, which exceedeth all the ways aforesaid: that they pine away through "confusion, and come to an end through shame," and burn through fear, in that they see the glory of the Most-High before whom they now sin in their life! 2 and before whom they are destined at the last to be judged. (Apocalypse of Ezra VII: 78 - 87).

Conversely, the righteous souls are made to patiently stay in their chambers after being shown what glory awaits them at the end of age:

> [88.] Of those, however, who have kept the way of the Most-High, this is the way, when 2 the day cometh that they shall be delivered from this corruptible vessel. [89.] For in the time when they dwelt therein they served the Most-High painfully, and at all hours endured danger, in order perfectly to keep his Law who had given them the Law. (90.) Wherefore this is the word concerning them. [91.] First they behold with great joy the glory of the Most-High, who hath guided them, and they rest [and come] 6 by seven ways. [92.] The first way: because with much toil they have striven to overcome the evil thought which was fashioned with them, that they might not go astray from life to death. [93.] The second way: that they see he whirl whereby the souls of the ungodly are whirled and driven about, and the torment reserved for them. (94.) The third way: that they see the witness which their fashioner witnesseth concerning them; because they kept the Law entrusted (to them). [95.] The fourth way: that they [see and] understand the rest in which they now, as soon as they have been gathered into their chambers, rest in

> profound rest, and are guarded by angels; and the glory which is reserved for them at the last. [96.] The fifth way: that they rejoice that they have fled now from what is corruptible, and that they inherit what is future; and further they see the straitness and much toil from which they have been freed, and the wide room which they are destined to receive, and the delights they shall gain, and be immortal. [97.] The sixth way: when it shall be shewed to them how their faces are destined to shine as the sun, and how they are destined to be made like the light of the stars, and no more corruptible. [98.] The seventh way which exceedeth all these aforesaid: that they exult with boldness, and are confident and not ashamed, and hasten to behold the face of him whom they served in their life and from whom they are destined to be glorified, and from whom they are destined to receive reward. [99.] These are the ways of the souls of the righteous which from henceforth are announced; and the way of tortures aforesaid shall the resisters receive. (Apocalypse of Ezra VII: 88 - 99).

These temporary places where the souls await the final judgement is not Heaven, even though they are in what may be classified as part of the spiritual realm. It is only at the final judgement that souls head off to their ultimate destination: either to the Kingdom of God (that will come down on earth) or to the lake of fire (Revelation 20: 11–15). These are Biblical facts that can easily be substantiated.

This is not to say that the souls of the righteous cannot travel to Heaven. Being in the spiritual realm grants a soul access to visit Heaven when necessary, and if permitted to do so. The point being presented here is that Heaven is not the place created for humans to permanently reside. Any human found in a Heaven is a visitor and not a permanent resident. Even the souls of those murdered during the Great Tribulation found in heaven will be brought down to the earth when Christ returns. To confirm that the destination of man is the earth, at the end of the age, Christ will come from heaven to first reign for one thousand years on earth and then establish the Kingdom of God here. The dead in Christ will be resurrected at this time to reign with Christ on earth. Following this, God will also come down to earth to establish his throne and rule the universe from here (Revelation 21: 1–6). In this renewed earth with the throne of God amidst it, there would be very close interaction between the heavenly and physical realms. The earth will literally fuse with cosmic realms, having been brought into concordance with the other realms. For a long time, the earth was playing discordant tune that is out of sync with the rest of God's creation, and needed to be brought under control, by ridding it of all impurities. This period when the earth has been restored and the throne of God, brought down to it, would be like the time of Adam, when he and Eve closely interacted with God. At the end of the Millennial Reign, paradise will be brought down to earth as the New Jerusalem with the tree of life nourishing the inhabitants of this city:

> On each side of the river stood the tree of life, bearing twelve crops of fruit, yielding its fruit every month. And the leaves of the tree are for the healing of the nations. ³ No longer will there be any curse. The throne of God and of the Lamb will be in the city, and his servants will serve him. ⁴ They will see his face, and his name will be on their foreheads. ⁵ There will be no more night. They will not need the light of a lamp or the light of the sun, for the Lord God will give them light. And they will reign for ever and ever. (Revelation 22: 2–5 NIV).

I am conscious of the notion that portends that when Christ rose from the dead, he emptied Abraham bosom and took the souls of the righteous to heaven. The closest passage in the Bible that alludes to such an event is in Mathew, which confirmed that many righteous people rose from the dead at the point of Christ's death when the earthquake shook Jerusalem and came out from their tombs at his resurrection:

> ⁵¹ And, behold, the veil of the temple was rent in twain from the top to the bottom; and the earth did quake, and the rocks rent; ⁵² And the graves were opened; and many bodies of the saints which slept arose, ⁵³ And came out of the graves after his resurrection, and went into the holy city, and appeared unto many. (Matthew 27:51–53 KJV).

However, there is no indication here that these people were taken to heaven afterwards. And the passage did not elaborate further on this. It is also doubtful that all righteous people or all the patriarchs in Abraham bosom were resurrected, considering that during the following Pentecost, Peter alluded that the tomb of David could still be found, suggesting that David was still in Sheol:

> ²⁹ "Brothers, I may say to you with confidence about the patriarch David that he both died and was buried, and his tomb is with us to this day. ³⁰ Being therefore a prophet, and knowing

> that God had sworn with an oath to him that he would set one of his descendants on his throne, [31] he foresaw and spoke about the resurrection of the Christ, that he was not abandoned to Hades, nor did his flesh see corruption. [32] This Jesus God raised up, and of that we all are witnesses. [33] Being therefore exalted at the right hand of God, and having received from the Father the promise of the Holy Spirit, he has poured out this that you yourselves are seeing and hearing. [34] For David did not ascend into the heavens (Acts 2: 29 -34 ESV).

It is hard to believe that if David was among those resurrected on the day Christ was crucified, Peter (and other residents of Jerusalem) would not have known. As a matter of fact, everyone in Jerusalem would have been talking about it.

One conclusion that could be derived from the available information in canonised Bible is that some righteous people were raised from the dead and lived with the people normally and died afterwards. This should not be farfetched, considering that Lazarus was also raised from the grave by Christ and lived. It is highly unlikely that these people went to heaven after being resurrected by Christ, otherwise the Bible would have mentioned it. Another conclusion could be that they were taken to another location after their resurrection. The Gospel of Nicodemus provided some insight in this respect about the whereabouts of the people resurrected at the death of Christ. It recorded an encounter between the Jewish leaders investigating the resurrection of Christ and two sons of Simeon (Karinus and Leucius), who were among those resurrected by Christ. According to the account presented in the book (Gospel of Nicodemus IX, X, XI), the people that were resurrected, were taken to paradise–essentially, they were admitted into the Garden of Eden. Even though the veracity of the account in the Gospel of Nicodemus is arguable, the account corresponds to what Christ alluded to on the cross, that he would take the thief to paradise.

Another argument that could be put forward is the promise Christ made that he was going to prepare a place for his followers that he was going to prepare a place for them:

> "Do not let your hearts be troubled. You believe in God; believe also in me. [2] My Father's house has many rooms; if that were not so, would I have told you that I am going there to prepare a place for you? [3] And if I go and prepare a place for you, I will come back and take you to be with me that you also may be where I

am. ⁴ You know the way to the place where I am going." (John 14: 1–4 NIV).

People usually conclude that Christ was going to Heaven to prepare a place there where humans will finally reside. However, the mere fact that Christ was going to prepare a place for humans means that there was a place for humans in Heaven prior this time. So, where have all the souls that died before this period go? Furthermore, Christ promise was to go to heaven to prepare a place where he and humans will reside. And we know from revelation that Christ is coming to earth to reign, and humans will be with him in this kingdom. To buttress this point, in Revelation 21, a new city (New Jerusalem) will descend from Heaven to earth:

> ² And I John saw the holy city, new Jerusalem, coming down from God out of heaven, prepared as a bride adorned for her husband. (Revelation 21: 2 KJV).

This magnificent city is tagged the bride of Christ, indicating that Christ has special relationship with it. This relationship emanates from the fact that Christ prepared it:

> ⁹ And there came unto me one of the seven angels which had the seven vials full of the seven last plagues, and talked with me, saying, Come hither, I will shew thee the bride, the Lamb's wife.
> ¹⁰ And he carried me away in the spirit to a great and high mountain, and shewed me that great city, the holy Jerusalem, descending out of heaven from God. (Revelation 21: 9–10 KJV).

This is the place Christ promised to go to Heaven to prepare. It is a city that will be prefabricated in Heaven and subsequently installed on earth. The magnificence of this city is described in Revelation 21: 11–27.

Even if we assume that the dead goes to heaven, they will eventually return to the earth to reign with Christ, because that is the destiny of man. Even God will eventually come to the earth to establish his throne:

> ³ And I heard a loud voice from the throne saying, "Look! God's dwelling place is now among the people, and he will dwell with them. They will be his people, and God himself will be with them and be their God. (Revelation 21:3 NIV).

The key point here is that the earth was originally created to be part of the heavens, however, the rebellion of Satan and the fall of Adam disconnected the earth from the rest of the heavens. Hence, the earth needs to be reconnected to the heavens. This is what Christ is coming to do–to reincorporate the earth into the Kingdom of God, by eradicating sin and vanquishing the rebellious angels (the enemies of God). Once the earth has been cleansed of sin, God will come over:

> And the seventh angel sounded; and there were great voices in heaven, saying, The kingdoms of this world are become the kingdoms of our Lord, and of his Christ; and he shall reign for ever and ever (Revelation 11:15 KJV).

Humanity will first be admitted into paradise, and from paradise they can access the Kingdom of God. In this regard, paradise is the first rung of the ladder into the Kingdom of God.

14.9 THE PARALLEL WORLDS DURING THE MILLENNIAL REIGN

Although details about this are sketchy, based on hints in the gospels and Revelation, there would be two diametrically opposed worlds operating on earth during the Millennial Reign of Christ. One part would be those loyal and under the authority of the Empire of Christ and the other are those disloyal to the authority of Christ. The loyal ones will live in peace and happiness. The disloyal ones will be at the fringes of the earth. These would be considered outsiders to the Kingdom of Christ, faced with the devastation and ruins on the earth (aftermath of the preceding events). Faced with this reality, they will be weeping and gnashing their teeth in frustration, having realised their errors, and seeing how peaceful those within the Empire of Christ are living. This outer world would be made up of mainly leftovers from the Beast System, who managed to survive the devastating impact of the wrath of God (possibly with varying levels of deformities), some extraterrestrial beings (some of the fallen angels chased down to earth with Satan, and other demonic entities unleashed on the world during the Great Tribulation, who survived), and any other individuals who were not accepted into the Empire of Christ. This alternate world was severally mentioned by Christ in parables as the "outer darkness" where there would be weeping and gnashing of teeth:

> 11 "But when the king came in to see the guests, he noticed a man there who was not wearing wedding clothes. 12 He asked, 'How did you get in here without wedding clothes, friend?' The man was speechless.

¹³ "Then the king told the attendants, 'Tie him hand and foot, and throw him outside, into the darkness, where there will be weeping and gnashing of teeth.' (Matthew 22:11–13 NIV).

This outer darkness will be hanging around the world during the Millennial Reign. These are the enemies of Christ who he will rule in their midst. It is from this part of the world that the nations coming to worship Christ will be drawn from:

> ¹⁶ And it shall come to pass that everyone who is left of all the nations which came against Jerusalem shall go up from year to year to worship the King, the Lord of hosts, and to keep the Feast of Tabernacles. 17 If any of the peoples of the earth do not go up to Jerusalem to worship the King, the Lord Almighty, they will have no rain. (Zechariah 14: 16–17 NIV).

It is also from this part of the world that Satan will gather an army to attack the camp of the saints at the end of the Millennial Reign:

> ⁷ When the thousand years are over, Satan will be released from his prison ⁸ and will go out to deceive the nations in the four corners of the earth—Gog and Magog—and to gather them for battle. In number they are like the sand on the seashore. *(Revelation 20: 78 NIV).*

These nations are remnants of the Beast System (hence, the reference to Gog and Magog here, to make the reader to realise that these people already have allegiance to Satan) who were subjected under the authority of Christ during the Millennial reign. At the end of the one thousand reign of Christ, this outer dark world will cease to exist as it will be destroyed in the lake of fire with all the enemies of God having been subdued and destroyed. Then will the Kingdom of God come into full swing on the earth with God at the head.

14.10 REGIMEN CHRISTUS–THE GOVERNMENT OF CHRIST

> ² And it shall come to pass in the last days, that the mountain of the Lord's house shall be established in the top of the mountains, and shall be exalted above the hills; and all nations shall flow unto it.

> ³ *And many people shall go and say, Come ye, and let us go up to the mountain of the Lord, to the house of the God of Jacob; and he will teach us of his ways, and we will walk in his paths: for out of Zion shall go forth the law, and the word of the Lord from Jerusalem.*
> ⁴ *And he shall judge among the nations, and shall rebuke many people: and they shall beat their swords into plowshares, and their spears into pruninghooks: nation shall not lift up sword against nation, neither shall they learn war any more.(Isaiah 2: 2-5 KJV)*

The government of Christ will be monarchical in nature, with Christ as the King, and other nations of the earth subject to the rule of Christ. It will function almost like any other empire, where one nation will be in charge of the rest of the nations on earth. In this case the nation of Israel will be the ruling country, while other nations at this time will be vassal states. The boundary of the nation of Israel at this time will encompass the boundary of the promised land which God showed Abraham extending from the River of Egypt to the Euphrates (Genesis 15:18).

At the initial stages of the establishment of this empire, there would be opposing forces aka the wicked, who are remnants of the Beast System, who would prefer not to subject themselves to the rulership of Christ. These will be crushed and used as a demonstration for others to fall in line:

> LXXII. Hear now also regarding the bright lightning which is to come at the consummation after these black (waters), this is the word: 2. After the signs have come, of which thou wast told before, when the nations become turbulent, and the time of My Messiah is come, He shall both summon all the nations, and some of them He shall spare, and some of them He shall slay. 3. These things therefore shall come upon the nations which are to be spared by Him. 4. Every nation which knoweth not Israel, and hath not trodden down the seed of Jacob, shall; indeed be spared. 5. And this because some of every nation shall be subjected to thy people. 6. But all those who have ruled over you, or have known you, shall be given up to the sword. (The Apocalypse of Baruch LXXII: 1-6).

Then will true peace exist in the world, with no country going against another:

> LXXIII. And it shall come to pass, when He hath brought low everything that is in the world, And hath sat down in peace for

the age on the throne of His kingdom, That joy shall then be revealed, And rest appear; 2. And then healing shall descend in dew, And disease shall withdraw, And anxiety and anguish and lamentation shall pass from amongst men, And gladness shall proceed through the whole earth 3. And no one shall again die untimely, Nor shall any adversity suddenly befall, 4. And judgements, and revilings, and contentions, and revenges, And blood, and passions, and envy, and hatred, And whatsoever things are like these shall go into condemnation when they are removed. 5. For it is these very things which have filled this world with evils, And on account of these the life of man has been greatly troubled. 6. And wild beasts shall come from the forest and minister unto men, And asps and dragons shall come forth from their holes to submit themselves to a little child, 7. And women shall no longer then have pain when they bear, Nor shall they suffer torment when they yield the fruit of the womb. LXXIV. And it shall come to pass in those days that the reapers shall not grow weary, Nor those that build be toilworn For the works shall of themselves speedily advance; With those who do them in much tranquillity. 2. For that time is the consummation of that which is corruptible, And the beginning of that which is not corruptible. 3. Therefore those things which were predicted shall belong to it Therefore it is far away from evils, and near to those things which die not. 4. This is the bright lightning which came after the last dark waters." (The Apocalypse of Baruch Chapter LXXIII–LXXIV).

[25] "'I will make a covenant of peace with them and rid the land of savage beasts so that they may live in the wilderness and sleep in the forests in safety. [26] I will make them and the places surrounding my hill a blessing. I will send down showers in season; there will be showers of blessing. [27] The trees will yield their fruit, and the ground will yield its crops; the people will be secure in their land. They will know that I am the Lord, when I break the bars of their yoke and rescue them from the hands of those who enslaved them. [28] They will no longer be plundered by the nations, nor will wild animals devour them. They will live in safety, and no one will make them afraid. [29] I will provide for them a land renowned for its crops, and they will no longer be victims of famine in the land or bear the scorn of the nations. [30] Then they will know that I, the Lord their God, am with them and that they, the Israelites, are my people, declares the Sovereign Lord. [31] You are my sheep, the sheep of

my pasture, and I am your God, declares the Sovereign Lord.'" (Ezekiel 34: 25-31 NIV).

Ezekiel 40 to 48 provides additional details about the Millennial Reign, especially how the land of Israel will be divided among the tribes, the design of the temple, and the sacrifices that will be offered during this period. Importantly, this prophecy gave an insight into the government structure of this period. Christ will be the King of the empire. However, there would be an administrator, who would function as a prime minister for the king. This individual is identified by Ezekiel as the prince, featured prominently in Ezekiel 44, 45, 46, and 47. There is almost a consensus that this prince referred to here is David. He would serve as the prime minister (a shepherd) for the house of Israel:

> [23] I will place over them one shepherd, my servant David, and he will tend them; he will tend them and be their shepherd. [24] I the Lord will be their God, and my servant David will be prince among them. I the Lord have spoken. (Ezekiel 34: 23-24 NIV).

In addition, there would be priests that would serve at the temple. These were identified as the sons of Zadok:

> [15] "But the Levitical priests, the sons of Zadok, who kept the charge of my sanctuary when the people of Israel went astray from me, shall come near to me to minister to me. And they shall stand before me to offer me the fat and the blood, declares the Lord God. [16] They shall enter my sanctuary, and they shall approach my table, to minister to me, and they shall keep my charge. (Ezekiel 44: 15-16 NIV).

It can also be extrapolated from the structure of governance in Israel at this time, will be replicated across other nations in the world. Hence, each nation will also have a prince overseeing the nation that would be subject to Christ. Again, this points back to the division of the earth after the dispersal at Babel, where a prince was assigned to each nation, with God taking Israel as his portion and assigning Archangel Michael as the prince of Israel (see Section 7.1).

14.11 OVERTHROWING OF THE ADVERSARIES OF GOD

A key agenda of Christ second coming is to complete the defeat and destruction of God's adversaries. But who are the adversaries of God?

Simple answer is all enemies of God, who opposes his will. As far as we know, this includes Satan and all the fallen angels who rebelled against God with him, the Watchers who came down to earth to fornicate with earthly women and give birth to the Nephilim, the false gods (the renegade sons of God, who were given charge over the nations of the world), the demons (disembodied spirits of the Nephilim), and their human collaborators, who execute the directives of these entities on earth. All these entities will be severely dealt with during this era. Hence, the second coming of Christ is a time of reckoning for all those opposed to the rule of God. God has patiently allowed all the rebellious entities to exercise all their powers before he deals with them in a decisive manner. The key agenda of the end times battles is to clear the heavens and the earth of all evil forces. After this period of cleansing, Christ will hand over the earth to God, hence bringing the earth fully under the rule of God:

> [24] Then comes the end, when he delivers the kingdom to God the Father after destroying every rule and every authority and power. [25] For he must reign until he has put all his enemies under his feet. [26] The last enemy to be destroyed is death. [27] For "God has put all things in subjection under his feet." But when it says, "all things are put in subjection," it is plain that he is excepted who put all things in subjection under him. [28] When all things are subjected to him, then the Son himself will also be subjected to him who put all things in subjection under him, that God may be all in all. (1 Corinthians 15: 24–28 ESV).

Hence, the earth will become fully reconnected with the heavens. Prior this time, the earth was partially connected to the heavens as sin ravaged the earth. But with the eradication of sin and evil forces, the earth regains full connection with the rest of the heavens. Hence, the kingdom of the earth will become the Kingdom of God:

> [15] When the seventh angel blew his trumpet, there were loud voices in heaven, saying,
>> "The kingdom of the world has become
>> the kingdom of our Lord and of his Messiah,
>> and he will rule as king forever and ever." (Revelation 11:15 GW).

Daniel also alluded to this when he provided the interpretation of Nebuchadnezzar's dream, where he stated that the kingdom of Christ will crush other worldly kingdoms:

⁴⁴ "In the time of those kings, the God of heaven will set up a kingdom that will never be destroyed, nor will it be left to another people. It will crush all those kingdoms and bring them to an end, but it will itself endure forever. ⁴⁵ This is the meaning of the vision of the rock cut out of a mountain, but not by human hands—a rock that broke the iron, the bronze, the clay, the silver and the gold to pieces. (Daniel 2: 44-45 IV).

14.12 JERUSALEM THE CAPITAL OF THE EMPIRE (WORLD CAPITAL)

The Empire of Christ will be headquartered in Jerusalem, hence making Jerusalem the capital city of the world (Isaiah 2:1-4). There are numerous prophecies pointing to this fact that the throne of Christ will be set up in Jerusalem:

> And in that day it shall be
> That living waters shall flow from Jerusalem,
> Half of them toward the eastern sea
> And half of them toward the western sea;
> In both summer and winter it shall occur.
> ⁹ And the *Lord* shall be King over all the earth.
> In that day it shall be—
> "The Lord is one,"
> And His name one (Zechariah 14: 8-9 NIV).

Hence, this city will tower above all others, in the same that Rome, Babylon and others towered above the cities of the world during their time of dominion:

> Jerusalem shall be raised up and inhabited in her place from Benjamin's Gate to the place of the First Gate and the Corner Gate, and from the Tower of Hananel to the king's winepresses.
>
> ¹¹ The people shall dwell in it;
> And no longer shall there be utter destruction,
> But Jerusalem shall be safely inhabited (Zechariah 14: 10-11 NIV).

Other nations will essentially be reduced to provinces of this empire. Inhabitants of other nations will be coming to Jerusalem to pay homage every year, to demonstrate their loyalty to Christ *(Zechariah 14: 1-21 KJV)*. Isaiah captured this moment in one of his prophesies:

"Arise, shine, for your light has come,
  and the glory of the Lord rises upon you.
² See, darkness covers the earth
  and thick darkness is over the peoples,
but the Lord rises upon you
  and his glory appears over you.
³ Nations will come to your light,
  and kings to the brightness of your dawn.
⁴ "Lift up your eyes and look about you:
  All assemble and come to you;
your sons come from afar,
  and your daughters are carried on the hip.
⁵ Then you will look and be radiant,
  your heart will throb and swell with joy;
the wealth on the seas will be brought to you,
  to you the riches of the nations will come.
⁶ Herds of camels will cover your land,
  young camels of Midian and Ephah.
And all from Sheba will come,
  bearing gold and incense
  and proclaiming the praise of the Lord.
⁷ All Kedar's flocks will be gathered to you,
  the rams of Nebaioth will serve you;
they will be accepted as offerings on my altar,
  and I will adorn my glorious temple.
⁸ "Who are these that fly along like clouds,
  like doves to their nests?
⁹ Surely the islands look to me;
  in the lead are the ships of Tarshish,
bringing your children from afar,
  with their silver and gold,
to the honor of the Lord your God,
  the Holy One of Israel,
  for he has endowed you with splendor.
¹⁰ "Foreigners will rebuild your walls,
  and their kings will serve you.
Though in anger I struck you,
  in favor I will show you compassion.
¹¹ Your gates will always stand open,
  they will never be shut, day or night,
so that people may bring you the wealth of the nations—
  their kings led in triumphal procession.
¹² For the nation or kingdom that will not serve you will perish;
  it will be utterly ruined.

> ¹³ "The glory of Lebanon will come to you,
>   the juniper, the fir and the cypress together,
> to adorn my sanctuary;
>   and I will glorify the place for my feet.
> ¹⁴ The children of your oppressors will come bowing before you;
>   all who despise you will bow down at your feet
> and will call you the City of the Lord,
>   Zion of the Holy One of Israel. (Isaiah 60: 1–14 NIV).

14.13 THE FINAL BATTLE–GOG AND MAGOG BATTLE II

The final battle is the last battle that will be waged on earth between Christ and Satan. This battle, which would take place after one thousand years of Christ rule on earth is setup to serve as the final test for humanity. Revelation briefly mentioned this battle:

> ⁷ And when the thousand years are ended, Satan will be released from his prison ⁸ and will come out to deceive the nations that are at the four corners of the earth, Gog and Magog, to gather them for battle; their number is like the sand of the sea. ⁹ And they marched up over the broad plain of the earth and surrounded the camp of the saints and the beloved city, but fire came down from heaven and consumed them, ¹⁰ and the devil who had deceived them was thrown into the lake of fire and sulfur where the beast and the false prophet were, and they will be tormented day and night forever and ever (Revelation 20: 7–10 ESV).

This final battle will be inspired by Satan at the end of the Millennial Reign. John alluded that this battle is a continuation of the Battle of Armageddon (mentioned in Ezekiel 38 and 39 as the Gog and Magog war), because the armies of Satan will be drawn from the remnants of the nations who fought alongside the antichrist a thousand years earlier. Many people tend to lump the Battle of Armageddon (see Section 13.9) with this war. This is based on the fact that there are certain similarities between these two battles. Firstly, the battleground for both is in Israel. Secondly, confederation of nations was mobilised against the inhabitants of Israel. Thirdly, God came to the rescue of the inhabitants of the land by fighting for them and defeating the enemy.

However, there are pointers in the prophesy to indicate that this battle is a different one. For instance, based on the allusions made in Revelation about these two wars, one can conclude that whereas the Battle of Armageddon will happen before the Millennial Reign, this final war will happen after the Millennial reign. Also, John cited Ezekiel's prophesy in Revelation 20:8 to enable people make the necessary connection that even though this battle is different, it is essentially linked with the first war, because it will be fought by the same nations.

There are other distinguishing factors between the two battles. In the Battle of Armageddon, Satan, the antichrist, and the false prophets would be the key players that would instigate the fight against the armies of Christ, whereas in this final war, Satan is the main character opposing Christ, because the antichrist and false prophet are already burning up in the lake of fire. Satan will insinuate among the nations who have been paying homage to Israel to go against them. The war is like a return match of the Battle of Armageddon, where Satan would be allowed to flex his final muscles before his final destruction.

One may wonder, what would have made some of the people living in the world at this time to have allowed themselves to be deceived by Satan to go against the inhabitants of the land after the Millenium Reign, when they have witnessed the harmonious rule of Christ. The crux here is the animosity of these nations towards Israel at this time, due to the fact that they are the ruling nation. It is usually natural for nations to rebel against the empire ruling them. Through Satan's instigation, the nations would be deceived to believe they can liberate themselves from the shackles of Christ and Israel and hence become free to do as they wish. However, this would be a debacle bring about their doom. This could also be a trap to test the peoples' loyalty to God. This war will serve as a final test that would be used to determine those that can be allowed into the kingdom of God. The end of this battle will culminate in the final judgement.

The nature of the war is decisive and brutal. John wrote that fire came from heaven to consume the armies of Satan:

> [9] And they marched up over the broad plain of the earth and surrounded the camp of the saints and the beloved city, but fire came down from heaven and consumed them, . (Revelation 20: 9 ESV).

14.14 THE SECOND RESURRECTION

Although the Second Resurrection was not directly mentioned, the mere fact that the Revelation mentioned the First Resurrection, suggests that there is more than one resurrection of the dead expected during the end times. It was hinted in Revelation 20 that only a select few (those that were beheaded for the sake of Christ and those who refused to bow down to the antichrist by accepting his mark), made it through, the first resurrection, the rest will have to wait for another one thousand years, to be resurrected:

> [5] The rest of the dead did not come to life until the thousand years were ended. This is the first resurrection. [6] Blessed and holy is the one who shares in the first resurrection! Over such the second death has no power, but they will be priests of God and of Christ, and they will reign with him for a thousand years. (Revelation 20: 5–6 ESV).

After, the final battle (see Section 14.13), which occurred at the end of the Millennial Reign, John recorded that he saw the dead standing before the white throne, which indicates that they have been raised from the dead. He went further to highlight that all the temporary holding places for the dead (the sea, Death, and Hades) released all the souls they have been holding:

> [12] And I saw the dead, great and small, standing before the throne, and books were opened. Then another book was opened, which is the book of life. And the dead were judged by what was written in the books, according to what they had done. [13] And the sea gave up the dead who were in it, Death and Hades gave up the dead who were in them, and they were judged, each one of them, according to what they had done. (Revelation 20: 12–13 ESV).

Unlike the First Resurrection, which occurred shortly before the commencement of the Millennial Reign, this Second Resurrection will occur after the final battle at the end of the Millennial Reign, in preparedness for the final judgement. This passage also seems to suggest that this second resurrection would be for the unrighteous dead who did not make it through the First Resurrection. These people would be raised in preparation for the final judgement, that would judge every human being and entity that has lived on the earth.

14.15 THE FINAL JUDGEMENT

At the end of all things, humans will be judged. This is the end of the matter! This judgement is a final assessment that would determine those than can progress into the Kingdom of God–the next phase of existence of humans, where only those with glorified bodies can be allowed in. This event is popularly known as the White Throne Judgement, due to the description of its settings in Revelation:

> [11] Then I saw a great white throne and him who was seated on it. From his presence earth and sky fled away, and no place was found for them. [12] And I saw the dead, great and small, standing before the throne, and books were opened. Then another book was opened, which is the book of life. And the dead were judged by what was written in the books, according to what they had done. [13] And the sea gave up the dead who were in it, Death and Hades gave up the dead who were in them, and they were judged, each one of them, according to what they had done. [14] Then Death and Hades were thrown into the lake of fire. This is the second death, the lake of fire. [15] And if anyone's name was not found written in the book of life, he was thrown into the lake of fire. (Revelation 20: 11–15 ESV).

This judgement is very critical. It will touch all entities *(And I saw the dead, great and small - Revelation 20:12)*: humans, angelic beings, pre-adamic beings, Nephilim, entities in the sea (the marine kingdom), those underground *(13 And the sea gave up the dead who were in it, Death and Hades gave up the dead who were in them–Revelation 20:13)*. All who at one point or the other had come in contact with the earth will be resurrected and judged accordingly. Those condemned will be incinerated in the lake of fire.

Christ will be the judge that is seated on this great white throne. He alluded to this in several passages in the gospels. Considering that he was the first fruit of those with glorified body, it makes sense that he will be the one to decide who can enter the Kingdom of God:

> [31] "When the Son of Man comes in his glory, and all the angels with him, then he will sit on his glorious throne. [32] Before him will be gathered all the nations, and he will separate people one from another as a shepherd separates the sheep from the goats. [33] And he will place the sheep on his right, but the goats on the left. [34] Then the King will say to those on his right, 'Come, you who are blessed by my Father, inherit the kingdom prepared

for you from the foundation of the world. (Mathew 25: 31–34 ESV).

He gave further insights about this event in the parable of the weeds, where he alluded to the fact that the *sons of God* will shine like stars, while the contraveners of the law will be destroyed:

> [37] He answered, "The one who sows the good seed is the Son of Man. [38] The field is the world, and the good seed is the sons of the kingdom. The weeds are the sons of the evil one, [39] and the enemy who sowed them is the devil. The harvest is the end of the age, and the reapers are angels. [40] Just as the weeds are gathered and burned with fire, so will it be at the end of the age. [41] The Son of Man will send his angels, and they will gather out of his kingdom all causes of sin and all law-breakers, [42] and throw them into the fiery furnace. In that place there will be weeping and gnashing of teeth. [43] Then the righteous will shine like the sun in the kingdom of their Father. He who has ears, let him hear. (Matthew 13:36–42 NIV).

To demonstrate the importance of this judgement, many extrabiblical texts extensively covered it. The Antiquities of Philo presented a narrative that closely matches the description in the Revelation:

> 10. But when the years of the world shall be fulfilled, then shall the light cease and the darkness be quenched: and I will quicken the dead and raise up from the earth them that sleep: and Hell shall pay his debt and destruction give back that which was committed unto him, that I may render unto every man according to his works and according to the fruit of their imaginations, even until I judge between the soul and the flesh. And the world shall rest, and death shall be quenched, and Hell shall shut his mouth. And the earth shall not be without birth, neither barren for them that dwell therein: and none shall be polluted that hath been justified in me. And there shall be another earth and another heaven, even an everlasting habitation. (Antiquities of Philo 3:9–10).

The Apocalypse of Baruch also touched on this:

> "For behold! the days come and the books shall be opened in which are written the sins of all those who have sinned; and, again, also the treasuries in which the righteousness of all those who have been righteous in creation is gathered. 2. For it shall come to pass at that time that thou shalt see —and many that

are with thee —the long-suffering of the Most-High, which hath been throughout all generations, Who hath been long-suffering towards all who righteous/' are born, (alike) those who sin and (those who) are (The Apocalypse of Baruch XXIV: 1–2).

The Apocalypse of Ezra delved into the bliss of the Kingdom of God that awaits the sons of God, while justifying the punishment that would be meted out to many people who would not make it into the kingdom but doomed in the lake of fire. He reiterated that only a fraction (few) of humanity who have lived on the earth will make it into the kingdom:

> But do thou (rather) consider thine own self and ask concerning the glories of those who are like thyself. 52. For for you is opened Paradise, and planted the Tree of life; and the future world prepared, and delight made ready; and a City builded, and a Rest ordained ; and good perfected, and wisdom completed;53. And the (evil) root is sealed up from you, and infirmity from you extinguished, and Death is hidden, and Sheol fled; and corruption is forgotten, and pains departed from you; 54. And in the consummation the treasures of life are manifested. 55. Do not thou, therefore, again ask any more concerning the many who perish; 56. because they have received liberty and they have despised the Most-High, his Law also they have scorned much, and have made his ways to cease. 57. Yea, his saints they have trampled upon, and 58. they have said in their heart that there is no God, while they verily know that they shall surely die. 59. Therefore as these things aforesaid await you, so also thirst and torment (are) destined for them. For the Most-High willed not that men should perish; 60. but these who have been created dishonoured the name of their Maker and were ungrateful {and confessed me not—]" who have prepared life for them. 61. Therefore my Judgement hath drawn nigh, 62. which (thing) I have not made known to the many, but (only) to thee and to the few like thee. (Apocalypse of Ezra VIII: 52–61).

> [37-] And then shall the Most-High say to those nations that have been raised: Gaze and see what ye have denied, or whom ye have not served, or whose commandments ye have despised! [38.] Look, therefore, over against you: behold here rest and enjoyments, and there fire and torment! Thus shall he speak to them in that Day of Judgement. (Apocalypse of Ezra VII: 37 - 38).

The preceding passages suggest that during the Millennial Reign there will still be some humans who have not been completely sold out to worshipping God, despite all that has happened in the world during the tribulation and wrath period. These sets of people will continue to do things that will profane God. These are the people that will join in the final rebellion of Satan, after he gets released from prison. Hence, these people will be taken out of the Kingdom of God (weed out of his kingdom everything that causes sin and all who do evil). Note that the language used here is different from the language used earlier in Mathew 8, when the unrighteous were being prevented from entering the kingdom. Mathew 8 and Luke 13:18-30 were referring to period when Christ was establishing his kingdom after the defeat of the antichrist, and the people who have qualified have been given the glorified body, which permits them to enter the kingdom of Christ (his empire), and the others prevented from entering the kingdom. However, Mathew 13: 40-43 is referring to the time after the Millennial Reign when the influence of the Empire of Christ has reached every corner of the earth. Hence, all the bad elements still hanging around the world are gathered out of the kingdom. Note that in Luke 13:18-30, the kingdom was still nascent and centerd around Jerusalem (the reason Christ compared it to a mustard seed, in Mathew 13, the kingdom has spread its influence around the world, hence the entire world has become the kingdom of God).

Although there is *weeping and gnashing of teeth* in both events, the distinguishing factor is that whereas in the first event the unrighteous were prevented from entering the kingdom (they were cast out into the outer darkness), in the second event, they will be removed from the kingdom and destroyed in the blazing furnace (*They will throw them into the blazing furnace, where there will be weeping and gnashing of teeth*). The blazing furnace here either refers to the lake of fire.

Another thing that confirms that these were referring to two different events, is that whereas the first was focusing on entrance into the kingdom (*the strive to enter through the narrow gate, the door being shut, people being shut out of the kingdom*), the other was focusing on removal of bad elements from the kingdom:

> [24] "Make every effort to enter through the narrow door, because many, I tell you, will try to enter and will not be able to. [25] Once the owner of the house gets up and closes the door, you will stand outside knocking and pleading, 'Sir, open the door for us.' (Luke 13:24-25 NIV).

Hence, we can safely conclude that the Parables of the Mustard Seed and the Yeast (Luke 13:18-30, Matthew 13: 31-34), refers to the physical establishment of the kingdom of Christ on earth soon after the defeat of the antichrist, while the parable of the weeds (Matthew 13: 24-29; 36-43) refers to the removal of every profane thing from the Kingdom of God at the end of the one thousand year reign of Christ. This is a purification process, to ensure that no bad element will enter the new earth and new heaven that God created for humans.

14.16 RESTORATION OF GOD'S KINGDOM

Following the final judgement, every evil entity (humans and non-humans) would have been eradicated from the heavens and the earth. At this point, the earth will fully be reconnected to the rest of God's kingdom. The disconnect that happened in the heavens and the earth, which commenced with the rebellion of Satan and his angels and culminated in the fall of Adam, would have been repaired by this time. Then will a new earth and new heaven, which God has prepared for his faithful servants and sons be made manifest:

> And I saw a new heaven and a new earth: for the first heaven and the first earth were passed away; and there was no more sea. (Revelation 21: 1 KJV).

There is an indication here that this new earth will be markedly different from the old way, as there would be *no more sea*. There may also be other physical changes.

The present earth has been marked for destruction. It was created perfect but was defiled by Satan and all the dark forces with him. However, before its destruction, God repurposed it as a training ground for a new set of beings he created. In this earth, humanity will be tested and tried in several ways so that only the best can emerge. These are those that would proceed to the new earth that God created. These are the sons of God that will inhabit the new earth. Those who made it will enjoy the everlasting bliss of this new earth:

> 11. For that which is to be shall be the object of desire, And on that which shall come afterwards do we place our hope. For it is a time that shall not pass away. 12. And the hour cometh which shall abide for ever, And the new world (cometh) which doth not turn to corruption those who depart to its blessedness. And

hath no mercy on those who depart to torment. And shall not lead to perdition those who live in it. 13. For these are they who shall inherit that time which hath been spoken of, And theirs is the inheritance of the promised time. 14. These are they who have acquired for themselves treasures of wisdom, And with them are found stores of understanding, And from mercy have they not withdrawn, And the truth of the Law have they preserved. 15. For to them shall be given the world to come. But the dwelling of the rest, who are many, shall XLV. be in the fire. Do ye, therefore, so far as ye are able, instruct the people, for that labour is yours. 2. For if ye teach them, ye will quicken them." (Apocalypse of Baruch XLIV: 11–14; XLIV: 1–2).

Although, the destruction of the present earth was not explicitly stated in Revelation, there were several allusions to it in the book. John records in Revelation 20 that he saw a new heaven and a new earth, because the first heaven and earth had passed away:

> Then I saw a new heaven and a new earth, for the first heaven and the first earth had passed away, and the sea was no more. (Revelation 21: 1 ESV).

Peter alluded that this present earth was destined to be burnt up:

> [6] Whereby the world that then was, being overflowed with water, perished:
> [7] But the heavens and the earth, which are now, by the same word are kept in store, reserved unto fire against the day of judgment and perdition of ungodly men. (2 Peter 3:6–7 KJV).
> [10] But the day of the Lord will come as a thief in the night; in the which the heavens shall pass away with a great noise, and the elements shall melt with fervent heat, the earth also and the works that are therein shall be burned up. (2 Peter 3:10 KJV).

One of the highlights of this period is the emergence of a new Jerusalem, where God and Christ will reside in the new earth. This city will emerge from the new heaven. In this new phase of life, the earth and heaven will be fully connected so that God's throne will be present on the earth:

> [2] I saw the Holy City, the new Jerusalem, coming down out of heaven from God, prepared as a bride beautifully dressed for her husband. [3] And I heard a loud voice from the throne saying, "Look! God's dwelling place is now among the people, and he will dwell with them. They will be his people, and God himself will be with them and be their God. [4] 'He will wipe every

tear from their eyes. There will be no more death' or mourning or crying or pain, for the old order of things has passed away." (Revelation 21: 2–4 NIV).

This new Jerusalem will be the citadel of the earth. It is beautifully crafted that it was metaphorized as the bride of Christ. John was given a preview of what this city looks like:

> [9] One of the seven angels who had the seven bowls full of the seven last plagues came and said to me, "Come, I will show you the bride, the wife of the Lamb." [10] And he carried me away in the Spirit to a mountain great and high, and showed me the Holy City, Jerusalem, coming down out of heaven from God. [11] It shone with the glory of God, and its brilliance was like that of a very precious jewel, like a jasper, clear as crystal. [12] It had a great, high wall with twelve gates, and with twelve angels at the gates. On the gates were written the names of the twelve tribes of Israel. [13] There were three gates on the east, three on the north, three on the south and three on the west. [14] The wall of the city had twelve foundations, and on them were the names of the twelve apostles of the Lamb.
>
> [15] The angel who talked with me had a measuring rod of gold to measure the city, its gates and its walls. [16] The city was laid out like a square, as long as it was wide. He measured the city with the rod and found it to be 12,000 stadia in length, and as wide and high as it is long. [17] The angel measured the wall using human measurement, and it was 144 cubits thick [18] The wall was made of jasper, and the city of pure gold, as pure as glass. [19] The foundations of the city walls were decorated with every kind of precious stone. The first foundation was jasper, the second sapphire, the third agate, the fourth emerald, [20] the fifth onyx, the sixth ruby, the seventh chrysolite, the eighth beryl, the ninth topaz, the tenth turquoise, the eleventh jacinth, and the twelfth amethyst. [21] The twelve gates were twelve pearls, each gate made of a single pearl. The great street of the city was of gold, as pure as transparent glass.
>
> [22] I did not see a temple in the city, because the Lord God Almighty and the Lamb are its temple. [23] The city does not need the sun or the moon to shine on it, for the glory of God gives it light, and the Lamb is its lamp. [24] The nations will walk by its light, and the kings of the earth will bring their splendor into it. [25] On no day will its gates ever be shut, for there will be no night there. [26] The glory and honor of the nations will be brought into it. [27] Nothing impure will ever enter it, nor will

anyone who does what is shameful or deceitful, but only those whose names are written in the Lamb's book of life. (Revelation 21: 9-26 NIV).

This passage alludes that in this new earth, people will still be organized into nations. This implies that there will be some form of racial divide on this earth, with every nation having its king, that would be coming to the new Jerusalem to pay homage to God and Christ:

> [24] The nations will walk by its light, and the kings of the earth will bring their splendor into it. [25] On no day will its gates ever be shut, for there will be no night there. [26] The glory and honor of the nations will be brought into it. (Revelation 21: 24-26 NIV).

This city where God's throne is will be like the Garden of Eden–beautiful, blissful and harmonious, with God in its midst. From it will the inhabitants of the earth be nourished:

> Then the angel showed me the river of the water of life, as clear as crystal, flowing from the throne of God and of the Lamb [2] down the middle of the great street of the city. On each side of the river stood the tree of life, bearing twelve crops of fruit, yielding its fruit every month. And the leaves of the tree are for the healing of the nations. [3] No longer will there be any curse. The throne of God and of the Lamb will be in the city, and his servants will serve him. [4] They will see his face, and his name will be on their foreheads. [5] There will be no more night. They will not need the light of a lamp or the light of the sun, for the Lord God will give them light. And they will reign for ever and ever. (Revelation 22: 1-5 NIV).

The unworthy will not be allowed into this blissful place as they will be burning in the fiery furnace. Everyone will be rewarded according to what they have done while they lived on the earth:

> [12] "Look, I am coming soon! My reward is with me, and I will give to each person according to what they have done. [13] I am the Alpha and the Omega, the First and the Last, the Beginning and the End.
> [14] "Blessed are those who wash their robes, that they may have the right to the tree of life and may go through the gates into the city. [15] Outside are the dogs, those who practice magic arts, the sexually immoral, the murderers, the idolaters and everyone who loves and practices falsehood. (Revelation 22: 12-14 NIV).

References

Aletia. "What did Paul VI mean by saying 'the smoke of Satan has entered the Church'"? (2018). https://aleteia.org/2018/07/06/what-did-paul-vi-mean-by-saying-the-smoke-of-satan-has-entered-the-church.

Anejionu, Obinna. "The Final Battle for Earth: Unlocking the Mysteries of the Coming Great Tribulation and Wrath of God. Resource Publications". ISBN: 978-1-6667-4812-3, 2022.

Archaeology World. "India: Archaeologists found 9,000 years old city beneath the surface of modern-day Dwarka". (2020). https://archaeology-world.com/india-archaeologists-found-9000-years-old-city-beneath-the-surface-of-modern-day-dwarka/.

Archi, Alfonso. "Translation of Gods: Kumarpi, Enlil, Dagan/NISABA, Ḫalki". Orientalia. 73 (4): 319–336. ISSN 0030-5367. JSTOR 43078173, 2004.

BBC. "Japan's mysterious underwater 'city'". (2021). https://www.bbc.com/travel/article/20210311-japans-mysterious-underwater-city.

BBC. *Dwarka: India's submerged ancient city.* (2022). https://www.bbc.com/travel/article/20220113-dwarka-indias-submerged-ancient-city.

BBC. "Elon Musk says Neuralink implanted wireless brain chip". (2024). https://www.bbc.co.uk/news/technology-68137046.

Becher, Brooke and Urwin, Mathew. 6G: "What Is It? When Can We Expect It"? (2023). https://builtin.com/hardware/6g.

Biblical Hermeneutics. "Is Lucifer a proper name of Satan according to Isaiah 14:12"? (2021). https://hermeneutics.stackexchange.com/questions/59388/is-lucifer-a-proper-name-of-satan-according-to-isaiah-1412.

Blakemore, Erin. "How archaeologists determine the date of ancient sites and artifacts". (2019). https://www.nationalgeographic.com/culture/article/archaeologist-methods-date-sites-artifacts.

Blakemore, Erin. "What were Neanderthals really like—and why did they go extinct?" (2023). https://www.nationalgeographic.com/history/article/who-were-the-neanderthals.

Bostrom, Nick. "The Transhumanist FAQ." (1999). https://nickbostrom.com/views/transhumanist.pdf.

Britannica. "Human sacrifice". Encyclopedia Britannica. (2024), https://www.britannica.com/topic/human-sacrifice.

Britannica. "Eridu Genesis". *Encyclopedia Britannica.* (2020). https://www.britannica.com/topic/Eridu-Genesis.

REFERENCES

Britannica, "Epic of Gilgamesh". Encyclopedia Britannica. (2023). https://www.britannica.com/topic/Epic-of-Gilgamesh.

Britannica, "Amon summary". *Encyclopedia Britannica*. (2021). https://www.britannica.com/summary/Amon.

Broussard, Gill. "Is Planet X Biblical?". https://www.timetobelieve.com/catastroph/is-planet-x-biblical/.(2025).

Burja, Samo. "The First World Government". (2024). https://www.palladiummag.com/2024/03/01/the-first-world-government/.

Catholic Adventurer. "The Choirs of Angels, According to Aquinas". (2023). https://catholicadventurer.com/theology/the-choirs-of-angels-according-to-aquinas.

Catholic Online. "The Nine Choirs of Angels". (2024). https://www.catholic.org/saints/angels/angelchoir.php.

CERN. "The Large Hadron Collider". (2023). https://home.cern/science/accelerators/large-hadron-collider.

Cohen, Julie. "A Cataclysmic Event of a Certain Age". (2015). https://news.ucsb.edu/2015/015778/cataclysmic-event-certain-age.

Cooke, Emily. "What's the difference between Neanderthals and Homo sapiens"? (2024). https://www.livescience.com/archaeology/whats-the-difference-between-neanderthals-and-homo-sapiens.

Charles, Jason. "The Six Types of Demons and Their Methods of Possession". (2017). https://wakethechurch.org/articles/the-six-types-of-demons-and-their-methods-of-possession.

Christian Pure. "Lucifer in Latin: An In-depth Etymological Analysis". (2024). https://christianpure.com/learn/lucifer-latin-meaning-analysis/#:~:text=The%20Latin%20term%20%27Lucifer%27%20makes%20its%20debut%20in,from%20%27lux%27%20%28light%29%20and%20%27ferre%27%20%28to%20bear%2Fto%20bring%29.

Christian Resource Centre. "The Lost Books of the Bible". (2024). https://www.crcnh.org/downloads/reference-guides/9-The-Lost-Books-of-the-Bible.pdf

Cosner, Lita. and Carter, Robert. "Were the Egyptian pyramids built before the Flood"? (2019). https://apologiaway1.wordpress.com/2019/12/16/were-the-egyptian-pyramids-built-before-the-flood/.

Croft, August. "Denisovan vs Neanderthal: What's the Difference"? (2023). https://a-z-animals.com/blog/denisovan-vs-neanderthal/.

Daley, Jason. "Did the Ancient Greeks Engage in Human Sacrifice"? (2016). https://www.smithsonianmag.com/smart-news/did-ancient-greeks-engage-human-sacrifice-180960111/.

Delbert, Caroline. "AI Will Hack Our Brains, Expert Says". (2021). https://www.popularmechanics.com/technology/security/a38147393/ai-hack-brains/.

DeLong William. "The Lost Continent of Lemuria Was A Myth — Then Scientists Found Evidence. (2024). https://allthatsinteresting.com/lemuria-continent.

DivineNarratives Team. The Gap Theory: Origins, Evidence, and Controversies. https://divinenarratives.org/the-gap-theory-origins-evidence-and-controversies/, 2024.

D-Wave. "The Most Connected and Powerful Quantum Computer Built for Business". (2024). https://www.dwavesys.com/solutions-and-products/systems/.

Economic Times. "Oracle's Larry Ellison says AI-driven cancer vaccine could be coming soon as Donald Trump announces a $500 billion investment". (2025). https://www.msn.com/en-in/health/other/oracle-s-larry-ellison-says-ai-driven-

REFERENCES

cancer-vaccine-could-be-coming-soon-as-donald-trump-announces-a-500-billion-investment/ar-AA1xDkoT?ocid=BingNewsSerp.

Emil G. Hirsch, M. Seligsohn, Wilhelm Bacher. "Nimrod". (2021). https://www.jewishencyclopedia.com/articles/11548-nimrod.

Emoto, Masaru. *The Hidden Messages in Water. Beyond Words*, United States. ISBN: 978-1-58-270114-1, 2004.

Emspak, Jesse. "Quantum Entanglement: Unlocking the Mysteries of Particle Connections". (2024). https://www.space.com/31933-quantum-entanglement-action-at-a-distance.html.

Encyclopedia.com. "Transhumanism and Posthumanism". (2024). https://www.encyclopedia.com/science/encyclopedias-almanacs-transcripts-and-maps/transhumanism-and-posthumanism.

Fairchild, Mary. "Exploring Gap Creationism." Learn Religions. (2025). https://www.learnreligions.com/what-is-the-gap-theory-701497.

Flores, Myles. "The New World Order: The Historical Origins of a Dangerous Modern Conspiracy Theory". (2022). https://www.middlebury.edu/institute/academics/centers-initiatives/ctec/ctec-publications/new-world-order-historical-origins-dangerous.

Forbes. "The Stargate Project: Trump Touts $500 Billion Bid For AI Dominance". (2025). https://www.forbes.com/sites/moorinsights/2025/01/30/the-stargate-project-trump-touts-500-billion-bid-for-ai-dominance/.

Futurism. "Artificial Superintelligence Could Arrive by 2027, Scientist Predicts". (2025). https://futurism.com/artificial-superintelligence-agi-2027-goertzel.

Gambetta, Jay. "The hardware and Software for the Era of Quantum Utility is here". (2023). https://www.ibm.com/quantum/blog/quantum-roadmap-2033.

Giacomazzo, Bernadette. "The Real Story of The Kandahar Giant, The 13-Foot Cryptid Purportedly Killed By U.S. Special Ops". (2023). https://allthatsinteresting.com/kandahar-giant.

Gillian, Joanna. "How DNA Testing Revealed European Ancestry in Elongated Paracas Skulls". (2023). How DNA Testing Revealed European Ancestry in Elongated Paracas Skulls | Ancient Origins (ancient-origins.net).

Goertzel, Ben. "Artificial Superintelligence Could Arrive by 2027, Scientist Predicts". (2025). https://futurism.com/artificial-superintelligence-agi-2027-goertzel.

Got Questions Ministries. "What is the marriage supper of the Lamb"? (2022). https://www.gotquestions.org/marriage-supper-Lamb.html.

Goswami, Manvi. "Did the Anunnaki Create Humans? Ancient Alien Origins of Humanity". (2024). https://lorelibrarymyth.com/did-anunnaki-create-humans-origin-of-humanity.

Grey, Orrin. "What Is the Lost World of Lemuria?" (2023). https://theportalist.com/lost-world-of-lemuria.

Halickman, Sharona. "Who Hitched a Ride on the Ark"? (2020). https://blogs.timesofisrael.com/who-hitched-a-ride-on-the-ark/.

Hamp, Douglas. "Tower of Babel: Stargate to the Abyss". (2023). https://www.douglashamp.com/tower-of-babel-stargate-to-the-abyss/.

Harari, Noah Harari. "AI and the future of humanity" Yuval Noah Harari at the Frontiers Forum. (2023). https://www.youtube.com/watch?v=LWiM-LuRe6w&t=2s.

Hart, Robert. "What Is Worldcoin? Here's What to Know about the Eyeball-Scanning Crypto Project Launched by OpenAI's Sam Altman". (2023). https://www.forbes.

com/sites/roberthart/2023/07/24/what-is-worldcoin-heres-what-to-know-about-the-eyeball-scanning-crypto-project-launched-by-openais-sam-altman/.

Harvey, Austin. "The true story of Atlantis, the fabled lost city that may lie on the floor of the Atlantic Ocean". (2024). https://allthatsinteresting.com/atlantis.

Heiser, Michael Steven. *The Unseen Realm: Recovering the Supernatural Worldview of the Bible*. Lexham, ISBN-13978-1577995562, 2015.

Heiser, Michael Steven. "The Tower of Babel Story: What Really Happened?" (2022). https://www.logos.com/grow/really-happened-tower-babel/?msockid=144f86c214cf6cc60d5e93da152f6d3f.

Heiser, Michael Steven. "Divine Council." *In Dictionary of the Old Testament: Wisdom, Poetry & Writings*. ed. Tremper Longman III and Peter Enns; Downers Grove, IL; Nottingham, England: IVP Academic; Inter-Varsity, 2008), 112, 2008.

Hendricks, Jonathan. R. "Geological time". In: *the Digital Encyclopedia of Ancient Life*. (2018). http://www.digitalatlasofancientlife.org/learn/geological-time/.

Hill, Jaden. "A Day is Not Always 24 Hours: How Earth's Shifting Systems Cause Day Length Variation". (2023). https://www.earthscope.org/news/a-day-is-not-always-24-hours-how-earths-shifting-systems-cause-day-length-variation/.

History.com Editors "Israel". (2023). https://www.history.com/topics/middle-east/history-of-israel.

History on the net. "Assyrian Empire: The Most Powerful Empire in the World". (2025). https://www.historyonthenet.com/assyrian-empire-the-most-powerful-empire-in-the-world.

History Tools. "The Destruction of Jerusalem: Inside the Brutal Roman Siege of 70 AD". (2024). https://www.historytools.org/stories/the-destruction-of-jerusalem-inside-the-brutal-roman-siege-of-70-ad#google_vignette.

Hodge, B. "Were the Pyramids Built Before the Flood"? (2012). https://answersingenesis.org/archaeology/ancient-egypt/were-the-pyramids-built-before-the-flood/.

Huawei. 6G: "The Next Horizon". https://www.huawei.com/en/huaweitech/future-technologies/6g-the-next-horizon, 2023.

Huss, Micha Van. *Secret Societies: Blood Never Sleeps*. Beacon Street Press. ASIN: B0CYYF597D, 2024.

InnoVirtuoso. "10 Remarkable Human Augmentation Companies Stocks to look at". (2023). https://innovirtuoso.com/technology/10-remarkable-human-augmentation-companies-stocks-to-look-at/.

Interesting Times with Ross Douthat. "A.I., Mars and Immortality: Are We Dreaming Big Enough?" (2025). https://www.youtube.com/watch?v=vV7YgnPUxcU&t=19s.

James, Montague Rhodes. "The Biblical Antiquities of Philo". (1917). https://sacred-texts.com/bib/bap/index.htm.

Jarrett, Ed. "What Kind of Authority Does Jesus Show in Matthew's Gospel"? (2023). https://www.biblestudytools.com/bible-study/topical-studies/what-kind-of-authority-does-jesus-show-in-matthews-gospel.html.

Jarus, Owen. "25 cultures that practiced human sacrifice". (2017). https://www.livescience.com/59514-cultures-that-practiced-human-sacrifice.html.

Jewish Virtual Library. "Zionist Congress: The Uganda Proposal". (1903). https://www.jewishvirtuallibrary.org/the-uganda-proposal-1903.

Jordan, Gina. "Projects aim for legal identity for everyone". (2016). Projects aim for legal identity for everyone - SecureIDNews.

REFERENCES

Josephus, Flavius. *Antiquities of the Jews*. (93 AD). https://gutenberg.org/files/2848/2848-h/2848-h.htm.

Khanum, Maryam. "Oracle Founder Larry Ellison Praises AI Surveillance State in Video Clip Resurfaced After Trump AI Infrastructure Announcement: 'Citizens Will Be On Their Best Behavior'". (2025). https://www.msn.com/en-us/news/technology/oracle-founder-larry-ellison-praises-ai-surveillance-state-in-video-clip-resurfaced-after-trump-ai-infrastructure-announcement-citizens-will-be-on-their-best-behavior/ar-AA1xJvnX?ocid=BingNewsSerp.

Leigh, Lex. "Blood for the Gods: 10 Cultures that Engaged in Ritual Sacrifice". (2022). https://www.ancient-origins.net/history-ancient-traditions/ritual-sacrifice-0017159#google_vignette.

Leigh, Lex. "Eri: Mythical King and Founder of the Igbo". (2022). https://www.ancient-origins.net/history-famous-people/king-eri-of-igbo-0016659.

Levi. "The Elite's are Planning to Shock the World | Whitney Webb BlackRock Exposed". (2024). https://www.youtube.com/watch?v=Y7IGs01U06k.

Lin, Christina. "CERN—looking for God particle, or opening portals of hell"? (2020). https://blogs.timesofisrael.com/cern-looking-for-god-particle-or-opening-portals-of-hell/.

Littman, Garry. Switzerland: "Gateway to the Alps and Gateway to Hell". (2016). https://www.bilan.ch/opinions/garry-littman/switzerland_gateway_to_the_alps_and_gateway_to_hell.

Livingston, Dave. "Who Was Nimrod"? (2003). http://www.davelivingston.com/nimrod.htm.

Lowth, M. 10 Ancient Sites That Might Be Stargates, Portals and Wormholes. (2016). https://listverse.com/2016/05/20/10-ancient-sites-that-might-be-stargates-portals-and-wormholes/.

Mack, Eric. "Elon Musk: 'We are summoning the demon' with artificial intelligence". (2014). https://www.cnet.com/science/elon-musk-we-are-summoning-the-demon-with-artificial-intelligence/.

Mark, Joshua J. "The Atrahasis Epic: The Great Flood & the Meaning of Suffering". *World History Encyclopedia*. (2011). https://www.worldhistory.org/article/227/the-atrahasis-epic-the-great-flood--the-meaning-of/.

Martin, Malachi. *Windswept House: A Vatican Novel*. Doubleday. New York. ISBN: 0-385-48408-9, 1996.

Martin, Malachi. *The Keys of This Blood: The Struggle for World Dominion between Pope John Paul II, Mikhail Gorbachev, and the Capitalist West*, Simon & Schuster, New York, 1990 ISBN 0-671-69174-0

Mindel, Nissan. "Abraham's Early Life". (2016). https://www.chabad.org/library/article_cdo/aid/112063/jewish/Abrahams-Early-Life.htm.

Minton. "What is the Divine Council and is it Biblical"? 2019 https://cerebralfaith.net/what-is-the-divine-council-and-is-it-biblical/.

Moon, Joshua. "Humans are hackable animals" - Yuval Noah Harari. (2022). https://www.youtube.com/watch?v=bRk3Wq9M1vI.

Mooney, Britt. "What is the Marriage Supper of the Lamb"? (2022). https://www.christianity.com/wiki/bible/what-is-the-marriage-supper-of-the-lamb.html.

Mucci, Tim. and Stryker, Cole. "What is artificial superintelligence"? (2023). https://www.ibm.com/think/topics/artificial-superintelligence.

REFERENCES

NASA. "Hidden Portals in Earth's Magnetic Field". (2012). https://www.nasa.gov/mission_pages/sunearth/news/mag-portals.html.

National Geographic Society. "How Did Scientists Calculate the Age of Earth"? (2023). https://education.nationalgeographic.org/resource/how-did-scientists-calculate-age-earth/.

Neuroba. "Can Consciousness Be Digitally Transferred? Exploring Mind Uploading". (2025). https://www.neuroba.com/post/can-consciousness-be-digitally-transferred-exploring-mind-uploading-neuroba.

O'Neal, Sam. "When Was the Bible Assembled?" (2021). https://www.learnreligions.com/when-was-the-bible-assembled-363293.

Oduah, Chika. "Nigeria's Igbo Jews: 'Lost tribe' of Israel"? (2013). https://edition.cnn.com/2013/02/01/world/africa/nigeria-jews-igbo/index.html.

Oracle Films. "The Agenda: Their Vision - Your Future. Full Documentary". (2025). https://www.youtube.com/watch?v=ZFHHOBiUrkg&t=3607s.

Patton, Patrick. "Is CERN Trying to Open the Bottomless Pit"? (2021). https://www.pspatton.com/post/is-cern-trying-to-open-the-bottomless-pit.

Political Incorrectness. "We Can Hack Humans Dr. Yuval Noah Harari and Klaus Schwab". (2022). https://www.youtube.com/watch?v=3vrkTl9Sv6Y.

Radin D, Hayssen G, Emoto M, Kizu T. *Double-blind test of the effects of distant intention on water crystal formation.* Explore (NY). Sep-Oct;2(5):408-11. doi: 10.1016/j.explore.2006.06.004. PMID: 16979104, 2006.

Rager, Maddy. "What Are the Gates of Hell Jesus Talked About"? (2023). https://www.biblestudytools.com/bible-study/topical-studies/what-are-gates-of-hell-jesus-talked-about.html#:~:text=Caesarea%20Philippi%20was%20home%20to%20a%20cave%20known,gods%20traveling%20in%20and%20out%20of%20the%20cave.

Ramos, Samuel. "Nimrod and the Tower of Babel". (2022). https://www.smashingpillarsinternational.org/single-post/nimrod-and-the-tower-of-babel.

Rannard, Georgina. "The asteroid that killed the dinosaurs was not alone". (2024). https://www.bbc.co.uk/news/articles/c62m04vokono.

Rao, Achintya. "AWAKE successfully accelerates electrons". (2018). https://home.cern/news/news/experiments/awake-successfully-accelerates-electrons#:~:text=AWAKE%2C%20which%20stands%20for%20%E2%80%9CAdvanced%20WAKEfield%20Experiment%E2%80%9D%2C%20is,energies%20than%20can%20be%20achieved%20using%20conventional%20technologies.

Reyna, M. "How Was The Bible Compiled". (2024). https://www.theholyscript.com/how-was-the-bible-compiled/?utm_content=cmp-true.

Reuters. "Turkey's Erdogan calls for Islamic alliance against Israel". (2024). Turkey's Erdogan calls for Islamic alliance against Israel (msn.com).

Revelation Now. "The People that Would Later Worship Baal Destroyed the Temple the Roman General Titus Attempted To Save The Temple". (2019). https://revelation-now.org/wp-content/uploads/The-People-of-Baal-Destroyed-the-Temple-in-70-AD.pdf.

Richardson, Joel. "Daniel 9:26: Who are the People of the Prince to Come"? (2010). https://prophezine.blogspot.com/2010/07/daniel-926-who-are-people-of-prince-to.html.

Ritchie, Hannah. "There have been five mass extinctions in Earth's history". (2022). https://ourworldindata.org/mass-extinctions.

REFERENCES

Riess, Adam. "Dark matter". Encyclopedia Britannica. (2024). https://www.britannica.com/science/dark-matter.

Rincon, Paul. "Stephen Hawking's warnings: What he predicted for the future". (2018). https://www.bbc.co.uk/news/science-environment-43408961.

Roat, Alyssa. "7 Facts You Didn't Know about Nimrod in the Bible". (2020). https://www.crosswalk.com/faith/bible-study/facts-about-nimrod-in-the-bible.html#google_vignette.

Rohl, David. "Was the Tower of Babel a Ziggurat"? Dr. David Rohl. (2021). https://www.youtube.com/watch?v=8vLlPbNv4Tk.

Roulette, Joey., and Taylor, Marisa. "Exclusive: Musk's SpaceX is building spy satellite network for US intelligence agency, sources say". (2024). https://www.reuters.com/technology/space/musks-spacex-is-building-spy-satellite-network-us-intelligence-agency-sources-2024-03-16/.

Schwemer, Daniel. "The Storm-Gods of the Ancient Near East: Summary, Synthesis, Recent Studies Part I" (PDF). Journal of Ancient Near Eastern Religions. 7 (2): doi:10.1163/156921207783876404. ISSN 1569-2116. 2007, 121–168.

60 Minutes. "Yuval Noah Harari: The 2021 60 Minutes interview". (2022). https://www.youtube.com/watch?v=EIVTf-C60Qo.

Sommerlad, Joe. "What is the 'New World Order' and why has Joe Biden caused uproar by using the phrase"? (2022). https://www.independent.co.uk/news/world/americas/us-politics/new-world-order-meaning-biden-b2043111.html.

Stringer, Chris. "Are Neanderthals the same species as us"? (2015). https://www.nhm.ac.uk/discover/are-neanderthals-same-species-as-us.html.

Study Country. "What are the 10 kingdoms of Atlantis"? (2025). https://www.studycountry.com/wiki/what-are-the-10-kingdoms-of-atlantis.

Suarez, Christophe. "Christophe Suarez on X: Friday night, a small supercell takes shape over #Geneva – Naissance". (2016). https://twitter.com/suarezphoto/status/747141377801216001.

Sus, Viktoriya. "Posthumanism vs Transhumanism: What Is the Difference"? (2024). https://www.thecollector.com/posthumanism-vs-transhumanism-difference.

Tabata, Mark. "How The Post-Flood Giants Returned". (2021). https://marktabata.com/2021/11/08/how-the-post-flood-giants-returned-2/#:~:text=Now%20it%20came%20to%20pass%2C%20when%20men%20began,of%20men%20and%20they%20bore%20children%20to%20them.

The Christian Realist. "How did we get the name Jesus when the Letter "J" didn't exist in Jesus' time"? (2018). https://thechristianrealist.com/2018/04/02/how-did-we-get-the-name-jesus-when-the-letter-j-didnt-exist-in-jesus-time/.

The Editors of Encyclopaedia Britannica. "Assyria". Encyclopedia Britannica. (2025). https://www.britannica.com/place/Assyria.

US Archives. "The Epic of Atraḥasis" (2450 B.C.E). (2024). https://ia802908.us.archive.org/31/items/HOLYBOOKS/Holy-Books/EpicofAtrahasis.pdf.

The Guardian. "No death and an enhanced life: Is the future transhuman?" (2018). https://www.theguardian.com/technology/2018/may/06/no-death-and-an-enhanced-life-is-the-future-transhuman.

This Is World. "All My Predictions Have Come True, So Far" | Ray Kurzweil (Time100)". (2025). https://www.youtube.com/watch?v=gGEu_5KbVe8&t=1457s.

UK Ministry of Defence. "Human Augmentation – The Dawn of a New Paradigm: A strategic implications project". (2025). https://assets.publishing.service.gov.uk/media/609d23c6e90e07357baa8388/Human_Augmentation_SIP_access2.pdf.

REFERENCES

Wagner, Paul. "AI and Consciousness Uploading: The Future of Human Consciousness and Artificial Intelligence". (2024). https://www.paulwagner.com/ai-and-consciousness-uploading-the-future-of-human-consciousness-and-artificial-intelligence/.

Waite, Mark. "What is Grace in The Bible Verses". (2024). *https://christian.net/theology-and-spirituality/what-is-grace-in-the-bible-verses/.*

Weber, Clas. "Could you move from your biological body to a computer? An expert explains 'mind uploading'". (2023). https://theconversation.com/could-you-move-from-your-biological-body-to-a-computer-an-expert-explains-mind-uploading-218035.

World Economic Forum. "What is transhumanism and how does it affect you?" (2018). *https://www.weforum.org/agenda/2018/04/transhumanism-advances-in-technology-could-already-put-evolution-into-hyperdrive-but-should-they/.*

Zuhlsdorf, John. "29 June 1972. Paul VI says, 'the smoke of Satan has entered the Church of God'". (2022). https://wdtprs.com/2022/06/29-june-1972-paul-vi-says-the-smoke-of-satan-has-entered-the-church-of-god/.